PROTECTING COMMUNITY INTERESTS
THROUGH INTERNATIONAL LAW

PROTECTING COMMUNITY INTERESTS THROUGH INTERNATIONAL LAW

Edited by
Gentian ZYBERI

INTERSENTIA

Cambridge – Antwerp – Chicago

Intersentia Ltd
8 Wellington Mews
Wellington Street | Cambridge
CB1 1HW | United Kingdom
Tel: +44 1223 736 170
Email: mail@intersentia.co.uk
www.intersentia.com | www.intersentia.co.uk

Distribution for the UK and
Rest of the World (incl. Eastern Europe)
NBN International
1 Deltic Avenue, Rooksley
Milton Keynes MK13 8LD
United Kingdom
Tel: +44 1752 202 301 | Fax: +44 1752 202 331
Email: orders@nbninternational.com

Distribution for Europe
Lefebvre Sarrut Belgium NV
Hoogstraat 139/6
1000 Brussels
Belgium
Tel: +32 (0)800 39 067
Email: mail@intersentia.be

Distribution for the USA and Canada
Independent Publishers Group
Order Department
814 North Franklin Street
Chicago, IL 60610
USA
Tel: +1 800 888 4741 (toll free) | Fax: +1 312 337 5985
Email: orders@ipgbook.com

Protecting Community Interests through International Law

Artwork on cover: clivewa / Shutterstock

ISBN 978-1-83970-112-2
D/2021/7849/132
NUR 828

British Library Cataloguing in Publication Data. A catalogue record for this book is available from the British Library.

To my family and friends who became family, with immense gratitude for their love and support throughout many years

Fetije Zyberi and Xhemal Zyberi
Judith Mundwiler and Peter Spinnler
Maria Hijman and Jan Weerdenburg

ACKNOWLEDGEMENTS

An edited volume, like other collective efforts, is built upon academic cooperation, goodwill, and a spirit of collegiality and common purpose. There are many to thank for enabling this volume to reach the publication stage. First, I would like to acknowledge the institutional support of the Norwegian Centre for Human Rights and the Faculty of Law of the University of Oslo, given in the framework of the activities of the Faculty Research Group on Human Rights, Armed Conflicts, and the Law of Peace and Security. I am grateful for the excellent work and support received by our research assistant at the Norwegian Centre for Human Rights, Eduardo Sánchez Madrigal, who painstakingly checked and formatted the footnotes, liaised with the authors and the language proofreader, and ensured that the chapters went through this important process in a timely and efficient manner. My sincere thanks go also to Jenifer Evans for her efforts and meticulous work on the language proofreading.

I am grateful to many colleagues and friends who kindly accepted to engage in a double-blind peer-review of the book's chapters and suggested other colleagues. In alphabetical order, I want to express my sincere thanks and gratitude to Zaker Ahmad, Mads Andenæs, Anna Andersson, Freya Baetens, Yifeng Chen, Priscilla Claeys, Thomas Cottier, Kjetil Mujezinović Larsen, Yuval Shany, Hélène Tigroudja, Dire Tladi, Christina Voigt, and Andreas Zimmermann.

I also want to thank my colleague Tom Scheirs (formerly of Intersentia) and Ahmed Hegazi for their generous and kind support with the publication process. I had previously published my first book with Tom, and it has been a pleasure to cooperate on pushing the second one to print.

Finally, I want to thank my partner, Lila Zotou, for her continuous support and patience with my habits and long work hours.

I hope that readers will enjoy the book and be inspired to pursue individual or joint research projects on this important topic of international law.

Gentian Zyberi
Oslo, May 2021

CONTENTS

LIST OF CASES

INTERNATIONAL COURTS AND TRIBUNALS

INTERNATIONAL COURT OF JUSTICE

PERMANENT COURT OF ARBITRATION

INTERNATIONAL CRIMINAL COURT

INTERNATIONAL CRIMINAL TRIBUNAL FOR THE FORMER YUGOSLAVIA

INTERNATIONAL TRIBUNAL FOR THE LAW OF THE SEA

AFRICAN COMMISSION ON HUMAN AND PEOPLE'S RIGHTS

AFRICAN COURT ON HUMAN AND PEOPLE'S RIGHTS

EUROPEAN COURT OF HUMAN RIGHTS

EUROPEAN COURT OF JUSTICE

INTER-AMERICAN COURT OF HUMAN RIGHTS

HUMAN RIGHTS COMMITTEE

COMMITTEE ON THE RIGHTS OF THE CHILD

NATIONAL COURTS

ARGENTINA

CANADA

FRANCE

GERMANY

ISRAEL

KENYA

UNITED KINGDOM

UNITED STATES OF AMERICA

RUSSIAN FEDERATION

SOUTH AFRICA

LIST OF TREATIES AND OTHER LEGAL INSTRUMENTS

INTERNATIONAL INSTRUMENTS

GENERAL INTERNATIONAL TREATIES

REGIONAL TREATIES

PEACE AGREEMENTS

SPACE LAW TREATIES

INTERNATIONAL HUMAN RIGHTS AND HUMANITARIAN LAW TREATIES

CULTURAL HERITAGE LAW

ENVIRONMENT AND BIODIVERSITY

LAW OF THE SEA

INTERNATIONAL TRADE AND INTELLECTUAL PROPERTY

CONVENTIONS AGAINST CORRUPTION

DOMESTIC LEGISLATION

GERMANY

UNITED STATES

REPORTS, RESOLUTIONS AND OTHER INTERNATIONAL ORGANISATION DOCUMENTS

AFRICAN UNION

COMMISSION OF THE EUROPEAN COMMUNITIES

COUNCIL OF EUROPE

COUNCIL OF THE EUROPEAN COMMUNITIES

COUNCIL OF THE EUROPEAN UNION

EUROPEAN COMMISSION

EUROPEAN PARLIAMENT

GENERAL AGREEMENT ON TARIFFS AND TRADE

UNITED NATIONS

Committee on Economic, Social and Cultural Rights

Committee on the Elimination of Racial Discrimination

Committee on the Rights of the Child

Conference of the Parties Serving as the Meeting of the Parties to the Paris Agreement

General Assembly

Human Rights Committee

Human Rights Council

International Commission on Intervention and State Sovereignty

International Seabed Authority

UN Office of Drugs and Crime

Office of the United Nations High Commissioner for Human Rights

UN Peacebuilding Commission

UN Secretary General

UN Security Council

United Nations Educational, Scientific and Cultural Organization

LEAGUE OF ARAB STATES

ORGANISATION FOR ECONOMIC CO-OPERATION AND DEVELOPMENT

ORGANIZATION OF AMERICAN STATES

ORGANIZATION FOR SECURITY AND CO-OPERATION IN EUROPE

UNIVERSAL POSTAL UNION

WORLD TRADE ORGANIZATION

LIST OF CONTRIBUTORS

Saeed Bagheri is a Lecturer in Law at the University of Reading, where he also served as Postdoctoral Research Fellow (2019–2021). Prior to this, he was a Max Weber Postdoctoral Fellow at the European University Institute (EUI) in Florence. Dr Bagheri undertook his doctoral studies at Ankara University and served as a visiting fellow at the Lauterpacht Centre for International Law (University of Cambridge) (Summer 2018), and a visiting scholar at the Grotius Centre for International Legal Studies (Leiden University) (Spring 2018). He also undertakes the role of Regional Correspondent for the University of Oxford Human Rights Hub. Dr Bagheri teaches and writes on peacebuilding and public international law issues. He has done research, published and taught in the areas of *jus in bello*, *jus ad bellum*, international human rights law and different fields of public international law.

Francesca Capone holds a Law Degree from the University of Naples Federico II and a Joint Ph.D. Degree from the Sant'Anna School of Advanced Studies and Tilburg University. In 2012–2013 she worked as a research fellow at the British Institute of International and Comparative Law in London. Currently she is Assistant Professor (tenure track position) of Public International Law at the Sant'Anna School of Advanced Studies, where from 2014 to 2018 she also served as Research Fellow, lecturer and Coordinator of the Master in Human Rights and Conflict Management. She has been a visiting fellow and guest lecturer at several academic institutions, including Leiden University, the Max Planck Institute for Comparative Public Law and International Law and Addis Ababa University. She has undertaken research on a wide range of topics, encompassing the law of remedies, climate change law, the law of State responsibility, the legal framework governing the response to CBRN events and the main issues connected to international law and terrorism.

Andreas Follesdal (PhD Harvard 1991) is a Professor of Political Philosophy at the Department of Public and International Law, University of Oslo. Follesdal is Co-Director of PluriCourts, a Centre of Excellence for the Study of the Legitimate Roles of the Judiciary in the Global Order.

He was Principal Investigator, European Research Council Advanced Grant MultiRights 2011–16, on the Legitimacy of Multi-Level Human rights Judiciary. Follesdal publishes in the field of political philosophy, mainly on issues of international political theory, globalisation/Europeanisation, Human Rights, and Socially Responsible Investing.

Friederycke Haijer (LL.M) has been a practitioner in both international law as well as criminal law since 2005. She is also a PhD candidate at Utrecht University (the Netherlands), where her research has focused on the extraterritorial enforcement of anticorruption laws in the Netherlands and the United States of America.

Corina Heri is a postdoctoral researcher at the Faculty of Law of the University of Zurich. She was previously a postdoctoral researcher at the Amsterdam Center for International Law (University of Amsterdam), and before that she completed her PhD at the University of Zurich in 2017. She has been a visiting researcher at the Human Rights Centre at Ghent University and has researched, taught and published on international human rights law for almost a decade. Her research interests cover various practical, theoretical and institutional aspects of international human rights law, including the work of the European Court of Human Rights, public interest litigation on discrimination, vulnerability and environmental interests, and the prohibition of torture and ill-treatment.

Rozemarijn Roland Holst is Assistant Professor of Public International Law at Utrecht University School of Law, and a senior research associate of the Netherlands Institute for the Law of the Sea and the Utrecht Centre for Water, Oceans and Sustainability Law. Her research focusses on contemporary challenges at the intersection of the law of the sea, environmental law, and international legal theory. She teaches public international law and legal skills and methodology courses at undergraduate and postgraduate levels. Rozemarijn was a visiting research fellow at the Graduate Institute of International and Development Studies in Geneva. She holds law degrees from the University of Amsterdam, the University of Edinburgh, and received her PhD *cum laude* from Utrecht University.

Lucas Lixinski is a Professor at the Faculty of Law & Justice, UNSW Sydney. Professor Lixinski is also Rapporteur to the International Law Association's Committee on Participation in Global Cultural Heritage Governance, and Vice President (Conference) of the Association of Critical Heritage Studies. He teaches, researches, and publishes primarily in the areas of international human rights and international cultural heritage law, with a range of projects across other facets of public international law, private international law, and comparative law. He has taught at universities in Australia, Brazil, Canada, Colombia, France, Italy, Switzerland, and many others. His current research focuses on the intersections between cultural heritage law and other fields of international law, as well as the ways in which international human rights adjudication shapes and is shaped by human rights social movements and advocacy groups.

Cedric Ryngaert (PhD Leuven 2007) is Chair of Public International Law at Utrecht University (Netherlands) and Head of the Department of International and European Law of the University's Law School. His research interests relate to the law of jurisdiction, immunities, sanctions, international responsibility, and international organizations. Among other publications, Professor Ryngaert has authored *Jurisdiction in International Law* (OUP 2015, 2nd ed) and *Selfless Intervention: The Exercise of Jurisdiction in the Common Interest* (OUP 2020). He is a member of the Dutch Advisory Council on International Law and editor-in-chief of the *Utrecht Law Review*. Previously, he taught at Leuven University and the Military Academy of Belgium.

Matthew Saul is Associate Professor in Law at Inland Norway University of Applied Sciences and a guest researcher at PluriCourts – Centre for the Study of the Legitimate Roles of the Judiciary in the Global Order. He publishes on aspects of general international law, international human rights law, and international adjudication. Saul is co-editor of *International Law and Dispute Settlement: New Techniques and Problems* (2010), *International Law and Post-Conflict Reconstruction Policy* (2015), and *The International Human Rights Judiciary and National Parliaments* (2017). His monograph *Popular Governance of Post-Conflict Reconstruction: The Role of International Law* was published by Cambridge University Press in 2014.

Bruno Simma has been teaching law at the University of Michigan Law School since 1986. He has a lifelong experience teaching and writing on international law, having served as dean of the Faculty of Law at the University of Munich (where he was a Professor for more than 30 years), as lecturer and director of studies at The Hague Academy of International Law (offering the General Course in 2009), and as a visiting professor at several European universities. Professor Simma is author, co-author or editor of around 150 scholarly articles and several influential books, including *Universelles Völkerrecht* and the leading *Commentary on the Charter of the United Nations*. He is a co-founder of the European Journal of International Law and the European Society of International Law and an associate member of the Institut de Droit International. From 1986 to 1996 he was a member of the UN Committee on Economic, Social, and Cultural Rights and, from 1997 to 2002 of the UN International Law Commission. He has served as counsel and arbitrator in various inter-state, foreign investment, international commercial, and sports law cases. From 2003 to 2012, he served as a judge at the International Court of Justice, followed by his appointment as one of the three third-party judges/arbitrators of the Iran-United States Claims Tribunal at The Hague. Professor Simma has been awarded honorary degrees by the universities of Macerata, Innsbruck and Glasgow, as well as a certificate of merit and the Manley O. Hudson Medal by the American Society of International Law in 2013.

Sarah Thin is a PhD Researcher and Tutor in International Law at Maastricht University and Hasselt University, where her research focuses on state responsibility and community interests in international law. She holds an LLB (1st Class) from the University of Durham, UK and an LLM in Public International Law (with Distinction) from the University of Nottingham, UK. At Maastricht University, she coaches several moot courts and coordinates a monthly reading and discussion group for students on Critical Approaches to International Law. She is also the Editorial Assistant for the Hague Yearbook of International Law. Her other areas of research interest and publication include international human rights law, international environmental law, international humanitarian law, and general issues of public international law.

Maruša T. Veber is a Teaching Assistant and a PhD candidate at the Department of International Law at the Faculty of Law, University of Ljubljana. She is pursuing her PhD in collaboration with the Manchester International Law Centre on the topic of sanctions adopted by international organisations in the defence of the general interest. Previously she was a junior visiting fellow at the Graduate Institute of International and Development Studies in Geneva, a visiting scholar at the University of Hull Law School and a researcher at the United Nations University Institute on Comparative Regional Integration Studies (UNU-CRIS) in Bruges. She is a member of Geneva International Sanctions Network and a member of Slovene branch of International Law Association.

Gentian Zyberi is a Professor of International Law and Human Rights and Head of Department of the Norwegian Center for Human Rights (University of Oslo). Professor Zyberi is a member of the UN Human Rights Committee (CCPR, 2019–2022) and a member of the Permanent Court of Arbitration, The Hague, the Netherlands (2016–2022). Over the last two decades, he has done research, published and taught in the areas of international human rights, international humanitarian law, international criminal law and public international law at different universities in the Netherlands, Albania, China, the US, and Norway. His research interests include the role of international courts and tribunals in developing international human rights law, international humanitarian law, and international criminal law; the protection of community interests in international law; operationalization of the responsibility to protect doctrine; transitional justice, especially in the Balkans.

PREFACE

From Bilateralism to Community Interests

I am pleased to write a preface for this volume, edited by my colleague and friend Gentian Zyberi, because the emergence and protection of community interests in international law has been an important topic for my scholarly work and research interests.[1] I am thrilled, though not surprised, that interest in this research topic has taken off in more recent years,[2] including my own *Festschrift*,[3] and hope this scholarly interest continues to grow.

Let me first say a few words about the concept of community interests. Then I will share some thoughts on the scope of the 'international community' and the relevance of international adjudication, before reflecting on potential new frontiers, and finishing with some concluding remarks. As I noted in my course at the Hague Academy of International Law, back in 1995, community interests express a consensus according to which respect for certain fundamental values is not left to the free disposition of states individually or *inter se*, but is recognised and sanctioned by international law as a matter of concern to all states.[4] International practice has shown that 'the identification of common interests does not derive from scientific abstraction but rather flows from the recognition of concrete problems. Besides, the articulation of community interests

---

1 Bruno Simma, 'From Bilateralism to Community Interest in International Law' (1994) 250 Recueil des Cours de l'Académie de Droit International 217–384 (The lecture was held in the summer of 1995, but published in one of the Recueil volumes for 1994).

2 See, among others, Giorgio Gaja, 'The Protection of General Interests in the International Community' (2011) 364 Recueil des Cours 9, Wolfgang Benedek and others (eds), *The Common Interest in International Law* (Intersentia 2014); Claire Buggenhoudt, *Common Interests in International Litigation: A Case Study on Natural Resource Exploitation Disputes* (Intersentia 2017); Eyal Benvenisti and Georg Nolte (eds), *Community Interests Across International Law* (Oxford University Press 2018).

3 Ulrich Fastenrath and others (eds), *From Bilateralism to Community Interest: Essays in Honour of Bruno Simma* (OUP 2011).

4 Simma (n 1) 233.

occupies a permanent place on the agenda of the United Nations and other international bodies or conferences.'[5] Samantha Besson has noted that community interests are best understood, in a nutshell, as interests that are common and/or belong to a community.[6] She has argued that it is best to approach state consent, sovereignty, and equality as contributing to the democratic legitimacy of the identification and protection of community interests in international law, and as community interests themselves.[7] Indeed, these elements are important for ensuring broad legitimacy for the confirmation of community interests in legal form, given some of the inherent shortcomings of international law-making.

Over the years, multilateral treaties have served as the vehicle *par excellence* of the formulation and protection of community interests. While the direction of this development – from bilateralism to community interests – might seem inherent to the nature of international law and result from sustained interaction among members of the international community, it is not necessarily unidirectional or subject to linear progress, as historical events have shown time and again. The success of these efforts hinges on the capacity and goodwill of the actors involved in the implementation of commonly agreed international legal commitments. If we look at international law as the basis for political discourse among members of the international system, as Paul Diehl and Charlotte Ku have pointed out, it performs two distinct functions: one is to provide the parameters and mechanisms for cross-border interactions, and the other is to shape the values and goals these interactions promote. The two authors call the first set of functions the operating system of international law, and the second set the normative system.[8] When it comes to identifying community interests, the normative system has developed considerably, whereas the operating system lags behind in some areas and continues to suffer from the endemic problems of effective enforcement of international legal obligations. That is why the worlds of what 'is' and what 'ought' to be still remain quite far apart. Nevertheless, international law has evolved from simply trying to ensure peaceful co-existence to a more developed stage where common global agendas are agreed and acted upon, such as

5 ibid 235.

6 Samantha Besson, 'Community Interests in International Law: Whose Interests Are They and How We Should Best Identify Them?' in Eyal Benvenisti and Georg Nolte (eds), *Community Interests Across International Law* (OUP 2018) 38.

7 ibid 49.

8 Paul F Diehl and Charlotte Ku, *The Dynamics of International Law* (Cambridge University Press 2010) 2 and especially 28–46.

the Sustainable Development Goals and the Agenda 2030 (as well as the Millennium Development Goals before that) and the international efforts to curb climate change through the 2015 Paris Accords.

A Need to Revisit the Concept of 'International Community'?

By sheer necessity, the quest to realize community interests has led to an ever-stronger institutionalisation or organisation of international society.[9] This process has unfolded over a long time period, from 1920 to the outbreak of World War II, through the League of Nations, and then from 1945 onwards mainly through the United Nations and its specialised agencies. The UN reflects the complex interaction between the various elements that comprise an international society: the realist emphasis on security and state interest, the institutionalist focus on functional cooperation, the cosmopolitan concern with human welfare, and the solidarist interest in promoting common values and principles among states.[10] These are not just elements comprising international society, but also the driving forces behind ongoing efforts to turn it into a community. To a large extent, the various agencies of the UN reflect the different community interests that they are established to foster and achieve.

Undeniably, international law has grown more inclusive in recent decades. But still, when speaking about the protection of community interests in international law, many understand the phrase 'international community' as denoting the organised community of states. After all, states are the primary custodians of such interests, given the state-centred system of international law. However, the concept of 'international community' on which that of 'community interest' is based comprises not only states and international organizations, but also important non-state actors like transnational corporations, and arguably other entities such as international civil society.[11] Many observers have pointed out the evolution of international law from the state-centred system just

9 Simma (n 1) 235.

10 Bruce Cronin, *Institutions for the Common Good: International Protection Regimes in International Society* (CUP 2003) 210.

11 See, among others, Bruno Simma and Andreas L. Paulus, 'The "International Community": Facing the Challenge of Globalization' (1998) 9(2) European Journal of International Law 266. For several relevant chapters, see Part II 'From Westphalia to World Community: Theoretical Perspectives on International Law' in Ulrich Fastenrath and others (eds), *From Bilateralism to Community Interest: Essays in Honour of Bruno Simma* (OUP 2011) 39–197.

mentioned towards one that is more focused on, and accounts better for, the interests of peoples or humanity as a whole.[12] The idea of an international community composed of various types of participants, even if states ostensibly retain a heightened status, would be closer to our notion of an 'international community'. Ultimately, it is the international community thus conceived that is the depository of fundamental values and interests transcending the state.

Community Interests in International Adjudication

The adjudicatory mechanisms of international law have multiplied since 1945,[13] though significant gaps remain. While this is not the place to provide a summary of international case law related to community interests,[14] a quick review of the jurisprudence of the International Court of Justice (ICJ), the principal judicial organ of the UN, shows that cases related to 'community interest', concerning the protection of human rights and accountability for mass atrocity crimes, though few and far in between,[15] have been gaining prominence, although some of the Court's findings might not always be encouraging. Elsewhere, I have pointed out that the intensity of community interests can and will vary due to differences in the geographical positions or economic potential of the states involved.[16]

---

12 See, among others, Theodor Meron, *The Humanization of International Law* (Martinus Nijhoff Publishers 2006); Antônio Augusto Cançado Trindade, *International Law for Humankind: Towards a New Jus Gentium* (2nd rev edn, Brill | Nijhoff 2010); John R Morss, *International Law as the Law of Collectives: Toward a Law of People* (Routledge 2013).

13 See, among others, Karen J Alter 'The Multiplication of International Courts and Tribunals After the End of the Cold War' in Cesare P R Romano, Karen J Alter, and Yuval Shany (eds), *The Oxford Handbook of International Adjudication* (OUP 2013) 63–89; Karin Oellers-Frahm, 'Proliferation' in William A Schabas and Shannonbrooke Murphy (eds), *Research Handbook on International Courts and Tribunals* (Edward Elgar Publishing 2017) 299–336.

14 See, among others, Eyal Benvenisti, 'Community Interests in International Adjudication' in Eyal Benvenisti and Georg Nolte (eds), *Community Interests Across International Law* (OUP 2018) 70–85.

15 See, among others, Bruno Simma, 'Human Rights Before the International Court of Justice: Community Interest Coming to Life?' in Christian J Tams and James Sloan (eds), *The Development of International Law by the International Court of Justice* (OUP 2013) 301–325; Gentian Zyberi 'The Interpretation and Development of International Human Rights Law by the International Court of Justice' in Martin Scheinin (ed), *The Relevance of Human Rights Norms before 'Other' International Courts and Tribunals* (CUP 2019) 28–61.

16 Simma (n 1) 242.

In a finding relevant to the issue of protection of fundamental human rights, the ICJ has confirmed this by holding that the responsibility of states to prevent genocide will depend on a number of factors, including '[t]he capacity to influence effectively the action of persons likely to commit, or already committing, genocide. This capacity itself depends, among other things, on the geographical distance of the State concerned from the scene of the events, and on the strength of the political links, as well as links of all other kinds, between the authorities of that State and the main actors in the events. The State's capacity to influence must also be assessed by legal criteria, since it is clear that every State may only act within the limits permitted by international law; seen thus, a State's capacity to influence may vary depending on its particular legal position vis-à-vis the situations and persons facing the danger, or the reality, of genocide.'[17] This finding points to the layered levels of responsibility for the protection of populations from mass atrocities, with primary responsibility resting on each individual state and residual responsibility resting with the organised international community. The ability to influence a situation also differs considerably from one state to another, with the permanent members of the UN Security Council retaining quite a lot of weight, formally and informally. Perhaps nowhere is this capacity to influence situations, and the dearth of the use thereof, more obvious than in the prolonged armed conflicts in the Middle East and the Great Lakes region in Africa.

Extending the Concept of Community Interest to New Research Frontiers?

In my earlier work I noted a few broad themes relevant to community interests, including international peace and security, the environment, and human rights. While these general areas are still quite relevant to the debates on protecting community interests, other areas have emerged due to technological developments and digitalisation, including the cross-border management of personal and other sensitive data, natural resources, global markets, international cooperation in countering pandemics, sharing of knowledge and advanced technologies, countering climate change and preserving biodiversity, and so on. These new areas need to

17 *Application of the Convention on the Prevention and Punishment of the Crime of Genocide (Bosnia and Herzegovina v Serbia and Montenegro)* (Judgment) [2007] ICJ Rep 43, para 430.

be further developed, also from the aspect of community interests, in the years and decades to come, preferably through a mixed or interdisciplinary approach, where legal methodologies are complemented by approaches from political sciences, international relations, economics, and so on.

Concluding Remarks

The emergence and protection of community interests under international law is an ongoing process of construction and reconstruction, determined by an interaction of various actors and the balancing of competing interests. As the international community develops and new global challenges emerge, so does international law, in an effort to respond to these challenges and secure a more satisfactory system. My hope is that international law scholars will continue to grapple with different aspects of community interests and further develop this important research area with qualitative, quantitative, and comparative studies in a critical spirit. I am heartened by these efforts, including the volume before us, and wish them the best of luck.

Bruno Simma
Munich/The Hague, May 2021

INTRODUCTION

Gentian Zyberi

BACKGROUND

The idea for this edited volume is part of continuous efforts over the last several years to obtain funding for a major research project on the topic, namely the emergence and protection of community interests under international law. Getting external research funding, as many scholars know, is a complex and demanding process, resulting in few successes and many frustrations. While my repeated fundraising efforts at the national and regional level have so far been in vain, the edited book project has come to fruition. Hopefully, it will give others working in this field some inspiration and ideas to pursue further research on the topic.

FROM THE CALL FOR PAPERS TO THE CURRENT EDITED VOLUME

As usual with edited volumes, this project started with a call for papers, made in early 2019, which attracted over 40 abstracts and expressions of interest. From these abstracts, eleven were selected and presented in a conference held in Oslo on 3 June 2019. The conference aimed at providing insights into the role and function of international law in a framework of increased global governance by focusing on how 'community interests' are articulated and protected and how global public goods are provided. Over time, community interests have come to encapsulate some of the global challenges facing the international community, such as ensuring collective human security, managing collective natural resources and countering climate change, and protecting world cultural heritage. Displaying differing degrees of normative intensity and institutional development, these broad areas of international law and governance involve the provision of different global public goods. The comprehensive impact of community interests visible today also reveals a fundamental tension in contemporary international law – the tension between the need to make international law adequately express and support what are assumed to be universally held values and beliefs and the need to make it firmly reflect its political context. The papers presented in the conference tried to address the following three questions:

1. Can international law mediate effectively between competing sovereign and collective concerns?
2. What are the main challenges and prospects of realizing community interests through and across international law?
3. What improvements are necessary to the normative framework and the operating system of international law to ensure an optimal protection of community interests?

While regrettably not all the draft papers presented in the conference could become part of this book, most of them are included. In preparation for publication, the chapters' revisions have benefited from a good exchange between the editor and the contributors and constructive feedback from the peer-reviewers. The draft chapters were discussed and feedback was first received during the conference. Then, in a second round, written editorial feedback was provided to all contributors, resulting in a first revision. Subsequently, the chapters were subjected to peer-review and to one or more further revisions by the authors. While the pandemic slowed down the publication process somewhat, I am very grateful to the contributors, all of whom responded swiftly to my inquiries and worked diligently on the necessary revisions.

OPEN ACCESS, CONTENT, AND RESEARCH ON THE TOPIC

The book is published as open access. The issue of open-access publication of scholarly work is very important and has rightly attracted significant attention and support, though more needs to be done in this regard.

Divided into four parts, the book first deals with general issues, in chapters written by Sarah Thin, Lucas Lixinski, and Andreas Føllesdal. Then, in Part II, the focus shifts onto global commons and concerns, with chapters written by Rozemarijn J. Roland Holst, Maruša T. Veber, Cedric Ryngaert and Friederycke Haijer, and Saeed Bagheri. Human rights and security-related issues are included in Part III, with chapters written by Matthew Saul, Francesca Capone, and Corina Heri. Part IV contains a concluding chapter from myself, containing some suggestions for potential research agendas on the topic.

Part I starts with the chapter by Sarah Thin. She focuses on three key questions in relation to the definition of community interest. First, what is meant by 'interest' in this context? Second, who or what is the 'international community' to which this interest is imputed? Finally, how are particular community interests identified? The answers to these questions serve to shore up the uncertain conceptual foundations upon which community interest is based. Thin concludes that the international community interest is a legal construct that facilitates the translation of commonly recognised values and concerns into legally effective normative statements without necessarily undermining a positivist approach or the fundamental tenets of international law, such as the exclusive law-making authority of states.

Lucas Lixinski's chapter contributes to the conversation about the international legal governance of global public goods by mapping out the various forms of governance created at the juncture of public and private international law. A key objective of his chapter is to inform public international lawyers, or international lawyers more generally invested in the safeguarding of global public goods, so that they can strategically and creatively tap into the possibilities of the private sphere. Cultural heritage is used as a key lens through which to unpack these issues, given the status of heritage as between public and private, and between global and local. Section three, which contains the bulk of this chapter, maps out various strategies of private international legal governance in relation to public values, and particularly shows the uses of language and institutional mechanisms typical of public international law in the pursuance of private international legal governance. Before concluding, Lixinski discusses strategies for reengaging the private in the governance of global public goods beyond cultural heritage.

Andreas Føllesdal's chapter discusses whether international law and international courts are effective in providing so-called global public goods. Section one of his chapter provides a sketch of the standard public goods theory. Section two gives a brief account of the several tasks of international courts, and considers various features and functions that distinguish them from other authorities. To illustrate their differences, the chapter considers three global public goods that pose quite different collective action problems, and where international courts and other bodies may take on distinct tasks: human rights protection, world trade, and the 'differentiated commitments' of the Paris Agreement to help states alleviate the climate crises. Section three seeks to incorporate game-theoretic contributions by various authors that the standard theory leaves untouched, underscoring how its exclusive focus on possible free riders shifts attention from crucial issues. Section four discusses some implications of lifting the constraints of the standard theory for how international courts may contribute to addressing challenges posed by global public goods. Many valuable contributions by international courts occur outside the scope conditions of the standard theory. The upshot is that the standard account ignores other functions of legitimate authorities, such as international courts, including allocating benefits and burdens, facilitating reasoned 'balancing' of conflicting objectives and norms, and addressing battles of the sexes and the need for assurance.

Part II focuses on global commons and concerns, starting with the chapter written by Rozemarijn J. Roland Holst. Her chapter seeks to unravel the oft-posited premise that the relationship between two central 'forces' in the law of the sea – 'sovereign' or individual state interests and community interests – is an inherently contentious one. Showing that sovereign interests and community interests continuously interact in the law of the sea, she proposes that a functional perception of sovereignty best explains the concept's role and functioning under the UN Convention on the Law of the Sea (UNCLOS), and in principle allows it to be aligned with the protection of other states' individual as well as community interests, both in theory and in positive international law. Four distinct ways in which community interests can be accommodated and balanced under UNCLOS are discussed, while persistent challenges are also highlighted. Finally, Holst draws some conclusions about how the reality of modern ocean governance provides examples of both consonance and dissonance between sovereignty and community interests, illustrating the potential and functionality, as well as the limitations, inherent in both concepts.

Maruša T. Veber's chapter seeks to demonstrate that international organizations do play a role in protecting community interests by virtue of the countermeasures they adopt in response to violations of *erga omnes* obligations and to pinpoint some of the controversies and discrepancies between the regime governing these activities of international organizations and their actual practice. First, the chapter clarifies the relevant basic concepts, including international organizations, community interests, and the distinctions and convergences between peremptory norms of international law (*jus cogens*) and *erga omnes* obligations. This is followed by a section on the protection of community interests by international organizations, in which a distinction is made between the invocation of responsibility and the adoption of countermeasures by injured international organizations and the invocation of responsibility and the adoption of countermeasures by organizations other than injured international organizations for the protection of community interests. Finally, Veber turns to an analysis of the relevant practice of international organizations when adopting countermeasures without the underlying communitarian norm breached being among the functions of the organization in question and situations where such norms are embedded in the constitutive act of the international organization.

Friederycke Haijer and Cedric Ryngaert's chapter makes the argument that preventing and punishing foreign corruption, in particular grand corruption by large corporations, reflects community interests. In order to maximize the fight against corruption, the OECD and UN Conventions give broad jurisdictional grants to states parties to take global anti-corruption enforcement action in relation to foreign corrupt practices. This allows states to act, at least potentially, as 'extraterritorial' enforcers of international community interests. Such enforcement comes with a number of problems, however. First, the expansive ways in which states, especially the United States, have construed jurisdictional grants, in particular the territoriality principle, may be in tension with the international law of jurisdiction. Bearing in mind that international law does not (yet) authorize the exercise of universal jurisdiction over corruption (that is, the jurisdictional ground *par excellence* in respect of the protection of community interests), it is uncertain whether the international criminalization of corruption can serve a justificatory role. While enforcement of anti-corruption norms potentially serves community interests in the abstract, it remains to be seen *which* interests of *which* communities are served in reality. Ideally, from an international community perspective, enforcement should serve the interests of those most victimized by foreign corrupt practices: the people who live in the countries affected by corrupt acts such as rigged tenders. By means of three case studies, Haijer and Ryngaert show that in practice, enforcement action rather serves the interests of the treasury of the enforcing states, and company shareholders allegedly injured by foreign corrupt practices.

Saeed Bagheri's chapter builds on the premise that the divisions and conflicts that have arisen in Iraq, particularly after the fall of the Islamic State, have roots in the weak governance and mismanagement of oil resources. A fair and sustainable management of these resources is key to ensuring and enhancing equality and political stability in federal Iraq's ethnically diverse society. His chapter tries to explain why good governance of resources in conflict-affected regions, through community initiatives ensuring equality, human rights, and the rule of law, is important. Certainly, resource management in line with the rule of law and the principle of equality inherently protects community interests, which in turn makes peacebuilding achievable. Focusing on the priority of common interests in natural resources, which belong to the whole community and to its individual members, over governments' interests, Bagheri examines his case study: how the uneven sharing of resources and the withholding of the regional government's proceeds from the national budget by the Iraqi central government disappointed the Kurdistan Regional Government (KRG) as part of the Iraqi community. He argues that ensuring trust and cooperation between the Iraqi government and the KRG is the basis for fairly sharing and protecting the common interests of the various ethnic communities in the country's natural resources, which is in turn the most effective way to achieve stability and peacebuilding in post-war Iraq. Finally, Bagheri evaluates several issues related to peacebuilding in Iraqi society after Islamic State as a matter of the *jus post bellum* and the good governance of energy resources as subject to the protection of community interests.

Part III is concerned with human rights and security-related issues. Matthew Saul's chapter analyses the right to self-determination and the prolonged occupation of Palestinian territory. Saul argues that when circumstances add complexity and uncertainty to the operation of a specialized legal regime, it is important to recognize that fundamental principles of international law continue to operate as a baseline securing protection of international community interests. The right to self-determination as a precept of non-domination provides legal protection in situations of prolonged occupation regardless of the haze that can form around the meaning and application of the law of occupation. The right to self-determination precludes practices that will pre-empt the choices available to the people at the end of an occupation with regard to the territory's organization, utilization, and status. Saul concludes that attempts to make sense of the law of occupation in situations of prolonged occupation should not come at the expense of attending to the meaning of, and legal consequences that result from, denial of the right to self-determination.

Francesca Capone's chapter deals with the issue of return of foreign terrorist fighters to their countries of origin. The presence of such fighters in Syria, Iraq, and to a far lesser extent Libya, triggers a number of questions that states, individually and collectively, seem unequipped or unwilling to address. So far the states most affected by the current situation, which include European states, have adopted heterogeneous and even contradictory strategies in relation to the repatriation of terrorist fighters and the women and children accompanying them. After clarifying who falls within this category and which specific issues emerge in relation to their accompanying family members, this chapter reflects on whether or not an obligation to repatriate terrorist fighters and their families can be inferred from one or more subfields of international law. The situation of foreigners, in particular women and children, deprived of liberty outside formal arrest and detention, appears much more complex and requires a closer look at states' obligations under the law of diplomatic and consular relations, as well as human rights law, which come into play when the states of origin of terrorist fighters are called on to protect their nationals abroad. This approach serves as the basis of this chapter. Finally, since the repatriation of foreign terrorist fighters is not just a legal challenge but also triggers important moral and security considerations, Capone tries, to the maximum degree possible, incorporate these perspectives too.

Corina Heri's chapter discusses some of the main novelties contained in the UN Declaration on the Rights of Peasants (UNDROP) – significantly, the right to food and seed sovereignty, the peasants' right to land, and environmental rights claims – and analyzes how, by gaining recognition of these rights specifically and the peasant rights project more generally, the peasant movement is exposing gaps in the interests protected by human rights law and using a human rights frame to seek to fill these lacunae. The chapter seeks to address some of the core indeterminacies of international law, and specifically of international human rights law, by showing how peasant human rights can help to contest not only the usefulness of the concept of community interests, but also some of the widely accepted constraints of liberal, Western, individualistic, universal, and state- and freedom-oriented human rights law with the injection of a mixture of radical, critical, third-world, and Marxist perspectives. The struggle by self-identified peasants from across the globe for the recognition of peasant human rights proposes some new insights for how to approach and address these issues. Heri's chapter discusses some of the novel claims made in this regard, which include the right to food sovereignty, the right to seed sovereignty, and the peasant right to land. A close look at peasant rights also shows that in the context of that system the concept of community interests is an ambiguous and therefore, in her view, a potentially harmful one.

Part IV contains my own chapter, which provides an analysis of the concept of 'community interests' in international law, before presenting a potential research agenda on three areas: ensuring collective human security, managing collective natural resources, and preserving world cultural heritage. While displaying different degrees of normative intensity and institutional development, these areas involve the provision of various important global public goods. The chapter discusses the nature and scope of the concepts of 'international community' and 'community interests' and the process through which certain issues of common international concern are elevated into constituting a 'community interest'. That process presupposes the elevation of a specific community interest to the level of representing common legal obligations incumbent upon the international community as a whole, and that such community interest is fostered and protected through appropriate institutional mechanisms or arrangements. An in-depth exploration of the formulation and protection of community interests has three interrelated aspects. First, it requires an understanding of the theoretical basis of the concept of 'community interests'. Second, it needs an analysis of the adequacy and effectiveness of the institutional framework and mechanisms established to protect and safeguard community interests. Third, the research must address challenges and prospects for ensuring community interests, be they concerned with efficiently managing public goods or with protecting common values. Research based on international law theories, combined with multi- or inter-disciplinary approaches on the processes of formulation and protection of community interests, can provide useful insights and answers to important questions for the future of humankind.

PART I

GENERAL ISSUES

IN SEARCH OF COMMUNITY

Towards a Definition of Community Interest

Sarah THIN*

1. INTRODUCTION

The notion of 'community interest' has the potential to revolutionise our understanding of international law. To look at international law through a traditionalist lens is to view it as a network of bilateral, horizontal relationships between sovereign states. Such a panorama is dependent upon the primacy of individual state interests as the basis for international law-making. The emergence of the international *community* interest has already caused cracks to form in this traditional image: individual state interest and bilateralism cannot explain, for example, laws protecting the human rights of individuals against interference by their own state, nor can they explain rules that oblige a state to conserve internationally significant biodiversity within its own territory. The traditional image cannot be reconciled with the limits that *jus cogens* places on the contractual freedom of states, or the existence of obligations *erga omnes*.

* PhD Researcher and Tutor in International Law at Maastricht University and Hasselt University.

Community interest therefore holds important potential, both to explain existing changes and as a normative basis for the progressive development of a new international legal order. However, an important barrier stands in the way of realising this potential: namely, the confusion surrounding what community interest is and how it works. Despite the popularity of the subject for scholars and students of international law,[1] the definitional step is often skipped or assumed, leaving room for uncertainty and diverging ideas.[2] This chapter seeks to provide the necessary clarity by focusing on three key questions in relation to the definition of the community interest. First, what is meant by 'interest' in this context (II)? Second, who or what is the 'international community' to which this interest is imputed (III)? Finally, how are particular community interests identified (IV)? The answers to these questions will serve to shore up the uncertain conceptual foundations upon which the community interest is based.

2. INTEREST

'Interest' is a difficult concept to pin down. The term is often used differently in legal and non-legal contexts. There is frequently confusion between the notion of an interest itself and the thing in which one may have an interest, or between a legal interest and a rule protecting that interest or the legal rights that derive therefrom. Furthermore, not all interests are of the same type, as will be discussed below.

---

1 See notably Bruno Simma, 'From Bilateralism to Community Interest in International Law' (1994) 250 Recueil des Cours de l'Académie de Droit International 217; Santiago Villalpando, 'The Legal Dimension of the International Community: How Community Interests Are Protected in International Law' (2010) 21(2) European Journal of International Law 387; Eyal Benvenisti and Georg Nolte (eds), *Community Interests Across International Law* (OUP 2018); Wolfgang Benedek and others (eds), *The Common Interest in International Law* (Intersentia 2014).

2 There are of course exceptions where definition has been attempted, although these are by no means uniform in their approach. Cf Samantha Besson, 'Community Interests in International Law: Whose Interests Are They and How Should We Best Identify Them?' in Eyal Benvenisti and Georg Nolte (eds), *Community Interests Across International Law* (OUP 2018); Isabel Feichtner, 'Community Interest' in Rüdiger Wolfrum (ed), *Max Planck Encyclopedia of International Law* (OUP 2007); Simma (n 1) 233; Wolfgang Benedek and others, 'Conclusions: The Common Interest in International Law – Perspectives for an Undervalued Concept' in Wolfgang Benedek and others (eds), *The Common Interest in International Law* (Intersentia 2014) 219.

An interest may be defined as the 'advantage or benefit of a person or group'; a 'stake or involvement in an undertaking'.[3] In this sense interests therefore exist only in relation to the subject to whom this benefit or advantage would accrue. Herein lies the main distinction between interests and values: while interests are inherently dependent on the actor or holder to whom they accrue, values exist independently of those who believe in them – although, certainly, one may have an interest in their protection or promotion.[4] An interest is normative in the sense that it 'always manifests itself in relation to a certain desired course of conduct'.[5] In this way, an interest translates a non-normative concept (a desired factual situation or an abstraction such as a value) into a normative proposition, dependent upon the holder of the interest.

In order for an interest to have legal effect, however, it must be granted such effect by a legal rule.[6] An interest has no integral or intrinsic legal force. Not all interests are protected by law: *non-legal interests* should be distinguished from *legal interests*, where only the latter benefit from legal protection.[7] This was affirmed by the ICJ in the *South West Africa* cases when it stressed that 'the existence of an "interest" does not of itself entail that this interest is specifically juridical in character.'[8] There must be something more: 'in order to generate legal rights and obligations, [an interest] must be given juridical expression and be clothed in legal form.'[9] It is *rules* that give interests legal force. Most categories of interest, including the community interest, straddle this divide between legal and non-legal interests. Some community interests benefit from legal protection, while others do not.

Legal rules protect or promote the community interest in two main ways. First, numerous primary rules have the effect of protecting or

---

3 Oxford English Dictionary <https://en.oxforddictionaries.com/definition/interest> accessed 15 January 2021.

4 Besson (n 2) 38; Giorgio Gaja, 'The Protection of General Interests in the International Community' (2013) 364 Recueil des Cours 9, 20.

5 Andreas De Hoogh, 'Obligations *Erga Omnes* and International Crimes: A Theoretical Inquiry into the Implementation and Enforcement of the International Responsibility of States' (Proefschrift, Radboud University, formerly Katholieke Universiteit Nijmegen 1995) 10.

6 *South West Africa Cases (Ethiopia v South Africa; Liberia v South Africa)* (Second Phase, Judgment) [1966] ICJ Rep 6, para 51.

7 Gaja (n 4) 21; De Hoogh (n 5) 12.

8 *South West Africa* (n 6) [50].

9 ibid [51].

promoting aspects of the community interest. This is the case with many rules of international human rights law or international environmental law, for example. A legal rule that stipulates that a state must take certain actions in order to protect internationally significant biodiversity within its territory can be said to further community interest with regard to such environmental concerns.[10] It does so incidentally, however, in the sense that the rule is inspired by the community interest, but does not protect the concept of community interest directly.

A different kind of legal rule grants legal force to the concept of the community interest itself. This is where the real transformative potential of community interest lies: at the intersection between community interest and the secondary rules of international law. Rules of *jus cogens* and obligations *erga omnes* in particular represent the most commonly accepted 'doctrinal expressions' of community interest.[11] Both are considered to belong to the same overarching idea: namely, the heightened protection of fundamental community interests.[12] They therefore relate not to *particular* community interests, but to the *concept of community interest* itself.

The emergence of such 'communitarian'[13] or community interest norms promises to imbed the notion within the normative structures of the international legal system. Thus, *jus cogens* (or peremptory[14]) norms

---

10 For instance, Convention on Biological Diversity (adopted 5 June 1992, entered into force 29 December 1993) 1760 UNTS 79 arts 5–14.

11 Simma (n 1) 285.

12 Santiago Villalpando, for example, sees obligations *erga omnes* and peremptory norms as having a 'racine commune', namely 'la protection des biens ou valeurs collectifs qui sont d'intérêt de la communauté internationale toute entière': Santiago Villalpando, *L'émergence de la communauté internationale dans la responsabilité des Etats* (Graduate Institute Publications 2005) 84. See also Maja Ménard, 'Circumstances Precluding Wrongfulness in the ILC Articles on State Responsibility: Compliance with Peremptory Norms' in James Crawford and others (eds), *The Law of International Responsibility* (OUP 2010) 449; ILC, 'Draft Articles on Responsibility of States for Internationally Wrongful Acts, with commentaries' in *Report of the International Law Commission on its 53rd Session* (23 April–1 June and 2 July–10 August 2001) UN Doc A/56/10 (ARSIWA) Commentary to Article 45 [4]; Vera Gowlland-Debbas, 'Judicial Insights into Fundamental Values and Interests of the International Community' in Muller, Raic and Thuransky (eds), *The International Court of Justice: Its Future Role after 50 Years* (Martinus Nijhoff 1997).

13 James Crawford, 'Responsibility for Breaches of Communitarian Norms: an Appraisal of Article 48 of the ILC Articles on Responsibility of States for Internationally Wrongful Acts' in Ulrich Fastenrath and others (eds), *From Bilateralism to Community Interest: Essays in Honour of Bruno Simma* (OUP 2011) 229.

14 See United Nations General Assembly 'Third report on peremptory norms of general international law (*jus cogens*) by Dire Tladi, Special Rapporteur' (12 February 2018) International Law Commission 17th session UN Doc A/CN.4/714.

prevent the creation of treaty rules that conflict with rules protecting fundamental community interests.[15] This protection is extended by the non-applicability of circumstances precluding wrongfulness as a means of avoiding or excluding responsibility for the breach of an obligation arising from a *jus cogens* norm.[16] The International Law Commission's Articles on State Responsibility also introduce a differentiated responsibility regime with additional legal consequences incurred in the case of a 'serious breach' of a *jus cogens* norm.[17] With regard to obligations *erga omnes*, the existence of a community interest in the fulfilment of a certain obligation creates a procedural right on the part of every state to invoke responsibility for the breach of that obligation.[18] This is not to say that the *right* to performance of the obligation has been violated in relation to each and every other state. It should be recalled that while the recognition of a legal interest may result in the generation of certain rights, the two concepts are distinct.[19]

The integrated protection of the community interest as a concept facilitates the dynamism of its content. As with any interest, community or individual, the substantive content of that interest is bound to evolve in accordance with what is considered to be a benefit or advantage in the given circumstance. The community interest is in a constant state of development 'in accordance with the changing requirements of the international community.'[20] There is therefore a movement or fluidity between what is in the community interest and what is not.[21] While the evolution of the interest and the corresponding community interest norms is hardly likely to happen overnight, it is important to highlight that it can and does change in accordance with international society. Its content is not static. Integration, through tools such as *jus cogens* and

---

15 Vienna Convention on the Law of Treaties (adopted 23 May 1969, entered into force 27 January 1980) 1155 UNTS 332 (VCLT) arts 53 and 64.

16 ARSIWA, art 26.

17 ibid arts 40, 41.

18 Crawford (n 13) 227.

19 See *Nicaragua v Colombia*, wherein the ICJ stated that, in order to intervene in judicial proceedings as a third party (Statute of the International Court of Justice (1946) UKTS 67, Article 62), a state need not 'establish that one of its rights may be affected,' but simply that it has an interest 'of a legal nature' that may be affected by the Court's decision in the main proceedings: *Territorial and Maritime Dispute (Nicaragua v Colombia)* (Application for Permission to Intervene, Judgment) [2011] ICJ Rep 420, para 37. See also *Barcelona Traction, Light and Power Company, Limited (Belgium v. Spain)* (Judgment) [1970] ICJ Rep 3, para 46.

20 Gowlland-Debbas (n 12) 363.

21 This is discussed further below, in section IV.

erga omnes, allows the legal protection of community interest (the *legal* community interest) to keep up with its changing content.

As noted above, not all interests are of the same type. There is an important distinction to be made between *individual interests* and *common interests*. The 'community interest' is a particular type of common interest, namely one that is held by the 'international community as a whole'.[22] The distinction between individual and common interests is sometimes misunderstood as a purely quantitative difference, that is, whether there is one or more holder of the interest in question. This approach tends to present common interests as collective interests: the lowest common denominator or shared individual interests of a group of actors.[23] While a quantitative element is clearly necessary – it would seem strange to say the least that a community interest could be held by an individual actor alone – this does not capture the full picture. The better approach is to understand the distinction between this and common interests as both quantitative and *qualitative*.[24] While 'individual interests' are private interests,[25] 'common interests' are those which are (a) shared by a group of actors and (b) transcend the individual interests of those actors.[26] They are greater than the sum of individual interests of the members of the group in question, and instead present a quality of commonality that goes beyond the mere coincidental lining up of individual interests.[27] In this sense, they 'transcend' individual interests.[28]

The superiority of this approach is grounded in the concept's utility. If a common interest is simply the lowest common denominator or aggregate form of the individual interests of all members of the commonality,

---

22 See e.g. ARSIWA, art 48; VCLT art 53.

23 See e.g. CW Cassinelli, 'Some Reflections on the Concept of the Public Interest' (1958) 69 Ethics 48, in relation to the public interest, at 50, 54.

24 Pavel Mates and Michal Bartoň, 'Public versus Private Interest – Can the Boundaries be Legally Defined?' (2011) Czech Yearbook of International Law 171, 181.

25 See Virginia Held, *The Public Interest and Private Interests* (Basic Books 1970) 18–19.

26 Judge Gaja draws an equivalent distinction between individual interests, collective interests (the aggregate of individual interests and 'general interests') which appear to be more or less synonymous with the concept of common interest outlined here: Gaja (n 4) 21.

27 Stephen M King, Bradley S Chilton and Gary E Roberts, 'Reflections on Defining the Public Interest' (2010) 41 Administration and Society 954, 957; see also *Reservations to the Convention on the Prevention and Punishment of the Crime of Genocide* (Advisory Opinion) [1951] ICJ Rep 15, para 23.

28 Benedict Kingsbury and Megan Donaldson, 'From Bilateralism to Publicness in International Law' in Ulrich Fastenrath and others (eds), *From Bilateralism to Community Interest: Essays in Honour of Bruno Simma* (OUP 2011) 81.

there will always be a confluence between the interests of individual states and the common interest. There is thus never any possibility of conflict between the common and individual interest.[29] The content of the community interest could never go beyond that which was shared, individually, by each and every member of the community. If this is the case, then the concept of common (and thus community) interest holds no utility: it is 'purely a rhetorical technique.'[30] This is quite clearly not the case with the community interest, however. As noted above, the community interest, through doctrinal innovations such as *jus cogens*, limits the traditionally unlimited freedom of states to act in pursuance of their individual interests. The balancing of interests between community and individual is inherent within, and an important aspect of, the concept of community interest.

In order to understand this fully, we turn next to the concept of 'community'. Who, or what, is the international community whose interest is balanced against that of individual states?

3. COMMUNITY

The term 'international community' appears in such a diversity of guises and contexts that it appears to mean both everything and nothing simultaneously. It is used to mean many different things, and in this sense, there is not one 'international community' that matters. It is clear that there are occasions on which the term is used purely rhetorically.[31] However, on other occasions, 'international community' (or occasionally 'international community of states') carries a distinct meaning, namely a collective term for those actors with law-making authority on the level of states. This is

---

29 This problem has been explored in relation to the public interest: see William D Zarecor, 'The Public Interest and Political Theory' (1959) 69 Ethics 277, 279; Frank J Sorauf, 'The Public Interest Reconsidered' (1957) 19 The Journal of Politics 616, 625; Mates and Bartoň (n 24) 181.

30 Gleider Hernandez, 'A Reluctant Guardian: The International Court of Justice and the Concept of "International Community"' (2013) 83(1) British Yearbook of International Law 13, 19.

31 See e.g. Foreign Ministers of Canada, France, Germany, Italy, Japan, the United Kingdom and the United States of America, and the EU High Representative, *Statement on the situation in the West of Libya (05.04.19)*, 2019 available at <https://www.diplomatie.gouv.fr/en/french-foreign-policy/french-g7-presidency/events/article/g7-foreign-ministers-statement-on-the-situation-in-the-west-of-libya-05-04-19> accessed 15 January 2021.

the case, for example, with the use of the term 'international community of states' in the context of the recognition of *jus cogens* norms.[32]

This state-focused approach to the identity of the international community has been criticised, particularly by those who argue that the increasing role of non-state entities in the formation of international law grants these entities the status of 'new subjects of international law', and thus makes them members of the international legal community alongside states.[33] McCorquodale argues that many non-state actors (including individuals, non-governmental organisations, and indeed multinational corporations) take an active part in the formation of international law, and should therefore be considered members of the legal community.[34] He rejects the 'exclusionary fiction'[35] of the binary notions of subjecthood and objecthood,[36] promoting instead a concept of 'participation'.[37] While it may indeed be true to say that individuals participate indirectly in international law-making, they do not, however, have true law-making capacity. Humans may well be the ultimate creators of international law,[38] but despite the indirect influence individuals surely have on the formation of international law,[39] they do not have the legal authority to create and consent to legal rules in the international legal order.

Alternatively, some have argued that individuals may now be considered 'subjects' of international law on the basis that they can now be said to have both rights[40] and obligations[41] under international law.[42]

---

32 VCLT art 53.

33 See e.g. Dino Kritsiotis, 'Imagining the International Community' (2002) 13(4) EJIL 961, 966.

34 Robert McCorquodale, 'International Community and State Sovereignty: An Uneasy Symbiotic Relationship' in Colin Warbrick and Stephen Tierney (eds), *Towards an 'International Community'? The Sovereignty of States and the Sovereignty of International Law* (BIICL 2006) 255, 257–261.

35 ibid 253.

36 See also Rosalyn Higgins, *Problems and Process: International Law and How We Use It* (OUP 1994), 48–50.

37 McCorquodale (n 34) 254.

38 Christian Tomuschat, 'Obligations Arising for States Without or Against Their Will' (1993) 241 Recueil des Cours 195 235–236.

39 See Robert McCorquodale, 'The Individual in International Law' in Malcolm D Evans (ed), *International Law* (4th edn, OUP 2014), 294–300; Andrew Clapham, 'The Role of the Individual in International Law' (2010) 21(1) EJIL 25, 25–26.

40 *LaGrand (Germany v United States of America)* (Judgment) [2001] ICJ Rep 466, para 77.

41 Most notably under international criminal law. See generally Rome Statute of the International Criminal Court (1998) 2187 UNTS 38544 arts 6–8 and 8*bis*.

42 Clapham (n 39); McCorquodale (n 34) 252; James Crawford 'Responsibility to the International Community as a Whole' (2001) 8(2) Indiana Journal of Global Legal Studies 303, 314.

Thus, international law is no longer exclusively a 'law between states'.[43] One might therefore suppose that, since there exist legal relationships between individuals and states under international law, the former are members of the international legal community. This is an interesting argument but flawed in two key ways. Firstly, in a strict sense, even the rights created under human rights treaties are not, in international legal terms, held by individuals: rather, these treaties create rights and obligations binding upon states, with individuals as the 'beneficiaries'.[44] Even if individuals were understood to hold rights under international law, they do not have the legal capacity to directly enforce those rights within the international system.[45] They are thus 'still "objects", not subjects of international law'.[46] Second, there is an important distinction to be made between international law and *public* international law. Whereas '[t]he law that applies *within* the international community may be called international law,'[47] *public* international law 'regulates relations between States, that is, between centrally organized entities having distinct existence and endowed with sovereign authority.'[48] Public international law 'emanates from the State, is organized around States and addresses reciprocal relations between States.'[49] Individuals 'are not direct subjects of public international law but are represented by States.'[50] They are therefore not directly governed by the rule of recognition; this position is reserved for states.

Perhaps the best illustration of this point is made through reference to the operation of the rules on statehood. As Tsagourias remarks, '[r]ecognition immortalizes States'.[51] Thus, when a territorial and political entity becomes

---

43 Stephen C Neff, 'A Short History of International Law' in Malcolm D Evans (ed), *International Law* (4th edn, OUP 2014) 14.

44 Clapham (n 39) 27.

45 Antonio Cassese, *International Law* (2nd edn, OUP 2003) 144–50. This should be distinguished from individual complain mechanisms and other such procedures that are exclusively treaty-based and do not amount to the invocation of the responsibility of a state under international law (see ARSIWA arts 42 and 48).

46 Bruno Simma and Andreas Paulus, 'The "International Community": Facing the Challenge of Globalization' (1998) 9(2) EJIL 266, 273.

47 Nicholas Tsagourias, 'International Community, Recognition of States, and Political Cloning' in Colin Warbrick and Stephen Tierney (eds), *Towards an 'International Community'? The Sovereignty of States and the Sovereignty of International Law* (BIICL 2006) 220 (emphasis added).

48 ibid 218 (citations omitted).

49 ibid.

50 ibid.

51 ibid 228.

a state under international law, its legal rights and obligations cannot be taken away without its express or implied consent. This is contrasted with the position of the individual, the rights and obligations of whom are created by states and constantly subject to alteration or abrogation by states. Thus, 'the state remains the basic unit in the world of public international law,'[52] and only states may be considered members of the international legal community.

Therefore, despite the great influence that other actors may have in international law,[53] states remain the only ones with law-making authority.[54] For this reason, the state-based nature of the international (law-making) community remains unchanged. This is not necessarily to say that other actors may not have law-making authority in the future, but for now, states remain 'the basic unit in the world of public international law.'[55]

However, the reluctance or aversion to the notion that the interest of the 'international community as a whole' should be limited to that of the international community of states is based on a perceived genuine problem.[56] A state-based approach certainly appears at first glance to limit the concept's scope and potential. Indeed, it seems scarcely reconcilable with much of the usage of the phrase 'interest of the international community' by international courts and by states themselves.

This concern is an unnecessary one. It is premised upon a misunderstanding of the commonality of common interests. As noted above, the community interest is a common interest. It is not, therefore, the sum total of the individual interests of the 'holders' of that interest. Instead, as explained above, it reflects the values[57] or concerns[58] that are shared by these actors and which *transcend* their individual interests. Thus, the identity of the 'holders' of the interest does not necessarily limit the content of that interest to what we perceive as state interests. In the

---

52 Simma and Paulus (n 46)273.

53 See McCorquodale (n 34) 255, 257–261.

54 With the notable exception of international organisations, although this can still be explaining in terms of state sovereignty as international organisations only enjoy this status or quality because they are inter-state institutions; they gain their subjecthood by being essentially groupings of states: See *Reparation for Injuries Suffered in the Service of the United Nations* (Advisory Opinion) [1949] ICJ Rep 174, para 185.

55 Simma and Paulus (n 46), 273.

56 See e.g. Kritsiotis (n 33) 973 *et seq*; Villalpando (n 12) 20.

57 Erika de Wet, 'The International Constitutional Order' (2006) 55 International & Comparative Law Quarterly 51; *Reservations to the Convention on Genocide* (n 27) 23.

58 E.g. the concept of the common concern of mankind in international environmental law: Convention on Biological Diversity (n 10) preamble.

same way that individuals in a society may hold both individual and 'social' interests[59] that do not necessarily coincide with one another – for example, a wealthy person may have a social interest in financial equality, or any number of people may have a social interest in the wellbeing of animals – so may states share common interests that do not necessarily coincide with their individual interests.[60] These social interests may reflect the wellbeing of individuals or the causes espoused by NGOs, but that does not make the latter members of the international legal community.

Thus, the 'holders' of the community interest may be limited to states. However, this is not to limit the understanding of the international community to whom the community interest attaches. At the end of the day, it is not so much a collection of legal actors but an *idea*. It is a legal fiction to which we impute interests, in very much the same way as we impute interests to the socio-legal construct of 'the public'. In this way, the 'international community' finds definition (at least for these purposes) in the international community interest, and not the other way around. The question of the identity of the community is less fundamental to the content of the interest than might otherwise be assumed. Despite this, it will be relevant to identifying that content, as is discussed in the following section.

4. IDENTIFICATION

Finally, we turn to the identification of particular community interests. This relates to the process by which particular interests are imputed to the 'legal fiction' or idea of the international community outlined above. How we understand this process necessarily impacts upon how we understand the nature and normative basis of the community interest, and vice versa.

Most approaches to this question boil down to two major schools of thought relating to the underlying philosophy of international law: natural law and positivism.[61] For the former, the community interest relates to a

59 See Cassinelli (n 23) 54.

60 See Besson (n 2) 46–47.

61 UNGA 'First report on *jus cogens* by Dire Tladi, Special Rapporteur' (8 March 2016) International Law Commission 68th session UN Doc A/CN.4/693 at 23 [42] and 30 [50].

higher law based on a shared international system of inherent values.[62] For the latter, it represents a legal fiction to which interests are imputed by means of (state) recognition.[63] As there has been next to no express guidance (judicial or otherwise) on identifying international public interests *per se*, the following analysis makes use of evidence pertaining to the identification of community interest norms,[64] most notably obligations *erga omnes* and *jus cogens*. As explained above, these are essentially the vector through which the concept of community interest takes legal effect. They therefore constitute a useful means by which to analyse the identification of the interest, even though they may only protect certain aspects of it.[65]

4.1. NATURAL LAW APPROACHES

Natural law approaches have several proponents. O'Connell and Dubois, for example, are prominent in arguing that peremptory norms 'bind all states (or even all subjects of international law) because of their intrinsic moral value, making them a legal necessary law.'[66] Similarly, Ragazzi has propounded a theory of obligations *erga omnes* based on the fact that they reflect 'an exceptionless moral norm (or moral absolute) prohibiting an act which, in moral terms, is intrinsically evil.'[67] This position is reflected in the ICJ's references to 'moral law',[68]

---

62 Mary E O'Connell, '*Jus Cogens*: International Law's Higher Ethical Norms' in Donald Earl Childress III (ed), *The Role of Ethics in International Law* (Cambridge University Press 2012) 93–94. Wolfgang Benedek and others also suggest 'the long-term survival of humankind' as a substantive principle upon which to found the international common interest: Wolfgang Benedek and others (eds), *The Common Interest in International Law* (Intersentia 2014) 221.

63 See Michael Byers, 'Conceptualising the Relationship between Jus Cogens and Erga Omnes Rules' (1997) 66(2–3) Nordic Journal of International Law 211.

64 See above, section II.

65 Jure Vidmar, 'Norm Conflicts and Hierarchy in International Law: Towards a Vertical International Legal System?' in Jure Vidmar and Erika de Wet (eds), *Hierarchy in International Law: The Place of Human Rights* (OUP 2012) 13, 26. See also Gaja (n 4) 53; Besson (n 2) 42.

66 Robert Kolb, *Peremptory International Law –* Jus Cogens*: A General Inventory* (Hart Publishing 2015) 30. See further O'Connell (n 62); Dan Dubois, 'The Authority of Peremptory Norms in International Law: State Consent or Natural Law' (2009) 78(2) Nordic Journal of International Law 133, 133.

67 Mauricio Ragazzi, *The Concept of Obligations Erga Omnes* (OUP 1997) 183.

68 *Reservations to the Convention on Genocide* (n 27) at 23; see also *Application of the Convention on the Prevention and Punishment of the Crime of Genocide (Bosnia and*

'elementary principles of morality',[69] 'elementary considerations of humanity',[70] and 'intransgressible principles' in the context of *jus cogens*, and the emphasis on 'the very nature'[71] of obligations *erga omnes* as the basis for their classification as such.[72] Similar language is used in international,[73] regional,[74] and domestic[75] court and tribunal decisions. However, the legal import of this phraseology is debatable. The use of these terms has not resulted in any direct legal effect,[76] and the content of these ideas is often analysed with reference to state practice rather than some kind of higher law.[77] It is therefore entirely possible to read them as simple rhetoric or 'ornament'.[78]

There are two major conceptual and practical problems with the natural law theory. As noted by the ILC's Special Rapporteur on peremptory norms, '[t]he primary difficulty [with this theory] remains the question of who determines the content of natural law.'[79] The idea of a higher

Herzegovina v Serbia and Montenegro) (Preliminary Objections, Judgment) [1996] ICJ Rep 595, para 31.

69 *Reservations to the Convention on Genocide* (n 27).

70 *Corfu Channel case (United Kingdom of Great Britain and Northern Ireland v. Albania)* (Merits) (Judgment) [1949] ICJ Rep 4, para 22; *Military and Paramilitary Activities in and Against Nicaragua (Nicaragua v United States)* (Merits) [1986] ICJ Rep 14, paras 215, 218.

71 *Barcelona Traction* (n 19) [33].

72 Ragazzi (n 67) 183.

73 E.g. *Prosecutor v Anto Furundzija* (Judgment) ICTY-95-17/1-T (10 December 1998) [153]; *Prosecutor v Stanislav Galić* (Judgment) ICTY-98-29-T (5 December 2003), para 98.

74 The Inter-American Court of Human Rights (IACHR) has similarly approached the peremptory status of the prohibitions of torture and forced disappearance on the basis of the seriousness of the act of rather than any state recognition. See *Tibi v Ecuador* (Judgment) [2004] IACHR Series C No 114 [143]; *Maritza Urrutia v Guatemala* (Judgment) [2003] IACHR Series C No 103, para 112; *Gómez-Paquiyauri Brothers v Peru* (Judgment) [2004] IACHR Series C No 110, para 92; *Goiburú et al v Paraguay* (Judgment) [2006] IACHR Series C No 153, para 84.

75 *Siderman de Blake v Argentina* (Judgment) 965 F2d 699 (United States Court of Appeal) (9th Cir. 1992), para 715; *Kenya Section of the International Commission of Jurists v Attorney General and Minister of State for Provincial Administration and Internal Security and Kenyans for Justice and Development Trust* (joining) (Final judgment) [2011] eKLR (High Court of Kenya), para 14. Given that these courts are integral parts of the state, these decisions can be viewed as state practice: see Statute of the International Court of Justice (1946) UKTS 67 art 38(1).

76 Hernandez (n 30) 27–37.

77 See e.g. Christian Tams, *Enforcing Obligations Erga Omnes in International Law* (CUP 2005) 149.

78 Hernandez (n 30) 27.

79 UNGA (n 61) [52].

natural law is of little use if we lack an appropriate means by which we can determine what it says.[80] Such indeterminacy threatens ineffectiveness and uncertainty, and invites abuse. It is worth flagging here the danger that a universal concept like community interest poses in the context of such a pluralist international society. Weil warns that such a concept may become a 'code word … under whose cloak certain states may strive to implant an ideological system of law that would be a negation of the inherent pluralism of international society.'[81] One need not look far for examples of the imposition of the ideology of the powerful in the name of universality. Turning to courts is not an attractive solution: it risks blurring the line between the identification and the determination of rules or interests.[82] It may end up asking that judicial bodies not only 'constatent leur existence, mais … participent aussi à leur naissance et à leur développement'.[83] This raises serious questions, primarily of legitimacy, but also of capacity and capability. To ask courts to determine questions of morality and the needs of humanity would be to burden them with a 'staggering' task,[84] one for which they are woefully ill-equipped.

A second problem is that the immutability of a 'higher' or 'moral' law is difficult to reconcile with the dynamism of the community interest as discussed above.[85] Moral law and value systems as conceived under natural law theory are absolute and unchanging. Conversely, the content of the international community interest evolves – as reflected, for example, in Article 64 of the Vienna Convention on the Law of Treaties ("VCLT"), which explicitly provides for the emergence of new rules

---

80 Robert Kolb (n 66) 31.

81 Prosper Weil, 'Towards Relative Normativity in International Law' (1983) 77(3) The American Journal of International Law 413, 441. For similar concerns, see Martti Koskenniemi, 'International Law in Europe: Between Tradition and Renewal' (2005) 16(1) EJIL 113, 114–116; Simma and Paulus (n 43) 268.

82 A comparison with courts' role in relation to customary international law is illustrative of this point. While their judgments may be used as a 'subsidiary means' to aid in the identification of customary (or indeed other) rules of international law, they are not in and of themselves law-creating. See Statute of the International Court of Justice (n 75) art 38(1)(d); ILC, 'Draft conclusions on Identification of Customary International Law' adopted by the International Law Commission at its seventieth session UN Doc A/73/10, Conclusion 13.

83 'determine their existence, but … also participate in their creation and development' (author's translation): Paul Tavernier, 'L'identification des règles fondamentales – un problème résolu?' in Christian Tomuschat and Jean-Marc Thouvenin (eds), *The Fundamental Rules of the International Legal Order: Jus Cogens and Obligations Erga Omnes* (Martinus Nijhoff Publishers/Brill Academic Publishers 2006) 5–6.

84 Hernandez (n 30) 25.

85 UNGA (n 61) [52].

of *jus cogens*.[86] Obligations *erga omnes* are considered to have a similar 'vitality,' even by those who purport to link them to natural-law-based ideas of morality.[87]

4.2. POSITIVIST APPROACHES

As noted above, positivist approaches focus on the role of recognition, usually by states. This is in line with the essential basis of legal positivism that the only valid law is that which is formed by established processes of law-making. It is the belief that 'the grounds of law are matters of (social) fact and hence that the law is *posited*'.[88] This does not necessarily imply that value-based considerations have no role to play; it simply leaves it to states (or those actors with law-making authority) to decide how such considerations should be applied.

This process of recognition is understood differently by different commentators. Byers understands it as similar to the formation of customary international law, arguing that 'the customary process determines the common interests of most if not all States, and then protects and promotes those common interests with rules.'[89] Others understand recognition of the community interest of a particular norm (e.g. a *jus cogens* norm) as an extra step: a 'double' acceptance or *opinio juris*.[90] This would also appear to be reflected in the VCLT.[91]

The ICJ has, on several occasions, followed a demonstrably positivist approach to the identification of public interest norms. In *Nicaragua*, the Court appeared to relate the *jus cogens* status of the prohibition of the use of force to the fact that it is widely and expressly recognised as such by state representatives.[92] Perhaps the clearest example of the Court following a positivist approach can be seen in *Belgium v Senegal*. In that case, the Court based its finding that the prohibition of torture

86 VCLT art 64.

87 Ragazzi (n 67) 163; see also Gowlland-Debbas (n 12) 363.

88 Samantha Besson, 'State Consent and Disagreement in International Law-Making: Dissolving the Paradox' (2016) 29(2) Leiden Journal of International Law 289, 303 (emphasis added).

89 Byers (n 63) 222.

90 Villalpando (n 12) 77; de Wet (n 57) 542; Vidmar (n 65) 25. See also UNGA 'Second Report on *Jus Cogens* by Dire Tladi, Special Rapporteur' (16 March 2017) ILC 69th session UN Doc A/CN.4/706 [77].

91 VCLT art 53.

92 *Nicaragua v United States* (n 70) [190].

was a *jus cogens* norm on the fact that '[t]hat prohibition is grounded in a widespread international practice and on the *opinio juris* of States'.[93] It outlined the materials it considered relevant, which included the inclusion of the prohibition in 'numerous international instruments of universal application,' and in domestic legal systems, and the fact that 'acts of torture are regularly denounced within national and international fora.'[94] This choice of materials clearly demonstrates the relevance of recognition by states of the international community interest in the prohibition of torture. Similar approaches have been taken by other international[95] and domestic[96] courts and tribunals. A host of examples of state practice demonstrates that states themselves hold the definition of the community interest to be their prerogative.[97]

It is not clear which states, or how many, are sufficient to represent the international community in the act of recognition.[98] It is apparent that there is no need for express recognition from each and every state.

---

93 *Questions Relating to the Obligation to Prosecute or Extradite (Belgium v Senegal)* (Judgment) [2012] ICJ Rep 422, para 99.

94 ibid [99].

95 See *Prosecutor v Germain Katanga* (Decision on the application for the interim release of detained witnesses) [2013] ICC-01/04-01/07-3405-tENG [30]; *Prosecutor v Milomir Stakić* (Judgment) IT-97-24-T (31 July 2003), para 500; *Osorio Rivera and Family Members v Peru* (Judgment) [2013] IACHR Series C No 274 [112]; *Mendoza et al v Argentina* (Judgment) [2013] IACHR Series C No 260 [199]; *Nadege Dorzema et al v Dominican Republic* (Judgment) [2012] IACHR Series C No 251 [225]; *Atala Riffo and Daughters v Chile* (Judgment) [2012] IACHR Series C No 239, para 79; *Dacosta Cadogan v Barbados* (Judgment) [2009] IACHR Series C No 204, para 5.

96 *Bouzari and Others v Islamic Republic of Iran* [2013] 71 OR (3d) 675 (Court of Appeal for Ontario, Canada), para 49; *On the Application of Universal Recognised Principles and Norms of International Law and of International Treaties of the Russian Federation by Courts of General Jurisdiction* (Decision of the Plenary Session of the Supreme Court of the Russian Federation, No. 5) [2003]; *Arancibia Clavel, Enrique Lautaro s/ Homicidio Calificado y Asociación Ilícita y Otros* (Causa No. 259, Judgment) [2004] (Supreme Court of Justice of Argentina) [29].

97 See e.g. United States of America, *Statement* (UN Doc A/C6/71/SR26) [125]; Netherlands, *Statement* (UN Doc A/C6/71/SR26) [43]; Netherlands, *Statement* (UN Doc A/C6/70/SR17) [78]; United States of America, *Statement* (UN Doc A/C6/70/SR19) [17] and [20]; Israel, *Statement* (UN Doc A/C6/70/SR18) [6]; China, *Statement* (UN Doc A/C6/70/SR18) [19]; France, *Statement* (UN Doc A/C6/70/SR20) [25]; France, *Statement* (UN Doc A/C6/71/SR20) [77]; UNGA (n 90) [10]. Faced with criticism that it did not take sufficient account of state practice, the ILC interestingly did not dispute the importance of state practice, but rather the special rapporteur responded to these criticisms by emphasising the extent of state practice relied upon, thus implicitly agreeing that state practice should have such a predominant role: ibid [17]. See also UNGA (n 61) [45].

98 Weil (n 81) 426.

In relation to *jus cogens* norms, the ILC has repeatedly maintained that the phrase 'international community of states *as a whole*'[99] is intended to underline that '[a]cceptance and recognition by a large majority of States is sufficient … Acceptance and recognition by all States is not required.'[100] There is a decided lack of transparency on this point in the practice of international judicial bodies, which tend to refer vaguely to recognition by 'the international community' or 'community of states' without further elaboration[101] – although there is a tendency to make reference to quasi-universal multilateral agreements, suggestive of a high bar for the number of states required. Wolfrum advocates the application of the doctrine of 'states whose interests are specially affected'.[102] This is arguably misplaced, however: the idea that recognition of a public interest could be prevented because of its relationship with a specific state's or states' private interest(s) seems illogical and indeed antithetical to the concept of *common* interest and the balancing act discussed above.

As with the natural law approach, this clearly raises the risk of abuse; there is a 'risk that the process of identification falls prey to power relationships'.[103] The tension between the universality of the public interest and the non-universality of its formation and identification is evident. While these unresolved questions are definitely troubling, these concerns do mirror those which relate to the formation and recognition of customary international law and general principles. The preponderance of European and Western practice in this regard has been well-documented.[104] Thus, while the concerns are indeed serious, they do not undermine the positivist approach *per se*. Rather, they present areas

99 VCLT art 53.

100 UNGA (n 90) Draft Conclusion 7(3).

101 Hernandez (n 30) 27 *et seq*.

102 Rüdiger Wolfrum, 'Identifying Community Interests in International Law: Common Spaces and Beyond' in Eyal Benvenisti and Georg Nolte (eds), *Community Interests Across International Law* (OUP 2018) 22: He suggests that recognition must come from a widespread selection of states, including 'those states which are meant to carry the burden of implementing the obligations which flow from the declaration that a particular issue is governed by community interest'; *North Sea Continental Shelf (Federal Republic of Germany/Denmark)* (Judgment) [1969] ICJ Rep 3, para 73.

103 Wolfgang Benedek and others (eds), *The Common Interest in International Law* (Intersentia 2014) 220.

104 See Bhupinder Chimni, 'Customary International Law: A Third World Perspective' (2018) 112 The American Journal of International Law 1; George Rodrigo Bandeira Galindo and César Yip, 'Customary International Law and the Third World: Do Not Step on the Grass' (2017) 16(2) Chinese Journal of International Law 251.

for further thought and study, and sound a note of caution with regard to practical application.

The fact that recognition is not required by every state raises a second potential problem, referred to by Dubois as the 'paradox' of consent.[105] This relates to the argument that a positivist approach is entirely irreconcilable with the non-consensual nature of certain community interest norms.[106] This is particularly evident with regard to *jus cogens*, as such rules are generally accepted to bind states without their express consent, even in the face of persistent objection.[107] Dubois argues that positivism fails to explain how such rules can take effect on a state without its consent, and that the 'only possible answer is that there exists some higher norm or rule that is above or prior to the will of states'.[108]

This, however, is based on a fundamental misunderstanding of legal positivism. Despite being often conflated with voluntarism by international scholars and even by the ILC,[109] positivism is *not* dependent on state consent.[110] As Besson observes, '[t]here are other ways of positing international law than consent. Even if consent plays a central role in that process … it is not a necessary condition thereof.'[111] Positivism, in essence, is concerned with the grounds of law as *fact* rather than *morality* (or humanity, religion, or internal reason).[112] Indeed, according

105 Dubois (n 66) 141.

106 In *Nicaragua v United States*, for example, the Court held that, regardless of whether Nicaragua had ratified international human rights agreements, 'the absence of such a commitment would not mean that Nicaragua could with impunity violate human rights' (at [267]. See also *Land and Maritime Boundary between Cameroon and Nigeria (Cameroon v Nigeria: Equatorial Guinea Intervening)* (Judgment) [2002] ICJ Rep 303 (Separate Opinion of Judge Ranjeva), para 3; *Armed Activities on the Territory of the Congo (New Application: 2002) (Democratic Republic of the Congo v. Rwanda)* (Jurisdiction and Admissibility) (Judgment) [2006] ICJ Rep 6 (Separate opinion of Judge *ad hoc* Dugard) [10]; *Jurisdictional Immunities of the State (Germany v Italy) (Counter-Claim, Order of 6 July 2010)* [2010] ICJ Rep 310 (Dissenting opinion of Judge Cançado Trindade), paras 134ff and 141.

107 UNGA (n 14) Draft Conclusion 15 (3); Tavernier (n 83) 14.

108 Dubois (n 66) 144.

109 UNGA (n 61) [53].

110 Liam Murphy, 'Law Beyond the State: Some Philosophical Questions' (2017) 28(1) EJIL 203, 205; Besson (n 88) 303–304.

111 Besson (n 2) 47. See also Besson (n 88) 303; H L A Hart, *The Concept of Law* (Clarendon Law Series, 3rd edn, OUP 2012) 223–226. See further Nico Krisch, 'The Decay of Consent: International Law in an Age of Global Public Goods' (2014) 108(1) The American Journal of International Law 1, where Krisch outlines how the community interest has resulted in a shift from 'consent to consensus' in various area of international law.

112 John Gardner, 'Legal Positivism: 5½ Myths' (2001) 46(1) American Journal of Jurisprudence 199.

to Murphy, '[i]t is just an accident of usage that 'positivism' has been understood to entail voluntarism.'[113] It is certainly possible to say that, in balancing generally recognised community interests against individual state interest, the concept of community interest and the development of community interest norms like *jus cogens* amounts to a partial overcoming of state consensualism. This does not, however, disprove the validity of the positivist approach.

Thus, it would appear that the identification of the substantive content of the community interest is best achieved through a form of 'value-inclusive positivism':[114] namely recognition by states (or other actors with law-making authority) of values and concerns that are imputed to the 'international community'. The community interest therefore provides a means of translating such values and concerns into legally effective normative statements within the international legal order without undermining the fundamental tenets of positivist legal thought.

5. CONCLUSION

This chapter set out to determine the conceptual and definitional parameters of the community interest. It has demonstrated that the community interest is a common interest, held by those actors possessing law-making authority in the international legal order, but which relates to a legal fiction that transcends the individual interests of all actors in the international sphere. It translates values and desired factual situations into normative statements that can then be given legal force by rules. These rules include community interest norms that integrate the concept of community interest into the international legal order, like obligations *erga omnes* and rules of *jus cogens*. The identification of the substantive content of the community interest is premised upon recognition. It thus undermines neither the exclusive law-making authority of states, nor the continued relevance of the positivist legal approach. By exploring these issues and providing answers to these essential questions, this chapter remedies the conceptual uncertainty that surrounds the community interest. In so doing, it helps pave the way to realising the full promise of the community interest.

---

113 Murphy (n 110) 205.

114 OA Elias and CL Lim, *The Paradox of Consensualism in International Law* (Kluwer Law International 1998) 224.

GLOBAL PUBLIC GOODS AND PRIVATE INTERNATIONAL LEGAL GOVERNANCE

Lessons from International Cultural Heritage Law

Lucas LIXINSKI*

---

* Professor, Faculty of Law & Justice, UNSW Sydney. Elements of this chapter have appeared as Lucas Lixinski, 'Across the Public/Private International Legal Divide in the Governance of Global Public Goods' 47(2) *Denver Journal of International Law and Policy* 1–28 (2018).

1. INTRODUCTION

This chapter contributes to the conversation about the international legal governance of global public goods by mapping out the various forms of governance created at the juncture of public and private international law. A key objective of this chapter is to inform public international lawyers, or international lawyers more generally invested in the safeguarding of global public goods,[1] so that they can strategically and creatively tap into the possibilities of the private sphere. Cultural heritage is used as a key lens through which to unpack these issues, given the status of heritage as between public and private, and between global and local.

A divide or schism has long existed between public and private international law.[2] It creates multiple shadow areas of self-regulation or regulation behind the curtains of national sovereignty, which render the private invisible and unregulated, or at least unregulated by traditional legal mechanisms.[3] A framework of international legal pluralism, because of its ability to engage with forms of non-state law in international regulatory spaces, has some potential to address such gaps and appears to promise an articulation transnational governance,[4] but it does not often engage with the private.[5] Elements of private international ordering thus end up written off as part of 'non-legality' as a structuring device, as pre- or post-legal.[6] For example, environmental protection is often proclaimed by states to be of utmost importance, but that proclamation means little if it is not translated into law regulating the conduct of private corporations who emit pollutants, and possibly even creating consumer protection safeguards that stimulate sustainable consumption by, hypothetically,

---

1 Paul A Samuelson 'The Pure Theory of Public Expenditure' (1954) 36(4) Review of Economics and Statistics 387; Paul A Samuelson, 'Diagrammatic Exposition of a Theory of Public Expenditure' (1955) 37(4) Review of Economics and Statistics 350 (the scholarship that originated the term 'public goods', and which has been extrapolated and refined to also encompass the connections among local, national, and global public goods, given the impacts of globalization).

2 Horatia Muir Watt, 'Private International Law Beyond the Schism' (2011) 2(3) Transnational Legal Theory 347.

3 ibid.

4 Robert Wai, 'The Interlegality of Transnational Private Law' (2008) 71 Law and Contemporary Problems 107, 108.

5 Paul Schiff Berman, 'Global Legal Pluralism' (2007) 80 Southern California Review 1155. See also Gregory Shaffer, 'International Law and Global Public Goods in a Legal Pluralist World' (2012) 23(3) European Journal of International Law 669.

6 Fleur Johns, *Non-Legality in International Law: Unruly Law* (Cambridge University Press 2013) 110, and more generally, 109–152.

creating a course of action available to consumers deceived when a product fails to meet advertised environmental commitments. Initiatives promoting international standard-setting on business and human rights still operate internationally as soft law and as self-regulation by businesses, while pushing for domestic legal reforms that have been relatively successful worldwide.[7]

Regardless of labeling, the public/private divide in international law persists for multiple reasons, ranging from the effects of regulatory framing,[8] to the nature of (classic) private international law as state law,[9] to questions about whether the legal field is public or private,[10] down to the training of those engaging in the field. As international law specializes and fragments, the divide between public and private is rendered even stronger, and so are its distributive effects. These distributive effects are felt particularly when speaking of global public goods,[11] which by their very nature seem to sit more easily within public (and sometimes quasi-constitutional) frameworks,[12] but the configuration of which as public values has two noteworthy consequences. First, private international regulatory spaces, by focusing on values like individual liberty and party autonomy, often disregard them. Second, even if the private sphere does engage with them, the engagement happens in sporadic ways that tend

7 Justine Nolan, 'Mapping the Movement: The Regulatory Framework for Business and Human Rights' in Justine Nolan and Dorothée Baumann-Pauly (eds), *Business and Human Rights: From Principles to Practice* (Routledge 2016) 32–50 (surveying the international movement towards regulating business activities in a human rights context).

8 André Nollkaemper, 'Aligning Frames for Elephant Extinction: Towards a New Role for the United Nations' (2014) 108 AJIL Unbound 158.

9 Alex Mills, 'Connecting Public and Private International Law' in Duncan French, Kasey McCall-Smith and Verónica Ruiz Abou-Nigm (eds), *Linkages and Boundaries in Private and Public International Law* (Hart Publishing 2018).

10 See, for instance, José E Alvarez, 'Is Investor-State Arbitration "Public"?' (2016) 7(3) Journal of International Dispute Settlement 534 (arguing that international investment law is best viewed as a 'hybrid' of public and private).

11 Daniel Bodansky, 'What's in a Concept? Global Public Goods, International Law, and Legitimacy' (2012) 23(3) EJIL 651; Francesco Francioni, 'Public and Private in the International Protection of Global Cultural Goods' (2012) 23(3) EJIL 719; Anne van Aaken, 'Behavioral Aspects of the International Law of Global Public Goods and Common Pool Resources' (2018) 112(1) American Journal of International Law 67. But for a critique of the uses of this terminology by international lawyers, see Samuel Barkin and Yuliya Rashchupkina, 'Public Goods, Common Pool Resources, and International Law' (2017) 111(2) American Journal of International Law 376.

12 Ernst-Ulrich Petersmann, 'International Economic Law, "Public Reason", and Multilevel Governance of Interdependent Public Goods' (2011) 14(1) Journal of International Economic Law 23.

to affect the public invisibly, due to private actors' myopia. For instance, mining companies may see a regulatory regime for deep-seabed mineral exploration as imposing business costs rather than safeguarding the 'common heritage of [hu]mankind'.[13]

Add to this the fragmentation not only of regimes but of regulatory models altogether, and the mapping of governance becomes difficult, with more and more 'shadow spaces' created. But that is not to say regulatory models need to be streamlined or harmonized: they fulfill different functions and speak to different stakeholders, and in doing so, they relate to different values that can be attributed to the global public good being engaged. We must therefore not undo diversity but rather to learn how to navigate it; then we will be able to strategically tap into the myriad possibilities while remaining aware of the different values and possibilities engaged in each.

I argue that international cultural heritage law can contribute to our thinking about global public goods governance due to two factors: first, because grounding cultural heritage more locally can increase engagement in, and consequently the safeguarding, of these global goods; secondly, because heritage law has a relatively easy (albeit still strained) relationship with private legal governance strategies. In order to advance my thesis, the chapter is divided in four additional parts. The next section makes the argument that cultural heritage should be treated as a global public good with associated community interests, and outlines the contribution it can make to thinking about global public goods more broadly. Section three, the bulk of this chapter, maps out various strategies of private international legal governance in relation to public values, and particularly shows the uses of language and institutional mechanisms typical of public international law in the pursuance of private international legal governance. Subsequently, before concluding, I discuss strategies for reengaging the private in the governance of global public goods beyond cultural heritage.

2. HERITAGE AS A GLOBAL PUBLIC GOOD

Francesco Francioni has argued that cultural heritage is a global public good because it is declared to be important to all of humankind, and that

[13] See also Jutta Brunnée, 'Common Areas, Common Heritage, and Common Concern' in Daniel Bodansky, Jutta Brunnée, and Ellen Hey (eds), *Oxford Handbook of International Environmental Law* (Oxford University Press 2008) (notably, being

the cultural heritage of each people contributes to the world.[14] Community interests are thus at the core of the raison d'être for safeguarding heritage. In this sense, cultural heritage is a global public good not because of its mere existence, but because of its creation: by creating heritage, each community adds to a sense of shared humanity that is important for promoting lasting peace, in the words of the UNESCO Constitution.[15] Cultural heritage is therefore different from other public goods, in that it is created by humans rather than predating their interaction with it. In other words, whereas the environment and outer space existed before human civilization, cultural heritage is a direct byproduct of humanity's existence. The objective of safeguarding heritage as a global public good should therefore focus on the ability to create and recreate heritage, rather than its protection against human interference. This insight into the nature of heritage puts community interests very much at the core of the conversation.

The value of cultural heritage is based on its connection to identity, which means its stakes are centered on human goals, in contrast to the protection of the environment, for instance, where 'anthropocentric v ecocentric' dimensions can add another layer of nuance. Further, culture, particularly cultural heritage, is often seen as a public concern: in defining a polity, it is equated with national identity and seen as a proxy for sovereignty.[16] The uses of heritage by nation-making projects, however, does not mean it is restricted to local or national public goods. At the very least, international interest and regulation as well as commitment to an idea of shared humanity make these goods global.

Those connections to human goals and the making of societies help cement the status of heritage as a public good, as does its non-excludability and non-rivalrous nature (meaning that individuals cannot be effectively

---

critical of the proprietary connotation of the term 'heritage' and using this tone to frame a general reluctance to common heritage as a pathway to frame community interests).

14 Francioni (n 11) 729.

15 Constitution of the United Nations Educational, Scientific and Cultural Organization (UNESCO) (adopted 16 November 1945, entered into force 4 November 1946) 4 UNTS 275 (UNESCO Constitution). Preamble: '… since wars begin in the minds of men, it is in the minds of men that the defences of peace must be constructed' and 'ignorance of each other's ways and lives has been a common cause, throughout the history of mankind, of that suspicion and mistrust between the peoples of the world through which their differences have all too often broken into war'.

16 cf Lorenzo Casini, 'Cultural Sites Between Nationhood and Mankind' in Eyal Benvenisti and Georg Nolte (eds), *Community Interests Across International Law* (Oxford University Press 2018) (arguing that, in fact, expertise-driven governance creates avenues against state sovereignty).

excluded from using heritage, and heritage being used by one individual does not reduce its availability to others).[17] Despite attempts to coopt cultural heritage by nation-making projects, it is still widely available for use by all, and, despite possible deterioration by excessive use (by tourists on World Heritage sites like Angkor Wat, for instance),[18] it is for the most part also non-rivalrous.

Although heritage is largely characterized as a global *public* good, most of the law around heritage, at least as far as dispute resolution is concerned, is actually located in the private domain, either happening outside of state institutions via arbitration and other alternative dispute-resolution mechanisms, or litigated on the basis of private law rules in property and contracts even when state courts are used. In the case of cultural heritage, property law in particular is present, whether in terms of intellectual property (IP) for intangibles,[19] chattels for cultural objects,[20] or 'classic' property for shipwrecks[21] and sites.[22] Private law on property, alongside transactional rules on contracts and the law of obligations, remains largely unaffected by and impervious to cultural considerations, however, and is thus unresponsive to what makes cultural heritage a public good.

The designation as global public good, encapsulated in the current term 'cultural heritage' adds gravitas and urgency to heritage safeguarding. 'Cultural property', which is regulated by private law,[23] was the terminology used in earlier international efforts to safeguard cultural sites, objects, and practices. While the term was drawn from international humanitarian law instruments and their protection of buildings like schools, churches, and hospitals as 'protected property', it nevertheless spoke directly to

17 See, generally, Inge Kaul, Isabelle Grunberg, and Marc Stern (eds), *Global Public Goods: International Cooperation in the 21st Century* (OUP 1999) (discussing these characteristics as essential to global public goods).

18 Tim Winter, 'Post-conflict Heritage and Tourism in Cambodia: The Burden of Angkor' (2008) 14(6) International Journal of Heritage Studies 524.

19 Convention for the Safeguarding of the Intangible Cultural Heritage (adopted 17 October 2003, entered into force 20 April 2006) 2368 UNTS 3 (ICHC).

20 Convention on the Means of Prohibiting and Preventing the Illicit Import, Export and Transfer of Ownership of Cultural Property (adopted 14 November 1970, entered into force 24 April 1972) 823 UNTS 231 (1970 Convention).

21 Convention on the Protection of the Underwater Cultural Heritage (adopted 2 November 2001, entered into force 2 January 2009) 2562 UNTS 3 (UCHC).

22 Convention Concerning the Protection of the World Cultural and Natural Heritage 1972 (adopted 16 November 1972, entered into force 17 December 1975) 1037 UNTS 151 (WHC).

23 For a discussion, see Lucas Lixinski, *International Heritage Law for Communities: Exclusion and Re-Imagination* (OUP 2019) 27–65.

property law, and the interaction between public and private law; one consequence was the idea that cultural heritage was the 'property' of states in international law. The shift toward the term 'heritage' added a global concern for these sites, objects, and practices, and aimed to transform the relevant community from a national community connected to cultural property to a global community connected to cultural heritage. 'Cultural heritage' thus embraces the ideas of (international) community interest and global public goods much more effectively than 'cultural property', even if it has unintentionally divorced local communities from their own heritage by making it harder to translate the commitments of states in public international law into the domestic, usually private law categories that are familiar and accessible to communities living in, with, or around heritage.[24] The disconnect between 'international community' interests and 'local community' interests is another reason why a clearer connection between public and private legal governance categories and mechanisms needs to be sought.

Conversely, cultural heritage and its regulation in international law can add to the thinking around global public goods because cultural heritage can be grounded more locally, which increases engagement with such goods, and consequently their safeguarding. In other words, the status of cultural heritage as a global public good functions as a reminder that, even though the stakes are global they are also local, and the local is an indispensable element in forming, regulating, and protecting these goods and the values they evoke. Likewise, the local element refocuses or at least problematizes the idea of 'community' and community interests in relation to global public goods.

Cultural heritage is best protected by focusing on the communities that live in, with, or around that heritage. If these communities are alienated from the public good, they have no reason to remain interested in or work towards safeguarding. This lesson articulated by international heritage law is one that the thinking around other public goods would do well to heed. An important frontline in the tensions between local and global consists of regulatory strategies, and private international law works as a bridge between domestic and international, community and state, global and local. Regulatory strategies in private international legal governance are therefore key to safeguarding global public goods. The next section maps out the diversity of possibilities contained within this realm.

---

24 ibid.

3. STRATEGIES OF PRIVATE INTERNATIONAL LEGAL GOVERNANCE AND PUBLIC VALUES

If delving into the private is key to ensuring the effectiveness of global public goods governance, understood as legal regimes' ability to protect or safeguard the public good and the objectives tied to such safeguarding, then a first key step is to map out the various strategies through which private international legal governance occurs. Private international legal governance, or transnational private law, can articulate a social vision of global public order and perform a public function of embedding private behavior into broader social ordering.[25] Identifying the place and role of public values in strategies of private international legal governance relates to these efforts. Five key strategies exist, and they will be addressed in turn: classic domestic conflict rules; international harmonization of conflict rules; international harmonization of substantive rules; international cooperation in civil or criminal legal matters; and industry self-regulation. Each favors certain values with respect to heritage, so each demonstrates a distinct set of objectives for public good safeguarding or protection.

3.1. DOMESTIC CONFLICT RULES: PUBLIC VALUES AS SOVEREIGNTY

Private international law is traditionally centered on the use of domestic conflict rules. Since conflict rules are domestic and of public law, that is why private international law is often discussed as being neither international nor private. Piercing the terminology and scrutinizing the nature of conflict rules as public reveals that some public values are contained in these rules, not only in their drafting, but first and foremost in their interaction with other rules of the forum. A key aspect of this interaction is the idea of public policy (*ordre public*), which prevents the application of the law the conflicts rule directs you to if that would negatively impact the forum's fundamental values. More broadly, as Alex Mills has suggested, private international law can be read through an

---

[25] Robert Wai, 'Transnational Private Law and Private Ordering in a Contested Global Society' (2005) 46(2) Harvard International Law Journal 471.

international rather than domestic prism, giving it the ability to engage with the 'public principles of global ordering it embodies'.[26]

Among existing conflict rules, the one that applies to the majority of situations involving cultural heritage is that which applies to property: *lex rei sitae*, or the law of the place where the thing is. In other words, domestic conflict rules more often than not suggest the application of the law of the place where the heritage is located, as long as the case is classified by the forum judge as being about property. In some cases of illicitly removed or looted cultural objects, limited recognition has been given to the idea of *lex originis*, or the application of the law of the place of origin of the property, but that rule is complicated by three factors: the difficulty of precisely identifying the country of origin of an object found to be looted; the fact that *lex originis* does not necessarily guarantee stronger protection to heritage; and the fact that the law of other states may provide better safeguarding.[27] The two latter objections, however, focus on a merits analysis that is not in line with the application of conflict rules, which should be mechanical and formalistic, and require a substantive analysis that is foreign to most understandings of the operation of domestic conflict rules. The last objection also perpetuates assumptions that the law of source nations (from where heritage is taken), because they are more often than not 'developing' countries, is necessarily inferior to the law of market nations (that is, to where heritage is taken), and gives the judge of the market nation an avenue to dismiss *lex originis* and render it stillborn. If *lex originis* is to be taken seriously, those objections must therefore be dismissed. The *lex originis* argument, further, focuses on the community interests of a specific community, and requires the identification of said community and its interests, whereas *lex rei sitae* concerns the thing and an abstract notion of property that may be too focused on the thing rather than the relationships communities form with it through their interests. The *lex originis* argument may better serve the idea of promoting and legally safeguarding community interests, by forcing the identification of a community, and thus being more closely connected to aspirations usually associated with global public goods. It may thus also serve the safeguarding of culture more broadly, if one identifies such safeguarding

26 Alex Mills, *The Confluence of Public and Private International Law: Justice, Pluralism and Subsidiarity in the International Constitutional Ordering of Private Law* (CUP 2009) 3.

27 As discussed in Alessandro Chechi, *The Settlement of International Cultural Heritage Disputes* (OUP 2014) 97–98. See also, generally, ibid 84–98.

as not just the preservation of the heritage site or artefact but of the ongoing relationships that give it cultural value and ongoing relevance. That said, other public goods may be best protected against human interaction, so rules like *lex rei sitae* may be most effective in the short term, even if that protection may come at the cost of excluding the formation and renewal of affective connections that serve as powerful incentives for safeguarding action on the ground.

For instance, if the classic and ongoing dispute about the Parthenon Marbles[28] were to be litigated in private international law, a *lex rei sitae* rule would consider them under the laws of England, which state that items of such status in the British Museum collection cannot be deaccessioned and should therefore stay in its possession. The *lex originis* rule would look at Greek law on items of the status of the Parthenon Marbles, which would necessarily reveal values behind these marbles that imbue them with significance far beyond property, possession, and bans on deaccession. A Greek law on objects with the status of the Parthenon Marbles would enunciate their importance to the community, and therefore better or at least more clearly articulate community interests.

The *lex rei sitae* rule, and the conflicts strategy more generally, align with public values inasmuch as they are about sovereignty. Conflict rules are chosen by the forum state (even if in practice there are many shared commonalities across states), and the public policy exception also protects the forum state from applying rules with which it disagrees on the basis of its public values. Therefore, in the protection of sovereignty on the basis of territoriality (*lex rei sitae*), this strategy aligns with public values in somewhat unexpected ways.

Values associated with public goods and heritage in particular have no clear place with respect to *lex rei sitae*, as the issue is largely about a mechanical application of a conflict rule, even if the state does have a certain degree of choice – choice about public values and sovereignty in attempting to predict the direction cases will take, and exercising preferences on the basis of those predictions. But another private international legal governance strategy seeks to remove this discretion by harmonizing different conflict rules. To this strategy, and its effects on global public goods, I move next.

---

28 For a recent discussion of the Marbles dispute, including the history of the Marbles and previous legal attempts at recovery, see Geoffrey Robertson, *Who Owns History? Elgin's Loot and the Case for Returning Plundered Treasure* (Knopf 2019).

3.2. HARMONIZATION OF CONFLICT RULES: PUBLIC VALUES AS LIMITED CERTAINTY

The harmonization of conflict rules is a process through which public international law starts to blur the public/private divide in private international legal governance. Specifically, this strategy consists of states agreeing to adopt the same conflict rule for the same classification of cases. In a case about torts, for instance, it may be that states agree through a treaty that all of them will apply the *lex loci delictii* rule, and not another option, like the law of nationality of the victim, regardless of where the tort occurred.[29]

The greatest draw of this strategy is to create a certain degree of certainty in the international space. States give up some sovereignty, particularly the sovereign interest of always defending the interests of their nationals regardless of the situation in which they are involved – since nationality is often the alternative and a trump to other conflict rules – in favor of international cooperation. But the mechanism's application is limited to conflict rather than substantive rules, so it still creates relatively little room for public values to enter directly into its workflow, save for the exceptions discussed above. States give up their ability to change their conflict rule, too, even though in practice these treaties are only ratified by states that already have the basic conflict rule contained in the treaty, with relatively few states changing their domestic law to reflect a new treaty commitment. Therefore, because in practice states only harmonize conflict rules when those rules are already in line with their domestic choices, this strategy may be seen as a pooling of sovereignty that can effectively strengthen sovereignty by enhancing legal certainty (especially if the harmonized conflict rule defers to *lex fori*).[30]

Use of the language and forms of public international law can encourage a shift in values or reinforce them. To revisit the example from the previous section on *lex rei sitae*, a harmonization of that conflict rule would allow market nations in particular to reinforce their assertion of sovereignty over other countries' cultural heritage that is currently in their territory. Conversely, a move towards *lex originis* would promote a significant shift in values in favor of source nations. Because market nations are unlikely

---

29 For an overview, see Heinz-Peter Mansel, 'Nationality' in Jürgen Basedow, Giesela Rühl, Franco Ferrari and Pedro de Miguel Asensio (eds), *Encyclopedia of Private International Law II* (Edward Elgar Publishing 2017) 1289–1301.

30 I am thankful to Gentian Zyberi for this insight.

to give up their ability to decide a dispute using their own sovereign laws, however, a shift to *lex originis* is unlikely. Further, with market nations also presenting themselves as the key exemplars of the application of private international law to heritage disputes, their 'superior' choice in favor of *lex rei sitae* will be reinforced, and with it their sovereignty, at the expense of certain community interests.

Most importantly for present purposes, though, the use of these mechanisms serves to test the waters for deepening private international legal governance through public and openly value-laden mechanisms. The next section discusses a strategy that largely builds on the idea of harmonization, but takes them further by looking at substantive rules.

3.3. HARMONIZATION OF SUBSTANTIVE RULES: PUBLIC VALUES AS INTERNATIONALIZATION

Harmonizing substantive rules is in some respects the next step from harmonizing conflict rules. Instead of making a uniform rule for judges to apply in deciding which law is applicable, the harmonization of substantive rules makes the applicable law itself uniform. The harmonization of substantive rules does not necessarily follow from the harmonization of conflict rules in the same area, and different fora can be used for one or the other strategy. Yet it does represent a more sophisticated strategy, at least on the surface, and one in which the forms and content of public international law have more of a bearing. In effect, thus, values from public international law have a clearer entry point to private international legal governance strategies than the two conflicts rules strategies outlined above.

Importantly, the harmonization of substantive rules internationalizes the values underlying those rules, which are more apparent and have greater influence than the values underlying conflict rules. As public policy, for example, is drawn from substantive rules rather than conflict rules, it underscores the importance of substantive law in enforcing public values, which are key when speaking of global public goods. Harmonizing substantive rules can also be a means for showcasing pluralism and responding to it.[31]

[31] Wai (n 4) 109; cf Mills (n 26) 21 (suggesting harmonization means the loss of pluralism, and may be too great a cost against the potential risk of regulatory conflict in conflict-based private international law).

The harmonization of substantive law also provides an opportunity to avoid the effects of classification, a necessary step in applying conflicts rules that, as indicated above, can and often does have the effect of stripping public values from public goods safeguarding, rendering them simply yet another property law issue or tort, for instance. This strategy is notorious in the field of intellectual property law, to give one example, and its consequent intersection with international trade and economic law. The TRIPS agreement annexed to the agreement establishing the World Trade Organization[32] is a quintessential example of a treaty that affects culture very directly, at least inasmuch as intellectual property rights are a way to legally regulate culture, a logic that does not always converge with cultural heritage priorities.[33] Nevertheless, the harmonization of substantive intellectual property law rules goes a long way toward promoting the protection of proprietary interests over culture and innovation, and, as initiatives in the area of public health and access to medicines have shown, at the very least the presence of this type of harmonization instrument creates opportunities to interface with global public priorities.[34] And, as harmonization of substantive rules happens more often than not in a relatively piecemeal fashion, rather than through large codifications of private international law, it also allows for the specialization of the substantive rule to reflect values specific to the global public good.

One instance of this latter effect, which I will call the harmonization of substantive rules with direct effect on global public goods, is the International Institute for the Unification of Private Law (UNIDROIT) 1995 Convention on Stolen or Illegally Exported Cultural Objects.[35]

---

32 Agreement on Trade-Related Aspects of Intellectual Property Rights, (adopted 15 April 1994), Annex 1C of the Marrakesh Agreement Establishing the World Trade Organization (1869) UNTS 299, 33 ILM 1197 (TRIPS).

33 Lucas Lixinski, 'Commercializing Traditional Culture: Promises and Pitfalls in the Convergence of Intellectual Property Law and Cultural Heritage Law' (2020) 29 Annali Italiani del Diritto d'Autore, della Cultura e dello Spettacolo (discussing the different logics of intellectual property and cultural heritage law for the regulation of culture, particularly in the areas of private international law and contracts).

34 Junaid Subhan 'Scrutinized: the TRIPS Agreement and Public Health' (2006) 9(2) McGill Journal of Medicine 152 (on the need for greater protection for global public health interests within the TRIPS agreement, and commenting on the World Trade Organization); WTO, 'Declaration on the TRIPS Agreement and Public Health' (20 November 2001) Doc WT/MIN(01)/DEC/2 <http://www.wto.org/english/thewto_e/minist_e/min01_e/mindecl_trips_e.pdf> accessed 15 January 2021.

35 UNIDROIT Convention on Stolen or Illegally Exported Cultural Objects (adopted 24 June 1995, entered into force 1 July 1998) 2421 UNTS 457, 34 ILM 1322. For a

This treaty fits squarely within the mandate of UNIDROIT, an institution created in 1940, which, as spelled out in its Statute, is to harmonize and coordinate private law, leading to the adoption of 'uniform rules of private law'.[36]

The 1995 Convention provides for the jurisdiction of the courts where the object is located, and for other states having possible jurisdiction over the object on the basis of their national rules.[37] The courts of the state where the object is located can issue provisional or protective measures that take precedence over the jurisdictional claims of any other state.[38] This provision, however, is not to be confused with *lex rei sitae*, discussed in the previous section, which is about applicable law. In disputes where the UNIDROIT Convention is applicable, the treaty itself is the applicable law.

The substantive rules harmonized or unified in the treaty have to do with ownership,[39] limitation periods,[40] compensation,[41] and the rights of possessors of good faith.[42] Certain public values can be seen in these substantive and procedural private law rules, such as the idea of enlarging limitation periods with respect to cultural objects 'forming an integral part of an identified monument or archaeological site, or belonging to a public collection'.[43] Likewise, the requirement for the exercise of due diligence in acquiring cultural objects implies a need to consider other parties' interests, and those of the public at large, prior to acquisition of property title.[44] The exercise of due diligence, to be discussed further in a subsection below, speaks to a public interest, but fundamentally creates a shield around private rights when exercised. This exercise of harmonizing private law, therefore, is centrally concerned with the protection of a global public good, even if it imbues public values somewhat obliquely in these instruments' framing of private interests, which is the central part of their mandate.

---

commentary, see Lyndel V Prott, *Biens Culturels Volés ou Illicitement Exportés: Commentaire Relatif à la Convention D'Unidroit* (Éditions UNESCO 2000).

36 Statute of UNIDROIT (adopted 15 March 1940) (incorporating the amendment to Article 6(1) which entered into force on 26 March 1993) art 1.

37 UNIDROIT Convention (n 35) art 8.

38 ibid.

39 ibid art 3.

40 ibid.

41 ibid art 4.

42 ibid.

43 ibid art 3(4).

44 ibid art 4(1).

But there are also other ways of harmonizing substantive rules with only indirect effects on global public goods. An example relevant here is the possibility of invoking instruments on civil liability for damage resulting from environmental activities in order to protect underwater cultural heritage. The Council of Europe Convention of March 1993 includes cultural heritage in its definition of the environment,[45] and gives provisions determining the liability of public or private actors for damage resulting from dangerous activities. Harm to underwater heritage resulting from oil spills, for instance, falls squarely within this regime's scope.[46] A regime thus established to address one global public good (the environment) refers to another (cultural heritage), while primarily regulating civil liability matters. Instead of a regime that focuses entirely on cultural heritage, heritage is made part of a treaty to harmonize law on certain types of liability more generally, in particular the environment as a global public good. This near 'mainstreaming' of cultural heritage should in theory make the regime more palatable for ratification.

Of the direct (UNIDROIT) and indirect (Environmental Liability Convention) instruments to harmonize private law rules on cultural heritage as a public good, it would seem that the Environmental Liability treaty would be more easily replicated and more desirable. It can direct harmonization towards a problem that on the surface is relatively technical and value-free (liability for pollution), while tying itself to important background political choices around safeguarding the global public good. Not being explicit about those political choices can lead to lack of clarity on the legal frameworks available for safeguarding the global public good, and to these tools getting lost in the cacophony of fragmented legal strategies. Yet by focusing on the legal mechanism rather than a specific public good, it can identify commonalities across different global public goods and the community interests underlying them. And working out a legal mechanism also assists in enabling those community interests to be properly articulated, therefore focusing on the community rather than the global public good, which can be sanctified and divorced from communities in specific regimes, which is what often happens to heritage.[47]

45 Council of Europe, Convention on Civil Liability for Damage resulting from Activities Dangerous to the Environment (adopted 21 June 1993) ETS No 150, art 2(10).

46 For a brief commentary in the context of underwater cultural heritage, see Vincent Négri 'Conventions and Laws Related to Submarine Archaeological Sites in the Mediterranean' in Mostafa Hassan Mostafa, Nicolas Grimal and Douglas Nakashima (eds) *Underwater Archaeology and Coastal Management: Focus on Alexandria* (UNESCO Publishing) 126–127.

47 For this critique see, generally, Lixinski (n 23).

Regardless of the choice of direct or indirect harmonization of substantive rules, it is important to note that this strategy also relies on the language and mechanisms of public international law to change private law. Underlying this strategy is thus the notion that 'private law assists in the circulation of ideas and norms among social systems, be they different functional areas, different identity groups, or different jurisdictions', and is thus an important component of global ordering projects.[48]

The safeguarding of global public goods comes to the fore more clearly because of the influence of substantive international law, but harmonized private law needs to give more guidance on how the public and the private mix, as opposed to only replicating the language of domestic private law – even if the latter is understandably the primary challenge, and a difficult one at that. Another factor to consider is whether the harmonization of substantive rules creates enough of an institutional framework through which to defend these values, and that may be part of the problem of background norm influence outlined above. Another strategy for private international legal governance would therefore put institutional frameworks at the forefront, and focus on cooperation in the joint pursuance of ever-changing values, rather than firmly setting those values without the institutional means to uphold them. To this idea of international cooperation as private international legal governance we move next.

3.4. INTERNATIONAL COOPERATION IN CIVIL (AND CRIMINAL) MATTERS: PUBLIC VALUES AS BEYOND SCRUTINY

Cooperation in civil and criminal matters means using international treaty frameworks to equalize procedures for obtaining access to information or people. These frameworks work on the assumption that substantive decisions about the law and its values are to be made elsewhere, and, for the sake of expediency and comity, it is up to the parties to mechanically promote certain outcomes without prejudging the merits in any given case. They are thus a type of private international law committed primarily to 'an allocation of regulatory authority, not a final judgment'.[49] This type

48 Wai (n 25) 481.
49 Mills (n 26) 18.

of framework blends private legal governance with administrative legal mechanisms,[50] but, because it eludes the forms of traditional public international law, and still has more purchase in private international law than public international law, I deal with it here as a strategy for private international legal governance.

For instance, the framework on the enforcement of foreign judgments or arbitral awards predetermines that the authority of the state where the judgment was first rendered was correct, bar formal defects or offense to public policy (*ordre public*).[51] Effectively, it means that the state where the judgment is being enforced is not able to question the judgment of the judge in the state of origin, and simply needs to guarantee its enforcement for the sake of comity and expediency. (International) public policy can apply here as a means of injecting substantive values, but it is the exception rather than the rule.[52]

Some, albeit limited, room emerges for discussing the substantive values, reverting back to the idea of public policy in the application of conflicts rules. Yet in many instances the idea of public policy is abused to promote sovereigntist outcomes by domestic authorities. In spite of these instances of the application of public policy, as a rule the strategy of international cooperation in civil or criminal affairs skirts any discussion of values. It brings to bear a fairly sophisticated institutional machinery, but only so it can give a domestic forum the opportunity to consider the merits of a case. However, it does seem that this machinery would not have been developed without its detachment from substantive values.

In the context of cultural heritage, the international framework on heritage crime and illicit trafficking is particularly useful. It involves a series of international institutions cooperating on issues like law enforcement, taking of evidence, customs, and taxation, among others.[53] Specific cooperation activities include training of police and customs officials, sharing of information on missing heritage artefacts in common

50 With respect to cultural heritage, on the administrative aspects, see Lorenzo Casini, '"Italian Hours": The Globalization of Cultural Property Law' (2011) 9(2) International Journal of Constitutional Law 369.

51 United Nations Convention on the Recognition and Enforcement of Foreign Arbitral Awards (adopted 10 June 1958, entered into force 1 July 1959) 330 UNTS 38,7 ILM 1046 (New York Arbitration Convention) art V.

52 Mills (n 26) 283.

53 For a useful summary, see United Nations Office of Drugs and Crime, 'Protection Against Trafficking in Cultural Property' (28 October 2009) UN Doc UNODC/CCPCJ/EG.1/2009/CRP.1.

databases, and facilitation of extradition and summons for persons involved in heritage crime.

This multifaceted framework prioritizes returning the object to the last jurisdiction where title could be lawfully established. In doing this, it overrides discussions of, inter alia, repatriation of objects that had once been looted and taken unlawfully from their countries of cultural origin, and therefore prevents a re-discussion of the values associated with specific cultural heritage items, and what they mean for contested identities. So, for instance, were someone outside of official channels to return to India the Koh-i-Noor diamond that currently adorns the British crown last worn by Queen Elizabeth's mother at Queen Elizabeth's coronation, but taken from India during British colonization, once British authorities made a complaint to the Indian government the cooperation framework would require that the object be sent back to the United Kingdom immediately, regardless of the colonial history and possibly legitimate claims that could be made on behalf of the Indian state. Likewise, were the Parthenon Marbles on loan in a third state and their return requested by Greece, they would need to be sent back to the United Kingdom immediately, disregarding the fairly unique opportunity for seizure of the marbles and their return to the country of origin.

With respect to public goods more generally, this strategy means the safeguarding of public goods is not scrutinized for meaning, which is a given. It suspends and defers a consideration of values as it gives way to the domestic institution's assessment of values. It thus resembles the conflicts strategies discussed above, with the key difference being that this strategy is focused on promoting the dispute resolution regardless of the law; instead of worrying about what the law and its values represent, international cooperation focuses on creating the material preconditions for the law to meaningfully bear on a situation to begin with. After all, without access to the cultural object, there is little to no point in pursuing a full legal case.

By divorcing the merits of a dispute from its preconditions, this strategy can be seen as assuming that values do not have a bearing on institutional design or the operation of international cooperation. It also presupposes that states have a shared interest in a neutral resolution of the dispute, rather than having individual interests that could be mediated through the harmonization of substantive rules. And because exceptions on the basis of public policy are still present, it gives certain states the ability to manipulate the system in favor of their own individual values, which may or may not coincide with other values connected to the safeguarding of global public goods. This strategy, thus, however functional, starts escaping the influence of public values by purporting to be about procedural mechanics, while it effectively perpetuates or allows the perpetuation of certain values.

Value neutrality as a strategy to avoid public interference in private international legal governance is, of course, not unique. Many other avenues exist, such as the operation of conflict rules which, in classifying a dispute for the purposes of determining the applicable conflict rule, ostensibly takes away the public values attached to the subject matter. Both these instances, however, require state mediation. What if the state could be done away with altogether? The next section explores a final strategy for private international legal governance, and queries the use of industry self-regulation to safeguard global public goods.

3.5. INDUSTRY SELF-REGULATION: PUBLIC VALUES AS BEYOND THE STATE

The use of industry standards[54] to influence governance and law-making is not unique to international law, nor does it go without official institutional endorsement by traditional public international law mechanisms.[55] Industry standards have the advantage of being more malleable and changeable, which means they can adjust to the latest developments and rely more directly on expertise that has an immediate and relevant bearing on the regulatory objective. They can also better make use of the possibilities within an industry without the burden of government-led regulation, and respond more quickly to changing circumstances, such as, in the area of cultural heritage, the issue of digital heritage and digitization.[56]

---

54 I am grateful to Julian Arato for reminding me of this category. For a collection of essays on the topic, see Panagiotis Delimatsis (ed), *The Law, Economics and Politics of International Standardisation* (CUP 2015).

55 The International Standardization Organization (ISO) is a quintessential example of an international organization created by states to facilitate industry self-regulation. For commentary on their role as law-makers, see José E Alvarez, *International Organizations as Law-Makers* (OUP 2005).

56 Lucas Lixinski, 'Digital Heritage Surrogates, Decolonization, and International Law: Restitution, Control, and the Creation of Value as Reparations and Emancipation' (2020) 6(2) Santander Art and Culture Law Review 65 (on the creation of digital surrogates of physical heritage); Sabine von Schorlemer, 'UNESCO and the Challenge of Preserving the Digital Cultural Heritage' (2020) 6(2) Santander Art and Culture Law Review 33 (on the general standard-setting framework for digital heritage within UNESCO).

Industry standards often have their values replicated in public legal instruments in the area, either because industry has led standardization and law-making in that area, or because their credibility depends on (at least ostensibly) abiding by certain public values, particularly when their activity relates to global public goods.

In cultural heritage, a useful example of industry self-regulation is the International Council of Museums (ICOM) Code of Ethics.[57] Voluntarily adopted by the museum profession, the code is the result of increasing public pressure in the aftermath of a series of high-profile cases involving museums and dealers in looted cultural objects.[58] It suggests that, prior to acquiring a cultural object, the collector or museum must perform due diligence to 'ensure that any object or specimen offered for purchase, gift, loan, bequest or exchange has not been illegally obtained in, or exported from its country of origin or any intermediate country in which it might have been owned legally'.[59] This is a particularly important commitment aimed especially at preventing trafficking of cultural objects to wealthy collectors or museums in market nations. The issue also concerns other private international legal governance strategies, since the UNIDROIT 1995 Convention on Stolen or Illegally Exported Cultural Objects likewise contains language on due diligence.[60] This standard allows for the public values of cultural heritage safeguarding to be directly considered in otherwise private transactions involving dealers, collectors, and cultural institutions. At the same time, though, it is unclear what exactly due diligence requires in practice, and the standard's oversight is performed by ICOM themselves, the constituency of which is not necessarily concerned with safeguarding the global public good, or at least not directly; rather,

---

57 International Council of Museums, Code of Ethics for Museums (adopted in 1986, revised in 2004).

58 Documented, for instance, in Jason Felch and Ralph Frammolino, *Chasing Aphrodite: The Hunt for Looted Antiquities at the World's Richest Museum* (Houghton Mifflin Harcourt 2011); and, for a more positive take, see James Cuno, 'View from the Universal Museum' in John Henry Merryman (ed), *Imperialism, Art and Restitution* (CUP 2006) 15–36; and James Cuno, *Who Owns Antiquity? Museums and the Battle over Our Ancient Heritage* (Princeton University Press 2010).

59 ICOM Code of Ethics (n 57) art 2.3.

60 UNIDROIT Convention (n 35) art 4(4): 'In determining whether the possessor exercised due diligence, regard shall be had to all the circumstances of the acquisition, including the character of the parties, the price paid, whether the possessor consulted any reasonably accessible register of stolen cultural objects, and any other relevant information and documentation which it could reasonably have obtained, and whether the possessor consulted accessible agencies or took any other step that a reasonable person would have taken in the circumstances.'

its central interest is in ensuring that museums can acquire objects they deem relevant for their collections. As museums themselves thus oversee compliance with their standard, self-regulation can be fraught, particularly amid calls for judges to defer to the expertise of museum and other cultural heritage experts.[61]

Clearly, even when it comes to an industry association devoted to the safeguarding of a global public good, there is still wide leeway for abuse and disregard of the public values the body purports to defend. Industry associations often avoid the public because the public means unwanted scrutiny; instead, they rely on the invisibility of the private to conduct their business, in a way that can fly in the face of public values associated with global public goods. Industry standards create blind spots within the private, and rely on the public for a feel-good veneer of legitimacy. They also lack the gravitas of public international law, as their normativity is always ephemeral, and they benefit from this state of affairs. Industry self-regulation is the strategy of private global legal governance where most cultural considerations take place, but these considerations occur outside the purview of all parties, only serving one specific industry – such as museums or archaeologists – at a time. The values of non-experts, because they do not organize in the same way, cannot form a competing form of discourse.

Industry self-regulation has largely been deemed insufficient and in need of supplementation by specific state-driven or state-enacted laws. Especially when speaking of global public goods like heritage, which necessitate the consideration of community interests, industry self-regulation falls desperately short. It is illogical to expect a dealer, who has an interest in enhancing their trade, to self-regulate their activity downwards on the basis of due diligence concerns, especially in an industry that does not receive much attention from the broad public, and in which reputation is grounded not on trade ethics, but on the quality and uniqueness of what is traded. The dealer's economic interests outweigh their reputational ones, so there is a self-interest in making self-regulation as lax and ineffective in practice as possible. There is a further argument to be made in relation to other public goods, in that when industry is heavily involved without much public scrutiny, values get translated into a business-case framework, and only those values that align with a good business case are promoted.[62]

61 For instance, Marett Leiboff, 'Clashing Things' (2001) 10(2) Griffith Law Review 294.

62 See, generally, Peter Dauvergne and Jane Lister, *Eco-Business: A Big-Brand Takeover of Sustainability* (The MIT Press 2013).

Therefore, out of the five possible strategies for private international legal governance, industry self-regulation seems least adept at promoting values associated with global public goods, even if it can safeguard aspects of these global public goods that speak directly to the industry's interests.

3.6. INTERNATIONAL PRIVATE LEGAL GOVERNANCE STRATEGIES AND PUBLIC VALUES

The five strategies outlined above respond to the idea of safeguarding global public goods in very different ways. None of them are specifically designed to protect global public goods, but some are better placed to do so, if adequately used – international harmonization of conflict rules, international harmonization of substantive rules, and international cooperation in civil or criminal legal matters. As public international law forms and mechanisms creep in,[63] however, these strategies become more open to directly engaging with the notion that they are pursuing values, rather than just mechanically applying conflict rules to safeguard state sovereignty while facilitating international comity.

In line with the idea of relying increasingly on public international law forms, harmonization processes are used more and more frequently. They allow for a more open discussion of the values to be promoted by legal instruments, and for identifying these values as goals rather than limits (which is what happens when public policy or foreign public law exceptions apply with respect to conflict rules). And if public values are put front and center, these strategies can more effectively bridge the public/private divide. Even in those instances, however, the private frame of state sovereignty and the private frame of technical or apolitical dispute resolution still creeps in, either as fallback norms when harmonized substantive law falls short, or through rendering institutional cooperation mechanisms ostensibly value-free.

There is something to be said about making values less apparent, and strategically using purported 'neutrality' to advance more sophisticated legal and institutional responses, as seen in the discussion of indirect harmonization of substantive rules with indirect effects on global public goods, and in international cooperation mechanisms. But the lack of normative commitment to safeguarding global public goods in these

---

63 A trend also noted by Mills (n 9).

instances means that lawyers, advocates, and decision-makers need to be more aware of the possible tools they can deploy. If fragmentation is one of the problems plaguing the public/private divide in this space, it may be that this strategy is less desirable and only compounds one of the field's key problems.

There are limits, then, to what the current strategies can do in terms of bringing public values into a conversation about safeguarding global public goods as part of private international legal governance efforts. What those limits mean for thinking about global public goods more generally, and the public/private divide, is the subject of the next section.

4. CULTURAL HERITAGE AND OTHER GLOBAL PUBLIC GOODS AS PUBLIC CONCERNS THAT NEED PRIVATE ARTICULATION

If we are serious about not undoing diversity but strategically tapping into it to safeguard global public goods, it is important that we are able to think more broadly about the ways in which the international private legal articulation of public concerns can gain traction and defend public values.[64] The private, as discussed above, brings novel techniques and strategies for addressing legal governance issues. While each of these strategies has its own normative preferences and limitations, they each also have the potential to serve different values associated with global public goods, and thereby advance a worthwhile diversity of mechanisms. Values can function to unify orientations, but not to change the mechanics of the strategies themselves.

Since the point of this discussion is to think more broadly and creatively about the possibilities of private international legal governance, it is worth

---

64 For essays engaging with the boundaries of public and private in the defense of public good such as finance, migration, and gender equality, see Bram van der Eem, 'Financial Stability as a Global Public Good and Private International Law as an Instrument for its Transnational Governance, Some Basic Thoughts' in Horatia Muir Watt and Diego P Fernández Arroyo (eds), *Private International Law and Global Governance* (OUP 2014) 293–300; Sabine Corneloup, 'Can Private International Law Contribute to Global Migration Governance?', in Horatia Muir Watt and Diego P Fernández Arroyo (eds), *Private International Law and Global Governance* (OUP 2014) 301–317; and Ivana Isailović, 'Political Recognition and Transnational Law: Gender Equality and Cultural Diversification in French Courts', in Horatia Muir Watt and Diego P Fernández Arroyo (eds), *Private International Law and Global Governance* (OUP 2014) 318–342.

recalling what the private domain brings to the table with respect to global public goods, and how to go about engaging it.

In terms of the advantages of the private law domain, some have already been mentioned: a diversity of strategies, an ability to generate discussion of the economics of global public goods, and greater effectiveness or enforcement potential. Among these advantages, the economics argument deserves more discussion. It is fairly common, as stated above, to think of global public goods as transcending economics.[65] If they are beyond the market, the reasoning goes, they can be protected in absolute terms, hermetically enclosed for the benefit of present and future generations. That is certainly a worthwhile ideal, but in effect the strategy is self-defeating. As I have argued elsewhere with respect to cultural heritage,[66] the fact that heritage is seen as beyond the reach of economics does not mean the market goes away: it just moves elsewhere. To turn a blind eye to the market is to enable it to act in the shadows; to think of the market as belonging more to the private than the public is to legitimize that move into the shadows. International law for public goods would therefore do well to engage more openly and aggressively with the market, so as to be able to regulate it while keeping the values associated with the global public good at front and center, rather than as afterthoughts which may or may not fit a market rationality. This engagement includes participation in legal fora that focus primarily on the market, and not only those that focus on the global public good. Because of the constitutional constraints under which they are created, legal institutions focused on the market often translate global public goods and community interests only when they serve a specific market rationality. If international law on global public goods were to be made a more central part of considerations in those regimes as well, the market would open itself up to values which are not driven necessarily by market rationality. Further, community interests would be more clearly articulated in fuller expression, rather than read only through the prism of defending free trade, promoting foreign investment, or some other market-related goal.

In addition to these advantages, other things can be gained from a greater engagement with private international legal governance for global public goods. The involvement of more stakeholders is an important factor to consider, as the investment of communities living in, with, or around global public goods is often a vital element in successful safeguarding.

---

65 See, generally, Barkin and Rashchupkina (n 11).

66 Lixinski (n 23) 127–167.

In other words, the involvement of non-state actors, which can be enabled via the language and strategies of private (international) law, can be crucial ways for these actors to gain a stake in the global public good, and contribute to its safeguarding, as long as private (international) legal mechanisms are set up in reference to public values that necessitate the safeguarding of the global public good. In this way the private can promote better outcomes for the global public good itself, and the possible uses and values of the public good are more clearly advanced or articulated throughout the entire legal system, as opposed to being relegated to the private.

How can this bridge between the public and the private be articulated, though? One possible pathway is through harmonizing agency and standing rules with respect to global public goods in contexts that do not necessarily speak directly to those goods, through the strategy of harmonizing substantive rules with indirect effects on global public goods. Doing so would enable the easier collectivization of the global public good's articulation outside of public international legal frameworks.

Further, public international legal governance fora and institutions where global public goods are discussed should become more transparent and accessible for feedback and increased participation to private (non-expert) parties. NGO and expert group participation already happens within a number of these institutions, but these instances of participation fall short of connecting the global public good with the groups that live in, with, or around it, thereby failing to engage these groups in venues where public values are put front and center, as opposed to private international legal governance strategies that, as discussed above, only engage these values indirectly. A range of strategies exist for participation in international bodies around the world, and their experiences teach us that participation should be determinative, and not just consultative (for instance, in international law the current standard is for consultation rather than consent from communities, and it should be the other way around); participation should be seen as a right rather than a concession; and participation should extend to the making of procedural rules as well, since they determine the parameters of possible participation by non-state actors who are better equipped to convey community interests.[67]

---

67 I am deeply thankful to the members of the International Law Association Committee on Participation in Global Cultural Heritage Governance, for their many insights in this area.

If the strategy of increasing participation is to be pursued, a significant threshold question is why states would agree to give up their power. As it stands, the public international legal governance of global public goods is done with significant deference to sovereignty, effectively meaning a monopoly of state (and sometimes expert) rule. However, if the commitment to safeguarding the global public good is to be prioritized, as opposed to being a pawn in a broader political game, then power-sharing should be possible. Experts could be a productive starting point for this shift, since they are already sympathetic to the idea of non-state actors in areas of public international legal governance, and are committed to the safeguarding of the global public good in more central ways. A key example in the heritage domain is in the World Heritage Convention, where the Operational Guidelines for its implementation have been significantly altered over the years, at the behest of experts, to include things like greater consultation with communities living in, with, or around heritage, as well as more intangible values associated with heritage in the consideration of the worthiness of heritage sites for inclusion on the World Heritage List.[68]

Once experts agree to power-sharing with communities, they can then put pressure on states as well in invisible ways. In the domain of international heritage law, the International Union for the Conservation of Nature, whose approval is necessary for natural or mixed sites to be added to the World Heritage List,[69] has increasingly chosen to consult local communities ahead of evaluating a site for inscription. This practice that is not required of it, but which engages communities in ways that are beneficial for the safeguarding of such sites, which are global public goods for both cultural heritage and environmental reasons.

Although the examples given here relate to cultural heritage, it is apparent that these strategies can be extended to other global public goods. Attempts have already been made in the environmental domain,[70]

---

68 See, generally, Francesco Francioni and Federico Lenzerini, 'Conclusions, The Future of the World Heritage Convention: Problems and Prospects' in Francesco Francioni (ed), *The 1972 World Heritage Convention: A Commentary* (OUP 2008).

69 WHC (n 22) arts 8, 11, 13 and 14.

70 See, for instance, United Nations Economic Commission for Europe 'Convention on Access to Information, Public Participation in Decision-Making and Access to Justice in Environmental Matters' (adopted 25 June 1998, entered into force 20 October 2001) 2161 UNTS 447, 38 ILM 517 (Aarhus Convention). For some commentary, see UNECE, *Commentary on the Convention on Access to Information, Public Participation in Decision-making and Access to Justice in Environmental Matters* (Jendroska Jerzmanski Bar i Wspólnicy 2016).

but the oceans and Antarctica, for instance, could also benefit from clearer engagement between the public and the private in their governance. After all, companies responsible for overfishing, marine pollution, and mineral exploitation in the oceans are for the most part private; public and private operators increasingly put pressure on the Antarctica regime's veto of economic exploitation,[71] and private presence in the area is growing.[72] The big question to be answered is whether it is feasible to expect states to give up their (near-) monopoly of power in favor of better safeguarding global public goods. As it stands, excluding the private legal domain from global public goods decisions renders the private legal governance dimension invisible, and community interests harder to gauge unless translated by the state, and, in some instances, experts. A case is thus to be made to not necessarily diminish public authority, but to pluralize it by increasing awareness of the ways in which private legal ordering necessarily affects global public goods in countless ways. In many respects, the state's cession of authority is therefore more of a broader recognition of the import of background norms in these debates than a bypassing of existing frameworks.

5. CONCLUDING REMARKS

This chapter illustrates the difficulties of blurring the public/private divide, particularly with respect to global public goods, which necessitate public values and the tools and engagement of private international legal governance strategies. Each side of this divide, and each strategy within private international legal governance, evokes different possibilities and priorities, creating a landscape that is often hard to navigate and highly fragmented. Rather than eliminating this diversity it is essential to strategically embrace it, for the benefit of those public global goods and the communities living in, with, or around them, which are the first to lose out

---

71 See, eg, Michael Atkin, 'China's Interest in Mining Antarctica Revealed as Evidence Points to Country's Desire to Become "Polar Great Power"', *ABC News* (20 January 2015) <http://www.abc.net.au/news/2015-01-20/chinas-desire-for-antarctic-mining-despite-international-ban/6029414> accessed 15 January 2021.

72 Alok Jha, 'As Antarctica Opens Up, will Privateer Explorers be Frozen Out?' *The Guardian* (28 February 2014) <https://www.theguardian.com/world/2014/feb/28/-sp-antarctica-privateer-explorers-scientific-research-territory-polar-code> accessed 15 January 2021.

when things go wrong with these public goods, and the ones upon whom the burden of safeguarding these goods weighs most heavily.

Further, this chapter shows that attaining objectives dictated by the values attributed to global public goods is only possible through blurring the public/private regulation divide, which justifies the excursion into these strategies and possibilities. The harmonization of conflict and substantive rules, as well as cooperation in international legal matters, can open up much-needed space for integrating other values and for enhancing the regulatory possibilities for safeguarding global public goods. Integrating private international legal governance strategies opens them up to the values of global public goods, while at the same time lending their greater effectiveness to create change on the ground to legal the safeguarding of strategies otherwise focused on (international) public law mechanisms.

Exploring these strategies, and their consequences for global public goods governance more broadly, reminds us that public international law must be more aware of the private's potential to actually make the lofty promises of treaties on public goods reality. At the same time, private international legal governance strategies need to stop hiding in their own shadows. Further work is required to map out the possibilities of private international legal governance for other global public goods, and, crucially, to articulate the possibilities for intersecting public values and private strategies. This articulation may make coordinated yet pluralistic action to safeguard global public goods possible, and these goods may be better safeguarded by taking into account more voices to translate community interest – not only increasing available tools, but also better embedding values and effectiveness.

HOW INTERNATIONAL COURTS CAN HELP SECURE GLOBAL PUBLIC GOODS WORTH HAVING

Pure Public Goods and Beyond

Andreas FOLLESDAL*

* Research for this chapter was partly supported by the Research Council of Norway through its Centres of Excellence Funding Scheme, project number 223274 – PluriCourts – on the Legitimacy of the International Judiciary. I am grateful for the opportunities to present earlier versions of these arguments at PluriCourts, Stockholm University, the University of Graz, and the Nordic Network on Political Theory, and for the many constructive suggestions received there. Particular thanks to Mark Pollack, Geir Ulfstein, Christina Voigt and anonymous readers for detailed comments and improvements.

1. INTRODUCTION

Debates about the legitimacy of international law and international courts (ICs)[1] revolve around whether, in various ways, they enable their subjects to act better.[2] One such debate concerns whether international law and ICs are effective in providing so-called global public goods (GPG). A central GPG is effective resolution of the climate crisis, and it is one for which international law and ICs are often found wanting.[3] This has often led scholars to focus on a particular diagnosis: the central legitimacy challenge is that *international law and ICs are too weak to prevent 'free riders' among states:*[4]

> Just as the state is needed to provide public goods at optimal levels nationally, international governance is needed to provide the optimal level of global public goods. For international organizations, global public goods thus provide a response to the growing questions that emerged in the 1990s about their legitimacy.[5]

---

1 See, among others, Nienke Grossman, Harlan Grant Cohen, Andreas Follesdal, and Geir Ulfstein (eds), *Legitimacy and International Courts* (Cambridge University Press 2018).

2 Joseph Raz, *The Morality of Freedom* (Clarendon Press 1986) 369–429; Andreas Follesdal, 'Survey Article: The Legitimacy of International Courts' (2020) 28(4) Journal of Political Philosophy 476.

3 cf Fabrizio Cafaggi and David D Caron, 'Global Public Goods Amidst a Plurality of Legal Orders: A Symposium' (2012) 23(3) European Journal of International Law 643 – several specific contributions are referenced below; Shirley V Scott, 'Climate Change and Peak Oil as Threats to International Peace and Security: Is it Time for the Security Council to Legislate?' (2008) 9(2) Melbourne Journal of International Law 495, 500; Ruth Gordon, 'The Triumph and Failure of International Law' (2011) 34(1) North Carolina Central Law Review 63; Nico Krisch, 'The Decay of Consent: International Law in an Age of Global Public Goods' (2014) 108(1) The American Journal of International Law 1; see also Tomer Broude, 'Warming to Crisis: The Climate Change Law of Unintended Opportunity' (2012) 44 Netherlands Yearbook of International Law 111.

4 These and other scholars often report such views without necessarily endorsing them; cf Clifford J Carrubba and Matthew J Gabel, 'Courts, Compliance, and the Quest for Legitimacy in International Law' (2013) 14(2) Theoretical Inquiries in Law 505.

5 Daniel Bodansky, 'What's in a Concept? Global Public Goods, International Law, and Legitimacy' (2012) 23(3) EJIL 651, 655.

> The major challenge for the production of many (but not all) global public goods, as well as those public goods that are transnational (but not global) in scope, [...] is collective action and free riding.[6]
>
> [T]he raison d'être and defining feature of public goods, in legal terms, lie in the need to provide for enforcement that cannot otherwise be provided.[7]

Concerns about free riding may be more salient for ICs than for international law in general, since states can easily avoid international adjudication by not ratifying the relevant treaty protocols.

I argue that this description, diagnosis, and prescription for how international law and ICs can and should enable GPG is unfortunate. The assumptions are too narrow, and distract our attention from other valuable contributions made by ICs – in terms of GPGs and beyond – and from other important challenges that ICs face. The shallow focus stifles our assessment of when international law and ICs may be legitimate authorities in general, and in relation to GPGs in particular. In fact, ICs' legitimacy does not depend on their ability to trigger sanctions against states; they serve several valuable functions for many objectives other than GPGs, including monitoring and providing information about other states' actions and preferences.

Even if we use the term 'global public goods' in a broader sense, heeding the efforts and publications of the UN Development Programme (UNDP), the tunnel vision remains unfortunate.[8] Broader lists include *inter alia* peace, world trade, eradication of infectious diseases, international solidarity, environmental protection, human rights, global justice, antitrust measures, food security, democracy, knowledge, the resolution of international disputes by ICs, and sovereignty itself.[9] Some scholars have questioned

---

6 Gregory Schaffer, 'International Law and Global Public Goods in a Legal Pluralist World' (2012) 23(3) European Journal of International Law 669, 674.

7 André Nollkaemper, 'International Adjudication of Global Public Goods: The Intersection of Substance and Procedure' (2012) 23(3) EJIL 769, 785–786.

8 Inge Kaul, Isabelle Grunberg and Marc A Stern (eds), *Global Public Goods: International Cooperation in the 21st Century* (Oxford University Press 1999). Other related concepts include 'common interest' cf Wolfgang Benedek and others (eds), *The Common Interest in International Law* (Intersentia 2014).

9 cf lists in Kaul, Grunberg and Stern (n 8) and Joel P Trachtman, *The Future of International Law: Global Government* (Cambridge University Press 2013); More specific discussions include Christian J Tams, 'World Courts as Guardians of Peace?' (2016) 15 Global Cooperation Research Papers 5, Petros C Mavroidis, 'Free Lunches? WTO as Public Good, and the WTO's View of Public Goods' (2012) 23(3) EJIL 731, Peter Burnell, 'International Democracy Promotion: A Role for Public Goods Theory?' (2008) 14(1) Contemporary Politics 37, 41.

the conceptual value of labelling this broad range of goods 'public goods.'[10] Long lists of GPGs have fostered attempts to provide all-encompassing categories,[11] but these appear disconnected to any overarching theory. The broader concept encompasses many outcomes considered by some to be good for individuals at large, for the international community in part or in whole,[12] or among parties that transcend national boundaries.

If the expansion of GPGs comes at the cost of accurate diagnoses and prescriptions – and of sound assessments of the legitimacy of ICs – what can be done? The need for sparse and stringent theories might prompt us to return to the narrower definition of 'public goods' present in 20th-century economic theory, as the quotes above apparently do. This chapter advises against that response. To be sure, the valuable and carefully justified insights of the by now standard 'public goods theory of authority' have had profound impact; it appears to be the origin of the recent popularity of the term 'global public goods.' More profoundly, the standard theory's focus on the problem of actors who free ride on others' collaborative efforts has achieved a central place in discussions, generating many analyses of the scope of challenges to collective action among states, and how the lack of legitimate authority over these sovereigns prevents easy solutions.

While the standard theory may be correct on its own terms, we should not dismiss a broader conception of GPGs as too analytically fuzzy. The standard theory is too incomplete to justify standards that help assess legitimate authority in general, including that of international law and ICs, and that of ICs regarding GPGs in particular.

One shared feature of GPGs may be that they are 'public' in the sense that they can benefit individuals or entities in more than one state, and require concerted action by multiple actors of different kinds for their provision.[13] The standard theory's limited scope leaves out large parts of game-theoretic modelling and important tasks for the legitimate authorities intending to secure such GPGs. The following argument seeks to justify these claims, largely by drawing together the many substantive findings of other scholars. Attention to broader game-theoretic insights helps understand and address the many challenges to collective action wrought by GPGs, and how ICs contribute and might contribute, as well as identifying tasks for which authoritative ICs may be neither feasible nor

---

10 Nollkaemper (n 7) 776.
11 Kaul, Grunberg and Stern (n 8).
12 Sometimes discussed as '*erga omnes* norms', cf Nollkaemper (n 7).
13 Kaul, Grunberg and Stern (n 8) 7.

suitable. The challenges of climate change and the possible contributions of the Paris Agreement illustrate this.

A further reason to downplay the significance of the standard public goods theory is to reduce its unfortunate framing effects. It leads scholars to regard other collective benefits, including GPGs, as 'impure' public goods, and to focus attention on problems that are similar to those that arise with GPGs.[14] But GPGs also raise quite different concerns, arguably at least as important as those around free riding, such as whether all states, or their citizens, have reason to secure an alleged GPG, and how to allocate the work of its provision and the resultant benefits and burdens. The standard theory also reenforces inaccurate accounts that may hinder our understanding and our strategies: it maintains that authorities' central and legitimating task with regard to GPGs is to employ sanctions, in order to shift the strategies of actors assumed to be motivated only by myopic, unconstrained, and immutable self-interest. We find traces of this narrow focus in seminal contributions to the study of international law. The framing of the standard theory hampers a broader, more justified appreciation of the complex and dynamic preferences and interests of states and other actors, and impedes a better sense of the many legitimate tasks of authorities and of ICs in particular.

Section 1 provides a sketch of the standard public goods theory. Its scope conditions help explain one discernable trend in the academic literature: justifying authority as necessary to prevent the free riding that undermines public goods. Its limited focus excludes several important issues, such as who decides what is of universal interest and who identifies matters of distributive justice. Section 2 gives a brief account of the several tasks of ICs, and considers various features and functions of ICs that distinguish them from other authorities. To illustrate their differences, it considers three GPGs which pose quite different collective action problems, and where ICs and other bodies may take on distinct tasks: human rights protection, world trade, and the 'differentiated commitments' of the Paris Agreement to help states alleviate the climate crises. Section 3 seeks to incorporate game-theoretic contributions by various authors that the standard theory leaves untouched, underscoring how its exclusive focus on possible free riders shifts attention from crucial issues. The 'free rider' problem itself merits more analysis and interpretation, and many urgent global challenges for states' pursuit of the GPGs they have reason to secure are better analyzed as mixes of other types of collective action

[14] ibid 4–5.

problems, such as assurance games and 'battles of the sexes', as shown by several scholars' contributions.

Section 4 discusses some implications of lifting the constraints of the standard theory for how ICs may contribute to addressing challenges posed by GPGs. It starts by challenging concern about the weak enforcement powers of ICs. Many valuable contributions by ICs occur outside the scope conditions of the standard theory. The upshot is that the standard account ignores other functions of legitimate authorities, such as ICs, including allocating benefits and burdens, facilitating reasoned 'balancing' of conflicting objectives and norms, and addressing battles of the sexes and the need for assurance.

The discussions yield both good and bad news for the legitimate authority of ICs. Broader perspectives complicate our assessment of whether existing and new ICs can contribute to securing a broader range of GPGs, where distributive conflicts and complex balancing of values occur among actors with opaque and changing preferences. On the one hand, their weak direct enforcement powers against free riders do not render ICs ineffective and hence illegitimate, and they serve other important tasks. But neither international law in general nor ICs in particular are a universal panacea for the challenges of international cooperation: international bodies without adjudicatory authority may often be better placed to act. To summarize and clarify the limited scope of tasks for which ICs may be helpful, section 5 considers the contributions of a quite different, non-adversarial, and less powerful body: the Compliance and Implementation Committee of the Paris Agreement. It illustrates important steps for furthering the GPG of combatting climate change that the standard theory ignores, and that might not need the authority of ICs.

2. GLOBAL PUBLIC GOODS AND THE STANDARD PUBLIC GOODS THEORY OF AUTHORITY

The link between authority, public goods, and free riders seems to have originated with economists' insights about a particular failure of voluntary market exchanges.[15] The central point of the standard public

---

15 The influential UNDP-based report that popularized 'GPGs' makes explicit reference to nonrivalry in consumption and nonexcludability, ibid. Prior and less formalized discussions include Plato, *The Republic and Other Works* (Benjamin Howlett tr, Anchor 1973), David Hume, *A Treatise of Human Nature* (Clarendon Press 1960);

goods theory is that even though certain benefits are desired by all, they cannot be provided by consensual market exchange. The reason for this consists of two features of what are often called 'pure' public goods.[16] Their consumption is *inexhaustible* – in the 'polar extreme case,'[17] use of the good by some does not reduce opportunities for use by others – and this cornucopian feature makes the production of such goods highly attractive.[18] But they are also *non-exclusive*: it is impossible or difficult to prevent their consumption by others.[19] Note that this standard conception of pure public goods is markedly different than the much broader concept of 'global public goods' presented above.

These two features leave rational actors without incentives to contribute to their production, but rather to free ride on others' efforts, with the result that the goods may not be produced. Voluntary, decentralized market exchanges cannot therefore yield an 'optimal' distribution of such public goods. Coercion may correct this market failure. This 'public goods theory of the state' maintains that authorities' main task is to deter free riders by means of sanctions. Thus the justification for a legitimate authority with coercive power over autonomous actors is to help them attain such public goods that each prefers.[20]

This justification of legitimate authority has stimulated, framed, and constrained much research and debate, about international law and ICs in particular. The legal scholars cited above appear to refer to a similar 'standard' global public goods theory of international law, but they do not necessarily accept either it or its diagnosis that the main problem

---

John Stuart Mill, *The Principles of Political Economy, With Some of their Applications to Social Philosophy* (Longmans, Greens and Co 1909); Vilfredo Pareto, *The Mind and Society* (Arthur Livingston ed, volume 3, Harcourt, Brace and Co 1935), 946–947, and – cf, for these and further discussions, Russell Hardin and Garrett Cullity, 'The Free Rider Problem' *Stanford Encyclopedia of Philosophy* (2020) <https://plato.stanford.edu/archives/win2020/entries/free-rider/> accessed 15 January 2021.

16 Originally called 'polar' public goods, see Paul A Samuelson, 'Diagrammatic Exposition of Public Expenditure' (1955) 37(4) The Review of Economics and Statistics 350.

17 ibid.

18 ibid; Paul A Samuelson, 'The Pure Theory of Public Expenditure' (1954) 36(4) The Review of Economics and Statistics 387.

19 Richard A Musgrave, *The Theory of Public Finance: A Study in Political Economy* (McGraw-Hill 1959) 8.

20 William J Baumol, *Welfare Economics and the Theory of the State* (Harvard University Press 1952) 57. Samuelson (n 16) analyzed 'the vital external interdependencies that no theory of government can do without'. He also acknowledged that he overstated the case in his first publication, as governments and taxation may have other legitimate tasks, 355–356.

of international law is its lack of sanctions against free-riding sovereign states.

I submit that the broader discussions of GPGs and institutional tasks may have suffered from the frame imposed by the economists' standard theory, which hides or hinders valuable insights. The challenge of securing public goods by preventing free riders is neither the sole or main justification for legitimate authority – for states, for international law, or for ICs. This focus may have detracted from other important tasks. We can observe this if we start with the standard theory and lift some of its restrictions, to understand better when international law and ICs may be beneficial and legitimate, and when they may not be justified. At least four *scope conditions* of the standard public goods theory do not extend easily to our broader concerns.

Firstly, the definition of 'public goods' as inexhaustible and non-exclusive is *ambiguous regarding normative commitments*. On the one hand it is *agnostic* about the normative value of the goods, and simply accepts actors' preferences regarding them. Those preferences may relate to one's own well-being, other-regarding sympathy, or complex mixes. States' concern for human rights violations by other states illustrate the latter: such violations may both be cause for humanitarian concern and challenge other states' benefits from economic trade and political cooperation. The definition simply helps explain why voluntary market exchanges cannot secure their supply or their restriction. On the other hand, central contributors to the theory express and acknowledge a range of normative positions. Thus Samuelson agrees that 'much public expenditure on education, hospitals, and so on, can be justified.'[21] The theory itself rests on several normative premises, including respect for consumer sovereignty and an allegedly weak normative claim about ethical distribution, discussed below. Notably, the theory does not address who should decide which such normative premises to accept.

Secondly, this account leaves aside issues of *preference formation* and modification. The parties' fundamental values, interests, and objectives are assumed to be stable. The acknowledged role of institutions and other actors is not to change these, but is rather limited to change the payoffs of some outcomes so that actors reorder their preferences among them.[22]

---

21 Samuelson (n 16) 356.

22 This bracketing of preference formation and change is not typical of economics as a whole. This public goods account and some other parts of economics regard preferences as exogenous. See Lionel Robbins, *An Essay in the Nature and Significance of Economic Science* (Macmillan 1932). But other economists do address such issues

Thirdly, this account brackets conflicts among values or interests *within* each actor. The preferences of each agent over the alternatives are supposed to already have accommodated any internal conflicts among the agent's values or objectives.

Fourthly, the standards for *optimal* distribution of goods in this account are quite limited. The answer to 'the ethically preferred final configuration'[23] of goods is simply any allocation where 'you can make one person better off only by making some other person worse off', that is, along the Pareto 'maximum utility frontier'.[24] The account does not address any inter-personal conflicts other than this concern. Any *further* issues relating to distribution of goods among actors are explicitly excluded from considerations about 'the best state of the world' as beyond the 'scientific' task of the economist.[25]

A more comprehensive account of legitimate authority, particularly that of ICs, often addresses these four topics; the origin of 'public good' analysis is therefore drastically incomplete. The following sections refer to various works of scholarship that have extended and challenged the constrained public goods account of legitimate authority, including for ICs. Authorities have other tasks, and there are reasons for ICs' authority over states other than to sanction free riders, even within the game-theoretic modelling of the standard theory.[26]

3. TASKS OF INTERNATIONAL COURTS

How may ICs enable states and individuals with regard to GPGs? Their core task is to adjudicate disputes through interpreting and applying international law by legal methods. This may be relevant to GPGs, insofar as the IC considers state violations that hinder objectives such as free trade or human rights. But the standard public goods theory creates low expectations about the impact of any such judgment for GPGs. First, international law generally and ICs in particular will not have jurisdiction over some non-cooperating states because they have not accepted the

head on, cf Amartya K Sen, 'Equality of What?' in Amartya K Sen (ed), *Choice, Welfare and Measurement* (The MIT Press 1980).

23 Samuelson (n 16) 351.

24 Samuelson (18).

25 ibid.

26 I leave aside how ICs may serve other legitimating tasks beyond facilitating cooperation and coordination among states, cf Follesdal 2020.

IC's jurisdiction to begin with, or have exited from it.[27] Second, relevant actors may not have 'standing' before the IC in the relevant case. Third, any judgment will only be binding for the parties to the case. Fourth, states can refuse to comply with the IC's judgment with little risk of sanctions from the IC.[28] Its legitimate authority stands to suffer, since it fails to enable states to meet objectives they have reason to pursue, such as protecting and promoting human rights, international trade, or the environment at home and abroad.

Such general pessimism on behalf of ICs is premature. Section 3 addresses their roles regarding sanctions, although ICs carry out several other tasks that may facilitate some GPGs.[29] To illustrate, I consider two types of ICs and an international body that does not adjudicate, but can still contribute. The WTO Dispute Settlement system and its Appellate Body (AB) may be closest to the standard theory's concern with free riders. The WTO AB determines whether states have violated trade rules. In contrast, the regional ICs that adjudicate human rights treaties make contributions and challenges that seldom concern free riders. The third contrasting case considers the potential contributions of the Compliance and Implementation Mechanism of the Paris Agreement (the 'Compliance Mechanism'), which despite ostensibly being even weaker than ICs, since it is not designed to adjudicate cases,[30] may facilitate cooperation and coordination among states – or so I shall argue.

The core task of ICs is adjudication. By adjudicating, ICs also contribute to reviewing and helping others monitor compliance. This is often necessary to facilitate cooperation among parties who are 'repeat players' and interact often – especially among those not seeking to free ride, as I return to below. Further important indirect effects of adjudication concern its impact on states' reputations. A state's express choice to allow cases to be brought against it may enhance its own credibility in the eyes of others, as it thus submits to future monitoring and scrutiny by an independent body.[31] Fear of future litigation may also help deter

27 Laurence Helfer, 'Exiting Treaties' (2005) 91 Virginia Law Review 1579.

28 Schaffer (n 6) 675.

29 For in depth and illuminating treatment of these issues cf Joshua Paine, 'International Adjudication as a Global Public Good?' (2019) 29(4) European Journal of International Law 1223.

30 Christina Voigt, 'The Compliance and Implementation Mechanism of the Paris Agreement' (2016) 25(2) Review of European, Comparative and International Environmental Law 161.

31 Laurence Helfer, 'Why States Create International Tribunals: A Theory of Constrained Independence' in Stefan Voigt, Max Albert and Dieter Schmidtchen (eds), *International Conflict Resolution* (Mohr Siebeck 2006).

free riders. The IC can provide more such assurance and deterrence if the state expands the potential pool of litigants to not only include states but also private parties, as in the case of human rights ICs.

Note that bodies other than ICs may perform similar tasks, such as international or domestic monitoring bodies, or competence-building agencies. The Compliance Mechanism is a case in point.[32] In comparison to some such bodies, ICs have limits: They adjudicate on the basis of agreed treaties, leaving many urgent issues out of reach. They are also mainly 'reactive' in that they consider cases brought before them by an actor. And they only address disputes between two parties who have accepted their jurisdiction, often without legally binding effect on others. Beneficial or disadvantageous effects on third parties may arise, but compete with the core task of settling the dispute among the parties. This process may therefore be less suited to alleviating collective problems wrought by multiple states. On the other hand, the risk of being found in violation of a treaty may nudge other states to defend their policies and legislation publicly, in light of possibly conflicting obligations. Thus the European Court of Human Rights appears to defer to states' assessments of violations in some cases, but only if they have performed a good faith 'proportionality test'.[33]

A second important task of ICs is that they must often *interpret*, develop, and specify international law in order to adjudicate. States agree to these treaties as 'incomplete contracts' either because of lack of time, or the impossibility to foresee all factual situations, or because they were unable to agree on details. They entrust some of these specific treaty details to IC judges.[34] Some even argue that ICs provide a GPG by completing

---

32 Elinor Ostrom, *Governing the Commons: The Evolution of Institutions for Collective Action* (CUP 1991); Elinor Ostrom, James Walker and Roy Gardner, 'Covenants with and Without a Sword: Self-Governance is Possible' (1992) 86(2) American Political Science Review 404; Oona Hathaway and Scott J Shapiro, *The internationalists: And their Plan to Outlaw War* (Allen Lane 2017); David G Victor, Kal Raustiala and Eugene B Skolnikoff, *The Implementation and Effectiveness of International Environmental Commitments: Theory and Practice* (The MIT Press 1998).

33 Janneke Gerards, 'How to Improve the Necessity Test of the European Court of Human Rights' (2013) 11(2) International Journal of Constitutional Law 466; Yutaka Arai-Takahashi, 'The Margin of Appreciation Doctrine: A Theoretical Analysis of Strasbourg's Variable Geometry' in Andreas Follesdal, Birgit Peters and Geir Ulfstein (eds), *Constituting Europe: The European Court of Human Rights in a National, European and Global Context* (CUP 2013); Andreas Follesdal, 'Appreciating the Margin of Appreciation' in Adam Etinson (ed), *Human Rights: Moral or Political?* (OUP 2018), 269–294.

34 Gregory Shaffer and Joel Trachtman, 'Interpretation and Institutional Choice at the WTO' (2011) 52 Virginia Journal of International Law 103; Joost Pauwelyn and

these treaties.[35] The impact of such interpretations may be significant, yet states sometimes explicitly leave it to the IC 'to clarify the existing provisions',[36] expecting that 'decisions through the convention's mechanism will create a significant new body of international law'.[37] When ICs 'fill in the gaps' in treaties they stabilize expectations about other actors' future conduct. They thereby help identify cases where free riding takes place, and where it does not. Through their interpretations, ICs also authoritatively set standards for how to allocate benefits and burdens, and they order and give priority to conflicting objectives and values. Their interpretations reframe and prioritize various issues, interpreting some cases of rape as acts of genocide,[38] for example, or specifying 'complementarity' vis-à-vis states[39] and 'constitutionalizing' a legal order. A prime example of the latter is how the Court of Justice of the European Union 'constitutionalized' EU law, going beyond the EU treaty texts to grant them direct effect and primacy over domestic legislation – and acknowledged human rights norms.[40] Note that this task of interpretation is not an obvious normative good, as parties may understandably disagree about the correctness and benefits of an IC's interpretation.

Manfred Elsig, 'The Politics of Treaty Interpretation' in Jeffrey L Dunoff and Mark A Pollack (eds), *Interdisciplinary Perspectives on International Law and International Relations: The State of the Art* (CUP 2013); Alec Stone Sweet and Thomas L Brunell, 'Trustee Courts and the Judicialization of International Regimes' (2013) 1(1) Journal of Law and Courts 61.

35 Mavroidis (n 9).

36 World Trade Organization, 'Dispute Settlement Understanding' (1994) 1869 UNTS 40, Annex 2 (DSU) art 3.2; see also Shaffer and Trachtman (n 34) 128, footnote 72.

37 Taylor St John attributes this to James Meeker, cf Taylor St John, *The Rise of Investor-State Arbitration: Politics, Law, and Unintended Consequences* (OUP 2018) 177, footnote 145.

38 *Prosecutor v Anto Furundzija* (Judgment) ICTY-95-17/1-T (10 December 1998) paras 164–186; *Prosecutor v Dragoljub Kunarac and others* (Judgment) ICTY IT-96-23-T and IT-96-23/1-T (22 February 2001) paras 436–464, 515–543; cf Patricia Viseur Sellers, 'The Prosecution of Sexual Violence in Conflict: The Importance of Human Rights as Means of Interpretation' (Office of the United Nations High Commissioner for Human Rights) <https://www2.ohchr.org/english/issues/women/docs/Paper_Prosecution_of_Sexual_Violence.pdf> accessed 15 January 2021.

39 Carsten Stahn and Mohamed M El Zeydi (eds), *The International Criminal Court and Complementarity: From Theory to Practice* (CUP 2011); Ignaz Stegmiller, 'Positive Complementarity and Legitimacy – is the International Criminal Court Shifting from Judicial Restraint Towards Intervention?' in Nobuo Hayashi and Cecilia M Bailliet (eds), *The Legitimacy of International Criminal Tribunals* (CUP 2017); Geir Ulfstein, 'Institutions and Competence' in Jan Klabbers, Anne Peters and Geir Ulfstein (eds), *The Constitutionalization of International Law* (OUP 2009).

40 J H H Weiler, *The Constitution of Europe: 'Do the New Clothes Have an Emperor?' and Other Essays on European Integration* (CUP 1999).

What, if any, comparative advantages do ICs have over other bodies in terms of interpreting and developing treaties? I start to address part of this question below, but several alternatives exist. Such (quasi-)legislative tasks may be carried out by states in the form of amendments to a treaty, or by other actors such as inter-state parliamentary committees or committees of the state parties, by coordination among domestic constitutional courts – or in dialogues with expert committees with fewer formal powers than ICs, as discussed below.

I now turn to how these IC tasks fit with the public goods theory of legitimate authority.

4. ASPECTS OF GAME THEORY: FREE RIDING AND BEYOND

The public goods theory of legitimate authority is exclusively concerned with free riders, and how sanctions may shift their preferences in order to secure the public goods. To understand the tasks of authorities in general, and of ICs in particular, I delve into the range of reactions ICs may trigger, other sorts of benefits from cooperation, and other parts of game theory. Many goods fall short of the 'pure case' Samuelson discusses, for many outcomes are not preferred by all parties and many goods are partly exhaustible or partly exclusive. I then note the existence of variations in the number of necessary contributors for various GPGs. Finally, because actors often have other preferences over outcomes than free riding, I consider other forms of 'games'. These distinctions are relevant when discerning ICs' possible contributions and limitations.

4.1. WHOSE PUBLIC GOODS?

Economists' interest in the standard account stemmed from the particular challenge of public goods. Many challenges facing international law today concern other objectives than these inexhaustible and non-excludable outcomes.

Firstly, many objectives are claimed by some actors to be of universal benefit, even though this is an open question. Some actors have the power to label certain objectives or outcomes GPGs and make other actors acquiesce to such labels, with important consequences. This power carries several risks. The idea that dominant powers easily conflate their interests with those of others is not new in international law: de Vitoria argued in 1539 for the Spaniards' right of freedom of movement and trade in 'the New World' based on everyone's interest in non-harmful travel and a corresponding universal duty of hospitality.[41] Arguably, he provided a justification for regulated imperialism in the name of GPGs regardless of the actual, informed preferences of the original inhabitants.

A second risk concerns framing. By calling certain outcomes '(global) public goods,' the standard account ascribes particular preferences to protesters, namely that they are unduly self-interested free riders. Such claims may well be false: the objectors may correctly deny any of the three scope conditions of the standard account: the outcome may harm them; or they may disagree that this particular shared objective – such as more liberalized trade or freedom of speech – should have priority other important values; or they may protest the distribution of burdens and benefits created by this particular way to produce and distribute the GPG. States may correctly hold that there are more equitable ways to allocate the costs and benefits of free trade, or of combatting climate change.

4.2. QUASI-PUBLIC GOODS

A second set of issues that merits our attention concern objectives that share some features with 'pure' public goods.[42] Some refer to these as 'impure' public goods, which unfortunately perpetrates a focus on the 'pure' cases.[43] Many benefits are exhaustible but non-excludable, and many GPGs of concern today are of this kind. Such *common-pool resources* include the world's fish stocks, and a clean environment. To prevent depletion, coordination may be required.[44] Other benefits are inexhaustible but

---

41 Francisco de Vitoria, 'On the American Indians' in Anthony Pagden and Jeremy Lawrance (eds), *Vitoria: Political Writings* (CUP 1992). Grotius developed such accounts further: Hugo Grotius, *On the Freedom of the Seas – Mare Liberum* (Brill 2009) 25; cf Vincent Chetail, 'Sovereignty and Migration in the Doctrine of the Law of Nations: An Intellectual History of Hospitality from Vitoria to Vattel' (2016) 27(4) EJIL 901; Antony Anghie, *Imperialism, Sovereignty and the Making of International Law* (CUP 2005).

42 For thorough and insightful discussions, cf Scott Barrett, *Why Cooperate? The Incentive to Supply Global Public Goods* (OUP 2007); Paine (n 29).

43 Kaul, Grunberg and Stern (n 8) 4–5.

44 Elinor Ostrom, *Understanding Institutional Diversity* (Princeton University Press 2005).

excludable. For instance, they may be available only within a geographical region, or only for 'club' members[45] – such as access to markets on specific terms among EU or WTO member states. I submit that ICs may have important roles in securing these GPGs.

4.3. WHEN PARTIAL COMPLIANCE IS ENOUGH

A third important departure from the standard theory's 'pure' case of public goods is that in many cases full compliance by all parties may not be required for the benefits to accrue.[46] The problem of 'free riders' can therefore vary. Consider common-pool resources. Some hold that all 'aggregate-effort' goods require compliance by every actor involved, be it climate change or sustainable fishing of tuna.[47] However, there is often a threshold or tipping point: as long as most parties restrain themselves, some actors may fish or harm the environment within limits. So the objective of, for example, environmental control or sustainable levels of fishing, is secured as long as the 'aggregate effort' of the parties is within a certain range. Satisfactory solutions may therefore only require compliance by a certain number of actors, often several 'big players', whose aggregate steps suffice. Indeed, efforts below or above a threshold may be unnecessary or unwarranted. This creates complex coordination problems, raises issues of fairness, and may challenge the legitimacy of international law and ICs that require general compliance. Compliance by a club of 'like-minded' actors might suffice, especially if they can provide club goods or side payments to members. A related issue arises for human rights: an IC that adjudicates human rights violations may still enable states to fulfil their human rights obligations even if certain states routinely fail to comply. However, an IC cannot help a state credibly pre-commit to human rights compliance if many states fail to defer. The IC is no longer better placed than the state to provide assurance, and its legitimacy may be at stake.

In other cases, in which any benefit depends on the 'weakest link', noncompliance by only one state may wreak havoc. Examples include preventing endemic diseases, nuclear weapons, or tax havens. Indeed, in

45 Todd Sandler, 'Regional Public Goods and International Organizations' (2006) 1 Review of International Organizations 5.
46 For further discussion, cf. Barrett, referenced in Bodansky (n 5), p. 652.
47 Nollkaemper (n 7) 778.

some such cases the incentives for a few to free ride increases with increased compliance by others.[48] ICs may help prevent such weakest links, serving a 'fire-alarm function' in allowing parties to trigger individual cases of suspected violations.[49] From this point of view, ICs should have a low threshold for considering cases. This may mean giving non-state actors a stake in the cases. Private parties may be awarded rights, as is the case with human rights, or they may benefit from treaties, such as trade agreements. Private parties may demand that their government brings cases or implements rulings.[50] They may also bring cases – and indeed this appears to be a trend among 'new style' ICs.[51]

A further variation on the number of required compliers is 'single-best-effort' public goods, which include efforts by a powerful player, possibly a hegemon, to establish or maintain regimes that are also beneficial to others or could be.[52] One example is when one actor can afford to bring a costly case to court to settle a controversial issue by means of an interpretation or judgment, with consequences for a broader community.[53] Note that this illustrates how the profound task of ICs in developing international law should make us wary of the risks of powerful actors using ICs to craft international law in their interest by bringing cases or submitting amicus briefs in favour of one interpretation or the other. Resourceful and informed actors may exploit such strategies to the detriment of other affected parties, who may have much at stake but be less powerful.

---

48 On the related issue of 'leakage', cf. Scott Barrett, 'Coordination vs. Voluntarism and Enforcement in Sustaining International Environmental Cooperation' (2016) 113(51) Proceedings of the National Academy of Sciences of the United States of America 14515.

49 Kal Raustiala, 'Police Patrols and Fire Alarms in the NAAEC' (2004) 26 Loyola of Los Angeles International and Comparative Law Review 389; Carrubba and Gabel (n 4). Some suggest that the value added of ICs may be greater in such cases than in the aggregate-efforts cases.

50 Helfer (n 31).

51 Karen J Alter, *The New Terrain of International Law: Courts Politics and Rights* (Princeton University Press 2014).

52 Across a range of theories of international relations. See Robert O Keohane, 'The Theory of Hegemonic Stability and Changes in International Economic Regimes' in Ole R Holsti, Randolph M Siverson and Alexander L George (eds), *Change in the International System* (Westview Press 1980); John J Mearsheimer, *The Tragedy of Great Power Politics* (WW Norton and Co 2001).

53 Bodansky (n 5) 663.

4.4. PROBLEM TYPES BEYOND FREE RIDING

The challenge of free riders occurs among actors with a particular configuration of preferences, in which free riders would prefer to not comply with the rules regardless of whether others do. Focusing on free riders risks drawing attention away from other common constellations of preferences. At least two problem types merit attention for our topic of concern.[54]

One important and frequent problem type is *assurance games*. These situations arise among individuals who each prefer to cooperate, but only under certain conditions: they must regard the rules as fair, and they must believe that most others also cooperate.[55] These *conditional cooperators* do not prefer free riding, and they do not require sanctions to comply. However, they may need reasons to hold that the system is fair, as well as trustworthy monitoring to confirm both others' belief in the fairness of the system and general compliance. Some features of human rights regimes have these characteristics. States within the European Union, for example, must all be subject to the European Convention on Human Rights; states may have no interest in free riding on other states' compliance with that treaty, but they may have good reason not to wish to pool decision-making for EU legislation with states who do routinely flout it. Even among able and willing states, each may need to be assured of each other's human rights compliance. ICs may contribute to such monitoring, although human rights ICs also perform valuable tasks for other actors than states. Since these ICs are somewhat independent of domestic government, they can perform similar important tasks for individuals and organizations *within* and *across* each state. These ICs provide both correction mechanisms and assurance about their

54 There are vastly more permutations of pay-offs, especially with more than two players in sequential and iterative games. For further details as regards the somewhat underdeveloped relationship of game theory to law, cf the classic Douglas G Baird, Robert H Gertner and Randal C Picker, *Game Theory and the Law* (Harvard University Press 1996); Gregory Shaffer and Mark Pollack, 'Hard and Soft Law' in Jeffrey L Dunoff and Mark A Pollack (eds), *Interdisciplinary Perspectives on International Law and International Relations: The State of the Art* (CUP 2012).

55 Ostrom, Walker and Gardner (n 32); Margaret Levi, 'A State of Trust' in Margaret Levi and Valerie Braithwaite (eds), *Trust and Governance* (Russell Sage 1998); Barrett (n 48); Niels Petersen, 'Customary International Law and Public Goods' in Curtis A Bradley (ed), *Custom's Future: International Law in a Changing World* (CUP 2016) 258.

government's compliance. These tasks are also overlooked by the public goods theory's exclusive focus on free riding.

A second problem type where the parties prefer to cooperate rather than free ride is known as the '*battle of the sexes.*' It denotes situations in which the parties disagree about *how* to cooperate, since each alternative allocates benefits and burdens differently among the parties. Such situations where the mode of cooperation is underdetermined are frequent in international relations and elsewhere.[56] Conflicts about the details of how to liberalize trade, or how to combat climate change, are cases in point. While it may be true that trade or investment treaties bring benefits to all states, critics maintain that the distribution of these benefits among states is grossly unfair, yet still better for the powerless states than no access to these markets.[57]

The public goods theory of authority brackets such distributive conflicts completely, rendering itself useless for understanding many real conflicts and even deadlocks. It may be argued that this statement is too pessimistic, since such bargaining problems are in some sense 'nested within' or limited by the parties' overarching commitment to comply with whatever alternative is agreed. It might appear that rational actors in such 'battle of the sexes' situations would be strongly motivated to agree since they have a strong preference for cooperation over non-cooperation. Thus, regarding environmental issues, Barrett writes:

> How would the emission limits for individual countries be chosen? This is the bargaining problem. If countries were 'symmetric', bargaining would be simple. [...] Asymmetry makes bargaining more complex, but so long as collective action promises all countries an aggregate gain, there will exist an allocation of responsibility that will be acceptable to every country (this allocation won't be unique and may require side payments, but these are relatively minor points compared with the imperative to avoid catastrophe).[58]

---

56 For fruitful elaboration, cf. Shaffer (n 6).

57 Daniel Behn, Ole Kristian Fauchald and Malcolm Langford, 'A Global Public Good? An Empirical Perspective on International Investment Law and Arbitration' (13th Annual Conference of the European Society of International Law, Naples, 7–9 September 2017) <https://www.jus.uio.no/ior/english/people/aca/malcolml/public-goods-final-submitted.pdf > accessed 15 January 2021; for some empirical evidence cf. Daniel Behn and Malcolm Langford, 'Trumping the Environment? An Empirical Perspective on Investment Treaty Arbitartion' (2017) 18(1) Journal of World Investment and Trade 14, 8.

58 Scott Barrett, 'Why Have Climate Negotiations Proved so Disappointing' in *Sustainable Humanity, Sustainable Nature: Our Responsibility* (Pontifical Academy of Sciences

Unfortunately, this type of collective action problem may occur even if the stakes are 'minor' compared with a non-cooperative outcome. The parties might not agree to their second-best alternative at the first-stage bargain, and so never reach the second stage where all would comply with the agreed rules – in effect creating a game of 'chicken'.[59] Thus Bodansky reports that: 'Many developing countries have been reluctant even to discuss the overall level of global emissions reductions without some agreement first on the burden-sharing issue'.[60]

Many real-life situations present mixes of these and other games. One additional confounding feature is that actors may be uncertain about each other's preferences, and hence about which type of game they are part of. Conditional cooperators may fear the existence of free riders among them, and parties may be unsure whether they are in a battle of the sexes, since there may not be any outcome which all parties will prefer over not cooperating at all.

5. DISCUSSION

How and when can ICs enable states to obtain the GPGs they seek, and have reason to secure? These comments largely draw on existing research, to indicate how a broader appreciation of game theory than employed by the standard theory may facilitate our assessment of the legitimacy of particular ICs, as well as their legitimacy in comparison to alternative institutions. I first consider how ICs may fit the standard theory by not only decreeing or permitting sanctions but also otherwise influencing states' payoffs from the various options. I then return to reconsider the four scope conditions of the standard theory and explore some implications for ICs. The fourth, affecting fair distribution of benefits and burdens among states, merits particular attention. I consider some of the challenges ICs face, and how some of tasks may be better performed by bodies other than ICs. The climate change challenge is a suitable example, and one that illustrates the limitations of the standard public goods theory.

2014) 263 <http://www.pas.va/content/dam/accademia/pdf/es41/es41-barrett.pdf> accessed 15 January 2021.

59 Stephen D Krasner, 'Global Communications and National Power: Life on the Pareto Frontier' (1991) 43(3) World Politics 336.

60 Bodansky (n 5) 657.

5.1. SANCTIONS

The standard public goods theory of legitimacy focuses on the role of sanctions in shifting actors' preferences over given alternatives. From that point of view, international law and ICs are often lamented as weak and without 'coercive power', making them ineffective in enabling states to secure GPGs. This is an overstatement on three counts: even if ICs lack 'coercive power,' some may trigger either direct or indirect sanctions, and ICs can add to states' alternatives.[61] Some ICs decree sanctions directly: regional human rights courts impose monetary awards, and the Inter-American Court of Human Rights (IACtHR) has required states to repeal laws, establish the crime of extrajudicial killing in its domestic law, grant victims' families' free health care, and erect a monument to the memory of the victims.[62] The risk of being found in violation of treaty obligations may itself promote state compliance, if only to avoid reactions from actors other than ICs. ICs have been designed and have themselves developed strategies so that many states will suffer repercussions from important international and domestic parties if they fail to comply to rulings. There are informal impacts: several, but not all,[63] states are vulnerable to reputational costs if they are not members of a treaty, or are found in violation of it – 'naming and shaming,' among either international peers and actors[64] or powerful domestic actors. In the case of human rights, a government found in violation of its obligations may expect reactions from civil society groups, opposition parties, and other 'compliance constituencies'. The IACtHR's choice of sanctions illustrate how the 'weak' IC may strategically trigger negative reactions from third parties with a more direct impact on the state.[65] Regarding trade, if the WTO AB rules in favour of a state, that state may impose carefully circumscribed 'countermeasures' otherwise prohibited.[66]

---

61 Helfer (n 31).

62 *Barrios Altos v. Peru* (Judgment) [2001] IACHR Series C No 75. This is not to say that all states comply with all sanctions, cf Cecilia M Bailliet, 'Measuring Compliance with the Inter-American Court of Human Rights: The Ongoing Challenge of Judicial Independence in Latin America' (2013) 31(4) Nordic Journal of Human Rights 477.

63 Emilie M Hafner-Burton, *Making Human Rights a Reality* (Princeton University Press 2013).

64 Thomas Risse, Stephen C Ropp and Kathryn Sikkink, *The Persistent Power of Human Rights: From Commitment to Compliance* (CUP 2013); Barrett (n 48); Beth A Simmons, *Mobilizing for Human Rights: International Law in Domestic Politics* (CUP 2009).

65 Xinyuan Dai, 'Why Comply? The Domestic Constituency Mechanism' (2005) 59(2) International Organization 363; Simmons (n 64); Alter (n 51).

66 DSU (n 36) art 22.2.

ICs may also help shift payoffs for states in other ways when they are part of *new* options created by other states. More formally, states sometimes set up treaties with ICs, so that, for example, only WTO members, who must be subject to the WTO AB, may enjoy WTO privileges.[67] Treaties may even rely on existing ICs as gatekeepers for the benefits that states are seeking; the most prominent example may be membership in the European Union, which requires that a state sign up to the European Convention on Human Rights and its court.

The upshot is that even by the terms of the standard public goods theory of legitimate authority, international law and ICs may enjoy legitimate authority insofar as they can influence states' preferences and hence actual choices among their alternative modes of action. ICs may do so by both triggering sanctions and contributing to new options that facilitate states' efforts and objectives. Several authors note that ICs' 'reactive' dispute-settlement function make them more effective in preventing defection by a few and when cases are not too costly, but less suitable when the GPG is prevented by many actors each adding only marginal damage to an aggregate with large harmful effects.[68]

I now turn to the possible functions of ICs in relation to collective action problems beyond those circumstances where the standard theory was intended to apply.

5.2. WHEN THE VALUE OF 'PUBLIC GOODS' IS CONTESTED

The standard theory takes actors' preferences regarding certain outcomes as given, and is exclusively concerned with cases where these preferences converge, meaning when all actors have the same (linear) payoff functions. To label an outcome as a '(global) public good' may deflect attention from the important issue of whether this scope condition actually holds in such cases:

> Most authors who use the term 'public goods' in international law discourse, use it to refer to values or interests that are considered to be good for the international community as a whole[69]

---

67 cf Barrett (n 42).

68 For attempts to hold parties responsible for aggregate harms, cf *Responsibilities and Obligations of States Sponsoring Persons and Entities with Respect to Activities in the Area* (Advisory Opinion) [2011] ITLOS Rep 10.

69 Nollkaemper (n 7).

Central points of concern for the legitimate role of ICs are *who* judges an objective to be a global public good and *on what grounds*. For instance, some states question the value of various treaties' objectives, be they more international trade or responsibilities to receive refugees or provide humanitarian assistance. At least three aspects merit mention regarding ICs.

Firstly, the existence of an IC that identifies and specifies GPGs may give states incentives to join a treaty in order to influence that interpretation.

Secondly, for the most part ICs will only perform tasks for the states who have agreed to the relevant treaties. Crucial states may refuse consent to treaties necessary to secure cooperation required for the GPG.[70] This is one reason why several authors note that state consent serves to undersupply treaties and their IC, and hence GPGs. Indeed, a recalcitrant powerful state may abuse its bargaining power so much that other states will not agree to a treaty at all – because it insists on options outside the domain of battle of the sexes.

Yet there are also reasons in favour of states' formal veto in the form of consent. It *sometimes* protects them against abject domination by more powerful states, although the latter sometimes get what they want and weak states consent to what they must. States who do not accept a particular treaty and an IC it establishes may not always be seeking to free ride, but simply not want the outcome, at least not as defined in the treaty. This has two implications for the legitimacy of an IC. First, even if it is authorized to interpret and adjudicate on the basis of a treaty, the question of whether that objective is actually shared by the states remains open. Second, even if states do consent, informed and freely, their objectives and choice of means merit scrutiny. The standard public goods theory takes those preferences of the parties as ultimate normative premises. It remains to be determined whether states have good reasons to pursue their stated objectives, such as more free trade, or more of the benefits that accrue from such an alleged GPG.

A third issue concerns fragmentation among ICs that states have agreed to in pursuit of particular GPG, say international trade and human rights. States have several objectives and strategies for pursuing them, by means of various treaties, ICs, domestic constitutions, and legislation.

---

[70] Andrew T Guzman, 'Against Consent' (2012) 52(4) Virginia Journal of International Law 747, 767, 789; Samantha Besson, 'State Consent and Disagreement in International Law-Making: Dissolving the Paradox' 2016 29(2) Leiden Journal of International Law 289; Krisch (n 3).

Consent to one IC does not indicate the relative value of this GPG or the treaty norms relative to these other important values and objectives. This general 'balancing' challenge applies among many objectives, including GPGs. There may be disagreements among states about these matters, such as the scope of human right norms versus free trade versus environmental protection. Still, different ICs must somehow perform the important tasks of interpreting and adjudicating on the basis of such fragmented international law.[71] Indeed, some may regard harmonization of international law as a GPG itself, and one that ICs contribute to. But we should be cautious. Some conflicts are resolved by means of *jus cogens* norms, the precise content of which is also contested.[72] Some treaties also recognize various conflicts when they specify exception clauses, such as for human rights or international trade.[73] Even in these cases ICs must exercise discretion in their 'balancing'. The judgments of ICs may exacerbate fragmentation, or contribute to harmonizing international law one way or the other, more systematically or less, more or less intentionally. ICs then extend and constrain some legal norms over others, and giving priority to some over others. This important task involves explicit and implicit, unavoidably value-laden choices by ICs that merit more scholarly attention.[74] The upshot for our discussion is that such tasks also arise among the different GPGs. Examples include how to specify the human

71 United Nations General Assembly, Martti Koskenniemi, 'Fragmentation of International Law: Difficulties Arising from the Diversification and Expansion of International Law, Report of the Study Group of the International Law Commission' (13 April 2006) UN Doc A/CN.4/L.682.

72 Hilary Charlesworth and Christine Chinkin, 'The Gender of *Jus Cogens*' (1993) 15(1) Human Rights Quarterly 63; Andreas Paulus, '*Jus Cogens* in a Time of Hegemony and Fragmentation: An Attempt at Re-Appraisal' (2005) 74 Nordic Journal of International Law 297; Matthew Saul, 'Identifying *Jus Cogens* Norms: The Interaction of Scholars and International Judges' (2015) 5(1) Asian Journal of International Law 26; UNGA, 'Third report on peremptory norms of general international law (*jus cogens*) by Dire Tladi, Special Rapporteur' (12 February 2018) International Law Commission Commission 17th session UN Doc A/CN.4/714.

73 cf Convention for the Protection of Human Rights and Fundamental Freedoms (European Convention on Human Rights, as amended) (opened for signature on 4 November 1950, entered into force on 3 September 1953) ETS 5, arts 7.2, 8.2, 9.2, 10.2 and General Agreement on Tariffs and Trade (GATT) (adopted 30 October 1947, entered into force 1 January 1948) 55 UNTS 194, arts XX–XXI.

74 Contributions include José E Alvarez, 'How Not to Link: Instutional Conundrums of an Expanded Trade Regime' (2001) 7 Widener Law Symposium Journal 1; José E Alvarez, 'Beware: Boundary Crossings – A Critical Appraisal of Public Law Approaches to International Investment Law' (2016) 17(2) Journal of World Investment and Trade 171; Pauwelyn and Elsig (n 34); Nollkaemper (n 7) 781–782.

right to strike relative to freedom of movement across borders in the EU, and rights to vaccines relative to intellectual property rights.[75]

5.3. ICs MAY AFFECT STATES' PREFERENCES

The standard public goods theory assumes that parties' fundamental values or objectives are static, and does not address how these are created or modified. Other theories in economics and social sciences do take on this subject, including both 'constructivist' and 'liberal' theories of international relations.[76] ICs contribute to these processes by serving several important functions for states' ability to secure GPGs as well as other objectives.

New treaties with judgement-issuing ICs create new opportunities for states. Club members might secure outcomes hitherto out of reach. ICs can foster new forms of reputation that states may value in order to appear more or less reliable and trustworthy. They can engage in strategic practices of naming, shaming, or 'outcasting'.[77] ICs' interpretive function, for GPGs but also more broadly, opens up completely new venues for states to influence the content of international law, such as joining treaties in order to change them from within, strategic litigation, amicus briefs, and so on.

ICs may also affect more profound changes in states' preferences: the monitoring, arguments, signaling, and sanctions that ICs contribute to may shift governments' perceptions of the games they are playing, and hence sometimes bring about changes in the game, as well as in states' longer-term interests and objectives.

---

75 Sybe A de Vries, 'Balancing Fundamental Rights with Economic Freedoms According to the European Court of Justice' 9(1) Utrecht Law Review 169; OHCHR, 'Resolution 2000/7: Intellectual Property Rights and Human Rights' UN Doc E/CN.4/SUB.2/RES/2000/7; Holger Hestermeyer, 'International Human Rights Law and Dispute Settlement in the World Trade Organisation' in Martin Scheinin (ed), *Human Rights in 'Other' International Courts* (CUP 2019); Laurence Helfer, 'Intellectual Property and Human Rights: Mapping an Evolving and Contested Relationship' in Rochelle Dreyfuss and Justine Pila (eds), *The Oxford Handbook of Intellectual Property Law* (OUP 2018).

76 For overviews, cf Jutta Brunnée and Stephen J Toope, 'Constructivism and International Law' in Jeffrey L Dunoff and Mark A Pollack (eds), *Interdisciplinary Perspectives on International Law and International Relations: The State of the Art* (CUP 2012); Andrew Moravcsik, 'Liberal Theories of International Law' in Jeffrey L Dunoff and Mark A Pollack (eds), *Interdisciplinary Perspectives on International Law and International Relations: The State of the Art* (CUP 2012).

77 Hathaway and Shapiro (n 32).

For example, states may realize that the collective action problems of climate change cannot be boiled down to a simple free rider problem but is actually genuine disagreement about proposed common actions and what fair distributions of burdens are. They may come to believe that the challenges are not so much in figuring out how to deal with shirkers, but how to provide credible assurance about others' compliance in a battle of the sexes.[78] The information ICs bring to the parties and the public at large may then leave states with different conceptions of their own long-term interests, since at least in some issue areas their environment is either less or more of a Hobbesian state of nature than they thought. They may need more or fewer sanctions against free riders, and more or fewer monitoring mechanisms. The monitoring and sanction-triggering by ICs may enable clubs of willing states to cooperate in fruitful ways even when other states refuse.[79]

Indeed, authoritative ICs sometimes help change not only states' objectives but what states and the system of states *are*. ICs are the creations of states, but they also specify state sovereignty. The legal powers of sovereignty as regulated by international law include both some forms of immunity from outside interference and an ability to enter inter-state agreements.[80] Some argue that this is part of one GPG, namely 'respect for sovereignty'.[81] ICs delineate the states' scope of immunity concerning how to treat their inhabitants, and the content of treaty obligations they may consent to. When effective, ICs thus specify the scope of sovereignty that states have, and consequently what they are.

> A State is not a fact in the sense that a chair is a fact; it is a fact in the sense in which it may be said a treaty is a fact: that is, a legal status attaching to a certain state of affairs by virtue of certain rules or practices.[82]

ICs may remove one obstacle H.L.A. Hart identified against regarding international law as a system of law, namely that it lacked a system

78 Petersen (n 55) 258–259; Vinod K Aggarwal and Cédric Dupont, 'Goods, Games, and Institutions' (1999) 20(4) International Political Science Review 393.
79 David G Victor, *Global Warming Gridlock: Creating More Effective Strategies for Protecting the Planet* (CUP 2011).
80 James Crawford, 'Sovereignty as a Legal Value' in James Crawford and Martti Koskenniemi (eds), *The Cambridge Companion to International Law* (CUP 2012).
81 Inge Kaul and Ronald U Mendoza, 'Advancing the Concept of Public Goods' in Inge Kaul and others, *Providing Global Public Goods: Managing Globalization* (OUP 2003).
82 James Crawford, *The Creation of States in International Law* (2nd edn, OUP 2007) 5.

of adjudication.[83] Optimists may therefore claim that ICs contribute to fundamentally transforming international relations, lamented for centuries as a nasty state of nature, toward a legal order among states with a 'common superior on earth, to judge between them'.[84]

5.4. ICs PROMOTE AND AFFECT DOMESTIC CONTESTATION

The standard public goods theory leaves aside how each actor comes to prefer some outcomes over others. For processes within states, several ICs serve important roles. At least two merit mention. ICs may affect decision-making and policy preferences within states. Regarding international trade agreements, a state may claim an exemption from the agreement in order to regulate certain products or services on certain grounds, such as if it is necessary to protect public morals or human, animal, or plant life or health, to conserve exhaustible natural resources, or for national security reasons.[85] The WTO AB may grant such exemptions, but to reduce the risk that they are disguised restrictions on international trade, the state must provide a convincing, good-faith justification to show their necessity. The ECtHR may likewise grant a 'margin of appreciation' to a state restricting certain human rights or 'balancing' among several. But it tends to require that state authorities have performed a good-faith 'proportionality test' in order to receive such a margin.[86]

Such calls by ICs for public justification nudges a state to more carefully consider plausible alternatives and their impact before arguing in favour of one. This may also hold for GPGs. Such deliberations would not always occur otherwise.

A second way that an IC affects domestic preferences for objectives and policies is when it mobilizes segments of the population and shifts political power and influence among them. States who ratify human rights treaties have experienced such effects.[87] The judgments and interpretations by ICs, and expectations thereof, may also influence

[83] HLA Hart, *The Concept of Law* (Clarendon Press 1961) 233.
[84] John Locke, *Two Treatises of Government* (New American Library, Mentor 1963) 2.19.
[85] GATT (n 73) art XX and – for security – art XXI.
[86] Kanstantsin Dzehtsiarou, *European Consensus and the Legitimacy of the Strasbourg Court* (CUP 2015); Follesdal (n 33).
[87] Simmons (n 64).

political and social processes broadly. Businesses, investors, human rights groups, or indigenous populations mobilize for strategic litigation to affect the political agenda, or to identify and authorize rules that will benefit them or their objectives in later political or legal settings. Groups may use IC judgments to call for political reforms, or for inclusion in domestic decision-making processes. A recent example in the environmental area is the case brought to the ECtHR by six young Portuguese people against 33 countries for failing to avert climate change and hence violating their human rights.[88]

The point here is not that the impact of ICs on domestic political and legal debates is always in favour of GPGs: their judgments and interpretations may also stimulate backlash and calls to renationalize authority, as well as opposition to international cooperation.[89] Either way, these impacts are important features when we assess the legitimate authority of ICs, in ways the standard public goods theory does not aspire to address.

5.5. ICs MAY PROMOTE MORE FAIR DISTRIBUTION

The standard theory of public goods for legitimate authority limits its standards of optimal distribution of goods to the Pareto principle: an ethically preferred allocation is one where no one can be made better off without making anyone else worse off. There is little reason to endorse this specific scope condition for research more generally. It is unclear why the Pareto principle is to be accepted as the unique distribution standard, for an allocation involving a small transfer from a vastly affluent person to prevent one death of starvation, contrary to the Pareto principle, is not obviously unethical. Other standards of distributive justice also appear justifiable, and certainly affect conceptions of legitimate authority as well as actors' preferences. Critical legal studies and other critics have identified how international law sustains colonialism and patriarchy.[90]

88 <https://youth4climatejustice.org/wp-content/uploads/2020/12/Application-form-annex.pdf> accessed 14 September 2021.

89 Erik Voeten, 'Populism and Backlashes Against International Courts' (2020) 18(2) Perspectives on Politics 407.

90 Anghie (n 41); Simon Chesterman, 'Asia's Ambivalence about International Law' in Simon Chesterman, Hisashi Owada and Ben Saul (eds), *The Oxford Handbook of International Law in Asia and the Pacific* (OUP 2019); Hilary Charlesworth, Christine Chinkin and Shelly Wright, 'Feminist Approaches to International Law' (1991) 85(4) The American Journal of International Law 613; Dianne Otto, 'Feminist Approaches to

They note the perceived significant impact of the injustice of the world trade system toward less developed states, leading to attempts to reform WTO procedures and rules in its Doha Round, starting in 2001. Likewise, the need for equity and a fair distribution of benefits and burdens are central challenges to international agreements for preventing climate change.[91]

How might ICs contribute to identifying and securing outcomes consistent with the relevant standards of distributive justice? They adjudicate according to relevant treaties and legal method and procedures; insofar as treaty negotiations have secured just distributions of benefits and burdens among the parties to a dispute, IC adjudicate trade or bilateral investment disputes. Legal procedures upheld by impartial judges may also reduce the influence of power imbalances among disputing states, or between accused state and complainant, due to such standards as the rule of law, hearing both sides, equality of arms, and so on.

At least two caveats merit concern regarding ICs and distributive justice, relating to the significance of unjust treaties and the interpretation of treaties. There is no clear reason to believe that an international treaty *per se* satisfies whatever defensible standards of distributive justice are relevant, among or within states. Treaty negotiations by domestic elites among international unequals may merely result in domination by new means. This raises important issues concerning how responsible international judges should interpret and adjudicate cases brought before them, not least the appropriate role of considerations of equity.[92]

Consider now how ICs interpret and develop international law, assessed by standards of distributive justice. ICs are often required to develop international law, if only to 'fill the gaps' left by states when agreeing to a treaty aimed at securing a GPG. One might expect and even support the idea that international judges should be primarily guided by the states' express 'object and purpose' with the treaty, but decide

---

International Law' in Anne Orford and Florian Hoffmann (eds), *The Oxford Handbook of the Theory of International Law* (OUP 2016).

91 Oran Young, 'Does Fairness Matter in International Environmental Governance? Creating an Effective and Equitable Climate Regime' in Todd L Cherry, Jon Hovi and David M McEvoy (eds), *Toward a New Climate Agreement: Conflict, Resolution and Governance* (Routledge 2014).

92 Vaughan Lowe, 'The Role of Equity in International Law' (1992) 12 Australian Yearbook of International Law 54; Robert Howse, 'The Concept of Odious Debt in Public International Law' (2007) United Nations Conference on Trade and Development, Discussion Paper UNCTAD/OSG/DP/2007/4.

among any remaining interpretive choices by considering distributive justice, as is consistent with standards of legal method. One drastic example mentioned above is the European Court of Justice retrofitting the GPG of human rights into the EU treaties.

While this account of how international judges should use their discretion may be laudable, in several of the cases surveyed above there are reasons to be wary concerning the authority and the qualifications of the IC. Firstly, international judges may see no reason to rely on such external standards; their professional specialist background and institutional setting may lead them to decide cases independent of outside references.

Secondly, if a treaty fails to detail the allocation of benefits and burdens among state parties, we may have low expectations of what ICs can actually do. Consider situations where an IC must choose among interpretations in 'battle of the sexes' circumstances. Any choice will benefit some parties to the detriment of others, compared to alternative interpretations. The losers are likely to question the IC's impartiality and authority, pointing out that alternative interpretations would be equally consistent with the text and equally efficacious in securing the GPG. In domestic legal orders the legislatures and executives address such issues; in democracies these bodies will be responsive to a broad range of the affected citizens. Disagreements about distributions of benefits and burdens are settled by democratic majority rule constrained by constitutional protections. But when an IC makes a judgment in such cases, the benefits or burdens can be distributed in different ways not specified by treaty because the states could not agree on this distributive conflict. Critical states would seem to have a good point: the authority of the IC is at stake, since it claims that its interpretation should count as a reason for that state to defer, excluding or displacing its reasons to act otherwise.[93]

A justification of this exercise of authority by the IC would presumably refer to the need for a well-qualified and suitably placed umpire in such settings, whose inevitably somewhat arbitrary choice of one among several acceptable options is decisive for the relevant states. One point in favour of authorizing ICs in this way is that they have some independence from states. They may therefore be aware of negative externalities for third parties, and may interpret treaties and allocate benefits and burdens in light of considerations of fairness and equity.

93 Bodansky (n 5) 652.

But such claims on behalf of an IC are overdrawn. Several premises concerning judges' professional backgrounds and features of how ICs function attest to this.

International judges are not necessarily experts on international relations or on public policy. They may therefore easily misjudge the consequences of their interpretations, compared to experts or democratically accountable bodies better positioned to predict the impact on various affected parties of the interpretive alternatives which 'balance' the conflicting values and objectives. To be sure, they do receive such information from the parties to the disputes brought before them, and some ICs permit amicus briefs that can identify further implications. Yet even these measures can perpetuate biased or partial information.

ICs are reactive, responding to cases brought before them. On one hand, the independent IC can address a single dispute about how to share benefits and burdens, and thereby set rules and settle expectations for many actors in ways that promote the GPG.[94] This renders them liable to develop international law in directions strategically important to those parties who have the will and resources to bring cases. For our purposes this may have implications for which GPGs the IC identifies, and how it specifies them.[95] A further risk is that any sector IC will favour concerns and GPGs within its domain – be it trade, investment, or human rights – in its attempt to 'balance' these against such GPGs as environmental concerns.[96]

We might hope that ICs would reduce their unintended bias and learn about the broader implications of their interpretations by admitting amicus briefs from third parties. Some ICs do accept amicus briefs. The WTO AB's decision to do so has provoked explicit protests from state parties, no doubt because they see that such briefs may influence the judgments, for better or worse.[97] To be sure, some parties may seek to intervene 'in the public interest' in pursuit of GPGs, and amici might identify and argue for GPGs.[98] But certainly there is a risk that those who engage and seek to influence an interpretation pursue their own other interests rather than GPGs, and seek certain specifications of a GPG rather than others. Amicus briefs do increase ICs' responsiveness, but may exacerbate bias.

94 ibid 660.
95 Nollkaemper (n 7) 781.
96 ibid 781; Behn, Fauchald and Langford (n 57).
97 CL Lim, 'The Amicus Brief Issue at the WTO' (2005) 4(1) Chinese Journal of International Law 85.
98 Nollkaemper (n 7) 778.

6. BEYOND BOTH THE STANDARD THEORY AND ICs: THE PARIS COMPLIANCE COMMITTEE AS A CASE

Honing in on the main point of this contribution requires considering the limitations of both the standard public goods theory and ICs. My reflections have sought to show how the limited scope conditions of the standard public goods theory has led to undue focus on free riders, and too much despair on behalf of international law and ICs who lack sanctioning power. This myopia and pessimism are not shared by recent literature. A main implication developed above is that ICs may still be legitimate due to a range of other functions they can carry out to alleviate collective action problems in pursuit of GPGs. In particular, they may provide valuable information and assurance among states.

These claims on behalf of ICs should not be overstated, however. They are legitimate only if their tasks require such adjudicatory authority, as they claim. To situate the more modest upshot of these reflections, I return to one issue they seem less suitable for: some of the challenges in combatting climate change.

ICs are not well-suited to settling 'battle of the sexes' problems among states who want to cooperate yet disagree about preferred solutions, that is, the burdens of climate policies. If states have not been able to agree to such specifics in a treaty, an IC is hard put to authoritatively and arbitrarily impose one solution on many in the form of an interpretation and judgment.

In such circumstances, bodies other than ICs may serve important tasks in bringing states toward sufficient agreement in the direction of GPGs without the need to claim adjudicatory authority to override states' preferences. The body's task may rather be to make noncompliance an option states avoid, rather than a choice for which they shall be punished.[99] This illustrates the importance of preference formation, as explored by constructivist and other scholarship.[100] These bodies may help avoid non-compliance by reducing uncertainty about other parties' preferences, by creating a reputational risk, and by increasing trust and information among them to help determine whether they are indeed moving toward a

99 And cf. Kal Raustiala and David G Victor, 'Conclusions' in David G Victor, Kal Raustiala and Eugene B Skolnikof (eds), *The Implementation and Effectiveness of International Environmental Commitments: Theory of Practice* (The MIT Press 1998).

100 Brunnée and Toope (n 77) and references therein, and Moravcsik (n 77).

battle of the sexes situation, so that some solutions may become sufficiently salient.[101] ICs may certainly assist in such monitoring, shaming, and fact-finding,[102] but other agents of management and coordination[103] need to claim less authority and are less judicialized 'systems of implementation review'.[104] Thus, importantly, there may be several GPGs for which yet another IC is not part of the solution, at least not for several of the challenges.

One recent example is the 'Compliance and Implementation Mechanism'[105] ('Compliance Committee') of the Paris Agreement.[106] A paramount challenge of the Paris Agreement is to secure enough participation by enough states to form a club with sufficient levels of commitment to avoid catastrophic climate change. Their coordination can help reach a tipping point that entices more states to join.[107] The complex condition for when the Agreement enters into force is part of the solution.

---

101 Andrew T Guzman and Timothy L Meyer, 'International Soft Law' (2010) 2(1) Journal of Legal Analysis 171; Gu Zihua, Christina Voigt and Jacob Werksman, 'Facilitating Implementation and Promoting Compliance with the Paris Agreement: Conceptual Challenges and Pragmatic Choices' (2019) 9 Climate Law 65; Christina Voigt and Gao Xiang, 'Accountability in the Paris Agreement: The Interplay Between Transparency and Compliance' (2020) 1 Nordic Environmental Law Journal 31.

102 Helfer (n 31).

103 Abram Chayes and Antonia H Chayes, *The New Sovereignty: Compliance with International Regulatory Agreements* (Harvard University Press 1998).

104 Victor, Raustiala and Skolnikof (n 32).

105 Paris Agreement (adopted 12 December 2016, entered into force 4 November 2016) UN Registration No I-54113, art 15.2; cf Voigt (n 30).

106 Other bodies with somewhat similar 'weak' powers and less legal authority than ICs, with important differences among them, are various UN human rights treaty bodies, and ASEAN instruments. cf Basak Cali, 'The Legitimacy of Human Rights Treaty Bodies: An Indirect-Instrumentalist Defense' in Andreas Follesdal, Johan K Schaffer and Geir Ulfstein (eds), *The Legitimacy of International Human Rights Regimes: Legal, Political and Philosophical Perspectives* (2013); Helen Keller and Geir Ulfstein (eds), *UN Human Rights Treaty Bodies: Law and Legitimacy* (CUP 2012); Gillian HL Goh, 'The 'ASEAN Way': Non-Intervention and ASEAN's Role in Conflict Management' (2003) 3(1) Stanford Journal of East Asian Affairs 113; Robert Beckman and others, *Promoting Compliance: The Role of Dispute Settlement and Monitoring Mechanisms in ASEAN Instruments* (CUP 2016); Geir Ulfstein, 'International Courts and Tribunals and the Rule of Law in Asia' in Takao Suami and others (eds), *Global Constitutionalism from European and East Asian Perspectives* (CUP 2018); Simon Chesterman, Hisashi Owada and Ben Saul (eds), *The Oxford Handbook of International Law in Asia and the Pacific* (OUP 2019).

107 The argument is reminiscent of the success of the Montreal Protocol to protect the ozone layer. This was apparently in part due to the Protocol's securing enough signatories to create such a tipping point. A central clause banned the parties from trading in chlorofluorocarbons with non-parties. While some question the likelihood of such successful linkages in other sectors, there are proposals to make trade

To reduce every state's risk that they would take on burdens to no avail, the agreement will only enter into force after

> ... at least 55 Parties to the Convention accounting in total for at least an estimated 55 per cent of the total global greenhouse gas emissions have deposited their instruments of ratification, acceptance, approval or accession.[108]

Note that this clause appears to address conditional cooperators. It does not *prevent* free riders who would not sign the Agreement anyway. They are surely also a problem, but not the only one, and not one that the Compliance Committee is tasked with resolving. The Committee is instead supposed to 'facilitate implementation of and promote compliance with' the agreement. It consists of experts, and has quite different tools and tasks than an IC: it is 'facilitative in nature and function in a manner that is transparent, non-adversarial and non-punitive'. It will thus not be a dispute settlement mechanism.[109] Its publicly stated role focuses not on the unwilling states, but on the club of willing yet possibly unable.[110]

The way forward that these states have agreed to contains a striking extent of *differentiation* among the various state parties' obligations, 'among de facto unequal states'.[111] The states have accepted that the agreement should be implemented to reflect equity and the principle of common but differentiated responsibilities and respective capabilities, in the light of diverse national circumstances.[112] In addition to 'equity', a term which itself is open to several interpretations,[113] possible parameters include 'past, current, and projected future emissions, but also financial

---

cooperation conditional on supplying the global public good of reducing greenhouse gas emissions. cf The Montreal Protocol on Substances that Deplete the Ozone Layer (adopted 16 September 1987, entered into force 1 January 1989) 1522 UNTS 3; Scott Barrett, *Environment and Statecraft: The Strategy of Environmental Treaty Making* (OUP 2005); Bodansky (n 5) 660.

108 Paris Agreement (n 106) art 21.1.

109 cf Decision 20/CMA.1 in UN, 'Report of the Conference of the Parties Serving as the Meeting of the Parties to the Paris Agreement on the Third Part of its First Session, held in Katowice from 2 to 15 December 2018' (19 March 2019) FCCC/PA/CMA/2018/3/Add.2, 59 <https://unfccc.int/sites/default/files/resource/cma2018_3_add2_new_advance.pdf> accessed 15 January 2021.

110 cf Victor (n 79).

111 Christina Voigt and Felipe Ferreira, 'Differentiation in the Paris Agreement' (2016) 6 Climate law 58, 59.

112 Paris Agreement (n 106) art 2.2.

113 Young (n 91); cf Christina Voigt, *Sustainable Development as a Principle of International Law: Resolving Conflicts between Climate Measures and WTO Law* (Brill | Nijhoff 2009).

and technical capabilities, human capacity, population size and other demographic criteria, abatement costs, opportunity costs, and so on.'[114] A further differentiation concerns development over time: states commit to progressively more ambitious efforts as time passes.[115]

The agreeing states clearly realized that several conflicting objectives and values must be balanced. This was so contentious that they could not agree on some ordering of these parameters among themselves. It was never discussed whether to entrust a separate body such as the Committee with such a quasi-legislative task, regardless of how independent, impartial, and expert it would be. Instead, it is for each state to declare its own milestones in its 'nationally determined contributions' (NDCs), updating and increasing them every 5 years, with transparent reporting leading to a global stocktaking to determine whether the achievements suffice to reach the GPG.[116] These obligations might not be expected to make any difference. Requiring states to do hardly anything different than they would in the absence of an agreement, they are 'shallow' obligations,[117] and mainly procedural rather than substantive. But the fact that states must make their NDCs publicly available in an online registry every 5 years, expressing the state's highest possible ambition and progression,[118] amounts to a public justification by the state of how the NDC reflects 'its common but differentiated responsibilities and respective capabilities, in the light of different national circumstances'.[119]

What tasks might the Compliance Committee perform? It may facilitate domestic implementation of efforts and legal compliance, and promote learning and best practices among the states.[120] Actual performance, such as emission cuts, is not directly reviewed by the Committee. But its contributions may facilitate other actors, such as opposition parties and civil society actors, to engage with governments in promoting actual performance on the ground. Although only coming from some states, these actual effects are especially important for the sort of collective action problems posed by climate change, where full compliance by

114 Voigt (n 30) 66.

115 Paris Agreement (n 106) art 3.

116 ibid arts 4.9, 7, 13, 14.

117 George W Downs, David M Rocke and Peter N Barsoom, 'Is the Good News about Compliance Good News about Cooperation?' (1996) 50(3) International Organization 379.

118 Paris Agreement (n 106) art 4.3.

119 ibid.

120 ibid art 15; See Decision 20/CMA.1 (n 110).

all is neither plausible in the short term nor required: what is needed is sufficient modification by a sufficient number of states. If those willing states engage 'deeper', at greater cost to themselves, this may be more effective than seeking full compliance with less 'costly' obligations. Again, the focus on full compliance and free riders may be misleading for many GPGs.[121]

Public justifications by each state that interpret and 'balance' the various parameters may also bring several benefits. They may bolster domestic and international pressure to reduce states' temptation to free ride or reduce stated ambitions by appealing to implausible national circumstances or balancing of considerations. They may (or may not) reduce such hypocrisy,[122] at least in states that allow freedom of speech and critical organizations. Indeed, states may transpose the international parameters into legally binding domestic provisions, which voters and other stakeholders can use to leverage more demanding NDCs in the next round. Some publicity may also nudge states to use their discretion in setting NDCs only in accordance with parameters they can expect other stakeholders to agree to.[123]

In due course states may have to give evidence of a public 'proportionality test', holding their NDCs up to more specified and 'balanced' parameters. Public justifications may also foster understanding of the dilemmas faced by other states and the tradeoffs they are making. They may increase mutual trust[124] and 'foster each state's own assessment of the fairness and equity of other states' contributions to addressing the problem.'[125] Crucially, the justifications also reinforce an assumption that the state parties are indeed willing, although sometimes unable, to cooperate more than they do.

Public reasoning may even lead to adjustments and even to some harmonization among the various domestic 'balancings' of parameters in order to achieve the aggregate improvements required. Such changes by states in light of what others do not require the Compliance Committee to play an active role, and certainly not any *adversarial* function, regarding

---

121 Raustiala and Victor (n 100) 688.

122 Jon Elster, 'Forces and Mechanisms in the Constitution-Making Process' (1995) 45 Duke Law Journal 364; Jon Elster, 'Arguing and Bargaining in Two Constituent Assemblies' (2000) 2(2) Journal of Constitutional Law 345.

123 Voigt and Ferreira (n 112) 74.

124 Paris Agreement (n 106) art 13.

125 Voigt and Ferreira (n 112) 60.

disputes concerning compliance.[126] To the contrary, at this stage, among actors not portrayed primarily as potential free riders, an adversarial independent body would be unnecessary and unhelpful if not destructive – and contrary to its mandate in Article 15.2.

Indeed, neither the Committee nor an IC would be equipped to perform these tasks, to test whether the balancing does indeed reach 'maximum achievable objectives', or determine issues of 'generalizability', that is, whether the same 'balancing' of various standards, applied by all states, would reach satisfactory objective.

For the purposes of appreciating the possible contributions to a GPG by a body that does not even have the authority to adjudicate, several comments are in order. Firstly, these optimistic expectations of how the Committee may foster harmonized 'differentiation' under the Paris agreement are of course not predictions. To unlock the Committee's potential requires several crucial scope conditions. The Committee and other parties must provide credible assurance that most parties believe most others to be conditional cooperators rather than free riders. Even though the Committee does not assess whether the DNCs are as ambitious as possible, the information it helps provide may reassure other states that another state's lack of ambition or implementation is due to inability rather than unwillingness. The Committee's public statements and procedures may bolster such reassurance. To foster such preferences among states, and correct beliefs about them, international and domestic civil society, rule of law, opposition parties, and free media may be crucial.[127] These 'compliance constituencies' play important roles by expressing, ensuring, and exploiting states' international commitments regarding human rights.[128] Yet domestic governments, social media, and other actors may hinder rather than help such critical voices.

A second, related observation is that optimism may also be premature concerning the beneficial impact of states' public reason-giving on the dynamic, progressive mutual acceptance and adaptation of ever more demanding DNCs. Deliberation may certainly shift preferences, sometimes in normatively preferable ways, but not always.[129] Still, the Committee

---

126 For possible adjudicatory tasks regarding noncompliance cf Voigt (n 30) 168.

127 Voigt and Ferreira (n 112) 72–73.

128 Simmons (n 64); Xinyuan Dai, *International Institutions and National Policies* (CUP 2007).

129 Jon Elster (ed), *Deliberative Democracy* (CUP 1998); Andreas Follesdal, 'The Value Added by Theories of Deliberative Democracy: Where (Not) to Look' in Samantha

holds parties accountable to whatever they have actually agreed to, and may nudge them toward more ambitious NDCs in the future.

These hesitations do not detract from the role of the Committee as an example of how bodies that cannot sanction free riders may still contribute in crucial ways – beyond the limits of the standard public goods theory – to solving collective action problems pertaining to GPGs.

Thirdly, even though the Committee and the ratchetting up of self-imposed NDCs by willing states may contribute to controlling climate change, several states may have mixed motives, and several clearly engage in a battle of the sexes. Assurance games are often unstable.[130] And many states, even parties to the Agreement, may seek to free ride.

The political challenges to averting climate change may be very large when faced with even just a few non-compliers, especially if they are heavy polluters, and able but unwilling.[131] But this sketch should indicate that several *other* challenges appear at least as urgent for the GPG of preventing catastrophic climate change. These challenges are beyond several of the scope conditions bracketed by the public goods theory of authority, and they underscore the fact that while ICs are sometimes necessary and legitimate, they may not always be needed. Neither the authority to discipline free riders nor the authority to adjudicate may be required to foster constructive preference formation, to facilitate a responsible domestic balancing of values and preferences, and to determine whether conflicts concerning the distribution of benefits among the parties are indeed cases of battles of the sexes.

7. CONCLUSION

One important source of legitimation for international law and international courts is that they enable states to secure certain 'global public goods'.

Besson and José Luis Martí (eds), *Deliberative Democracy and Its Discontents* (Ashgate 2005) <http://follesdal.net/ms/Follesdal-2006-delib-dem.rtf> accessed 15 January 2020; Jane J Mansbridge, 'Conflict and Self-Interest in Deliberation' in Samantha Besson and Jose Luis Marti (eds), *Deliberative Democracy and Its Discontents* (Ashgate 2005).

130 Petersen (n 55).

131 Bodansky (n 5) 662.

International law *may* help, and optimists might draw the unwarranted conclusion that it therefore *will* help if sufficiently transformed:

> The power of international law comes from our belief in it and the purposes it serves: the promotion of peace, human rights, prosperity and the natural environment.[132]

On the other hand, several critics lament the lack of sanctioning power as an Achilles' heel of international law and ICs. Their premise and conclusions are likewise ill-founded. In response, the present reflections have sought to show that the choice of the concept of 'public good' may have had unfortunate framing effects. Economists' 'standard' public goods theory of authority is theoretically and practically incomplete: its scope conditions exclude vast expanses of game-theoretic modelling – and brackets important tasks for legitimate authorities, including ICs.

The risk of uncontrollable free riders has received too much attention from scholars and politicians. This may have occurred to the detriment of several other challenges to secure mutually beneficial outcomes among states with partially concurring and partly conflicting interests. The standard theory is not mistaken, but it misguides our attention. Fortunately, recent literature has brought broader game-theoretic perspectives back into international law, to help us understand and address the many collective action problems for different GPGs.

This discussion has sought to show some of the functions ICs may serve even when they lack enforcement power over free riders. There are many further tasks in the pursuit of truly global public goods for which ICs would be illegitimate. Beyond the scope of the standard public goods theory, ICs may contribute to determining who gets to define and specify global public goods, how states develop and change their preferences and accommodate the needs of their inhabitants, and how the international legal order can reduce the domination of powerful states over others. This is not to say that ICs are a universal solution to all ills in the pursuit of global public goods, but that legitimate ICs may perform a broad range of tasks in enabling states to act better in that pursuit.

---

132 Mary Ellen O'Connell, 'Binding on All States All of the Time' (*Opinio Juris*, 20 November 2008) <http://opiniojuris.org/2008/11/20/binding-on-all-states-all-of-the-time/> accessed 15 January 2021.

PART II

GLOBAL COMMONS AND INTERNATIONAL CONCERNS

COMMUNITY INTERESTS AND SOVEREIGNTY

On Consonance and Dissonance in the Law of the Sea

Rozemarijn Roland HOLST*

1. INTRODUCTION

The development of the law of the sea is characterised by the continuous struggle between the ever further seaward expanding sovereignty of

* Assistant professor, University of Utrecht, the Netherlands. Research for this contribution was funded by the European Research Council under the European Union's Horizon 2020 research and innovation programme (Grant Agreement No 639070 – SUSTAINABLEOCEAN).

coastal states on the one hand, and the freedoms of the high seas as the biggest 'global commons' on the other. The inheritance of this classic 'sovereignty *versus* freedom' narrative is reflected in the fundamental structure of the modern law of the sea set out in the UN Convention on the Law of the Sea (UNCLOS or 'the Convention'[1]) in two different ways. First, in its 'zonal approach' to jurisdiction. Second, in its attempts to balance interacting state interests and community interests within and across these jurisdictional zones. While the traditional legal bases, epitomised in terms of 'sovereignty' (internal waters, territorial sea), 'sovereign rights' (exclusive economic zone (EEZ), continental shelf) and 'freedoms' (high seas), are maintained under the Convention, the implications of these rights and freedoms have also been transformed and transcended in various ways and to varying degrees. All rights and freedoms granted under the Convention are inherently conditional; subject to a complex web of limitations contained in the Convention itself and in other instruments of international law.

At the same time, tensions between the traditional connotations of both the sovereignty and freedom principles and interests shared by the international community at large persist, and continue to emerge in the light of fundamentally changing circumstances. Global challenges, such as the impacts of climate change, ocean acidification, large-scale biodiversity loss, and (plastic) pollution, are having a profound impact on the functioning of the ocean as a global ecosystem, and consequently on our current and future use thereof. When it comes to protecting the interests shared by the international community in sustaining the variety of global public goods for which we rely on our oceans, both sovereignty and freedoms-based models of jurisdiction, or indeed the zonal approach derived therefrom, are perceived as an obstacle to governing them effectively.[2] This chapter seeks to unravel the oft-posited premise that the relationship between two central 'forces' in the law of the sea – 'sovereign' or individual state interests and community interests – is an inherently contentious one. Showing that sovereign interests and community interests continuously interact in the law of the sea, it is proposed that a functional perception of sovereignty best explains the concept's role

1 United Nations Convention on the Law of the Sea (adopted 10 December 1982, entered into force 16 November 1994) 1833 UNTS 397 (UNCLOS).

2 See also Yoshifumi Tanaka, *A Dual Approach to Ocean Governance: The Cases of Zonal and Integrated Management in International Law of the Sea* (Routledge 2009).

and functioning under the Convention, and in principle allows it to be aligned with the protection of other states' individual as well as community interests, both in theory and in positive international law (2). Four distinct ways in which community interests can be accommodated and balanced under UNCLOS are discussed, while also highlighting some persistent challenges (3). Finally, some conclusions are drawn as to how the reality of modern ocean governance provides examples of both consonance and dissonance between sovereignty and community interests, illustrating the potential and functionality, as well as the limitations, inherent in both concepts (4).

2. COMMUNITY INTERESTS AND SOVEREIGNTY: AN INTERACTION OF INTERESTS

The relationship between sovereign interests and community interests is often perceived as an inherently contentious one, because 'sovereignty' and 'sovereign rights' are seen as the primary vessel for the protection and furtherance of individual state interests, whereas the concept of 'community interests' typically transcends these individual interests.[3] 'State interest' or 'sovereign interest' confers the traditional idea of a common set of factors that are important to the existence of a state as an abstract entity.[4] As it is states that make, implement, and enforce international law, their interests are determinative in these processes. However, that does not mean that state interests are static, nor that states are necessarily exclusively self-interested.[5] While positive international law is at present undeniably the law of states, it is evident that states not only have individual interests that are unique to them, but also – and increasingly – share interests that are common to the international community of states, or a large part

3 See for a discussion e.g. Samantha Besson, 'Community Interests in International Law: Whose Interests Are They and How Should We Best Identify Them?' in Eyal Benvenisti and Georg Nolte (eds), *Community Interests Across International Law* (Oxford University Press 2018); Christina Voigt, 'Delineating the Common Interest in International Law' in Wolfgang Benedek and others (eds), *The Common Interest in International Law* (Intersentia 2014) 17.

4 See also Markus P Beham, *State Interest and the Sources of International Law* (Routledge 2018) 124.

5 See also Besson (n 3) 37, 46–47, who problematises the analogy of states as individuals.

thereof, as well as to their (trans)national communities.[6] Furthermore, issues of interest to the wider international community may simultaneously be relevant to the existence and welfare of an individual state. In that sense, there is 'nothing extraordinary' about states acting in the interest of the community.[7]

For the present purposes, the term 'community interests' is used in a broad sense to include those interests shared by the international community of states, or a part thereof, but which may simultaneously transcend the interests of state actors *per se* as they coincide with wider interests of 'humanity'.[8] Although strictly speaking the treaty-based examples of commonality discussed in this chapter primarily concern interests shared by the community of *states*,[9] it should be borne in mind that it is inherent in the shared use of ocean space that, more often than not, these interests coincide with or directly affect concerns such as the health, safety, environment, and livelihoods of wider (transnational) communities of *people*. As such, the identification of community interests in the ocean governance context is interlinked with environmental, social and economic development considerations as contained in the concept

---

6 The widely referenced move away from an 'international law of coexistence' towards a 'law of cooperation' bears witness thereto, see i.a. Wolfgang Friedmann, *The Changing Structures of International Law* (Columbia University Press 1964) 410; Bruno Simma, 'From Bilateralism to Community Interest in International Law' (1994) 250 Recueil des Cours de l'Académie de Droit International 217; *Legality of the Threat or Use of Nuclear Weapons* (Advisory Opinion, Declaration of President Bedjaoui) [1996] ICJ Rep 226, 270–271; and *Case Concerning the Gabčíkovo-Nagymaros Project (Hungary v. Slovakia)*, (Judgment, Separate Opinion of Vice-President Weeramantry) [1997] ICJ Rep 118.

7 See also Samantha Besson, 'Community Interests in the Identification of International Law: With a Special Emphasis on Treaty Interpretation and Customary Law Identification' in Eyal Benvenisti and Georg Nolte (eds), *Community Interests Across International Law* (OUP 2018) 51, referring to Giorgio Gaja, 'The Protection of General Interests in the International Community' (2013) 364 Recueil des Cours 31.

8 Wolfrum poses the valid question whether it is possible to distinguish between the sum of the interests of states individually and the interest of the 'community' of states as such, suggesting the latter reflects a common value whereas the former do not. However, as will be argued below, this distinction may be more theoretical than practical. Rüdiger Wolfrum, 'Enforcing Community Interests through International Dispute Settlement: Reality or Utopia?' in Ulrich Fastenrath and others (eds), *From Bilateralism to Community Interest: Essays in Honour of Bruno Simma* (OUP 2011) 1133–1134.

9 As opposed to instances where international law makes the protection of the rights of individuals or groups the concern of the international community of states. See on this distinction also ibid 1136.

of sustainable development.[10] As stressed by Simma, 'the identification of common interests does not derive from scientific abstraction but rather flows from the recognition of concrete problems'.[11] The preamble of UNCLOS recognises that 'the problems of ocean space are closely interrelated and need to be considered as a whole'.[12] Hence the law of the sea provides ample examples where individual state interests, states' common interests, and wider interests beyond the state align or overlap, but it also provides examples where they coexist or diverge.

2.1. ON CONSONANCE AND DISSONANCE

It should be noted at this point that the conceptual distinction between individual state interest and community interests will often be easier to make in theory than in practice. Many (if not most) cases can be said to fall within a large grey area. For many reasons, states may choose to frame their individual interests as community interest, and – even when they give effect to what could objectively be recognised as a community interest – the underlying reasons are difficult to discern and not necessarily altruistic in nature. Although the result may ultimately be the same, this has prompted critical notes to be raised in respect of the community interest concept. Wolfrum poses the question whether a single state (or limited number of states) could declare that, for example, a certain resource or area needs to be preserved in the common interest of biodiversity preservation, despite express objection thereto by other states.[13] This situation arose in the *Chagos* arbitration, where the UK argued it was acting in the common interest when establishing a no-take marine protected area (MPA) around the Chagos archipelago, despite Mauritius' objection thereto.[14] The tribunal concluded that the UK had breached its obligations under UNCLOS for failing to consult with Mauritius in the process, but not for the substance or goal of the measure as such, namely

---

10 See also e.g. Rüdiger Wolfrum, 'Identifying Community Interests in International Law: Common Spaces and Beyond' in Eyal Benvenisti and Georg Nolte (eds), *Community Interests Across International Law* (OUP 2018).

11 Simma (n 6) 235.

12 UNCLOS, Preamble.

13 Wolfrum (n 10) 20.

14 Mauritius also claimed sovereignty over the archipelago, but had not been consulted in the MPA designation process. *Chagos Marine Protected Area Arbitration* (*Mauritius v UK*) [2015] PCA Case No 2011-03.

designating the no-take MPA to preserve the marine environment.[15] While the identification or invocation of an issue as a community interest might be open to debate in particular instances, it does not appear to be too problematic in cases where the qualification is both well-founded in fact and accepted through some 'legitimising process'.[16] A clear example is when it is incorporated in a treaty regime with a wide membership, but subsequent 'political' recognition in soft law documents may also be of significance.[17] The point for the present discussion being that also community interests may be pluralistic, indeterminate at times, and that they may conflict across or within different regimes.[18]

As a result, tensions between sovereign interests and interests shared by the international community continue to emerge. These tensions are not only visible on the broader level in the need for enhanced cooperation and an integrated (as opposed to a zonal) governance approach to effectively tackle global challenges like climate change, ocean acidification, or plastic pollution, they are also visible on the individual state level.[19] Characteristic of these kinds of global challenges is that, despite the explicitly recognised community interest in addressing them, the pursuit of individual states' rights, interests, and priorities is not necessarily conducive to the shared goal.[20] When it comes to effectively protecting

---

15 ibid [544].

16 Wolfrum (n 10) 21. Also Besson (n 3) 43 on the question of legitimacy.

17 E.g. General Assembly Resolutions adopted by consensus. The UNGA, for example, declared the method of driftnet fishing contrary to community interests in sustainable fishing, and the call for a moratorium thereon proved highly influential. See e.g. UNGA, Res 44/225: 'Large-Scale Pelagic Drift-Net Fishing and its Impact on the Living Marine Resources of the World's Oceans and Seas' (22 December 1989) Resolution Adopted by the UN General Assembly in its 85th plenary meeting, UN Doc A/RES/44/225, and Res 46/215: 'Large-Scale Pelagic Drift-Net Fishing and its Impact on the Living Marine Resources of the World's Oceans and Seas' (20 December 1991) Resolution Adopted by the UN General Assembly in its 46th Session, UN Doc A/RES/46/215.

18 See also e.g. Besson (n 3).

19 For example, sea level rise and the imminent loss of territory pose questions as to what happens to established baselines and existing maritime entitlements that are measured from these baselines. See e.g. International Law Association Committee on International Law and Sea Level Rise, 'International Law and Sea Level Rise' Final Report of the Sydney Conference (2018); Signe Veierud Busch, 'Sea Level Rise and Shifting Maritime Limits: Stable Baselines as a Response to Unstable Coastlines' (2018) 9 Arctic Review on Law and Politics 174.

20 To stay with the example of climate change, neither the impacts of climate change nor the costs and benefits of mitigation are equally shared among cooperating states. As a result, their individual short-term interests and priorities inevitably diverge. For a discussion of the limits inherent in the 'self-interest approach' to issues of common

the interests shared by the international community in addressing these global challenges, models of jurisdiction based on 'sovereignty' or 'sovereign rights' have therefore been observed to fall short, or are seen as an obstacle to governing them effectively. Sovereignty has been subject to sociological and ecological critiques in that it fails to articulate the factual interdependencies that link social and ecosystems across the globe, and to functional objections in that it fails to deal effectively with global challenges such as those mentioned above.[21] What Viñuales calls the 'binary approach' to managing sovereign powers, where sovereignty is asserted first and then an 'additional layer' of limitations is added by law, is problematised for implying that 'the environment' (or indeed 'society') is something 'external' to the sphere of sovereignty.[22] Scholarly attempts to move beyond this 'externalisation' or disconnection of law and nature (or law and society) therefore often involve some reconceptualization of sovereignty based on a 'common interest' presumption.[23] However, a reconceptualization of the Westphalian 'state-centred' notion of sovereignty does not have to imply the end of state sovereignty or legal principles derived therefrom altogether.[24] It is proposed here that a functional perception of sovereignty in principle allows it to be aligned with the protection of community interests, as is visible in the various conceptions of 'commonality' already present in UNCLOS and in positive international law more generally.

---

concern, see Alexander Gillespie, *International Environmental Law, Policy, and Ethics* (2nd edn, OUP 2014) 23–24.

21 See Martti Koskenniemi, 'What Use for Sovereignty Today?' (2011) 1(1) Asian Journal of International Law 61, 61.

22 Jorge E Viñuales, *The Organisation of the Anthropocene: In Our Hands?* (Brill 2018) 23–24.

23 An example can be found in Scelle's 'domaine public international', which is based on the unity of ocean space, and a common interest and use by all states. See Georges Scelle, *Manuel Élémentaire de Droit International Public: Avec les Textes Essentiels* (Domat-Montchrestien 1943); for a discussion also Tanaka (n 2) 9–11. Other examples are the application of public trust doctrine or related concepts, see e.g. Peter H Sand, 'Public Trusteeship for the Oceans' in Rüdiger Wolfrum and Tafsir Malick Ndiaye (eds), *Law of the Sea, Environmental Law, and Settlement of Disputes: Liber Amicorum Judge Thomas A. Mensah* (Brill | Nijhoff 2007) 534–535.

24 Benvenisti's theory of 'sovereign trusteeship', for example, recognises the 'crucial role of sovereignty in the evolving global architecture of governance', and does not propose that sovereignty should be disparaged, but rather that it should be exercised in an 'other regarding' way. Eyal Benvenisti, 'Sovereigns as Trustees of Humanity: On the Accountability of States to Foreign Stakeholders' (2013) 107(2) The American Journal of International Law 295, 301.

2.2. A FUNCTIONAL PERCEPTION OF SOVEREIGNTY

It is generally recognised that in contemporary international law sovereignty is connoted not only with rights but also with obligations that stem from an increasingly complex web of normative and institutional frameworks. Globalisation, scientific and technological developments, and cumulative human impacts on the global environment have all contributed to a greater understanding of the complex interdependencies in today's interconnected world, to the effect that individual states' rights and interests have inevitably become more nuanced.[25] This is reflected in a range of developments over the past decades in which community interests have been woven into the fabric of international law.[26] The expansive development of, for example, human rights law and international environmental law bears witness to the fact that international law increasingly reflects the interests of 'humanity' more widely: conceptualising states as 'protectors' of these interests by focusing on their 'functional role'.[27] A functional perception of sovereignty thus perceives the concept as inherently conditional and linked to the functional role of the state.

The conditions imposed on the exercise of sovereignty are often seen as constituting or shaping the legal status of sovereignty itself, but Peters suggests they are better understood as legal *consequences* of the status of state sovereignty.[28] Scholarship engaging with this more realistic perception of what is also referred to as 'relative sovereignty' thus describes sovereign authority as diffuse and manifested through various interactions within the international legal system.[29] Young suggests

25 See also, e.g., Eyal Benvenisti and Georg Nolte (eds), *Community Interests Across International Law* (OUP 2018) 4; Stephen Stec, 'Humanitarian Limits to Sovereignty: Common Concern and Common Heritage Approaches to Natural Resources and Environment' (2010) 12(3) International Community Law Review 361, 364.

26 See for an extensive discussion i.a. Simma (n 6); Santiago Villalpando, 'The Legal Dimension of the International Community: How Community Interests Are Protected in International Law' (2010) 21(2) European Journal of International Law 387; Ulrich Fastenrath and others (eds), *From Bilateralism to Community Interest: Essays in Honour of Bruno Simma* (OUP 2011); Eyal Benvenisti and Georg Nolte (eds), *Community Interests Across International Law* (OUP 2018).

27 See Ellen Hey, 'Global Environmental Law: Common Interests and the (Re)Construction of Public Space' (2009) 1 Iustum Aequum Salutare 41, 42ff.

28 Anne Peters, 'Humanity as the A and Ω of Sovereignty' (2009) 20(3) EJIL 513, 516.

29 See e.g. Abram Chayes and Antonia H Chayes, *The New Sovereignty: Compliance with International Regulatory Agreements* (Harvard University Press 1998). Also, Richard

that 'an account of sovereignty that allows international law to confront issues of global concern, even as those issues traverse multiple regimes with disparate (and sometimes non-existing) state membership and differing organisational structures, is a necessary part of an open system of international law'.[30] In this perception, sovereignty implies a set of 'sovereign responsibilities' that require states to be 'other-regarding' in the exercise of their rights within intersecting regimes.[31] As the next section will illustrate, UNCLOS already contains a number of express obligations and mechanisms to that effect.

3. ACCOMMODATING COMMUNITY INTERESTS IN THE LAW OF THE SEA

UNCLOS distinguishes itself from other regimes incorporating community interests, such as the Convention on Biological Diversity (CBD) or the United Nations Framework Convention on Climate Change (UNFCCC), as the latter focus less on the allocation and balancing of rights and interests and more on facilitating cooperation to address specific 'common concerns'.[32] UNCLOS does both, and does so for a broad range of issue areas. It uniquely contains a variety of community interest manifestations within a single regime, including general references to the interests of 'mankind' or 'the international community' as a whole.[33] Four distinct ways in which community interests can be accommodated under UNCLOS will be highlighted here. First of all, 'balancing principles' contained in the substantive provisions require rights and freedoms under the Convention to be exercised in an 'other regarding' way. Not only do they allow for individual states' rights and interests to be balanced on

---

Barnes, 'Energy Sovereignty in Marine Spaces' (2014) 29(4) The International Journal of Marine and Coastal Law 573, 582.

30 Margaret A Young, 'Fragmentation, Regime Interaction and Sovereignty', in Christine Chinkin and Freya Baetens (eds), *Sovereignty, Statehood and State Responsibility: Essays in Honour of James Crawford* (Cambridge University Press 2015) 73.

31 ibid 87; Similarly, Benvenisti (n 24) 300ff.

32 The CBD declares the conservation of biodiversity a 'common concern of humankind', and the UNFCCC declares the impacts of climate change a 'common concern of humankind', see preamble of CBD and UNFCCC respectively. See also Patricia Birnie, Alan Boyle and Catherine Redgwell, *International Law & the Environment* (3rd edn, OUP 2009) 260.

33 See e.g. UNCLOS art 59 and the preamble.

a reciprocal basis, they also allow for shared interests to be taken into account, including those protected by other regimes of international law. Secondly, the Convention elaborates two regimes based on distinct conceptions of commonality in areas beyond national jurisdiction (the high seas and the deep seabed beyond national jurisdiction, or 'the Area'), both characterised by the absence of sovereign entitlements. Thirdly, obligations *erga omnes* can be found in the general provisions of Part XII on the protection of the marine environment. Finally, the protection of community interests under the Convention is (partly) supported by enforcement mechanisms and the compulsory dispute settlement system.

3.1. BALANCING MECHANISMS WITHIN AND ACROSS JURISDICTIONAL ZONES

Under the Convention, coastal states have 'sovereignty' over their internal waters,[34] or archipelagic waters in the case of archipelagic states,[35] and over their territorial sea.[36] The concept of sovereignty over ocean space originally emerged as a simple 'extension' of the territorial sovereignty of the coastal state over the sea, based on notions such as 'appropriation' or 'effective control'.[37] The 'sovereign rights' concept, on the other hand, emerged during the second half of the twentieth century, with the development of the continental shelf regime and the expanding coastal state claims over natural resources.[38] 'Sovereign rights' is a functional term.

---

34 UNCLOS art. 2(1) and 8.

35 ibid art. 2(1) and 46–54.

36 ibid art 2. This includes the air space, seabed and subsoil, and all the living and non-living resources therein.

37 This goes back to the earliest development of territorial sea claims around the turn of the 17th century, see e.g. Tullio Scovazzi, 'The Origin of the Theory of Sovereignty of the Sea' in Lilian del Castillo and Hugo Caminos (eds), *Law of the Sea, From Grotius to the International Tribunal for the Law of the Sea: Liber Amicorum Judge Hugo Caminos* (Brill | Nijhoff 2015); AV Lowe, 'Reflection on the Waters Changing Conceptions of Property Rights in the Law of the Sea' (1986) 1 International Journal of Estuarine and Coastal Law 1.

38 Starting with the 1945 Truman Proclamation. It is noteworthy that the Truman Proclamation did not use the word 'sovereignty', rather it spoke of natural resources 'appertaining to the United States' and being 'subject to its jurisdiction and control' to make it clear that the rights claimed were limited in purpose to the particular category of resources and expressly did not seek to affect the freedom of navigation and other rights of third states applicable in the water column. United States Presidential

Under UNCLOS, coastal states enjoy sovereign rights '*for the purpose of* exploring and exploiting, conserving and managing the natural resources' of the EEZ,[39] and over their continental shelf, again, '*for the purpose of* exploring and exploiting the natural resources'.[40] Contrary to what the traditional connotations of 'sovereignty' and 'sovereign rights' might suggest, these rights are inevitably of a limited and conditional character. While they are granted to the exclusion of other states, 'exclusive' does not mean 'absolute'. This is of course inevitable in any use of ocean space where, due to the inherent interconnectedness of the marine environment, one state's exercise of sovereign rights has consequences for how another state can enjoy its equally sovereign rights in what is ultimately still a single shared pool of water. While sovereignty has a long history in the law of the sea, it has thus never been absolute,[41] and its inherently conditional character is perhaps even more visible in ocean space than it is on land.[42]

Allott explained the structure of the Convention as one that 'delegates powers', conceiving of rights and freedoms as 'powers' shared between the holder of the right, other states, and the international community of states, to whose interests regard is to be had in the exercise of that 'power'.[43] Rights and freedoms granted under the Convention are subject to a web of limitations contained in the Convention itself, as well as in other applicable instruments of international law.[44] The 'boundaries' between different rights and interests are furthermore not static, but often determined by recourse to certain 'balancing principles' (such as 'due regard', 'taking account of', 'reasonable', or 'equitable').[45] As a result, the

---

Proclamation No 2667: 'Policy of the United States with Respect to the Natural Resources of the Subsoil and the Sea Bed of the Continental Shelf', 28 September 1945.

39 UNCLOS art 56.

40 ibid art 76.

41 From the outset it has been subject to the right of innocent passage through the territorial sea. See for a detailed discussion e.g. Scovazzi (n 37).

42 While the exercise of sovereignty over land territory has also become subject to increasing limitations over time, the unique character of ocean space makes that sovereignty over the sea can arguably not be regarded as ever having been identical to sovereignty over land. See also Lea Brilmayer and Natalie Klein, 'Land and Sea: Two Sovereignty Regimes in Search of a Common Denominator' (2001) 33 NYU Journal of International Law and Politics 703.

43 Philip Allott, 'Power Sharing in the Law of the Sea' (1983) 77(1) The American Journal of International Law 1, 27.

44 It falls outside the scope of this chapter to provide a comprehensive overview of these conditions and limitations.

45 Allott refers to these principles as 'power modifiers', Allott (n 43).

substance of a specific right or legal relationship is ultimately determined by the sum of these conditions and balancing principles, rather than the allocation of the 'sovereign right' or 'freedom' as such.

An important example of a recurrent balancing mechanism is the duty to have 'due regard' to the rights and interests of other states and relevant rules of international law beyond the Convention: an obligation that (in slightly different wordings) is provided in each of the different jurisdictional zones, and applies to both flag states and coastal states. As explained by the tribunal in the *Chagos* arbitration:

> Looking across the various maritime zones created by the Convention, the Tribunal notes that each of the territorial sea (Article 2(3)), international straits (Article 34(2)), the exclusive economic zone (Article 56(2), the continental shelf (Article 78(2)) and the high seas (Article 87(2)) includes a provision to the effect that States will exercise their rights under the Convention subject to or with regard to the rights and duties of other States or rules of international law beyond the Convention itself. While the language of these provisions is not harmonised, *a renvoi* to material beyond the Convention must be interpreted in a manner that is coherent with respect to all the foregoing maritime zones.[46]

The tribunal interpreted this duty to entail a positive obligation on states to engage in a 'balancing exercise',[47] but which duties exactly are 'due' depends on the circumstances of the specific case. As an open-ended mechanism, the function of the duty of due regard is not limited to the accommodation of interests explicitly protected by the Convention, but may also include other states' rights and interests under international law beyond the Convention, allowing evolving standards to be taken into account. Importantly, as the due regard concept is context-dependent, its function is also not limited to mediating conflicting interests between two states on a reciprocal basis, but may include (by implication or directly) the consideration of community interests.[48] For example, the tribunal in the

46 *Chagos* (n 14) para 503.

47 ibid [535].

48 See also e.g. Julia Gaunce, 'On the Interpretation of the General Duty of "Due Regard"' (2018) 32 Ocean Yearbook Online 27, 59; David Anderson, 'The Principle of Reasonableness in the Law of the Sea' in Holger P Hestermeyer and others (eds), *Coexistence, Cooperation and Solidarity: Liber Amicorum Rüdiger Wolfrum* (Brill | Nijhoff 2012) 662; Joshua Paine, 'The Judicial Dimension of Regime Interaction beyond Systemic Integration' in Seline Trevisanut, Nikolaos Giannopoulos and

South China Sea arbitration, by reference to the ITLOS' *Fisheries Advisory Opinion*, interpreted the obligation of due regard of the flag state to extend to a duty to 'take the necessary measures' to ensure that its nationals and vessels are not engaged in illegal, unreported, and unregulated (IUU) fishing in the EEZ of another state.[49]

Also the exercise of high seas freedoms is subject to the obligation of due regard. Already pre-UNCLOS, the ICJ found in the *Fisheries Jurisdiction* cases that:

> it is one of the advances in maritime international law, resulting from the intensification of fishing, that the former *laissez-faire* treatment of the living resources of the sea in the high seas has been replaced by a recognition of a duty to have due regard to the rights of other States and the needs of conservation for the benefit of all.[50]

This dictum already reflected that the duty of 'due regard' extends to the interests of other states in both the conservation and equitable exploitation of high seas resources, and that this duty applies not only between states, but also between every state and the international community as a whole.[51] At the very least, to the extent that the mutual duty of due regard qualifies the exercise of sovereign rights, jurisdiction, and freedoms across the Convention, it acknowledges and serves the shared interest in the accommodation of competing interests in ocean space.[52]

Rozemarijn Roland Holst (eds), *Regime Interaction in Ocean Governance: Problems, Theories and Methods* (Brill | Nijhoff 2020) 210.

49 *South China Sea Arbitration (Philippines v China)* (Merits) [2016] PCA Case No 2013–19, para 743, referring to *Request for Advisory Opinion submitted by the Sub-Regional Fisheries Commission* (Advisory Opinion) [2015] ITLOS Rep 2015, 4, paras 124 and 129, where this obligation is interpreted as an obligation of 'due diligence'. Accordingly, the tribunal in *South China Sea* considered that 'anything less than due diligence by a State in preventing its nationals from unlawfully fishing in the exclusive economic zone of another would fall short of the regard due pursuant to Article 58(3)', para 744.

50 This obligation was found in art 2 of the 1958 High Seas Convention and applied here as a rule of customary international law. See *Fisheries Jurisdiction (UK v. Iceland)* (Merits, Judgement) [1974] ICJ Rep 3, para 72; and *Fisheries Jurisdiction (Germany v. Iceland)* (Merits, Judgement) [1974] ICJ Rep 175, para 64.

51 See also Anderson (n 48) 662.

52 See also Bernard H Oxman, 'The Principle of Due Regard', in International Tribunal for the Law of the Sea, *The Contribution of the International Tribunal for the Law of the Sea to the Rule of Law: 1996–2016* (Brill | Nijhoff 2018) 108.

3.2. AREAS BEYOND NATIONAL JURISDICTION

3.2.1. *Freedom of the High Seas*

The high seas are a classic example of 'the commons', where all states enjoy high seas freedoms on an equal basis.[53] A common area implies the absence of sovereign entitlements, as expressly prohibited by Article 89.[54] Instead, the Convention grants non-discriminatory access to the high seas, with special regard to the geographical position of states.[55] At least rhetorically, the freedoms-based regime implies a decentralised 'sharing' of this ocean space and its resources, which are therefore traditionally regarded as 'common property' resources or *res communis*.[56] All states thus share an interest in both the exploitation and the conservation of high seas resources. As observed above, also high seas freedoms are not absolute or unrestricted, but defined by the rules contained in the Convention, including the obligation of due regard, and other rules of international law.[57]

An important consequence of the absence of sovereign rights on the high seas is that the only jurisdiction that can be exercised there remains exclusively with the flag state over ships flying its flag.[58] Certain exceptions exist for the purposes of combatting particular activities, such as piracy, drugs trafficking, transporting slaves, and unauthorised broadcasting,[59] acknowledging the community interest in the effective enforcement of these issues. Yet many persistent highs seas governance challenges remain, including IUU fishing, forced labour, and sub-standard shipping, and the principle of exclusive flag state jurisdiction is often perceived as an obstacle to effective enforcement.[60] The challenges

---

53 These freedoms include navigation, overflight, the laying of cables and pipelines and the construction of installations, fishing, and scientific research, but the list in art 87(1) is non-exhaustive.

54 Paradoxically, this follows from the sovereign equality of states. As each state enjoys equal rights of access and use of the high seas, exclusive claims would prevent other states from deriving the same benefits. See also Djamchid Momtaz, 'The High Seas' in RJ Dupuy and Daniel Vignes (eds), *A Handbook on the New Law of the Sea* (Volume 1, Martinus Nijhoff 1991) 399.

55 See e.g. UNCLOS art 90.

56 See also Birnie, Boyle and Redgwell (n 32) 194ff.

57 UNCLOS art 87(2).

58 ibid art 94.

59 ibid art. 100–109. See art 110 for right of visit and 111 for hot pursuit.

60 See e.g. Osvaldo Urrutia, 'Combating Unregulated Fishing through Unilateral Trade Measures: A Time for Change in International Fisheries Law?' (2018) 49(4) Victoria

of a freedoms-based regime became evident early on in relation to the management of high seas fisheries. Whereas the Convention itself contains only a few general provisions on the management and conservation of high seas living resources, entailing little more than a duty to cooperate,[61] the adoption of the 1995 Fish Stocks Agreement (FSA) was meant to remedy some of these deficiencies.[62] The FSA introduced more extensive provisions on conservation and sustainable use, as well as the precautionary approach, but its application is limited to straddling and highly migratory stocks and does not cover all high seas fisheries.[63] Under the FSA, states are required to cooperate through regional fisheries management organisations (RFMOs), and to comply with the relevant RFMO's conservation and management measures in order to get access to the fish stocks in question.[64] As a result, it is the intricate political process within RFMOs that ultimately determines the participation requirements and quota allocations.[65] It is questionable to what extent the traditional notion of 'equal access' to high seas fish stocks is preserved under this system in practice, and it has been observed to encourage IUU fishing outside the relevant regimes.[66] Alternatively, one could argue that the FSA and the rules and practices of RFMOs might well (in the future) become regarded as the stipulation of new rules on access to high seas fisheries that are no longer based on the traditional notion of equal access, but on mandatory cooperation. This would mean that states not participating in or adhering to RFMO rules effectively lose their right to

University of Wellington Law Review 671; Arron N Honniball, 'The Exclusive Jurisdiction of Flag States: A Limitation on Pro-Active Port States?' (2016) 31(3) The International Journal of Marine and Coastal Law 499.

61 See UNCLOS art. 117–120.

62 UNGA, 'Agreement for the Implementation of the Provisions of the United Nations Convention on the Law of the Sea of 10 December 1982 relating to the Conservation and Management of Straddling Fish Stocks and Highly Migratory Fish Stocks' (8 September 1995) 6th Session (1995) UN Doc A/Conf.164/37 (FSA).

63 See FSA art. 5, 6.

64 See UNCLOS art 118, and FSA art 8.

65 Erik J Molenaar, 'Participation in Regional Fisheries Management Organizations' in Richard Caddell and Erik J Molenaar (eds), *Strengthening International Fisheries Law in an Era of Changing Oceans* (Hart Publishing 2019).

66 Access will often ultimately depend on the technological and financial resources of states. With the current over-capacity, fisheries are often already fully utilised and allocations to new members thus inevitably involve reduced allocations for existing members, which results in an obvious measure of reluctance on their part and a conflict of interests. See ibid. See also Jutta Brunnée, 'Common Areas, Common Heritage, and Common Concern' in Jutta Brunnée, Daniel Bodansky and Ellen Hey (eds), *The Oxford Handbook of International Environmental Law* (OUP 2008) 562.

fish on the high seas, which arguably goes beyond a mere 'limitation' of this freedom and would constitute an altogether new conception of the 'common' character of high seas fisheries.[67]

Today, more than ever, the high seas constitute a 'managed common area', rather than a place where unfettered freedoms can be exercised.[68] A host of regional and global treaties apply to the high seas, dealing with issues ranging from dumping to maritime safety and security or standards for ship operations.[69] Several multilateral environmental agreements, such as the CBD, as well as a host of global and regional species-specific agreements and institutions also regulate activities on the high seas.[70] This is hardly surprising, as it is inevitable that the management of 'common resources' depends entirely on international cooperation. Yet despite the increase in governance of the high seas, the freedoms-based regime set out in UNCLOS inevitably leaves gaps and outstanding questions regarding the regulation of particular (shared) interests and emerging activities, such the use and conservation of marine genetic resources and biodiversity.[71] The latter is, for that reason, the subject of currently ongoing negotiations with the aim of adopting a new

---

67 See also Birnie, Boyle and Redgwell (n 32) 740.

68 See also Donald R Rothwell and Tim Stephens, *The International Law of the Sea* (2nd edn, Hart Publishing 2016) 155.

69 See, i.a., IMO Conventions such as the International Convention for the Prevention of Pollution from Ships (as amended) (adopted 2 November 1973, entered into force 2 October 1983) 1340 UNTS 61, the International Convention for the Safety of Life at Sea (as amended) (adopted 1 November 1974, entered into force 25 May 1980) 1184 UNTS 2, the International Convention on Standards of Training, Certification and Watchkeeping for Seafarers (as amended) (adopted 7 July 1978, entered into force 28 April 1984) 1361 UNTS 2, the Convention Relating to Intervention on the High Seas in Cases of Oil Pollution Casualties (adopted 29 November 1969, entered into force 6 May 1975) 970 UNTS 211, the International Convention on Oil Pollution Preparedness, Response and Co-operation (adopted 30 November 1990, entered into force 13 May 1995) 1891 UNTS, and the Convention on the Prevention of Marine Pollution by Dumping of Wastes and Other Matter (as amended) (adopted 13 November 1972, entered into force 30 August 1975) 1046 UNTS 120.

70 See, e.g., Convention for the Regulation of Whaling (adopted 2 December 1946, entered into force 10 November 1948) 161 UNTS 72, the International Convention for the Conservation of Atlantic Tunas (adopted 14 May 1966, entered into force 21 March 1969) 673 UNTS 63, and the Convention for the Conservation of Salmon in the North Atlantic (adopted 2 March 1982, entered into force 1 October 1983) 1338 UNTS 33.

71 See e.g. Ane Jørem and Morten Walløe Tvedt, 'Bioprospecting in the High Seas: Existing Rights and Obligations in View of a New Legal Regime for Marine Areas beyond National Jurisdiction' (2014) 29(2) The International Journal of Marine and Coastal Law 321.

implementing agreement under UNCLOS on biodiversity in areas beyond national jurisdiction.[72]

3.2.2. *The Area as Common Heritage of Mankind*

The Area and its resources are 'common heritage of mankind'.[73] What the Area and the high seas regime have in common is the absence of sovereign rights. At least on the face of it, 'common heritage' points to a wider conception of commonality by vesting all rights in the mineral resources of the Area in 'mankind as a whole'.[74] 'Mankind' is a trans-temporal concept in that it includes both present and future generations,[75] which accords an important role to the concept of sustainable development.[76] The principle of common heritage arose out of the view that both the traditional sovereignty and freedom principles were unable to provide a politically acceptable legal framework for governing deep seabed resources.[77] The regime thereby makes a clean break with the traditional 'sovereignty versus freedom' narrative. It also provides a unique example of 'institutionalised' protection of community interests. The International Seabed Authority (ISA) is the international organisation established by UNCLOS to act on behalf of mankind in managing activities (deep seabed

72 The UNGA convened the intergovernmental conference on this topic for the first time in 2017, see UNGA Res. 72/249 (24 December 2017) with the aim of developing an 'International legally binding instrument under the United Nations Convention on the Law of the Sea on the conservation and sustainable use of marine biological diversity of areas beyond national jurisdiction'. See also Report of the Preparatory Committee established by General Assembly resolution 69/292, UN Doc A/AC.287/2017/PC.4/2 (31 July 2017). See, for the latest version of the text Revised Draft Text of the Agreement, UN Doc A/Conf.232/2020/3 (18 November 2019).

73 UNCLOS art 136 and rest of Part XI of the Convention; and the 1994 Part XI Implementing Agreement.

74 UNCLOS art 137(2).

75 See Yoshifumi Tanaka, 'Protection of Community Interests in International Law: The Case of the Law of the Sea' (2011) 15 Max Planck Yearbook of United Nations Law 329, 339.

76 See also Wolfrum (n 10) 29.

77 See e.g. Catherine Redgwell, 'Property Law Sources and Analogies in International Law' in Aileen McHarg and others (eds), *Property and the Law in Energy and Natural Resources* (OUP 2010) 111; Surabhi Ranganathan, 'The Law of the Sea and Natural Resources' in Eyal Benvenisti and Georg Nolte (eds), *Community Interests Across International Law* (OUP 2018); Isabel Feichtner, 'Sharing the Riches of the Sea: The Redistributive and Fiscal Dimension of Deep Seabed Exploitation' (2019) 30(2) EJIL 601.

mining) in the Area.[78] To this end, the ISA has exclusive legislative and enforcement jurisdiction over a wide range of issues; from environmental protection to financial terms and benefit sharing.[79] The ISA has thus far adopted regulations governing the prospecting and exploration phase,[80] and is currently working on draft regulations for the – yet to commence – commercial exploitation phase.[81]

At least in theory, the main difference between the regimes of the high seas and the Area is that high seas freedoms have to be exercised with 'due regard' to the interests of other states (collectively), while activities in the Area are meant to be carried out 'for the benefit of mankind as a whole'.[82] In practical terms, this means that activities in the Area can only be conducted by entering into a regulated contractual relationship with the ISA, which will monitor compliance with applicable regulations, and, once commercial exploitation commences, distribute part of the proceeds among the international community.[83] Although it is the ISA's primary task to safeguard the interests of 'mankind as a whole', the ITLOS Seabed Disputes Chamber in its Advisory Opinion also stressed the 'common-interest role' of sponsoring states in contributing to 'the realization of the common interest of all states in the proper application of the principle of common heritage of mankind'.[84] The sponsoring states (and contractors) thus also carry international responsibility and liability for implementing

78 UNCLOS art 137.

79 ibid art 157.

80 International Seabed Authority, 'Regulations on Prospecting and Exploration for Polymetallic Nodules in the Area' (22 July 2013) UN Doc ISBA/19/C/17, 'Regulations on Prospecting and Exploration for Polymetallic Sulphides in the Area' (15 November 2010) UN Doc ISBA/16/A/12/Rev.1, 'Regulations on Prospecting and Exploration for Cobalt-Rich Crusts' (22 October 2012) UN Doc ISBA/18/A/11. For an overview of prospecting and exploration activities that are/have been taking place, see: <https://www.isa.org.jm/deep-seabed-minerals-contractors> accessed 15 January 2021.

81 This concerns all aspects of the exploitation phase. See further below.

82 UNCLOS art. 87 and 140 respectively.

83 Contractors can be states parties, or public or private enterprises sponsored by a state party. The Enterprise (an organ of the ISA) can currently only participate through joint ventures, see UNCLOS art 153.

84 See *Responsibilities and obligations of States sponsoring persons and entities with respect to activities in the Area* (Advisory Opinion) [2011] ITLOS Rep 10, para 76 and 226. It adds that the sponsoring state does not have absolute discretion with respect to the action it is required to take: 'in the sphere of the obligation to assist the Authority acting on behalf of mankind as a whole, while deciding what measures are reasonably appropriate, the sponsoring State must take into account, objectively, the relevant options in a manner that is reasonable, relevant and conducive to the benefit of mankind as a whole', para 230.

the common heritage principle, making it a prime example of a shared responsibility regime under international law.[85]

Still, this begs the question what exactly 'benefits' mankind. States may argue from diametrically opposed positions, and a sharp distinction between the interests of industrialised and developing countries has marked the development of the regime from the outset.[86] Perhaps the most crucial question outstanding at the moment is how to strike a balance between economic interests and the environmental preservation component of the common heritage principle.[87] While the deep seabed regime is firmly established as a 'common interest'-based regime, Ranganathan notes that 'the relationship between international law and the commons is not linear: on the one hand, international law is a medium to advance equitable (and, to a more limited extent, sustainable) use of the commons, but on the other, it is also the means through which ideas counter to that of the commons are asserted.'[88] The community interests that the common heritage principle purports to protect are not necessarily easy to pin down, and may mean different things to different actors depending on their political agenda. Hence Collins and French observe that the ISA:

> has evolved to ensure that no one understanding of the collective interest, as reflected in disagreement about the very idea of (common heritage of mankind) itself, can take precedence over others. The regime accommodates substantive disagreement and competing political interests by incorporating them within the evolving institutional framework of the Authority itself.[89]

85 See also Ilias Plakokefalos, 'Environmental Protection of the Deep Seabed' in André Nollkaemper and Ilias Plakokefalos (eds), *The Practice of Shared Responsibility in International Law* (CUP 2017).

86 See on the substantial changes to the original Part XI regime brought about by the 1994 Implementing Agreement to accommodate the demands of industrialised states e.g. Michael C Wood, 'International Seabed Authority: The First Four Years' (1999) 3 Max Planck Yearbook of United Nations Law 173; Surabhi Ranganathan, *Strategically Created Treaty Conflicts and the Politics of International Law* (CUP 2014) 175 and Appendix 3.

87 The need to protect the marine environment of the Area has been recognised from the outset, see UNCLOS art 145. See for a discussion also Karin Mickelson, 'Common Heritage of Mankind as a Limit to Exploitation of the Global Commons' (2019) 30(2) EJIL 635.

88 Ranganathan (n 86) 149.

89 Richard Collins and Duncan French, 'A Guardian of Universal Interest or Increasingly Out of Its Depth: The International Seabed Authority Turns 25' (2020) 17(3) International Organizations Law Review 633, 650.

Brunnée suggests, however, that a main weakness inherent in the common heritage concept is that it is motivated in the first place by states' interest in *access* to resources, rather than some *a priori* common interest in their conservation or sustainable use.[90] After all, the concept emerged as a device for developing countries to secure access to deep sea resources.[91] Hence, the common heritage principle can also be understood as a jurisdictional principle which merely serves to allocate exploitation rights.[92] The focus on access and exploitation may get the concept entangled in and side-lined by the competition it inevitably entails, possibly to the detriment of the environmental or re-distributional components of the common heritage principle.[93] In any event, it is clear that the common heritage principle is not 'self-executing', nor do particular legal relations flow from it.[94] It requires further arrangements and institutional mechanisms to be operationalised and implemented.

In this respect, the ISA currently finds itself in a crucial phase in its regulatory work. The development of the Draft Exploitation Regulations does not take place within a legal and contextual vacuum, but is interwoven with evolving scientific knowledge, political interests and evolving international law.[95] While there is renewed commercial interest in the Area, knowledge of its fragile ecosystem is only starting to emerge and a number of serious concerns about the impacts of seabed mining have been raised, ranging from consequences for food security, local livelihoods and human health, to impacts on the ecosystem and biodiversity at large.[96] These issues in turn constitute valid community

90 Brunnée (n 66) 563.

91 In line with the New International Economic Order idea, see also Ranganathan (n 86); Martti Koskenniemi and Marja Lehto, 'The Privilege of Universality' (1996) 65 Nordic Journal of International Law 533.

92 Feichtner (n 77) 604.

93 See also Brunnée (n 66) 563–564; Feichtner (n 77) 607.

94 See also Redgwell (n 77).

95 See also Till Markus and Pradeep Singh, 'Promoting Consistency in the Deep Seabed: Addressing Regulatory Dimensions in Designing the International Seabed Authority's Exploitation Code' (2016) 25 Review of European Community & International Environmental Law 347.

96 See, e.g., L Cuyvers and others, 'Deep Seabed Mining: A Rising Environmental Challenge' (IUCN 2018) <https://portals.iucn.org/library/node/47761> accessed 15 January 2021; Ann Vanreusel and others, 'Threatened by Mining, Polymetallic Nodules Are Required to Preserve Abyssal Epifauna' (2016) 6 Scientific Reports 1; Aline Jaeckel and Rosemary Rayfuse, 'Conceptions of Risk in an Institutional Context: Deep Seabed Mining and the International Seabed Authority' in Monika Ambrus, Rosemary Rayfuse and Wouter Werner (eds), *Risk and the Regulation of Uncertainty in International Law* (OUP 2017).

interests that arguably warrant limits on purely commercial interests,[97] and at least require the precautionary approach to be front and centre of any next step.[98] It is now the ISA's task to take the elaboration of all aspects of its mandate forward and devise future-proof regulations that not only balance shared economic interests with shared environmental interests in preserving the common heritage, but do so in a way that is responsive to evolving scientific knowledge. Of course, the proof of the pudding will be in the yet-to-be elaborated details that will determine how effectively and equitably this can be realised in practice. This is an ongoing and evolving dialogue between the various bodies of the ISA, member states, and (industry) stakeholders, with input from science and civil society.[99]

3.3. OBLIGATIONS ERGA OMNES: THE PROTECTION OF THE MARINE ENVIRONMENT

Perhaps the most important example of a community interest to be taken into account at all times is the protection of the marine environment. The obligation to protect and preserve the marine environment is elaborated in Part XII of the Convention and reflects customary international law.[100] Regardless in which zone an activity takes place, and regardless of whether it has effects in or outside national jurisdiction, all states are under a general obligation to protect the marine environment. This obligation is thus not subject to the zonal approach and is of an *erga omnes* character,[101] which means that, as stressed by the tribunal in *South China Sea*,

97 See also Ranganathan (n 77) 132.

98 See extensively Aline Jaeckel, *The International Seabed Authority and the Precautionary Principle: Balancing Deep Seabed Mineral Mining and Marine Environmental Protection* (Brill | Nijhoff 2017). The matter also has some political momentum. The European Parliament adopted a Resolution calling on Member States to support an international moratorium on commercial deep-sea mining exploitation licences, at least until the effects on the marine environment, biodiversity and human activities at sea have been thoroughly studied and better understood. EP resolution of 16 January 2018 on international ocean governance: an agenda for the future of our oceans in the context of the 2030 SDGs (2017/2055(INI)) para 42.

99 For updates on the process, including stakeholder consultations, see ISA, 'Draft Exploitation Regulations' <https://www.isa.org.jm/instruments-juridiques/ongoing-development-regulations-exploitation-mineral-resources-area> accessed 15 January 2021.

100 See UNCLOS art 192ff.

101 See also James Harrison, *Saving the Oceans Through Law: The International Legal Framework for the Protection of the Marine Environment* (OUP 2017) 24–25. And *Seabed Advisory Opinion* (n 84) para 180.

'questions of sovereignty are irrelevant to the application of Part XII'.[102] It has furthermore been stressed repeatedly in UNCLOS case law that the obligation relates not only to activities undertaken by states or their organs directly, but also requires states to ensure that activities carried out by other actors within their jurisdiction and control do not cause harm to the marine environment.[103] The general obligations of Part XII have been interpreted as an obligation of 'due diligence', rather than an obligation of result.[104] It requires states to take the 'necessary and appropriate measures', which requires vigilance in the monitoring and enforcement of applicable standards,[105] and may trigger specific obligations, such as the duty to cooperate[106] or to conduct an environmental impact assessment.[107] Exactly what measures are required depends on the circumstances of the case. UNCLOS tribunals have also interpreted the content of the obligation of due diligence by reference to 'external' standards of international law, notably under the CBD and the Convention on International Trade in Endangered Species (CITES).[108] Barnes has explained the essence of the concept of due diligence as establishing 'positive obligations of conduct that are to be assessed in the light of a general regulatory position that *extends* beyond immediate treaty obligations'.[109] The emphasis on due diligence thereby makes the obligation to protect the marine environment under UNCLOS undeniably more complex than a mere specification of the 'no harm' rule found in general international law,[110] and allows its content to be responsive to developments in international law more widely.

---

102 *South China Sea* (n 49) para 940.

103 ibid [944].

104 *Seabed Advisory Opinion* (n 84) para 110; *South China Sea* (n 49) para 944.

105 *Fisheries Advisory Opinion* (n 49) paras 131–138 (in relation to illegal fishing); referring to *Pulp Mills on the River Uruguay (Argentina v. Uruguay)* (Judgment) [2010] ICJ Rep 14, para 197. See also *Seabed Advisory Opinion* (n 84) para 110ff; *South China Sea* (n 49) para 944.

106 *Fisheries Advisory Opinion* (n 49) para 140. See also *Chagos* (n 14).

107 UNCLOS art 206. See, generally, *Certain Activities Carried Out by Nicaragua in the Border Area (Costa Rica v. Nicaragua)* (Judgment) [2015] ICJ Rep 354 and *Construction of a Road in Costa Rica along the San Juan River (Nicaragua v. Costa Rica)* (Judgment) [2013] ICJ Rep 354, para 101–105 (proceedings joined); *Pulp Mills* (n 105) para 204.

108 *South China Sea* (n 49) paras 945 and 956.

109 Richard Barnes, 'The Continuing Vitality of UNCLOS' in Jill Barrett and Richard Barnes (eds), *Law of the Sea: UNCLOS as a Living Treaty* (BIICL 2016) 480.

110 See for a discussion Nele Matz-Lück and Erik van Doorn, 'Due Diligence Obligations and the Protection of the Marine Environment' (2017) 42 L'Observateur des Nations Unies 177, 181–182.

3.4. ENFORCEMENT AND DISPUTE SETTLEMENT

The effective enforcement of community interests is a crucial aspect of their protection. A mechanism provided by the Convention to remedy some of the limitations inherent in exclusive flag state jurisdiction is the concept of port state jurisdiction and port state control (PSC).[111] This allows port states to exercise enforcement jurisdiction over vessels that are voluntarily in port, and verify compliance of merchant vessels with applicable international law on matters such as maritime safety, security, labour standards, and environmental standards, or international fisheries law when it concerns fishing vessels. As port state jurisdiction and PSC arrangements give expression to the need for 'policing' on topics of clear interest to the international community, some authors suggest that the port state takes on the role of an organ of the international community.[112] Gavouneli describes port state jurisdiction as a 'cooperative jurisdiction' in the sense that, while the territorial sovereignty and discretion of the port state are maintained, the obligations to uphold international standards have in fact converted the port into the primary 'control point' for environmental protection, fisheries regulation, and maritime safety and security.[113] Port state jurisdiction is an attractive mechanism because it does not interfere with navigational freedoms or the sovereign rights of coastal states.[114] It is also an example where national interest and interests of the international community often coincide. If the international community shares an interest in preventing unseaworthy vessels from posing a threat to the environment or human safety on the high seas, a port state has a – possibly even greater – interest in not having such a vessel in its port. On the other hand, incentives on the port state to

111 See UNCLOS art 218. More specifically, most IMO conventions provide for port state control to ensure compliance. See e.g. Bevan Marten, *Port State Jurisdiction and the Regulation of International Merchant Shipping* (Springer 2014).

112 See e.g. Christian J Tams, 'Individual States as Guardians of Community Interests' in Ulrich Fastenrath and others (eds), *From Bilateralism to Community Interest: Essays in Honour of Bruno Simma* (OUP 2011). Tanaka likens it to Scelle's theory of 'dédoublement fonctionnel', Tanaka (n 75) 351ff.

113 Maria Gavouneli, 'State Jurisdiction in Relation to the Protection and Preservation of the Marine Environment' in David J Attard, Malgosia Fitzmaurice, Norman Martínez and Riyaz Hamza (eds), *The IMLI Manual on International Maritime Law, Volume III: Marine Environmental Law and Maritime Security Law* (OUP 2016) 27.

114 It should be noted, however, that the primacy of the flag state, or the coastal state in whose waters the violation occurred, is recognised in cases where proceedings against a vessel are instituted. See art 128(2–4).

exercise jurisdiction may be lacking when no direct damage occurs.[115] The effectiveness of PSC as a complementary mechanism is dependent on the discretion of the port state and limited to instances when a vessel suspected of violations is voluntarily in port.[116] Both flags and ports of convenience remain a serious problem, as is evident from the persistent struggles with issues such as IUU fishing, forced labour, and sub-standard shipping.[117]

A final feature of community interest protection under UNCLOS to be mentioned here is the role of dispute settlement. The traditional bilateral means of resorting to dispute settlement are often not available when a dispute relates to community interests.[118] Even when certain obligations are recognised as having an *erga omnes* character, and thus in theory enforceable by any state, the consent of the respondent state is still required to establish jurisdiction. While the dispute settlement system under UNCLOS is certainly not fully equipped to accommodate community interests,[119] it does contain several unique features in this respect. First of all, the Convention provides for compulsory dispute settlement for any dispute 'concerning the interpretation or application of the Convention' before either the ITLOS, the ICJ or an *ad hoc* arbitral tribunal.[120] This includes disputes relating to common interests such as high seas fisheries or states' obligations to protect the marine environment.[121] Underlining the importance of marine environmental protection, the Convention also provides for provisional measures that can be requested from the ITLOS to prevent serious harm to the marine environment pending a final decision on the merits.[122] In terms of litigating 'in the public interest',

---

115 Tanaka (n 75) 363.

116 There are a number of regional port state control agreements, memoranda of understanding (MoUs), through which states coordinate inspection and control, e.g. the Paris MoU for Europe and the North Atlantic, or the Tokyo MoU for Asia and the Pacific.

117 See further e.g. Honniball (n 60); Marten (n 111); Erik J Molenaar, 'Port State Jurisdiction: Towards Mandatory and Comprehensive Use' in David Freestone, Richard Barnes and David Ong (eds), *The Law of the Sea: Progress and Prospects* (OUP 2006).

118 See also Brunnée (n 66) 570; Wolfrum (n 8).

119 See also Wolfrum (n 10) 33.

120 UNCLOS art. 286, 287, 288 and 297. This applies only if alternative arrangements between the parties have failed, see art. 281, 282.

121 UNCLOS art 297 (1)(a), (c). EEZ fisheries disputes are excluded from compulsory dispute settlement.

122 UNCLOS art 290. This option has been used on a number of occasions, see *Southern Bluefin Tuna (New Zealand v Japan; Australia v Japan)* (Provisional Measures) [1999]

it is furthermore noteworthy that the ISA, acting on behalf of humanity as whole, is the only international organisation with the express power to instigate proceedings against states.[123] The ISA can furthermore claim compensation for damage to the marine environment and resources of the Area.[124]

For the establishment of jurisdiction under the Convention, Article 288 does not explicitly require the applicant state to act exclusively in defence of its individual rights or interests. It merely requires a disagreement 'concerning the interpretation and application' of the Convention. As argued convincingly by Wolfrum, 'allowing a case to be filed without the necessity to prove that individual interests of the applicant State are at stake would be in line with a literal interpretation as well as with the general community orientation of the Convention.'[125] Yet it should be noted that in practice there will inevitably be a combination of individual and community interest at play, regardless of how the submissions are framed.[126] Boyle notes that UNCLOS' compulsory dispute settlement mechanism is particularly meaningful when it comes to the protection of the rights and interests of weaker states.[127] Compulsory dispute settlement is rare in other international (environmental) agreements, and reinforces, among other things, the *erga omnes* character of the environmental obligations under the Convention.

4. CONCLUSION

Due to its nature and vast substantive scope, the law of the sea provides an example of a regime that was designed to accommodate and mediate

ITLOS Rep 280; *MOX Plant (Ireland v United Kingdom)* (Provisional Measures) [2001] ITLOS Rep 95; *Land Reclamation by Singapore in and around the Straits of Johor (Malaysia v. Singapore)* (Provisional Measures) [2003] ITLOS Rep 10.

123 Limited of course to the scope of its competence concerning activities in the Area and the protection of the marine environment from such activities These cases will be heard by the ITLOS Seabed Disputes Chamber. UNCLOS art 187(b)(i).

124 *Seabed Advisory Opinion* (n 84) paras 179–180.

125 Wolfrum (n 8) 1145.

126 Beham critically notes that "just as states will bulldoze over public image considerations, whenever their survival interests are at stake, states will limit their activism with regard to *ius cogens* and *erga omnes* obligations to situations, in which their own interest are concerned". Beham (n 4) 132.

127 Alan Boyle, 'The Tribunal and the Rule of Law' in International Tribunal for the Law of the Sea, *The Contribution of the International Tribunal for the Law of the Sea to the Rule of Law: 1996–2016* (Brill | Nijhoff 2018).

an ever-evolving balance of competing interests. It has been shown that a functional perception of sovereignty best describes its contemporary position under the Convention, and in principle allows it to be aligned with a wider range of interests, including community interests. That does not mean, however, that this functional perception eliminates all limitations inherent in the concept. Some authors have observed that the 'reduction to purpose' implies that the sovereignty concept has no intrinsic normative value, but that its justification is rather to be found in the objectives it fulfils.[128] The possible 'functions' it serves may of course vary widely from time to time and depend on the circumstances, making it per definition a changing notion: a vehicle to serve the changing individual *and* collective interests of states. This 'openness' of the sovereignty concept does not have to be a bad thing. Like most legal concepts, if it were a rigid notion it would arguably have long surpassed its use.

What constitutes the 'community interest' in any particular context and who exactly have this interest in common, is not a given either. Also community interests are pluralistic and subject to change. The example of the deep seabed shows that even within a single regime states may have starkly diverging views as to what constitutes the 'interest of mankind' and how to operationalise it. Complex and multifaceted global challenges, be it 'old' ones like IUU fishing or 'new' ones like climate change, furthermore show that even when there is a clearly recognised community interest and a common goal, the political will and individual priorities of a state do not always make them harness their sovereign competences to live up to those commitments in practice. After all, the difference with domestic legal systems is that international law has no central public authority with enforcement powers, and it inevitably remains an inter-state order in the sense that legal obligations that give effect to community interests are 'left to the play of individual auto-determination of duties and self-enforcement'.[129]

It is submitted, however, that the role of international law is to give expression and recognition to (emerging) trans-temporal considerations of common interest, that in turn inform decision-making and qualify the exercise of existing rights. The growing importance and (pragmatic) recognition of community interests is thus perhaps best qualified as a shift in discourse – in the rationales that inform decision-making on

128 Peters (n 28) 518; Koskenniemi (n 21) 64.
129 Simma (n 6) 249.

the international level.[130] The legal principles, scientific knowledge, and interests that inform this discourse and their respective weight evolve. Hence any conception of sovereignty as a foundational notion underpinning the Convention, and as a constitutive element of the state as an actor in the international legal order, cannot be a static one but must be responsive to changes in law and fact – as it has been over time. Aligning this 'other regarding' sovereignty with contemporary interests is thus more about reconfiguring the principles of international debate. And, as the contributions to this volume illustrate, these can and increasingly do reflect community interests in various manifestations.

130 Similarly, Peters (n 28) and Emma Dunlop, 'Humanity as the A and Ω of Sovereignty: Four Replies to Anne Peters' (2009) 20(3) EJIL 556.

THE PROTECTION OF COMMUNITY INTERESTS THROUGH COUNTERMEASURES ADOPTED BY INTERNATIONAL ORGANIZATIONS

Maruša T. VEBER*

* PhD candidate and Teaching Assistant at the Faculty of Law, University of Ljubljana, Slovenia (marusa.veber@pf.uni-lj.si).

1. INTRODUCTION

International organisations are often perceived as platforms for promoting community interests and, in some ways, as embodying community interests.[1] Yet their active contribution to protecting community interests is often disregarded. This chapter seeks to demonstrate that international organisations do play a role in protecting community interests by virtue of the countermeasures they adopt in response to violations of *erga omnes* obligations and to pinpoint to some of the controversies and discrepancies between the regime governing these activities of international organisations and actual practice of international organisations. In particular, this chapter seeks to demonstrate that the restrictive approach of the International Law Commission (ILC) towards the standing of non-injured international organisations to invoke responsibility and subsequently adopt countermeasures in response to violations of *erga omnes* violations is not warranted. It will be explained that limiting this standing of international organisations to instances where safeguarding against a breach of a particular communitarian norm falls under the functions of that organisation[2] is based on an inconclusive understanding of distinctions between the capacities of international organisations under general international law and the competences embedded in the rules of individual international organisations.

Various kinds of measures are adopted by international organisations in cases where they cannot be considered as being individually injured by a certain breach of international law. In this respect we have to differentiate between 1) measures adopted by international organisations against their member states, on the basis of the constitutive act of

1 See, e.g., Charter of the United Nations (opened for signature 24 June 1945, entered into force 24 October 1945) 1 UNTS XVI (UN Charter) art 1; Statute of the Council of Europe (opened for signature 5 May 1949, entered into force 3 August 1949) ETS No 001, art 1; Constitutive Act of the African Union (opened for signature 11 July 2000, entered into force 26 May 2001) OAU Doc CAB/LEG/23.15, art 3. See also Jan Klabbers, 'What Role for International Organizations in the Promotion of Community Interests? Reflections on the Ideology of Functionalism' in Eyal Benvenisti and Georg Nolte (eds), *Community Interests Across International Law* (Oxford University Press 2018) 86.

2 'Draft Articles on the Responsibility of International Organisations' (ARIO) in *Report of the International Law Commission on its 63rd Session* (26 April – 3 June and 4 July–12 August 2011), supplement No 10 A/66/10, art 49.3; See section 3.2 below.

a particular international organisation and 2) measures adopted by international organisations on the basis of the general international law of countermeasures. Examples of the former are sanctions adopted by the United Nations Security Council (UNSC) on the basis of the Article 41 under the Chapter VII of the United Nations Charter in cases of a threat to the peace, breach of the peace, or act of aggression;[3] European Union (EU) sanctions on the basis of the Article 7 of the Treaty of the European Union (TEU) in response to a clear risk of a serious breach or a serious and persistent breach of the EU's fundamental values;[4] and African Union (AU) sanctions in response to unconstitutional changes of government on the basis of Article 30 of the Constitutive Act of the AU.[5] In these instances international organisations protect community interests as embodied in their constitutive acts. More important for the purpose of

3 UN Charter, art 39. UN's collective security system is commonly considered as an important regime governing the protection of the community interest of the international peace and security. See, e.g., Giorgio Gaja, 'The Protection of General Interests in the International Community' (2011) 364 Recueil des Cours de l'Académie de Droit International 74–96; Bruno Simma, 'From Bilateralism to Community Interest in International Law' (1994) 250 Recueil des Cours de l'Académie de Droit International 236. For more on UN sanctions, see e.g.: Vera Gowlland-Debbas, *United Nations Sanctions and International Law* (Volume 1, Brill | Nijhoff 2001) and Larissa van den Herik (ed), *Research Handbook on UN Sanctions and International Law* (Edward Elgar Publishing 2017).

4 Consolidated version of the Treaty on European Union (adopted 26 October 2012) OJ C 326 (TEU) art. 2 and 7. For more on this, see: Maruša T Veber, 'Safeguarding Fundamental Values of the EU Through the Adoption of Sanctions' (2020) 4 University of Vienna Law Review 37; Stelio Mangiameli, 'Article 2 [The Homogeneity Clause]' in Hermann-Josef Blanke and Stelio Mangiameli (eds), *The Treaty on European Union (TEU). A Commentary* (Springer 2013); Stelio Mangiameli and Gabrialla Saputelli, 'Article 7 [The Principles of the Federal Coercion]' in Hermann-Josef Blanke and Stelio Mangiameli (eds), *The Treaty on European Union (TEU), A Commentary* (Springer 2013).

5 Constitutive Act of the AU art 30. See also Protocol Relating to the Establishment of the Peace and Security Council of the African Union (opened for signature 9 July 2002, entered into force 26 December 2003) art 7(g); African Charter on Democracy, Elections and Governance (opened for signature 30 January 2007, entered into force 15 February 2012) DOC EX CL /301 (X), art. 23 and 25; Rules of Procedure of the Assembly of the Union (9–10 July 2002) AU Doc ASS/AU/2(I) – a Rule 37; Assembly of the African Union, Decision on the Prevention of Unconstitutional Changes of Government and Strengthening of the Capacity of the AU to Manage such Situations (2 February 2010) Assembly/AU/Dec 269(XIV) Rev 1, 2. See also Konstantinos Magliveras 'The Sanctioning System of the African Union: Part Success, Part Failure?' (2011) an Institute of Security Studies Expert Roundtable on The African Union: The First Ten Years, Addis Ababa, Ethiopia.

this chapter, however, are situations in which international organisations adopt measures for the protection of community interests against their members or non-members – not on the basis of their constitutive acts, but on the basis of the general international law of countermeasures. This was the case in the following examples: the expulsion of South Africa from the Universal Postal Union (UPU) and its suspension from the World Health Organisation (WHO) and World Meteorological Organisation (WMO) due to its apartheid policies; the suspension of Liberia from the Economic Community of West African States (ECOWAS) in response to human rights violations in the country; the suspension of Syria's Arab League (AL) membership and the AL's adoption of economic sanctions in response to violence and human rights violations in Syria; and EU's economic measures against third states (such as Argentina, Myanmar, Syria, and Zimbabwe) in response to violations of human rights, humanitarian law, and the prohibition of aggression.[6] Under the general international law of responsibility, all these measures – occasionally referred to as 'solidarity measures',[7] 'collective countermeasures',[8] 'community measures',[9] or 'third-party countermeasures'[10] – can arguably be termed as countermeasures[11] adopted by a subject other than an injured subject.[12]

The following preliminary caveats further delineate the aim of this contribution. It aims to clarify the interpretation of secondary rules applicable to the adoption of countermeasures by international organisations and pinpoint the controversies embodied in these rules. While I acknowledge that international organisations can protect

6 For more on this, see section 3.3. below.

7 James Crawford, 'The Relationship Between Sanctions and Countermeasures' in Vera Gowlland-Debbas, *United Nations Sanctions and International Law* (Volume 1, Brill | Nijhoff 2001) 57–68.

8 Linos-Alexandre Sicilianos, 'Countermeasures in Response to grave violations of obligations owed to the international community' in James Crawford and others (eds), *The Law of International Responsibility* (OUP 2010) 1137.

9 Jarna Petman, 'Resort to Economic Sanctions by not Directly Affected States' in Laura Picchio Forlati and Linos-Alexandre Sicilianos (eds), *Economic Sanctions in International Law* (Brill | Njihoff 2004) 315.

10 Martin Dawidowicz, *Third-Party Countermeasures in International Law* (CUP 2017).

11 These measures are termed in this chapter as 'countermeasures', although the ILC uses the notion of 'lawful measures.' See ILC, 'Draft Articles on Responsibility of States for Internationally Wrongful Acts, with commentaries' in *Report of the International Law Commission on its 53rd Session* (23 April–1 June and 2 July–10 August 2001) UN Doc A/56/10, (ARSIWA) art 54 and ARIO, art 57. See, however, commentary to Article 57 ARIO where the term 'countermeasures' is used instead of 'lawful measures.'

12 See ARSIWA art. 48 and 54; ARIO art. 49 and 57. See also section 3.2 below.

community interests by adopting measures under other relevant international legal regimes, such as treaty law,[13] those will not be elaborated on in this chapter, which is confined to the adoption of countermeasures in response to *erga omnes* obligations. It is also acknowledged that expressions of community interests other than *erga omnes* and *jus cogens* exist, such as *erga omnes partes* obligations, but their protection is not explored here. Finally, this chapter is not meant to provide an exhaustive overview of practice relating to the adoption of countermeasures by international organisations in the defence of the community interest, but is confined to some selected cases considered important for our discussion.

This chapter first clarifies the relevant basic concepts, including international organisations, community interests, and the distinctions and convergences between peremptory norms of international law (*jus cogens*) and *erga omnes* obligations (section 2). This is followed by a section on the protection of community interests by international organisations (section 3) in which a distinction is made between the invocation of responsibility and the adoption of countermeasures by injured international organisations (section 3.1) and the invocation of responsibility and the adoption of countermeasures by organisations other than injured international organisations for the protection of the community interest (section 3.2). The chapter then turns to an analysis of the relevant practice of international organisations when adopting countermeasures without the underlying communitarian norm breached being among the functions of the organisation in question (section 3.3.1.) and situations where such norms are embedded in the constitutive act of the international organisation (section 3.3.2.). Finally, the chapter offers some concluding remarks (section 4).

2. CLARIFYING BASIC CONCEPTS

2.1. COMMUNITY INTERESTS

The idea of community interests has been acknowledged in international law since the very beginnings of the modern sovereignty-based

13 E.g., Human rights clauses in EU development aid agreements. See, e.g., Eibe Riedel and Martin Will, 'Human Rights Clauses in External Agreements of the EC', in Philip Alston (ed) *The EU and Human Rights* (OUP 1999) 723; Lorand Bartels, *Human Rights Conditionality in the EU's International Agreements* (OUP 2005).

international legal order.[14] However, it is only recently that the protection of individual interests in bilateral relationships has shifted towards a greater recognition of community interests, and that these interests have come to be recognised as legally protected – allowing for their protection not only by injured subjects, but also by those not considered injured by the breach.[15]

While the existence of community interests is uncontested, the notion remains evasive and its exact scope, identification, and coming into being are controversial. For the purpose of this chapter, community interests are understood as those that are (i) shared among multiple stakeholders and (ii) bestow subjects that are not necessarily injured by the breach of the norm encompassing the interest with standing to protect them. This chapter is therefore confined to an analysis of arguably one of the most prominent normative expressions of community interests, *erga omnes* obligations. It also, however, touches upon peremptory norms of international law (*jus cogens*) where appropriate or necessary. *Erga omnes* and *jus cogens* are interrelated but distinct concepts, and their understanding or comparison is sometimes warranted for the analysis of the role played by international organisations in the protection of community interests.

2.1.1. *Standing to Protect Community Interest*

Legal interests correspond to standing under international law, sometimes also referred to as the entitlement[16] of subjects that are holders of

---

14 See Santiago Villalpando, 'The Legal Dimension of the International Community: How Community Interests are Protected in International Law' (2010) 21(2) EJIL 387, 390; Georges Abi-Saab, 'Whither the International Community?' (1998) 9(2) EJIL 248, 249–251; Georg Nolte, 'The International Law Commission and Community Interests' (2017) KFG Working Paper Series No 7, Berlin Potsdam Research Group 'The International Rule of Law – Rise or Decline?' 5 <https://papers.ssrn.com/sol3/papers.cfm?abstract_id=3136943> accessed 15 January 2021; Laura Picchio Forlati, 'The Legal Core of International Economic Sanctions' in Laura Picchio Forlati and Linos-Alexandre Sicilianos (eds), *Economic Sanctions in International Law* (Brill | Njihoff 2004) 144; Simma (n 3) 217; Samantha Besson, 'Community Interests in International Law: Whose Interests Are They and How Should We Best Identify Them?' in Eyal Benvenisti and Georg Nolte (eds), *Community Interests Across International Law* (OUP 2018); Ulrich Fastenrath and others (eds), *From Bilateralism to Community Interest: Essays in Honour of Bruno Simma* (OUP 2011); Wolfgang Benedek and others (eds), *The Common Interest in International Law* (Intersentia 2014).

15 See ARSIWA art 54 and ARIO art 57. See also Simma (n 3); Fastenrath and others (n 14); Nolte (n 14).

16 See e.g., ARIO, commentary to Article 43, para 3; VCLT art 60.1. See also Lori Fisler Damrosch, 'Enforcing International Law Through Non-Forcible Measures' (1997)

a particular interest. There is no uniform concept of standing in international law and it is a notion that is used in many different ways, but it usually corresponds to the notion of 'right' – the right to make a claim, the right to enforce duty, or the right to invoke responsibility. Multiple relevant standings exist in relation to subjects having a legal interest in the observance of particular international rule, such as standing to start international proceedings (at the International Court of Justice (ICJ), for example)[17] or to request reparations.[18] This chapter only focuses on standing related to the right to enforce international legal rules through the adoption of countermeasures.

Standing to adopt sanctions has traditionally been perceived as a right of the victim of an illegal act[19] based on the reciprocity of rights and duties, stemming from the classical theory of international responsibility.[20] In these situations the injured subject has an individual interest in seeing the concerned obligation being complied with by the wrongdoing subject and is entitled, among other things, to adopt certain measures against that subject. This organisation of relations oriented around bilateral and individual interests[21] worked well in interactions based on the fulfilment of individual interests, but faced difficulties in cases where common values such as human rights needed to be protected.[22] Historical changes and the development of international law, including through the case law of

---

269 Recueil des Cours 53; Christian J Tams, *Enforcing Obligations Erga Omnes in International Law* (Cambridge University Press 2005) 12. The notion of entitlement is often used interchangeably with the notion of standing. See, e.g., Jean d'Aspremont, 'The Multifaceted Concept of the Autonomy of International Organizations and International Legal Discourse,' in Richard Collins and Nigel D White (eds), *International Organizations and the Idea of Autonomy* (Routledge 2011) 71.

17 See James Crawford, 'The Standing of States: A Critique of Article 40 of the ILC's Draft Articles on State Responsibility' in Mads Andenas and Duncan Fairgrieve, *Judicial Review in International Perspective: Liber Amicorum in Honour of Lord Slynn of Hadley* (Volume 2, Kluwer Law International 2000) 23; Angela Del Vecchio, 'International Courts and Tribunals, Standing' Max Planck Encyclopedia of International Law (OUP 2010).

18 See ARSIWA art 31.

19 Kay Hailbronner, 'Sanctions and Third Parties and the Concept of International Public Order' (1992) 30 Archiv des Völkerrechts 2, 3. See also Karl Zemanek, 'The Unilateral Enforcement of International Obligations' (1987) 47 Heidelberg Journal of International Law 32, 37, 720; Villalpando (n 14) 405; Tams (n 16) 48.

20 See, e.g., Dionisio Anzilotti, 'La Responsabilité Internationale des Etats à Raison des Dommages Soufferts par des Étrangers' (1906) 13 Revue Générale de Droit International Public 5, 13; Clyde Eagleton, *The Responsibility of States in International Law* (New York University Press 1928) 3, 5; Villalpando (n 14) 400.

21 Villalpando (n 14) 400.

22 ibid 405.

the ICJ[23] and the work of the ILC on the law of treaties and the law of responsibility, have led to the acknowledgement of rules that do not fit the pattern of bilateralism and subsequently also of rules giving standing to subjects other than injured by the underlying breach, as is the case with *erga omnes* obligations.[24]

2.1.2. Erga Omnes *Obligations*

The ICJ famously introduced the idea of *erga omnes* obligations in the *Barcelona Traction* case as obligations 'owed towards international community as a whole', thereby distinguishing them from obligations 'arising vis-à-vis another State'.[25] Due to their fundamental character, 'all States can be held to have a legal interest in their protection' and accordingly have to be distinguished from their treaty-based counterpart, *erga omnes partes*, which is not elaborated in this chapter.[26] Two parts of Court's pronouncement are important: 1) the confirmation of the universality of *erga omnes* obligations, meaning these obligations are owed to the international community as a whole; and 2) the solidarity of *erga omnes* obligations, that is, because they are owed to the international community as a whole, non-injured subjects can be held to have a legal interest in their protection.[27] *Erga omnes* obligations therefore transcend the traditional bilateral nature of obligations by affecting the rules of

---

23 *Barcelona Traction, Light and Power Company, Limited, (Belgium v Spain)* (Judgment) [1970] ICJ Rep 3, paras 33–34; *Application of the Convention on the Prevention and Punishment of the Crime of Genocide (Bosnia and Herzegovina v Serbia and Montenegro)* (Preliminary Objections, Judgment) [1996] ICJ Rep 595, para 31; *Application of the Convention on the Prevention and Punishment of the Crime of Genocide (Croatia v Serbia)* (Judgment) [2015] ICJ Rep 3, para 87; *Questions relating to the Obligation to Prosecute or Extradite (Belgium v Senegal)* (Judgment) [2012] ICJ Rep 422, paras 68–69; *Application of the Convention on the Prevention and Punishment of the Crime of Genocide (The Gambia v Myanmar)* (Order of 23 January 2020) [2020] ICJ Rep 69, 12–13; *Obligations concerning Negotiations relating to Cessation of the Nuclear Arms Race and to Nuclear Disarmament (Marshall Islands v Pakistan)* (Application) [2014] General List No 159, para 35.

24 ARSIWA art. 42 and 48; ARIO art. 43 and 49. ILC, 'Fourth report on State responsibility, by Mr. Gaetano Arangio-Ruiz, Special Rapporteur' (1992) Yearbook of the International Law Commission, UN Doc A/CN.4/444 and Add.1–3, Volume II(1), para 130.

25 *Barcelona Traction* (n 23) [33–34]. For an in-depth analysis of the *erga omnes* obligations see Maurizio Ragazzi, *The Concept of International Obligations Erga Omnes* (OUP 1997).

26 *Erga omnes partes* is not perceived as conventional equivalent of obligations *erga omnes*. Tams (n 16) 125.

27 Ragazzi (n 25) 17.

standing to enforce such rights and the invocation of responsibility.[28] This manifests itself in the right of subjects other than an injured subject to invoke responsibility and institute judicial proceedings, or to adopt countermeasures to enforce such rights.[29] It is on the latter consequence that this paper focuses (see section 3).

Examples of existing obligations that have *erga omnes* status include the prohibition on the act of aggression and genocide, principles and rules concerning the basic rights of the human person, including protection from slavery, racial discrimination,[30] self-determination of peoples,[31] and some obligations of international humanitarian law.[32]

The notion of the 'international community as a whole', with interests, values, principles and procedures common to all it members[33] and towards which *erga omnes* obligations are owed, is not a separate juridical entity,[34] but is composed of the international legal subjects which are addressees of such obligations. The scope of subjects forming this community has been subject to debate. Some scholars have advocated for a state-centric view of the 'international community as a whole',[35] but it seems more

---

28 *Barcelona Traction* (n 23) [33–34]; Tams (n 16) 99. For other effects see ibid 106–116. See also, ARSIWA art 48 and corresponding commentary.

29 ARSIWA art. 48 and 54; ARIO art. 49 and 57. Gaja (n 3) 21; Sicilianos (n 8) 1137. For relevant ICJ practice see n 23. See also Gentian Zyberi, 'The Role and Contribution of International Courts in Furthering Peace as an Essential Community Interest' in Cecilia M Bailliet (ed), *Research Handbook on International Law and Peace* (Edward Elgar Publishing 2019) 424–448; Bruno Simma, 'Human Rights Before the International Court of Justice: Community Interest Coming to Life?' in Christian J Tams and James Sloan (eds), *The Development of International Law by the International Court of Justice* (OUP 2013) 301–325; James Crawford 'Responsibility for Breaches of Communitarian Norms: An Appraisal of Article 48 of the ILC Articles on Responsibility of States for Internationally Wrongful Acts' in Ulrich Fastenrath and others (eds), *From Bilateralism to Community Interest: Essays in Honour of Bruno Simma* (OUP 2011) 230; Erika De Wet, 'Invoking Obligations *Erga Omnes* in the Twenty-First Century: Progressive Developments Since Barcelona Traction' (2013) 38 South African Yearbook of International Law 1, 2–19.

30 *Barcelona Traction* (n 23) [34]; Ragazzi (n 25) 74–117.

31 *Case Concerning East Timor (Portugal v. Australia)* (Judgement) [1995] ICJ Rep 90, para 29.

32 *Legal Consequences of the Construction of a Wall in the Occupied Palestinian Territory* (Advisory Opinion) [2004] ICJ Rep 136, paras 155–157.

33 Bruno Simma and Andreas L Paulus, 'The "International Community": Facing the Challenge of Globalization' (1998) 9(2) EJIL 266, 268.

34 *Legal Consequences for States of the Continued Presence of South Africa in Namibia (South West Africa) Notwithstanding Security Council Resolution 276 (1970)* (Advisory Opinion, dissenting opinion of Judge Sir Gerald Fitzmaurice) [1971] ICJ Rep 56, para 229. On this discussion, see also Gaja (n 3) 26–33.

35 Abi-Saab (n 14) 248–265, 249; Hermann Mosler, 'The International Society as a Legal Community' (1974) 140 Recueil des Cours 140, 32; Roberto Ago, 'The International

accurate to also include international organisations, being as they are independent subjects of international law.[36] This has been acknowledged by the ILC[37] and can be implied from the *Barcelona Traction* case, in which the court refrained from including specific reference to states in its wording.[38] With the exception of the Vienna Convention on the Law of Treaties (VCLT)[39] and the Vienna Convention on the Law of Treaties between States and International Organizations or between International Organizations,[40] which relate to *jus cogens* norms, the phrase 'international community as a whole' without the mention of 'states' is included in the relevant documents.[41] We can therefore conclude that international organisations form part of the international community as a whole, meaning that *erga omnes* obligations are owed not only to all states but also to international organisations.[42]

Community and the International Organization' in René-Jean Dupuy (ed) *A Handbook on International Organizations* (Brill | Nijhoff 1998) 3.

36 See, e.g., James Crawford, 'Responsibility to the International Community as a Whole' (2001) 8(2) Indiana Journal of Global Legal Studies 303, 314.

37 Some States have advocated for the inclusion of expression 'international community of States as a whole' in ARSIWA, however, the Special Rapporteur rejected their views and expressly acknowledged that international community also includes entities other than States, e.g., the EU. See UNGA, 'Fourth Report on State Responsibility by Mr. James Crawford, Special Rapporteur' (2 April 2001) International Law Commission fifty-third session UN Doc A/CN.4/517, para 36; ARSIWA commentary, para 18. See also ARIO art 49 with commentaries, 78–79.

38 *Barcelona Traction* (n 23) [32–33].

39 VCLT art 53, confines *jus cogens* norms to those 'accepted and recognized by the international community of States as a whole'. The possibility to replace this phrase with 'international community as a whole' was the subject of debate in the ILC during its work on the draft convention on treaties between States and international organisations or between international organisations. The Special Rapporteur Reuter, however, was of the view that a wider notion of international community would not be accepted by some states and therefore retained expression from Article 53 of VCLT. ILC, 'Draft Articles on the Law of Treaties Between States and International Organizations or Between International Organizations' (1982) YILC, Volume II(2) (Commentary to Article 53) 56. See also Paolo Palchetti, 'Reactions by the European Union to Breaches of *Erga Omnes* Obligations' in Enzo Cannizzaro, *The European Union as an Actor in International Relations* (Kluwer Law International 2002) 219–230.

40 Vienna Convention on the Law of Treaties between States and International Organizations or between International Organizations (adopted 21 March 1986, not yet in force) art 53.

41 For a list of treaties, see ARSIWA commentary to Article 25, para 18, ft 404.

42 Eglantine Cujo, 'Invocation of Responsibility by International Organisations', in Crawford and others (eds), *The Law of International Responsibility* (OUP 2010) 977. See also Gaja (n 3) 25.

Together with the notion of *erga omnes*, peremptory norms of international law (*jus cogens*) are considered as the most important 'doctrinal expressions' of community interest.[43] Both concepts share the underlying idea of heightened protection of fundamental interests in the international community which transcend traditional bilateral relationships.[44] However, a distinction between two concepts is warranted at least in relation to their emphasis and focus, for the notion of *jus cogens* arguably relates to the very substance of particular norms and their non-derogability or priority,[45] whereas the focus of *erga omnes* relates more to the nature of the legal relationship deriving from that substantive obligation, to the fact that certain obligations are legally indivisible since a certain type of rule 'provides for obligations which bind simultaneously each and every State concerned with respect to all the others'.[46] Thus *erga omnes* obligations create certain procedural rights, standing on the part of subjects to invoke responsibility for the breach of that obligation.[47] As regards the relationship between *erga omnes* obligations and *jus cogens* norms, the most commonly adopted position is that all *jus cogens* norms have *erga omnes* effect, but in contrast not all *erga omnes* obligations have the status of *jus cogens* norms.[48] This view acknowledges that there exist *erga omnes* obligations which do not derive from *jus cogens* norms, such as those relating to environmental protection, human rights, and

---

43 Simma (n 3) 285.

44 See the contribution by Sarah Thin in this volume.

45 VCLT art. 53 and 64; Vienna Convention on the Law of Treaties between States and International Organizations or between International Organizations, art 53; ARSIWA, Part Two, Chapter Three; *Case Concerning Armed Activities on the Territory of the Congo (Democratic Republic of the Congo v Uganda)* (Judgment) [2005] ICJ Rep 168. See also, ILC, 'Statement of the Chairman of the Drafting Committee' (2016) Sixty-eight session, Draft Conclusion 2.

46 ILC (n 24) para 92. See also ARSIWA commentary, 111–112, par. 7; Alain Pellet, 'Conclusions' in Christian Tomuschat and Jean-Marc Thouvenin, *The Fundamental Rules of the International Legal Order* (Brill | Nijhoff 2006) 418.

47 Crawford (n 29) 227.

48 See, e.g., Santiago Villalpando, *L'émergence de la communauté internationale dans de la responsabilité des États* (Graduate Institute Publications 2005) 107; ILC (n 24) 34. For the link between *jus cogens* norms and *erga omnes* character of these norms see *Croatia v Serbia* (n 23) [87]. The ILC dealt with the two concepts separately and did not expressly mention the *erga omnes* nature of *jus cogen* norms. However, this can be inferred from the paragraph 3 of Article 41 ARSIWA stating that other consequences than those described in the Article, can be entailed in a breach of *jus cogens* norms. See also UNGA, 'Third report on peremptory norms of general international law (*jus cogens*) by Dire Tladi, Special Rapporteur' (12 February 2018) ILC seventieth session UN Doc A/CN.4/714, 30, 40–43.

common spaces.[49] The exact modalities of the relationship between the two concepts are not of fundamental importance for the present chapter; it rather suffices to make a conclusion that seems to be undisputed: peremptory norms of international law (*jus cogens*) establish obligations *erga omnes*, the breach of which concerns the international community as a whole.[50] For the purposes of this chapter *jus cogens* norms are therefore relevant only in so far as they overlap with *erga omnes* obligations, that is in terms of their effect on the rules of standing to adopt countermeasures and not their legal consequences *per se* (their non-derogability and voidness).

2.2. INTERNATIONAL ORGANISATIONS

When dealing with questions of the responsibility of international organisations, the ILC introduced the following definition of international organisations:[51]

> 'international organization' means an organization established by a treaty or other instrument governed by international law and possessing its own international legal personality.[52]

49 See, e.g., Gabčikovo-*Nagymaros Project (Hungary/Slovakia)* (Judgment, Separate Opinion of Vice-President Weeramantry) [1997] ICJ Rep 7, 117–118; Dinstein Yoram, 'The *Erga Omnes* Applicability of Human Rights' (1992) 30 Archiv des Völkerrechts 16; ILC, 'Conclusions of the Work of the Study Group on the Fragmentation of International Law: Difficulties Arising from the Diversification and Expansion of International Law' in *Report of the International Law Commission on its 58th Session* (1 May–9 June and 3 July–11 August 2006) UN Doc A/61/10, 421, para. 38.

50 UNGA (n 48) 40–43.

51 This chapter uses the term 'international organisations' as opposed to other terms such as 'public international organisation' and 'intergovernmental organisation' which are used by some scholars and instruments. See, e.g., International Court of Justice (ICJ) Statute in its Article 34 (using the term 'public international organisation'); Article 124 of the Charter of the Organisation of American States (uses the term 'intergovernmental organization.'). The term 'intergovernmental organization' is also used in, e.g., Article 2/1(i) of the VCLT (1969); Article 1/1(1) of the Vienna Convention on the Representation of States in their Relations with International Organizations of a Universal Character (1975); art 2.1 of the Vienna Convention on Succession of States in respect of Treaties (1978) and Article 2 of the Vienna Convention on the Law of Treaties between States and International Organizations or between International Organizations (1986). See also Henry Schermers and Niels Blokker, *International Institutional Law: Unity Within Diversity* (5th rev edn, Brill | Nijhoff 2011), 30, ft 115.

52 ARIO art 2. This is not considered as a general definition of international organisations for all purposes, but only for the purposes of ARIO. ARIO, commentary to Article 2, 6, para 1. For a critique of the ILC's definition, see Maurice Mendelson, 'The Definition of "International Organization" in the International Law Commission's Current

This chapter adopts the ILC definition and is therefore limited to the study of international organisations possessing international legal personality. This does not imply that all international organisations necessarily have such legal personality, but it does mean that international organisations with no legal personality cannot adopt countermeasures as subjects, separate from their member states.[53] In the absence of legal personality, only member states would be entitled to adopt countermeasures,[54] and that is not the subject of this chapter. The notion of legal personality is understood as a general international law attire, enabling international organisations to function in the international legal order, to bear rights and obligations on the international plane as distinct from their members.[55] Consequently international organisations are deemed to have access to coercive measures in the form of countermeasures to enforce such rights. This has been confirmed in the case law of the ICJ[56] and the work of the ILC on the responsibility of international organisations.[57]

It has to be acknowledged, however, that the question of which consequences stem from the international legal personality of international organisations is far more controversial than the scope of legal personality of states.[58] In particular, we have to distinguish between the notion of capacities and the notion of competences. The capacities of international organisations to operate on the international plane[59] encompass rights

Project on the Responsibility of International Organizations' in Maurizio Ragazzi (ed), *International Responsibility Today: Essays in Memory of Oscar Schachter* (Brill | Nijhoff 2005) 371.

53 Catherine Brölmann, *The Institutional Veil in Public International Law: International Organisations and the Law of Treaties* (Hart Publishing 2007) 72.

54 Schermers and Blokker (n 51) 32.

55 ibid para 44; *Reparation for Injuries Suffered in the Service of the United Nations* (Advisory Opinion) [1949] ICJ Rep 174, 179; Christiane Ahlborn, 'The Rules of International Organizations and the Law of International Responsibility' (2011) 8 International Organizations Law Review 397, 416–417; Chittharanjan Felix Amerasinghe, *Principles of the Institutional Law of International Organizations* (2nd rev edn, CUP 2005) 78.

56 *Reparation for Injuries Suffered in the Service of the UN* (n 55) 177–179. See also Frédéric Dopagne, 'Sanctions and Countermeasures by International Organisations' in Richard Collins and Nigel D White (eds), *International Organizations and the Idea of Autonomy* (Routledge 2011) 181.

57 ARIO art 2(a).

58 See *Reparation for Injuries Suffered in the Service of the UN* (n 55), where the ICJ recognised, e.g., that the UN has international personality, however this '[is not the same thing as saying that it is a State, which it certainly is not, or that its legal personality and rights and duties are the same as those of a State.'

59 ibid.

and duties which flow from general international law, for example to be active or passive subjects of responsibility.[60] Capacity is therefore not dependent on the internal law of a particular international organisation but on general international law. Competences to adopt concrete acts and decisions, on the other hand, are determined by the rules of the organisation.[61] The notion of competences therefore relates to the powers of an international organisation, as defined by its constitutive act, and are therefore dependent on the rules of the organisation rather than upon general international law. International organisations are established for specific purposes and with certain functions. As opposed to states, which possesses a 'totality of international rights and duties recognised by international law',[62] it is generally accepted that the competences of international organisations are functionally defined.[63] This is often referred as the principle of speciality,[64] the principle of functional limitation,[65] the attribution principle,[66] or the doctrine of functional necessity.[67] In essence it means that while international organisations possess certain capacities to act in general international law[68] *ipso facto*, on the basis of their legal personality, exercise of capacities in concrete cases is dependent upon the competences of international organisations, which are determined by their internal rules.[69] Capacities are therefore sometimes referred

60 Other capacities include, e.g., treaty-making capacity. See Amerasinghe (n 55) 101; Manuel Rama-Montaldo, 'International Legal Personality and Implied Powers of International Organizations' (1970) 44 British Yearbook of International Law 111, 139–140.

61 Brölmann (n 53) 91. Article 2(b) ARIO defines the rules of the organisation as including 'in particular, the constituent instruments, decisions, resolutions and other acts of the international organization adopted in accordance with those instruments, and established practice of the organization.'

62 *Reparation for Injuries Suffered in the Service of the UN* (n 55) 180.

63 *Legality of the Use by a State of Nuclear Weapons in Armed Conflict* (Advisory Opinion) [1996] ICJ Rep 66, para 25; *Jurisdiction of the European Commission of the Danube Between Galatz and Braila* (Advisory Opinion) [1927] PCIJ Rep Series B No 14, 64; Schermers, and Blokker (n 51) 18, paras 16 and 158; Brölmann (n 53) 285–312.

64 *Legality of the Use by a State of Nuclear Weapons in Armed Conflict* (n 63); *Jurisdiction of the European Commission of the Danube* (n 63); ARIO commentary, 47, para 7.

65 Rama-Montaldo (n 60) 141; Brölmann (n 53) 82.

66 Schermers and Blokker (n 51) 159.

67 Jan Klabbers, 'Constitutionalism Lite' (2004) 1 International Organizations Law Review 31, 39–40.

68 Brölmann (n 53) 25.

69 The exact scope of competences of international organsiations has been subject to different theories, e.g., doctrine of attributed competences (international organisations possess only those competences expressly foreseen in the constitutive acts); doctrine of implied competences (competences can be implied from the provisions of

to as 'skeletal in their incidence, their content and extent being subject to implication or express grant'.[70] As will be explained below, the legal capacity of international organisations under general international law to adopt countermeasures should be considered as 'inherent' to their international legal personality.[71] On the other hand, the competence of an organisation to adopt a particular countermeasure in a concrete situation pertains to the rules of that particular organisation. Thus international organisations must comply with their own internal rules when adopting concrete countermeasures.[72]

However, the above-described distinction between capacity and competences is commonly disregarded, and the functions and the rules of organisation of a particular international organisation are thought to delimit not only its competences but also its capacities. Even the ICJ, in the famous *Reparations* case, failed to distinguish between these two notions and seemed to confine its reasoning to the question of competences; it did not explain the capacities of international organisations.[73] This reasoning was also adopted by the ILC when discussing the capacity of international organisations to invoke international responsibility in its Articles on Responsibility of International Organisations (ARIO). The ILC therein distinguishes between two situations: 1) invocation of responsibility by international organisations as injured subjects and as subjects other than the injured subject for the protection of collective interest; and 2) invocation of responsibility by international organisations as subjects other than the injured subject for the protection of obligations owed to the international community as a whole. While in the first situations international organisations are entitled to invoke responsibility and adopt countermeasures on an equal footing with states, their ability to protect

constitutive acts or the object and purposes of the organization) and doctrine of inherent competences (competences are inherent to international organisations, i.e. deriving from their organisationhood). More on this, see Schermers and Blokker (n 51) 155–162; Nigel D White, *The Law of International Organisations* (3rd edn, Manchester University Press 2016) 121–146.

70 Amerasinghe (n 55) 99.

71 Frédéric Dopagne, *Les Contre-Mesures des Organisations Internationals* (Anthemis 2010); Frédéric Dopagne, 'Countermeasures by International Organisations: the Decentralised Society in the Heart of the Institutionalised Society' in Hélène Ruiz Fabri, Rüdiger Wolfrum and Jana Gogolin, *Select Proceedings of the European Society of International Law* (Volume 2, Hart Publishing 2010) 205. For a contrary view, see' Palchetti (n 39).

72 Dopagne (n 56) 178–195.

73 *Reparation for Injuries Suffered in the Service of the UN* (n 55) 180.

the community interest through invoking responsibility and adopting countermeasures is curtailed by the functions of the organisation (see section 3 below).

Finally, it has to be acknowledged that scholars nurture caution when it comes to assessing the activities of international organisations as autonomous subjects of international law, since it is sometimes difficult to differentiate between the activities and practice of states and of international organisations as such.[74] When international organisations adopt countermeasures in their own capacity as subjects of international law, the conduct must be attributable to them specifically, and not to their member states. This chapter demonstrates that occasions exist in which international organisations adopt countermeasures in response to breaches of *erga omnes* obligations and subsequently contribute to the protection of community interests.

Under the law of responsibility the basic relevant rule regarding the attribution of conduct to international organisations states that 'conduct of an organ or agent of an international organization in the performance of functions of that organ or agent shall be considered an act of that organization under international law, whatever position the organ or agent holds in respect of the organization.'[75] Sanctions amounting to countermeasures are typically adopted by organs of international organisations. One case where this question seems to be fairly straightforward, is the adoption of countermeasures by the EU. It is accepted today that the EU, as a supranational organisation, often acts as an independent subject of international law, separate from its member states.[76] This is especially the case when EU adopts countermeasures in the form of economic measures which fall into the common commercial policy and are therefore under the exclusive competence of the EU. Such measures are adopted by a regulation which is an act of legislation binding on all member states and

---

74 See, e.g., in relation to customary international law: UNGA, 'Second report on identification of customary international law by Michael Wood, Special Rapporteur' (22 May 2014) ILC sixty-sixth session UN Doc A/CN.4/672, para 43; UNGA, 'Third report on the identification of customary international law by Michael Wood, Special Rapporteur' (27 March 2015) ILC Sixty-seventh session UN Doc A/CN.4/682, para 71; Tullio Treves, 'Customary International Law' Max Planck Encyclopedia of International Law (OUP 2006) para 50.

75 ARIO art 6. See also UNGA, 'Report of the International Law Commission (sixty-first session)' (4 May – 5 June and 6 July – 7 August 2009) UN Doc A/64/10, 60 and ft 79, with regards to the decision of the Swiss Federal Council of 30 October 1996, document VPB 61.75. See ARIO Commentary to Article 6, 55, para 4 ft 103.

76 See UNGA (n 74) para 77.

has specific features of EU law. This was acknowledged by the EU itself[77] and is supported in scholarly writing.[78]

3. THE PROTECTION OF COMMUNITY INTERESTS BY INTERNATIONAL ORGANISATIONS THROUGH THE ADOPTION OF COUNTERMEASURES

Countermeasures are one of the circumstances precluding wrongfulness, giving a subject injured by a wrongful act a right to take measures that would otherwise be contrary to international law.[79] They are governed by the Articles on Responsibility of States for Internationally Wrongful Acts (ARSIWA),[80] ARIO,[81] and customary international law.[82] In essence, their aim is to ensure cessation of the alleged breach and where appropriate ensure reparation for injury.[83] Apart from 'traditional' countermeasures that can be adopted by states or international organisations injured by a previous breach of international law, in Article 54 of the ARSIWA and Article 57 of ARIO the ILC presupposed a 'saving clause' opening up the possibility of states and international organisations other than injured state or international organisation adopting measures in response to breaches of obligations 'owed to the international community as a whole', that is, *erga omnes* obligations. The ILC left the legality of the adoption of such countermeasures by not directly injured subjects to be determined by the further development of international law.[84] In the meantime, due to increased practice in this respect, acceptance of the legality of such measures is becoming firmly established among international lawyers[85]

---

77 See the statement on behalf of the European Union in 'Summary Record of the 23rd Meeting' (Sixth Committee, 5 December 2013) UN doc A/C.6/68/SR.23, para 37.

78 See, e.g., Palchetti (n 39).

79 ARSIWA art 22 and Part Three, Chapter II.

80 ARSIWA Part Two.

81 ARIO Part Two.

82 *Naulilaa Incident Arbitration (Portugal v. Germany)* [1928] 2 RIAA 1012; *Gabčíkovo-Nagymaros Project* (n 57); *Air Services Agreement of 27 March 1946 between the United States of America and France* [1978] RIAA Vol. XVIII.

83 ARSIWA art. 22 and 49.

84 ARSIWA Commentary, 139.

85 Dawidowicz (n 10); Martin Dawidowicz, 'Third-Party Countermeasures: A Progressive Development of International Law?' (2016) 29 Questions of International Law, Zoom-In 3 <http://www.qil-qdi.org/third-party-countermeasures-progressive-development-international-law/> accessed 15 January 2021; Tams (n 16); Dopagne (n 71); Dopagne

and other important professional organisations on international law, such as the Institut de droit international.[86] It is therefore premised here that such a standing exists in international law.

Countermeasures are traditionally studied from the perspective of interstate relations, but the possibility of international organisations adopting such measures has been confirmed through practice (see section below) and was explicitly acknowledged by the ILC in its work on responsibility of international organisations.[87] States' and international organisations' regimes of 'classical' countermeasures are strikingly similar, the latter being more or less a reproduction of relevant articles from ARSIWA. An important difference, however, exists between the two regimes in relation to the possibility of countermeasures adopted by states or international organisations not directly injured by a previous breach,[88] namely in cases of breaches of *erga omnes* obligations. It is on these differences that this chapter focuses.

A wide range of types of countermeasures are adopted by international organisations. These include but are not limited to complete or partial interruption of economic relations, import and export restrictions, freezing of foreign assets, embargoes, travel restrictions, expulsion from or suspension of membership, suspension of aviation agreements, and severance of diplomatic relations.[89]

3.1. THE INVOCATION OF RESPONSIBILITY AND THE ADOPTION OF COUNTERMEASURES BY INJURED INTERNATIONAL ORGANISATIONS

It is uncontested that an international organisation, like a state, has a standing to adopt countermeasures when it is considered injured by previous

---

(n 56) 178–195; d'Aspremont (n 16) 63–86; Elena Katselli Proukaki, *The Problem of Enforcement in International Law: Countermeasures, the Non-Injured State and the Idea of International Community* (Routledge 2010); Sicilianos (n 8) 1137–1148. For the contrary view, see James Crawford, *State Responsibility: The General Part* (CUP 2013) 706, 709.

86 Institut de Droit International, 'Obligations and Rights *Erga Omnes* in International Law' (2005) Fifth Commission, Krakow sessions.

87 ARIO art 21(1).

88 ARSIWA art 54.

89 See, e.g., Council of the European Union (CEU) (Press Office), 'EU Restrictive Measures' (2014) Factsheet <http://www.consilium.europa.eu/uedocs/cms_data/docs/pressdata/EN/foraff/135804.pdf> accessed 15 January 2021.

internationally wrongful act either because the obligation breached is owed to it individually or because it is specially affected by a breach of *erga omnes (partes)* obligation.[90] On such occasions it enjoys general capacity under international law to invoke responsibility and subsequently adopt countermeasures. In other words, international organisations enjoy such capacity on an equal footing with states.[91] As subjects of international law, international organisations can partake in mechanisms of international responsibility in a similar way as states, as confirmed by the ICJ in the *Reparations for injuries* advisory opinion in relation to standing to invoke responsibility:

> It cannot be doubted that the Organization has the capacity to bring an international claim against one of its Members which has caused injury to it by a breach of its international obligations towards it.[92]

This is not controversial, and it is supported by legal writings.[93] Special Rapporteur Gaja has therefore proposed to adapt the existing meaning of 'injured State' in Article 42 ARSIWA to include injured international organisations for the purposes of ARIO. Article 43 ARIO, governing the invocation of responsibility by international organisations, exclude reference to the rules or particular functions of the organisation.

> While the rules of the internal law of a State will determine which is the State organ that is competent for bringing a claim, in the case of an international organization reference would have to be made to the rules of the organization … Since the requirement that the conduct of the organization be appraised according to its pertinent rules is of general application, it seems preferable not to make a specific reference to the rules of the organization in part three. This would also be consistent with the fact that the articles on responsibility of States for internationally wrongful acts do not address the question of which State organ is to be regarded as competent for bringing or withdrawing a claim.[94]

This passage reveals that indeed there exists a general capacity of international organisations to invoke responsibility, but in order to make

90 ARSIWA art 42. See: Dopagne (n 56) 180–181; d'Aspremont (n 16); see also *Reparation for Injuries Suffered in the Service of the UN* (n 55) 177–179.

91 UNGA, 'Sixth Report on Responsibility of International Organizations by Mr. Giorgio Gaja, Special Rapporteur' (1 April 2008) ILC sixtieth session UN Doc A/CN.4/597, 23, paras 28–29.

92 *Reparation for Injuries Suffered in the Service of the UN* (n 55) 180.

93 d'Aspremont (n 16); Dopagne (n 56); Dopagne (n 71).

94 UNGA (n 91) 20, para 11.

a claim in a concrete situation, the rules of the organisation will have to be applied; it will depend on the concrete competences of the organisation and powers of its organs.

3.2. THE INVOCATION OF RESPONSIBILITY AND THE ADOPTION OF COUNTERMEASURES BY INTERNATIONAL ORGANISATIONS OTHER THAN AN INJURED INTERNATIONAL ORGANISATION FOR THE PROTECTION OF COMMUNITY INTEREST

What is disputed and less clear is whether, and to what extent, these organisations have standing to adopt countermeasures to vindicate a community interest. In other words, controversy pertains to situations where international organisations cannot be perceived as individually injured but where the breach that triggers the measures concerned is of such nature that it allows a response of a broader category of international legal subjects (the international community as a whole). As opposed to states, which are by definition entitled to adopt countermeasures in the community interest, it is not entirely settled in the international legal scholarship whether international organisations too can be perceived to have such capacity inherent within their legal personality, or whether this is something that has to be provided for in their constitutive acts.[95]

In relation to this question, the ILC has adopted an approach different from the one described above. When preparing draft articles, Special Rapporteur Gaja has noted that as opposed to the first situation, the question of whether an international organisation has standing to invoke the responsibility of another international organisation (or state) for the breach of an obligation owed to the international community as a whole is much more difficult and complex, and the relevant practice scarce.[96] Finally, the ILC has limited the capacity of international organisations to invoke responsibility with their functions:

> An international organization other than an injured international organization is entitled to invoke the responsibility of another international organization in accordance with paragraph 4 if the obligation breached is owed to the international community as a whole and safeguarding the interest of the

[95] Jan Klabbers, *An Introduction to International Institutional Law* (2nd edn, CUP 2009) 53.

[96] UNGA (n 91) 23–24, paras 31–33.

> international community as a whole underlying the obligation breached is within the functions of the international organization invoking responsibility.[97]

While Article 49 ARIO is based on and corresponds to Article 48 ARSIWA governing the invocation of responsibility by states other than an injured state, there is one important difference between the two. Article 49 ARIO provides for an additional requirement: the obligation breached, to which an international organisation is responding by invoking responsibility, has to be within the functions of a concerned international organisation. In other words international organisations will have standing to invoke responsibility as a response to a breach of an obligation owed to the international community as a whole, and subsequently to adopt countermeasures under Article 57 ARIO, only in cases where they act in the 'exercise of functions that have been attributed to it by member States.'[98] This means that an international organisation is precluded from reacting to those breaches of *erga omnes* obligations which are not among the functions attributed to it by its member states. In terms of adopting countermeasures, which complements the invocation of responsibility, this means that an international organisation not having competence in the areas of, for example, the prohibition of genocide or apartheid, will not have standing to adopt measures in protection of these obligations regardless of their community nature, that is, their being owed to the international community as a whole. While this view has gained some support in the ILC discussions,[99] it is not endorsed in the practice of international organisations and has been criticised by some scholars.[100]

In Article 49(3) ARIO the ILC made a general international law capacity of international organisations to invoke responsibility

---

97 ARIO art 49(3).

98 ARIO, Commentary to Article 49, para 7.

99 See, e.g., discussion in the UNGA Sixth Committee summary records of meetings (2007): Argentina (UN Doc A/C.6/62/SR.18, para 64), Denmark, (UN Doc A/C.6/62/SR.18, para 100), Italy (UN Doc A/C.6/62/SR.19, para 40), Japan (UN Doc A/C.6/62/SR.19, para 100), the Netherlands (UN Doc A/C.6/62/SR.20, para 39), the Russian Federation (UN Doc A/C.6/62/SR.21, para 70) and Switzerland (UN Doc A/C.6/62/SR.21, para 85); statements made by the Organisation for the Prohibition of the Chemical Weapons and the European Commission to the ILC on the topic of responsibility of international organisations, in ILC, 'Responsibility of International Organizations: Comments and Observations Received from International Organizations' (31 March and 28 April 2008) Documents of the Sixtieth Session, UN Doc A/CN.4/593.

100 Dopagne (n 71); d'Aspremont (n 16); Christian Tomuschat, 'Artikel 210' in Hans von der Groeben and others (eds), *Kommentar zum EU-/EG-Vertrag* (Volume 5, Nomos 1997) 28–29. For a view endorsing a restrictive ILC position see Cujo (n 42) 980–981.

dependent upon the functions of the organisation as deriving from that organisation's rules.[101] It is argued here that such a restriction is not justified, and that international organisations should have a general capacity to respond to violations of *erga omnes* obligations. The ILC's limitation is not in line with the very nature of *erga omnes* obligations, which are by definition owed to the international community as a whole, including international organisations. The ILC seems to confuse the notion of the capacity of an international organisation under general international law and the competences of an international organisation to invoke responsibility and adopt countermeasures in a concrete situation which derives from the rules of the organisation.[102]

It is interesting to note that the ILC has adopted different approach in relation to obligations stemming from *jus cognes* norms which, as explained above, are necessarily of *erga omnes* nature. On particular consequences of a serious breach of *jus cogens* norms, Article 42 ARIO stipulates that international organisations shall cooperate to bring to an end through lawful means any serious breach of *jus cogens* norms.[103] As opposed to Article 49(3) ARIO, Article 42 ARIO does not include any limitation in relation to the functions of those organisations. In terms of capacities, international organisations should therefore cooperate to bring to an end through lawful means any serious breach of *jus cogens* norms on an equal footing with states. The commentary to this article states, however, that this provision is 'not designed to vest international organizations with functions that are outside their respective mandates.'[104] Concrete ways in which such cooperation is actually done are therefore limited to the functions of the concerned organisation.[105]

Concurrent reading of both relevant articles brings us to the conclusion that, while all international organisations are under obligation to cooperate to bring to an end through lawful means any serious breach of *jus cogens* norms, when it comes to the invocation of responsibility of breaches of *jus cogens* norms, they are on the other hand limited with their functions – they only have standing to invoke responsibility and

---

101 See also Gaja (n 3) 106.

102 d'Aspremont (n 16) 72.

103 ARIO art 42(1). See also *Israeli Wall* case (n 32) [202].

104 ARIO Commentary to Article 42, para 4.

105 ibid paras 3–4; UNGA, 'Fifth Report on Responsibility of International Organizations, by Mr. Giorgio Gaja, Special Rapporteur' (2 May 2007) ILC Fifty-ninth session UN Doc A/CN.4/583, 14, para 61; UNGA, 'Seventh report on responsibility of international organizations, by Mr. Giorgio Gaja, Special Rapporteur' (27 March 2009) ILC Sixty-first session UN Doc A/CN.4/610, 91, para 100.

adopt countermeasures if the underlying obligation breached falls under their competences. While the ILC differentiated between capacities and competences in Article 42 ARIO, it failed to do so in Article 49 ARIO. I argue that this inconsistency could best be reconciled by deleting the reference to the functions of an organisation in Article 49 ARIO, thereby implicitly recognising the important difference between the two notions.

Finally, it has to be acknowledged that in principle Article 49 ARIO only relates to situations where an international organisation invokes the responsibility of another international organisation which breached an obligation owed to the international community as a whole, and not to the invocation of responsibility of states for breaches of *erga omnes* obligations. The fact that the adoption of countermeasures by international organisations against States is not explicitly governed neither by ARSIWA nor by ARIO,[106] was acknowledged during the drafting of ARIO, whereby it was concluded that this matter pertains to state responsibility and could be covered by analogy.[107] In this respect ARIO excludes from its ambit the regulation of issues relating to the international responsibility that a state may incur towards an international organisation. It focuses on the responsibility of international organisations towards states or other international organisations and not on the invocation of responsibility of states[108] and the taking of countermeasures by international organisations against states.[109] This would imply that the above-mentioned condition from Article 48(3) ARIO only applies to situations in which an international organisation invokes the responsibility of another international organisation. It is unclear why the ILC decided to introduce this distinction. Regulation of countermeasures adopted by international organisations in response to violations of *erga omnes* obligations should be uniform regardless of who the target of the countermeasure is (a state or another international organisation). The above-mentioned ARIO provisions are commonly considered as *mutatis mutandis* relevant in situations in which an international organisation invokes the responsibility of another state.[110]

106 ARSIWA art. 1 and 57; ARIO art 1. See also ARSIWA Commentary to Article 57, 141, para 1.
107 ARIO Commentary to Article 1, para 10. See also ARIO art 22 and coresponding commentary, 47, para 2.
108 ARIO Commentary to Article 43, 69, para 3. See also ARIO Commentary to Part Four, 68, para 2.
109 ARIO, Commentary to Article 22, 47, para 2.
110 See, for example, d'Aspremont (n 16) 71–72.

3.3. EVALUATION OF PRACTICE

Regardless of the controversies shrouding the capacity of international organisations to protect community interests through the adoption of countermeasures, practice in this respect includes instances in which an international organisation reacts to breaches of *erga omnes* obligations whose protection is not among its functions. Practice also shows that international organisations adopt countermeasures in defence of the community interest against their member states as well as against third states. The prime example of the former are EU sanctions, while the latter have been adopted by the UPU, the WMO, the WHO, the ECOWAS, and the AL, among others.

3.3.1. *Cases in which the Underlying Communitarian Norm is not Among the Functions of the Concerned International Organisation*

An international organisation may react to a breach of an *erga omnes* obligation by one of its members with the adoption of coercive measures not on the basis of its constitutive act and rules of organisation, but on the basis of general international law. Article 22 ARIO acknowledges the possibility of adopting countermeasures in such instances, but with two additional restrictions: 1) the measures adopted must remain consistent with the rules of the organisation,[111] and 2) there must be no other available means appropriate for inducing compliance with the obligations of the responsible state.[112] In relation to the first restriction, the ILC made the ability of international organisations to adopt countermeasures against their members conditional upon the internal rules of a particular organisation, failing to distinguish between internal relations between an international organisation and its members and external relations that an international organisation may have with states, including its members.[113] While a detailed analysis of this issue is beyond the scope of this chapter, it suffices to mention that international organisations have commonly adopted sanctions which could be classified as countermeasures against their members in the form of expulsion or suspension in the absence of specific provisions on expulsion or suspension in their constitutive acts. It has been argued that this does not affect the international legality

---

111 ARIO art 22.2(b).
112 ARIO art 22.2(c).
113 Ahlborn (n 55) 471.

of such countermeasures.[114] Regardless of these controversies, practice below shows that international organisations should have capacity under general international law to protect community interests without them necessarily being among the functions of a concerned organisation.

An example of this practice, whereby an international organisation adopted countermeasures against one of its members in the defence of the community interest without the underlying communitarian norm being among the functions of that organisation, include the expulsion of South Africa from the UPU in 1979 due to its discriminatory apartheid policies. South Africa was first excluded from the Vienna XV Congress (1964)[115] and the Lausanne XVII Congress (1974),[116] and then at the 1979 XVII Rio de Janeiro Congress of the UPU South Africa it was expelled from the organisation, despite the absence of a provision on either apartheid or the expulsion of member states.[117] The expulsion of South Africa despite the fact that apartheid is not mentioned in the UPU constitution and without an explicit provision on expulsion in the UPU acts was met with some opposition.[118] An attempt to introduce a clause allowing for the expulsion of members in the event of apartheid in the UPU constitution was unsuccessful.[119] Nevertheless, the expulsion decision was reaffirmed by Resolution C7 adopted at the Hamburg XIX Congress in 1984.[120] The UPU is a technical organisation with limited purposes and functions – 'to secure the organization and improvement of the postal services and to promote in this sphere the

114 Philippe Sands and Pierre Klein, *Bowett's Law of International Institutions* (Sweet & Maxwell, 2009) 549–550.

115 See reference to the Universal Postal Union (UPU), 'Declaration C 1/1964' in Konstantinos Magliveras, *Exclusion from Participation in International Organisations: The Theory and Practice Behind Member States' Expulsion and Suspension of Membership* (Volume 5, Brill | Nijhoff 1999) 69 ft 30.

116 UPU, 'Resolution C 2/1974: Exclusion of the Republic of South Africa from the 17th Congress of the UPU and from all other Congresses and meetings of the Universal Postal Union' (1974) Lausanne Congress, Volume 2, 953, and Volume 3, 834.

117 UPU, 'Resolution C 6: Expulsion of the Republic of South Africa from UPU' (1979) United Nations Juridical Yearbook 90, <http://legal.un.org/unjuridicalyearbook/pdfs/english/volumes/1979.pdf> accessed 15 January 2021. See also Dopagne (n 56) 181. According to Magliveras, however, South Africa was not expelled, but rather excluded from the organisation the effect of which can be eqated with that of wide-ranging suspension. Magliveras (n 115) 74.

118 See, e.g., European Commission Reply to Written Question No. 948/79 of the European Parliament, OJ 1980 C 41/17. See also Magliveras (n 115) 74.

119 See Magliveras (n 115) 76–68.

120 UPU, 'Resolution C 7' Doc Cg Hamburg XIX Congress, Volume 3, 932.

development of international collaboration'[121] – yet it nevertheless adopted countermeasures in response to one of its members' violations of international obligations that can be considered a community interest, that is, the prohibition of apartheid and human rights violations. At the UN level, UNGA condemned the South Africa's apartheid policies and requested member states to adopt sanctions against South Africa in the form of trade embargoes and suspension of landing rights for all South African aircraft.[122] The UNSC adopted a resolution calling on all states to impose arms embargoes against South Africa.[123] There was, however, no international legal justification for the adoption of measures by the UPU against South Africa in these resolutions. The UNGA appeal to its specialised agencies to withhold from the government of South Africa financial, economic, technical, and other assistance until they had renounced their policies of colonial domination[124] and its request to deny membership or privileges of membership to South Africa[125] cannot be considered as providing a legal basis for the UPU's adoption of measures against South Africa. The UPU's sanctions could therefore arguably only be justified by the law of countermeasures in response to violations of *erga omnes* obligations.[126]

Similarly, in 1964 South Africa was suspended from the WHO on the basis of Article 7 of the WHO Constitution, which permits the suspension of voting privileges and services to which a member is entitled if it fails to meet its financial obligations to the WHO or in other exception circumstances.[127] The underlying reason consisted of South Africa's apartheid policies, but the prohibition of apartheid is not among the

---

121 Constitution of the Universal Postal Union (10 July 1964) UNTS 1967, art 1(2).

122 UNGA, Res 1761 (XVII): 'The Policies of *Apartheid* of the Government of the Republic of South Africa' (6 November 1962) UN Doc A/RES/1761(XVII).

123 UN Security Council, 'Policies of *Apartheid* of the Government of the Republic of South Africa' (7 August 1963) S/RES/181 and S/RES/182 (4 December 1963).

124 UNGA, Res 2426 (XXIII): 'Implementation of the Declaration on the Granting of Independence to Colonial Countries and Peoples by the Specialized Agencies and the International Institutions Associated with the United Nations' (18 December 1968) UN Doc A/RES/2426(XXII).

125 UNGA, Res 3151 (XXVIII): 'Policies of *Apartheid* of the Government of the Republic of South Africa' (14 December 1973) UN Doc A/RES/3151 (XXVIII), para 13.

126 For a similar conclusion with regard to measures against South Africa adopted by individual States see Dawidowicz (n 10) 117. Magliveras, however, claims that the adoption of resolution C 6 lead to a *sui generis* situation, 'which lied outside the constitutional framework of the UPU.' Magliveras (n 115) 74.

127 World Health Assembly (WHA) Resolution 17.50 (19 March 1964) Assembly Seventeenth session, Meetings of the Regional Committee for Africa. See also Magliveras (n 115), 151–152.

purposes of the WHO. Again, it could be argued that the WHO suspension was justified by the concept of countermeasures adopted in response to a violation of *erga omnes* obligations. South Africa was also suspended from the WMO from 1975 until it renounced its racial discrimination policies, even though prohibition of racial discrimination is not among the WMO's functions and purposes.[128]

Another example relates to the 1980 coup in Liberia and human rights violations following it, which were the underlying reason for ECOWAS banning the incumbent Liberian president from participating in the ECOWAS summit in Lomé, which was considered as *de facto* suspension from the organisation. This was done even though protection of human rights was not foreseen among the organisation's functions and purposes, and suspension of a member was not presupposed in the relevant treaty. Again, this could be seen as a countermeasure in response to *erga omnes* obligations.[129]

More recent example includes the AL measures against Syria in the form of suspension of membership and economic sanctions, including travel bans, freezing of assets belonging to the Syrian government and senior regime officials, suspension of dealings with the central bank of Syria, and a ban on civil aviation.[130] These measures were adopted in responses to violence and human rights violations in Syria,[131] although protecting human rights and respect of humanitarian law is not among the AL's functions. The AL pact only includes provision on the exclusion of members in cases of failure to fulfil the obligations resulting from the pact,[132] and there exists no provision on suspension of members. These sanctions were adopted in the absence of the UNSC response to the outbreak of violence and it has been argued that they can be termed countermeasures in response to *erga omnes* violations, namely to the continuous suppression of civilians and violations of human rights by the Syrian regime.[133]

It has to be acknowledged, however, that there were occasions on which a proposal was made within an international organisation for an action

128 'Resolution 38 (Cg-VII): Suspension of the Government of the Republic of South Africa from Membership of the World Meteorological Organization' (1975) Seventh World Meteorological Congress, Geneva.

129 See also Dawidowicz (n 10) 126–127.

130 Arab League Resolution 7442 (27 November 2011).

131 Arab League Resolution 7438 (12 November 2011).

132 Pact of the League of Arab States (22 March 1945) art 18.

133 See also Dawidowicz (n 10) 224–225.

similar to those just described, but no sanction was ultimately adopted. Such was the case with the proposal of Arab states to exclude Israel from the UPU at the Hamburg Congress in 1984, which did not receive enough support.[134]

3.3.2. *Cases in which the Underlying Communitarian Norm is Among the Functions of the Concerned International Organisation*

The EU regularly adopts sanctions against non-member states[135] in reaction to violations of obligations that are of community interest. Restrictive measures,[136] as such sanctions are referred to under EU law, are one of the EU's tools to uphold respect for human rights, democracy, the rule of law, good governance, international law, and the preservation of peace, prevention of conflicts, and strengthening of international security in the wider world.[137] The adoption of restrictive measures forms an 'integral part of the EU's external relations toolbox',[138] their aim being to bring about a change in activities or policies of targeted states.[139] Unlike the practice described in the previous section, the underlying communitarian norm breached in such instances is included among the functions of the EU.[140] This EU practice therefore serves mostly as a general confirmation that international organisations do have a role to play in protecting community interests.

---

134 See Magliveras (n 115) 75.

135 The possibility of relying on self-help mechanisms by the EU in relation to its members under general international law, including the adoption of countermeasures, was, however, ruled out by the CJEU in Joined Cases 90/63 and 91/63 *Commission of the European Economic Community v Grand Duchy of Luxembourg and Kingdom of Belgium* (*the Dairy Products* case) [1964] para 631. See also Case C-5/94 *The Queen v Ministry of Agriculture, Fisheries and Food, ex parte: Hedley Lomas (Ireland) Ltd* [1996] EC Rep I-02553, para 20.

136 TEU art 29; Treaty on the Functioning of the European Union (adopted 13 December 2007, entered into force on 1 December 2009) OJ C 83/47 (TFEU).

137 CEU, 'Basic Principles on the Use of Restrictive Measures (Sanctions)' (7 June 2004) 10198/1/04 rev 1, 2; CEU 'Sanctions: how and when the EU adopts restrictive measures' <https://www.consilium.europa.eu/en/policies/sanctions/> accessed 15 January 2021.

138 European Parliament, 'Resolution of 14 March 2019 on a European Human Rights Violations Sanctions Regime' 2019/2580(RSP), para C. For an overview of current sanctions in force see EU Sanctions map, <https://www.sanctionsmap.eu/#/main> accessed 21 January 2021.

139 European Commission, 'Restrictive Measures' (2008) 1 <http://eeas.europa.eu/archives/docs/cfsp/sanctions/docs/index_en.pdf> accessed 21 January 2021.

140 See, e.g., TEU preamble, art. 2–3 and 6.

Currently there are over 40 different EU restrictive measures in place against 34 countries.[141] The EU adopts two types of restrictive measures: 1) so-called non-autonomous sanctions, whereby it merely implements existing UN sanctions, and 2) autonomous sanctions.[142] For the purposes of this chapter, it is the adoption of autonomous sanctions that are of particular interest. When non-autonomous sanctions are adopted, it is the UNSC who decides and justifies their adoption and the EU merely implements that decision,[143] while in cases of autonomous sanctions the EU decides on the need and underlying reasons. In these latter situations the EU's legal basis for adopting measures cannot be found in a UNSC resolution adopted under Chapter VII of the UN Charter,[144] but it arguably can be found under the law of countermeasures.

The EU's autonomous sanctions are typically economic – such as the complete or partial interruption of economic relations, import and export restrictions and the freezing of foreign assets and embargoes, bans on the provision of financial services, and investment bans[145] – and are commonly in breach of the EU's GATT obligations towards targeted states[146] or its obligations from bilateral trade agreements with targeted states.[147] The EU therefore necessitates an international legal basis for

141 European Parliament (n 138). For an overview of current sanctions in force, see 'EU Sanctions map' <https://www.sanctionsmap.eu/#/main> accessed 21 January 2021, and European Commission (n 139).

142 The EU has adopted autonomous sanctions against numerous States, including China, Iran, Libya, Myanmar, Russia, Syria, Turkey, United States, Venezuela, and Zimbabwe. EU sometimes adopts autonomous sanctions in parallel to the UN, imposing measures additional to or different from the ones called for in the UNSC resolution. These autonomous sanctions are sometimes referred to as supplementary measures or mixed sanctions regimes. Thomas Biersteker and Clara Portela, 'EU Sanctions in Context: Three Types' (2015) 26 European Union Institute for Security Studies (Brief Issue) 1; European Council, Council of the European Union, 'Different Types of Sanctions' <https://www.consilium.europa.eu/en/policies/sanctions/different-types/> accessed 21 January 2021. Such sanctions were for example adopted against the Federal Republic of Yugoslavia, Côte d'Ivoire, the Democratic Republic of the Congo, Guinea-Bissau, Iran, Libya, North Korea, South Sudan, and Sudan. See, e.g., 'EU sanctions map' (n 141).

143 CEU, 'Sanctions Guidelines – Update' (4 May 2018) 5664/18, 5, para 3.

144 UN Charter art. 39–51.

145 See CEU (n 137) 8, para 14; CEU (Press Office) (n 89).

146 See General Agreement on Tariffs and Trade (GATT), 'Trade Restrictions Affecting Argentina Applied for Non-Economic Reasons – Revision' (18 May 1982) L/5319/Rev.1 and 'Minutes of the Meeting Held in the Centre William Rappard on 7 May 1982' (22 June 1982) C/M/157, 10 (in relation to sanctions adopted against Argentina).

147 See, e.g., See Council of the European Communities (CEC), 'Agreement between the European Economic Community and the Argentine Republic on trade in textile

justifying the adoption of such measures.[148] The EU regularly justifies the adoption of autonomous measures by citing breaches of human rights, international humanitarian law and prohibition of aggression by the targeted states. For example, the EU adopted economic measures against Argentina because it invaded part of the Falkland Islands (Malvinas), a non-self-governing territory administered by the United Kingdom.[149] It suspended certain iron and steel products originating in South Africa in response to South Africa's apartheid policies.[150] The European Community froze Iraqi assets in the territory of its member states in response to Iraq's invasion of Kuwait.[151] The EU adopted restrictive measures against the Federal Republic of Yugoslavia (FRY) due to violations of

---

products' (26 November 1979) OJ L 298, art 16.3; CEC, 'Council Regulation (EEC) No 2557/79 of 30 October 1979 concerning the conclusion of the Agreement between the European Economic Community and the Argentine Republic on trade in textile products' (26 November 1979) OJ L 298, 1; CEC, 'Arrangement in the form of an exchange of letters between the European Economic Community and the Argentine Republic on trade in mutton and lamb' (18 October 1980) OJ L 275, 14–19; See also CEC, 'Agreement on Partnership and Cooperation establishing a partnership between the European Communities and their Member States, of one part, and the Russian Federation, of the other part' (28 November 1997) OJ L 327.

148 It has to be acknowledged, that international legal justification is not necessary for all EU's measures. In case of, e.g., diplomatic sanctions such as, e.g., suspension of bilateral talks with the Russian Federation on visa matters and talks on a new comprehensive Agreement, are qualified under international law as act of retorsion. These are unfriendly conducts 'not inconsistent with any international obligation of the State engaging in it even though it may be response to an internationally wrongful act.' See ARIO Commentary to Chapter II, 128; CEC, 'Council Decision 2014/145/CFSP of 17 March 2014 Concerning Restrictive Measures in Respect of Actions Undermining or Threatening the Territorial Integrity, Sovereignty and Independence of Ukraine' (17 March 2014) OJ L 78, para 2; CEU, 'EU restrictive measures in view of the situation in Eastern Ukraine and the illegal annexation of Crimea' (Background note, 29 July 2014).

149 CEC, 'Council Regulation No 877/82 of 16 April 1982 Suspending Imports of All Products Originating in Argentina' (16 April 1982) OJ L 102; CEC, 'Council Regulation No 1176/82 Extending the Suspension of Imports of all Products Originating in Argentina' (18 May 1982) OJ L 136; CEC, 'Council Regulation No 1254/82 of 24 May 1982 Extending the Suspension of Imports of All Products Originating in Argentina' (24 May 1982) OJ L 146. Commission of the European Communities, 'Commission Regulation 1254/83 of 20 May 1983 Fixing the Components Used to Calculate the Differential Amounts for Colza, Rape and Sunflower Seed' (21 May 1983) OJ L 133; ARSIWA Commentary to Article 54, 138, para 3; Dawidowicz (n 10) 141.

150 CEC, 'Decision of the Representatives of the Governments of the Member States, Meeting within the Council of 16 September 1986 Suspending Imports of Certain Iron and Steel Products Originating in South Africa' (19 September 1986) OJ L 268.

151 Dawidowicz (n 10) 159. See also ARSIWA Commentary to Article 54, 138.

the human rights of the Kosovar Albanian community in Kosovo.[152] It adopted restrictive measures against Myanmar (Burma) due to its undemocratic practices and gross violations of human rights against the Rohingya population,[153] as well as against Syria due to violence and continued widespread and systematic gross violations of human rights

---

152 CEC, 'Common Position of 19 March 1998 defined by the Council on the basis of Article J.2 of the Treaty on European Union on restrictive measures against the Federal Republic of Yugoslavia (98/240/CFSP)' (27 March 1998) OJ L 95 and 'Council Regulation (EC) No. 926/98 of 27 April 1998 concerning the reduction of certain economic relations with the Federal Republic of Yugoslavia' (1 May 1998) OJ L 130; CEC, 'Common Position of 7 May 1998 defined by the Council on the basis of Article J.2 of the Treaty on European Union concerning the freezing of funds held abroad by the Federal Republic of Yugoslavia (FRY) and Serbian Governments (98/326/CFSP)' (14 May 1998) OJ L 143 and 'Council Regulation (EC) No 1295/98 of 22 June 1998 concerning the freezing of funds held abroad by the Governments of the Federal Republic of Yugoslavia and the Republic of Serbia' (23 June 1998) OJ L 178; CEC, 'Common Position of 8 June 1998 defined by the Council on the basis of Article J.2 of the Treaty on European Union concerning the prohibition of new investment in Serbia (98/374/CFSP)' (10 June 1998) OJ L 165 and 'Council Regulation (EC) No 1607/98 of 24 July 1998 concerning the prohibition of new investment in the Republic of Serbia' (25 July 1998) Council Regulation (EC) No 1901/98 of 7 September 1998 Concerning a Ban on Flights of Yugoslav Carriers; CEC, 'Common Position of 29 June 1998 defined by the Council on the basis of Article J.2 of the Treaty on European Union concerning a ban on flights by Yugoslav carriers between the Federal Republic of Yugoslavia and the European Community (98/426/CFSP)' (4 July 1998) OJ L 190 and 'Council Regulation (EC) No 1901/98 of 7 September 1998 concerning a ban on flights of Yugoslav carriers between the Federal Republic of Yugoslavia and the European Community' (8 September 1998) OJ L 248; CEC, 'Common Position of 14 December 1998 defined by the Council on the basis of Article J.2 of the Treaty on European Union on restrictive measures to be taken against persons in the Federal Republic of Yugoslavia acting against the independent media (98/725/CFSP)' (19 December 1998) OJ L 345; CEC, 'Common Position of 23 April 1999 defined by the Council on the basis of Article J.2 of the Treaty on European Union concerning a ban on the supply and sale of petroleum and petroleum products to the Federal Republic of Yugoslavia (FRY) (1999/273/CFSP)' (27 April 1999) OJ L 108 and 'Council Regulation (EC) No 900/1999 of 29 April 1999 prohibiting the sale and supply of petroleum and certain petroleum products to the Federal Republic of Yugoslavia (FRY)' (1 May 1999) OJ L 114. See also Palchetti (n 39).

153 See CEC, 'Common Position of 26 April 2000 extending and amending Common Position 96/635/CFSP on Burma/Myanmar (2000/346/CFSP)' (24 May 2000) OJ L 122 and 'Council Regulation (EC) No 1081/2000 of 22 May 2000 prohibiting the sale, supply and export to Burma/Myanmar of equipment which might be used for internal repression or terrorism, and freezing the funds of certain persons related to important governmental functions in that country' (24 May 2000) OJ L 122; CEC, 'Council Regulation (EC) 194/2008 of 25 February 2008 Renewing and Strengthening the Restrictive Measures in respect of Burma/Myanmar and Repealing Regulation (EC) No 817/2006' (10 March 2008) OJ L 66, 1; CEU, 'Council Decision 2013/184/CFSP of 22 April 2013 concerning restrictive measures against Myanmar/Burma and repealing

and of international humanitarian law.[154] The EU also adopted restrictive measures against Zimbabwe due to escalating violence and worrying legislation regulating the media, which infringed on the freedoms of speech and of assembly and association, as well as denying democracy.[155]

The international legal justification for adopting such autonomous sanctions has been subject to numerous debates, and most commonly they are seen as measures taken by a subject other than an injured subject under the law of responsibility as a response to a violation of an *erga omnes* obligation.[156] It has to be acknowledged, however, that not all measures adopted by the EU against third states can be justified by the law of countermeasures. The European Community, for example, responded to the outbreak of violence in FRY by suspending and later denouncing the Cooperation Agreement between the European Economic Community and the Socialist Federal Republic of Yugoslavia.[157] These trade measures went beyond those of the UNSC weapons embargo,[158] and their legality was subject to legal proceedings in which the European Commission relied on the treaty law doctrine of fundamental change of circumstances, arguing that warfare in Yugoslavia made it impossible to perform the agreement, rather than the law of countermeasures.[159]

Decision 2010/232/CFSP' (23 April 2013) OJ L 111 and 'Council Regulation (EU) No 401/2013 of 2 May 2013 concerning restrictive measures in respect of Myanmar/Burma and repealing Regulation (EC) No 194/2008' (3 May 2013) OJ L 121.

154 See CEU, 'Council Decision 2013/255/CFSP of 31 May 2013 concerning restrictive measures against Syria' (1 June 2013) OJ L 147 and 'Council Regulation (EU) No 36/2012 of 18 January 2012 concerning restrictive measures in view of the situation in Syria and repealing Regulation (EU) No 442/2011' (19 January 2012) OJ L 16.

155 See CEU, 'Council Decision 2011/101/CFSP of 15 February 2011 concerning restrictive measures against Zimbabwe' (16 February 2011) OJ L 42 and 'Council Regulation (EC) No 314/2004 of 19 February 2004 concerning certain restrictive measures in respect of Zimbabwe' (24 February 2004) OJ L 55.

156 Crawford (n 7); Dawidowicz (n 10); Petman (n 9); Sicilianos (n 8) 1137. See also ARIO commentary to Article 43, 69, para 3, and 89.

157 CEC, 'Cooperation Agreement between the European Economic Community and the Socialist Federal Republic of Yugoslavia' (14 February 1982) OJ L 41. CEC, 'Decision of the Council and the Representatives of the Governments of the Member states, meeting within the Council of 11 November 1991 suspending the application of the Agreements between the European Community, its Member states and the Socialist Federal Republic of Yugoslavia (91/586/ECSC)' (15 November 1991) OJ L 315; CEC, 'Council Decision of 25 November 1991 denouncing the Cooperation Agreement between the European Economic Community and the Socialist Federal Republic of Yugoslavia (91/602/EEC)' (27 November 1991) OJ L 325.

158 See UNSC, Res 713 (25 September 1991) UN Doc S/RES/713.

159 Case C-162/96 *A Racke GmbH & Co v Hauptzollamt Mainz* [1998] ECR I-3655, paras 52–59.

It also has to be acknowledged that in the past the EU adopted measures against third states in response to their violations of *erga omnes* obligations outside the framework of restrictive measures. This was the case especially before the EU started to introduce 'basic human rights clauses',[160] 'essential elements clauses', and 'non-execution clauses'[161] in its international agreements concluded with third states. One of the first instances in which the EU adopted such measures was in 1967 when the Community suspended the Association Agreement concluded with Greece on account of its military regime.[162] There was no provision for such a suspension in the agreement, so Community's legal basis for doing so was questioned; it has been argued that the EU's suspension could be based on the law of countermeasures in response to breaches of *erga omnes* obligations under general international law.[163] In 1977 the Community similarly responded to human right violations in Uganda by suspending development aid under the 1975 Lomé Convention I,[164]

---

160 E.g., CEC, 'Framework Agreement for trade and economic cooperation between the European Economic Community and the Argentine Republic' (26 October 1990) OJ L 295; CEC, 'Framework Agreement for Cooperation between the European Economic Community and the Republic of Chile' (26 March 1991) OJ L 79; CEC, 'Framework Agreement for cooperation between the European Economic Community and the Republic of Paraguay' (30 October 1992) OJ L 313; CEC, 'Council decision of 8 February 1993 on the conclusion of an Agreement on trade and economic cooperation between the European Economic Community and Mongolia (93/101/EEC)' (18 February 1993) OJ L 41. See also Bartels (n 13) 15–17.

161 See, e.g., art 96 of the Cotonou Agreement, providing for the adoption of 'appropriate measures' in case of non-fulfilment of an obligation stemming from respect for human rights, democratic principles, and the rule of law. CEC, 'Partnership agreement between the members of the African, Caribbean and Pacific Group of states of the one part, and the European Community and its Member states, of the other part, signed in Cotonou on 23 June 2000' (15 December 2000) OJ L 317. See also Commission of the European Communities, 'Communication from the Commission to the Council and the European Parliament – the European Union's role in promoting human rights and democratisation in third countries' (8 May 2001) COM(2001) 252 final, 4; European Parliament, 'Resolution on the Communication from the Commission on the inclusion of respect for democratic principles and human rights in agreements between the Community and third countries (COM(95)0216 – C4-0197/95)' (28 October 1996) OJ C 320, 261, paras 3–4.

162 The Association Agreement provided for common external tariff, elimination of quantitative restrictions on trade, free movement of services, movement and capital and possibility of taking loans from the Community. See also Tams (n 16) 91.

163 Martin Dawidowicz, 'Public Law Enforcement Without Public Law Safeguards? An Analysis of State Practice on Third-Party Countermeasures and Their Relationship to the UN Security Council' (2007) 77 The British Yearbook of International Law 333, 356; Dawidowicz (n 10) 119; Proukaki (n 85) 210 and Tams (n 16) 91.

164 The ACP-EEC Convention (signed at Lomé on 28 February 1975, entered into force 1 April 1976) OJ L 25 (The Lomé Convention I) was concluded between the EU and

through which Uganda, as a party, benefitted from financial aid and export stabilization payments.[165] The Community again lacked proper legal justification for doing so under the Convention, which did not mention human rights, democracy, and the rule of law. Suspension of aid to Uganda in the absence of concrete treaty provision, thereby violating the Lomé Convention I, could be classified as a countermeasure in response to violation of an *erga omnes* obligation.[166] In a similar way the Community suspended its aid under the Lomé Convention I to the Central African Republic in 1979 in response to serious human rights abuses in the country after Colonel Bokasa assumed power through a military coup in 1966; and to Liberia due to human rights violations there after a coup in April 1980 and the occupation of the French embassy in May 1980.[167] It is worth mentioning that in these situations no UNSC enforcement measures were adopted that could justify the Community's measures.[168] These measures are therefore commonly seen as amounting to countermeasures in response to violation of *erga omnes* obligations.[169]

Finally, it must be acknowledged that international organisations, like states,[170] avoid clearly stipulating the legal framework of their coercive actions. These are often politically motivated and do not include proper legal assessment[171] or identification of the underlying communitarian

46 African, Caribbean and Pacific (ACP) countries. Membership was later expanded with successive Lomé Conventions II, III and IV to 69 countries. The Community *de facto* suspended aid to Uganda, without claiming official suspension of the convention, by paying only 5 percent of development assistance owed to Uganda under the Lomé Convention I, stating that development assistance should not contribute to human rights violations in Uganda; Dawidowicz (n 10) 121; Tams (n 16) 211; Bartels (n 13) 10–11.

165 Lomé Convention I art. 19 and 40.

166 Dawidowicz (n 10) 121–123. See also Proukaki (n 85) 130–131; Tams (n 16) 210–211.

167 See references to the Statement by the Commissioner Cheysson in Dawidowicz (n 10) 127 ft 88 and Tams (n 16) 211 ft 52. For a more detailed overview, see Bartels (n 13) 7–12.

168 See UNGA, 'Official Record of the thirty fourth session,' 14th plenary meeting (28 September 1979) UN Doc A/34/PV.14, 270 para 13. For example, it was only in 1979, after the overthrow of the Idi Amin's brutal regime in Uganda, that the UNGA adopted resolution concerning the situation in the country; UNGA, Res 34/122: 'Assistance for the Reconstruction, Rehabilitation and Development of Uganda' (14 December 1979) UN Doc A/RES/34/122.

169 Dawidowicz (n 10) Tams (n 16) 211; Proukaki (n 85) 132–135.

170 Proukaki (n 85) 93.

171 *Colombian-Peruvian Asylum Case (Colombia v Peru)* (Judgment) [1950] ICJ Rep 266, 277.

norm that prompted them. The exact content of protected community interest is thus sometimes unclear. When adopting sanctions against Russia, for example, the EU did so *inter alia* on the basis of 'Russia's actions destabilising the situation in Ukraine'.[172] In cases like this, it is not clear in what way the EU perceives the actions of Russia to be contrary to international law or the exact content of the protected communitarian norm. Likewise, when adopting sanctions against Libya, the EU argued they were necessary due to the 'threat that continues to be posed to the peace, stability or security of Libya' and 'seriousness of the situation in Libya.'[173] In such instances the role of international organisations in protecting concrete community interests seems limited.

4. CONCLUDING REMARKS

International organisations can play an active role in protecting community interest through the adoption of countermeasures in response to violations of *erga omnes* obligations. This chapter discussed the ILC's decision to make the general international law capacity of international organisations to invoke responsibility dependent upon the functions of each organisation as deriving from the rules of that organisation.[174] It has been argued that this restriction is not justified and that international organisations should have a general capacity to respond to violations of *erga omnes* obligations. The restriction is not in line with the very nature of *erga omnes* obligations, which are by definition owed to the international community as a whole, including international organisations. The ILC seemed to confuse the notion of the capacity of international organisations under general international law, which cannot be dependent upon the rules of the organisation, and the competences of an international organisation to invoke responsibility and adopt countermeasures in a concrete situation, which do derive from the organisation's rules. It was argued here that this inconsistency may best be reconciled by deleting reference to the functions of an organisation in Article 49 ARIO, thereby

172 CEU, 'Council Decision 2014/512/CFSP of 31 July 2014 concerning restrictive measures in view of Russia's actions destabilising the situation in Ukraine' (31 July 2014) OJ L 229 and CEU, 'Council Regulation (EU) No 833/2014 of 31 July 2014 concerning restrictive measures in view of Russia's actions destabilising the situation in Ukraine' (31 July 2014) OJ L 22.

173 CEU (n 172).

174 ARIO art 49.3.

implicitly recognising the important difference between the two notions. Practice shows that instances in which an international organisation reacts to breaches of obligations whose protection is not among the functions of that organisation do exist. Such was the case when South Africa was expelled and suspended from technical international organisations such as the UPU, the WHO, and the WMO due to its apartheid policies. Similarly, ECOWAS suspended Liberia's membership due to human rights violations even though it is an organisation whose primary function is economic cooperation, and the AL suspended Syria and adopted economic sanctions against it in response to human rights violations, despite the AL having no provision on the protection of human rights among its functions. This chapter has also discussed EU practice relevant to the protection of community interests.

It has been argued by some scholars that peculiarities of the decision-making process and functioning of an international organisation, such as objectivity, coordination, and centralisation, water down the *justice privée* nature of countermeasures by international organisations. This means that international organisations could even be considered better positioned than states to react to breaches affecting community interests.[175] However, the assessment of international organisations' contribution to protecting community interests must be approached with caution. In practice, international organisations often avoid clearly stipulating the legal framework of their coercive conduct. In such situations, it is not entirely clear if and when they are responding to a violation of community interests, that is, *erga omnes* obligations, or what the exact content of such communitarian norms is.[176]

---

175 Eglantine Cujo, *Les réactions décentralisées de l'Union européenne à l'illicite* (Thèse de doctorat, Université de Paris Nanterre 2002) 635–637.

176 See also Maruša T Veber, 'The Making of Custom Through Sanctions of International Organisations' in Sufyan Droubi and Jean d'Aspremont (eds), *International Organizations, Non-State Actors, and The Formation of Customary International Law* (Manchester University Press 2020) 303–305.

PROSECUTING FOREIGN CORRUPT PRACTICES

Is Extraterritoriality a Tool to Protect Community Interests?

Friederycke HAIJER* and Cedric RYNGAERT**

1. INTRODUCTION

It may come as a surprise that the public international law literature on community interests contains hardly any reference to the prevention and punishment of foreign corrupt practices as a community interest.[1] There is little doubt, however, that preventing and punishing foreign

* PhD candidate at Utrecht University (Ucall research programme).

** Professor of Public International Law at Utrecht University (Ucall research programme).

1 We have studied the following key sources in this respect: Bruno Simma, 'From Bilateralism to Community Interest in International Law' (1994) 250 Recueil des Cours de l'Académie de Droit International; Ulrich Fastenrath and others (eds),

corruption, in particular grand corruption by large corporations, reflects community interests. Corruption is one of the few 'international wrongs' to be internationally criminalized on the basis of transnational crime conventions, in particular in the OECD Anti-Bribery Convention and the UN Convention against Corruption (UNCAC).[2] The preamble to the UNCAC considers corruption, including bribery, as a global scourge that threatens the stability and security of societies, undermining the institutions and values of democracy, ethical values, and justice, and jeopardizing sustainable development and the rule of law.[3] In addition, some recent literature has even characterized corruption as a violation of international human rights.[4] Accordingly, corruption not only limits competitive opportunities for *bona fide* businesses and stunts economic development as resources are diverted and not put to their most efficient use, but it also endangers undeniable international community interests such as democracy, the rule of law, human rights, and sustainable development. It is this direct link with these interests which arguably makes the global fight against transnational corruption a community interest in itself.

In order to maximize the fight against corruption, the OECD and UN Conventions give broad jurisdictional grants to states parties to take global anti-corruption enforcement action in relation to foreign corrupt practices. This allows states to act, at least potentially, as 'extraterritorial' enforcers of international community interests (section 2). Such enforcement comes with a number of problems, however. First, the expansive ways in which states, especially the United States, have construed jurisdictional grants, in particular the territoriality principle, may be in tension with the

From Bilateralism to Community Interest: Essays in Honour of Bruno Simma (Oxford University Press 2011); Giorgio Gaja, 'The Protection of General Interests in the International Community' (2013) 364 Recueil des Cours 9, 20; Wolfgang Benedek, Koen De Feyter, Matthias C Kettemann and Christina Voigt (eds), *The Common Interest in International Law* (Intersentia 2014); Claire Buggenhoudt, *Common Interests in International Litigation: A Case Study on Natural Resource Exploitation Disputes* (Intersentia 2017); Eyal Benvenisti and Georg Nolte (eds), *Community Interests Across International Law* (OUP 2018).

2 Organisation for Economic Co-operation and Development, 'Convention on Combating Bribery of Foreign Public Officials in International Business Transactions' (adopted 21 November 1997, entered into force 15 February 1999) (OECD Convention); United Nations Convention Against Corruption (adopted 31 October 2003, entered into force 14 December 2005) 2349 UNTS 41 (UNCAC).

3 See, e.g., UNCAC, preamble.

4 Anne Peters, 'Corruption as a Violation of International Human Rights' (2018) 29 European Journal of International Law 1251.

international law of jurisdiction (section 3). Indeed, some jurisdictional assertions appear to lack any substantial connection with the enforcing state. Bearing in mind that international law does not (yet) authorize the exercise of universal jurisdiction over corruption (that is, the jurisdictional ground *par excellence* in respect of the protection of community interests), it is uncertain whether the international criminalization of corruption can serve a justificatory role.

Even if such assertions would pass muster with the international law of jurisdiction, a second challenge arises. While enforcement of anti-corruption norms potentially serves community interests in the abstract, it remains to be seen *which* interests of *which* communities are served in reality. Ideally, from an international community perspective, enforcement should serve the interests of those most victimized by foreign corrupt practices: the people who live in the countries affected by corrupt acts such as rigged tenders. By means of three case studies, we show that in practice, enforcement action rather serves the interests of the treasury of the enforcing states, and company shareholders allegedly injured by foreign corrupt practices (section 4).

2. PROSECUTING FOREIGN CORRUPT PRACTICES: CASTING A WIDE JURISDICTIONAL NET

The substantive international criminalization of corruption in the UN and OECD conventions is accompanied by relatively elaborate jurisdictional provisions.[5] These aim to limit safe havens for corrupt practices, and allow, or even require, the exercise of jurisdiction by states over *foreign* corrupt practices, meaning acts of corruption that take place extraterritorially, outside the forum state.[6]

The relevant grounds on which states can or must rely to exercise their jurisdiction over corrupt practices pursuant to the OECD and

5 See, for a general jurisdictional discussion: Jan Wouters, Cedric Ryngaert and Ann Sofie Cloots, 'The International Legal Framework Against Corruption: Achievements and Challenges' (2013) 14 Melbourne Journal of International Law 205, 248–261.

6 It is noted that national law-enforcement agencies, exercising state jurisdiction under international law, are key players in combating corruption, as there is no international court with criminal jurisdiction over acts of corruption. See, however, for a proposal to establish an international anti-corruption court: Mark L Wolf, 'The World Needs an International Anti-Corruption Court' (2018) 147 Dædalus 144.

UN Conventions largely reflect the permissive principles of jurisdiction: territoriality, nationality, passive personality, and protection.[7] The conventions do not as such provide for universal jurisdiction, meaning the classic jurisdictional ground to protect community interests, the operation of which is based on the gravity of the crime rather than the strength of state connections. Still, the conventions allow, and in some situations mandate, the exercise of jurisdiction on the basis of an *aut dedere aut judicare* clause. This clause grounds presence-based jurisdiction in case of the non-extradition of the presumed offender.[8] The conventions also feature a jurisdictional savings clause, which may allow for even more expansive assertions of jurisdiction.[9] It is not clear how expansive these assertions could be, however, given current limitations under the customary international law of jurisdiction.

As corrupt practices often have a transnational dimension, multiple states may in principle have jurisdiction on the basis of the aforementioned principles. Casting the jurisdictional net wide serves community interests in combating corruption: giving multiple states prosecutorial authority may prevent impunity and offer accountability, and thus address the prevailing under-enforcement of anticorruption law in respect of foreign practices.[10] Community interests are served even better if states give a broad interpretation to the jurisdictional principles. For instance, according to the drafters of the OECD Convention, 'the territorial basis for jurisdiction should be interpreted broadly so that an extensive physical connection to the bribery act is not required.'[11] This implies that even

---

7 E.g., UNCAC art. 42(1)-(2). See, for a discussion, Cedric Ryngaert and Friederycke Haijer, 'Art. 42: Jurisdiction', in Cecily Rose and others (eds), *Commentary on the UN Convention Against Corruption* (OUP 2019).

8 UNCAC art. 42(3)-(4) (mandating such jurisdiction if the person is not extradited on the ground that he is a national).

9 UNCAC art 42(6) ('Without prejudice to norms of general international law, this Convention shall not exclude the exercise of any criminal jurisdiction established by a State Party in accordance with its domestic law.').

10 Recently, there have indeed been signs of increased enforcement activity. See OECD Working Group on Bribery, '2016 Data on Enforcement of the Anti-Bribery Convention: Special Focus on International Co-operation' (November 2017); See, for a fine example, the US prosecution of the FIFA bribery scandal, discussed in Connor Slattery, 'A New World Order: FIFA Fiscal Scandal Opens the Door for the United States Department of Justice to Prosecute Crimes Committed across the Globe through the Use of Extraterritorial Jurisdiction' (2018) 41 Suffolk Transnational Law Review 201.

11 Commentaries on the Convention on Combating Bribery of Foreign Public Officials in International Business Transactions (Adopted by the Negotiating Conference on 21 November 1997), para 25, in relation to art 4.1 of the OECD Convention.

relative bystander states – states which only have a tenuous connection to the matter – may be authorized to exercise their jurisdiction. The most important bystander state is the US, which has at times considered incidental or fleeting territorial connections as sufficient for a finding of jurisdiction over non-US corporations under the 1977 Foreign Corrupt Practices Act (FPCA),[12] an act which the US has not failed to vigorously enforce.

One should be careful what one wishes for, however. While vigorous enforcement of anti-corruption law regarding foreign corrupt practices may further community interests theoretically, it may also be in tension with certain principles of international law, and may have unwelcome governance consequences. In particular, domestic enforcement activity based only on tenuous connections with the enforcing state may be incompatible with the law of jurisdiction, amount to intervention in other states' internal affairs, and may create a smokescreen for the defense of national interests. All this may belie the international community orientation of national anti-corruption enforcement. In the next section, we review the anti-corruption enforcement practice of the US in light of the international law of jurisdiction.

3. CHALLENGES OF JURISDICTIONAL OVERREACH

From the perspective of the international law of jurisdiction, the main issue with respect to the extraterritoriality of anti-corruption enforcement activity pertains to the *strength of the required nexus* to ground jurisdiction over foreign corrupt practices, notably of the type exercised by the US.[13]

Under the FCPA, two US jurisdictional triggers are relevant for non-US persons. First, since 1977 the FCPA applies to 'issuers', namely to corporations that trade on a US stock exchange, including non-US corporations.[14] Second, the FPCA prohibits any person, including a non-US person, from 'using mail or interstate commerce in the US

12 The Foreign Corrupt Practices Act of 1977 (FCPA), Pub L 95-213, 91 Stat 1494 (1977) 15 United States Code (USC). See below for relevant US practice.

13 This section is partly based on Cedric Ryngaert, 'Extraterritorial Liability for Corrupt Practices' (*Blog van het Utrecht Centre for Accountability and Liability Law*, 17 June 2019) <http://blog.ucall.nl/index.php/2019/06/extraterritorial-liability-for-corrupt-practices/> accessed 15 January 2021.

14 15 USC Section 78dd-1.

in furtherance of any act that constitutes bribery of a foreign official'.[15] The first trigger is not wholly unproblematic, as a US listing does not turn a foreign corporation into a US corporation, but such a corporation can at least be considered 'resident' in the US, and can anticipate the liability consequences of trading stock there. Much more controversial is the second trigger, which is based on territoriality and which has been interpreted very broadly by US law-enforcement agencies, which have considered tenuous connections to the US as sufficing for the application of US law. They have considered as sufficient such 'incidental' connections as using a correspondent bank account in the US to clear transactions in US dollars[16] and sending an email through a US server.[17] On this basis, and bearing in mind the reality of US financial and technological dominance, many international transactions become subject to US law.[18]

One may argue that such a broad construction of territoriality is desirable from the perspective of stamping out foreign corrupt practices as a global ill – and for that matter, that it is an obligation under UNCAC and the OECD Convention. Arguably, the US is simply implementing the conventions which mandate the exercise of territorial jurisdiction as soon as a constituent element of the offence takes place in its territory. Nevertheless, while it is indeed true that the international community has considered corruption to be globally reprehensible, there is no consensus on what acts precisely constitute corruption or how they should be penalized. Concerns over jurisdictional overreach are brought into particularly stark relief when substantive law applied by a bystander state, such as the US, differs from local law (for example, regarding the permissibility of facilitation payments), when state preferences regarding suitable accountability mechanisms diverge (for example, when the bystander state prefers prosecution, and the local state a negotiated settlement),[19] or when

---

15 15 USC Section 78dd-3.

16 See, for an overview of relevant case-law, 'Supreme Court Questions Whether Dollar-Denominated Transactions or Other Financial Transactions In The U.S. Are Sufficient To Assert Jurisdiction Over Foreign Corporations' (*FCPA Professor*, 8 May 2018) <http://fcpaprofessor.com/supreme-court-questions-whether-dollar-denominated-transactions-financial-transactions-u-s-sufficient-assert-jurisdiction-foreign-corporations/> accessed 15 January 2021.

17 *SEC v Straub*, 921 F Supp 2d 244 (United States District Court, SDNY 2013).

18 Compare also the global reach of US sanctions legislation. See Tom Ruys and Cedric Ryngaert, 'Secondary Sanctions: A Weapon Out of Control? International Legality of, and European Responses to, US Secondary Sanctions' (2020) 0 British Yearbook of International Law 1 <https://doi.org/10.1093/bybil/braa007>.

19 Abiola O Makinwa, 'The Value of Negotiated Settlements in International Bribery Cases' (2017) Draft prepared for Symposium on Exercising Extraterritoriality in

the bystander state does not share the proceeds of fines or settlements with the local state and its population.[20]

Idiosyncratic interpretations of national anti-corruption legislation are obviously difficult to defend under a 'community interest' rationale of expansive jurisdiction. This is especially so if a situation has almost no link with the US, but is much more closely tied to another state, namely the state whose public official was bribed and whose local society bears the adverse developmental consequences of corruption. Such projection of US law may impinge on other states' sovereignty. Moreover, from an individual rights perspective, states exercising jurisdiction on the basis of a weak nexus may violate the criminal law principles of legality, due process, and foreseeability of the law, as foreign persons may be caught unawares by another state's laws.[21] Such persons may also be subject to multiple prosecutions for the same act of corruption.[22] Furthermore, it should be borne in mind that jurisdictional assertions over corruption may have major economic consequences in the local state. If a relative bystander state applies strict anti-corruption legislation, it may well deter much-needed investment in local states, and thus adversely affect the latter's development opportunities.[23] These distributive consequences cannot be justified by facile recourse to the mantra of the 'international criminalization' of corruption in various treaties.

At the same time, these concerns should not be overstated. First, the charge that a foreign state's prosecution of corrupt practices was not foreseeable for the defendant is weakened to the extent that corruption is

---

Anti-Corruption Regulation, held at Utrecht University School of Law on 14 December 2017, 7 <https://papers.ssrn.com/sol3/papers.cfm?abstract_id=3088555> accessed 15 January 2021.

20 See, for mechanisms to allow the local state and population to share in the proceeds of extraterritorial enforcement activity: *United States v Giffen* (*Mercator/Giffin case*) 326 F Supp 2d 497 (SDNY 2004) and 'Memorandum of Understanding Among the Governments of the United States of America, the Swiss Confederation, and the Republic of Kazakhstan' (2 May 2007). Thanks to Cecily Rose for pointing this out to us.

21 Michael Farbiarz, 'Accuracy and Adjudication: The Promise of Extraterritorial Due Process' (2016) 116 Columbia Law Review 625.

22 Note, however, that, under international law, there is no transnational principle of *ne bis in idem*. But compare with The Schengen Acquis – Convention Implementing the Schengen Agreement of 14 June 1985 Between the Governments of the States of the Benelux Economic Union, the Federal Republic of Germany and the French Republic on the Gradual Abolition of Checks at their Common Borders (22 September 2000) OJ L 239, art 54.

23 Kevin E Davis, 'Why Does the United States Regulate Foreign Bribery: Moralism, Self-Interest or Altruism?' (2012) 67 NYU Annual Survey of American Law 497, 508.

indeed internationally criminalized, and the basic elements of the offense of corruption are generally similar or even identical in the prosecuting country and the defendant's country of origin (thereby satisfying the dual criminality requirement). Second, given the prevailing under-enforcement of anti-corruption norms, it is not particularly likely that a person will be prosecuted twice. It is more probable that states will 'jointly prosecute' presumed offenders, as is for instance demonstrated by US involvement in Dutch prosecutions, described in section 4. Third, there is no clear empirical evidence that vigorous extraterritorial enforcement of anti-corruption law limits developmental opportunities in host countries. Even if investment decreases, this does not automatically mean that local communities will be worse off. In fact, as the OECD has observed, foreign direct investment may at times negatively affect legal communities.[24] As the literature has showed, if coupled with corruption, these negative effects may increase.[25]

From a public international law perspective, it is striking that there has been little foreign protest against vigorous FCPA assertions by the US to date.[26] This is probably because foreign states, especially those parties to the conventions, do not want to be seen to condone as odious a practice as corruption. The domestic judicial level in the US has also seen little contestation by non-US persons of US agencies' wide interpretation of the geographic scope of the FCPA. Agencies ordinarily enter into out-of-court settlements, and for reasons of costs and legal uncertainty, foreign firms do not seek judicial review, and put their efforts instead into complying with the FPCA. The result is that there is little to no case-law on the permissible reach of the FCPA; the enforcement agencies largely decide for themselves, without guidance from the courts. So far there has been only one successful legal challenge to US law-enforcement agencies' broad interpretation of US jurisdiction under the FCPA.[27]

The takeaway of the above discussion is that while corruption may have been internationally criminalized as an offense that jeopardizes community

---

24 OECD, 'Foreign Direct Investment for Development: Maximising Benefits, Minimising Costs' (2002) 6.

25 Olatunde Julius Otusanya, 'Corruption as an obstacle to development in developing countries: a review of literature' (2011) 14(4) Journal of Money Laundering Control 387.

26 However, there may be substantial foreign resentment, and foreign firms have delisted from US stock exchanges to avoid application of the FCPA. See Annalisa Leibold, 'Extraterritorial Application of the FCPA under International Law' (2015) 51 Willamette Law Review 225, 258.

27 *United States v Hoskins*, No 16-1010 (United States Court of Appeals, 2d Cir 2018).

interests, and the relevant conventions give broad jurisdictional powers to states, this is not a blank cheque for states to exercise quasi-universal jurisdiction over foreign acts of corruption. Under the international law of jurisdiction, a substantial connection with the state is required. Somewhat similarly, under the presumption against extraterritoriality (a canon of statutory construction used notably in the US), statutes are only intended to apply in the territory, unless a contrary congressional intent appears. The combined effect of the law of jurisdiction and the presumption may narrow the geographic scope of states' foreign anti-corruption legislation. It remains, obviously, that overly narrow interpretations of jurisdictional mandates may result in dangerous under-enforcement – a throwback to a bygone era when foreign corrupt practices were essentially allowed to proceed unchecked, with dire consequences for business reputation and developmental opportunities.

The way forward is for states to exercise jurisdictional restraint, to encourage more closely connected states to exercise their jurisdiction,[28] and to strengthen international cooperation.[29] Cooperation with other states is in any event called for in cases of complex practices, in respect of which the evidence needed to sustain a conviction, or propose a settlement, and the corporate assets against which subsequent enforcement can be taken (asset recovery) are spread over multiple jurisdictions. Given the pernicious effects of foreign corrupt practices on local societies, it is of particular importance that bystander states pay heed to the views of those societies where the officials were bribed.[30]

4. CHALLENGES FACING THE PROTECTION OF COMMUNITY INTERESTS

In sections 2 and 3, we explained how expansive jurisdictional assertions could serve the community interest of stamping out foreign corrupt practices. At the same time, we warned against an encroachment of

---

28 Sarah Routh, 'Tweet to Defeat Government Bribes: Limiting Extraterritorial Jurisdiction under the Foreign Corrupt Practices Act to Combat Global Corporate Corruption' (2018) 51 Vanderbilt Journal of Transnational Law 625, 628.

29 The relevant treaties in fact provide for international consultation between jurisdictionally competent states, in the very article on jurisdiction: OECD Convention, art 4.3; UNCAC art 42.5.

30 Kevin E Davis, *Between Impunity and Imperialism: The Regulation of Transnational Bribery* (OUP 2019), Chapter 10.

such assertions on *another* international community interest, namely the geographic demarcation of sovereign powers safeguarded by the international law of jurisdiction. A second challenge addressed in this contribution pertains to the *actual* community or communities served by raising vigorous enforcement action in respect of foreign corrupt practices. Positing that global anti-corruption enforcement serves global interests may amount to a belief or pious wish rather than a reality. The preambles of the UN and OECD anti-corruption conventions certainly mention concepts such as stability, sustainable development, and the rule of law, which in theory benefit the world community at large, or all communities around the world. However, they are also abstract concepts that are difficult to substantiate at the community level.

We already mentioned the existence of differing views on what constitutes corruption and how and by whom it should be penalized. When extraterritorial anti-corruption measures are evaluated from the perspective of community interests, however, additional questions come up relating to exactly which community interests are being served. This is best clarified by taking a closer look at specific extraterritorial anti-corruption enforcement actions, and investigating retrospectively how certain communities benefited from them and others did not. Since we focused the first half of our chapter on the US, we will look at three multinational enforcement actions with US involvement: Bridgestone (4.1), VimpelCom (4.2), and Petrobras (4.3). We go on to make an overall evaluation of whose community interests were served in those cases, and whose were not (4.4).[31]

4.1. BRIDGESTONE

The first two decades of the 21st century were an active period for the two major US anti-corruption enforcement agencies, the Securities and Exchange Commission (SEC) and the Department of Justice (DOJ). With hundreds of enforcement actions, the anti-corruption field was bustling with activity. Many of these enforcement actions followed a

31 The second half of this chapter partly builds upon a post one of the authors published earlier. See Friederycke Haijer 'Towards a system of compensation for the victims of foreign corruption' (23 October 2018) Public Administration Review: Blog Symposium on corruption <https://www.publicadministrationreview.com/2018/10/23/686/> accessed 15 January 2021.

corresponding path, of which the Bridgestone case (2011) offers just one example.

On September 15, 2011, the DOJ released an announcement in relation to its settlement agreement with the Bridgestone Corporation, a multinational corporation headquartered in Japan that manufactures rubber products. The corporation was being prosecuted on foreign corruption charges:

> Bridgestone Corporation has agreed to plead guilty and to pay a $28 million criminal fine for its role in conspiracies to rig bids and to make corrupt payments to foreign government officials in Latin America related to the sale of marine hose and other industrial products manufactured by the company and sold throughout the world.[32]

The prelude to this settlement happened in 2007, when the Yokohama Rubber Company Limited reported itself and six other companies – Bridgestone among them – to the European Commission as having been engaged in a global foreign corruption cartel. Yokohama's disclosure revealed a global cartel in the provision of marine hose, a valuable industrial product used for loading and unloading oil tankers. It was disclosed that the cartel had been in place since at least 1986.[33]

By coming forward, Yokohama wished to qualify for the European Commission's leniency program, under which companies cooperating with cartel investigations could obtain immunity from fines or a reduction of fines. Yokohama's exposure of the cartel kick-started not only European investigations but also global anti-trust enforcement actions, including in Japan, Australia, the UK, and the US.[34] Accordingly, several individuals and multinational corporations involved in the cartel were eventually prosecuted by the DOJ for violations of the Sherman anti-trust act.

---

32 The United States Department of Justice, 'Bridgestone Corporation Agrees to Plead Guilty to Participating in Conspiracies to Rig Bids and Bribe Foreign Government Officials [press release]' (15 September 2011) Office of Public Affairs <https://www.justice.gov/opa/pr/bridgestone-corporation-agrees-plead-guilty-participating-conspiracies-rig-bids-and-bribe-0> accessed 15 January 2021.

33 European Commission, 'Summary of Commission Decision of 28 January 2009 relating to a proceeding under Article 81 of the Treaty and Article 53 of the EEA Agreement' (21 July 2009) OJ C 168.

34 Australian Competition & Consumer Commission, '$8 million plus penalty imposed on cartel members [press release]' (14 April 2010) Release NR 074/10 <https://www.accc.gov.au/media-release/8-million-plus-penalty-imposed-on-cartel-members> accessed 15 January 2021.

Bridgestone Corporation and one of its local managers, Misao Hioki, pleaded guilty to anti-trust violations and to violations of the US Foreign Corrupt Practices Acts (FCPA).[35] According to the plea agreements, between 1999 and 2007, Bridgestone authorized and approved corrupt payments to foreign government officials employed at state-owned entities in Argentina, Brazil, Ecuador, Mexico, Venezuela, and other countries, in order to secure large sale contracts for the supply of marine hose. The bribes were made through local sales agents and disguised as commission payments in the accounts.[36] Bridgestone's US subsidiary had offices in Texas and Tennessee, but the payments did not take place on US territory. The only direct connections to US territory were fax and email communications that were read and printed there. Yet both the individual as well as the corporate criminal investigations were settled in the US.

To make sure these plea agreements would not be challenged, the DOJ had insisted on a uniform clause in which the defendants waived their rights to jurisdictional defenses to the prosecution of their cases, and agreed to consent to the jurisdiction of the US to prosecute the cases against them in the Southern District of Texas. The defendants also waived their right to file any appeal.[37] In the settlement agreement, Bridgestone agreed to pay 28 million US dollars, which at the time was among the highest FCPA fines of all time. A three-page standard judgment form, filled out and signed by a single judge, rendered the agreement final.[38]

The Bridgestone settlement, just one of hundreds of FCPA enforcement actions between 2001 and 2017, contains many elements that were typical and representative of FCPA enforcement actions in those years: the investigations started with a voluntary disclosure, the settlement involved a foreign company, there was limited territorial connection to the US, a high fine was involved, the case was settled rather than litigated, and there was no appeal. These combined elements have led to the criticism that the US has been using the FCPA as a tool to protect its domestic industries, or even as an 'international anti-corruption business tax'.[39]

---

35 *United States v Bridgestone Corporation*, 11-cr-00651 (Criminal Information) (United States District Court, S D Tex 2011) 9–12.

36 ibid 10.

37 ibid 2.

38 *United States v Bridgestone Corporation*, 4:11-cr-00651 (Plea Agreement) (United States District Court, S D Tex 2011).

39 Leibold (n 26).

Community Interests and the Bridgestone Case

Some of the monetary penalties that the DOJ collected went to the treasury of Texas, the state where the case was formally settled, and the rest to the US federal Treasury. The federal Treasury, which manages the federal budget and tax revenue, usually puts fines in a general fund with federal taxes, which can be used for any item in the national budget, as authorized by the US Congress. Consequently, the financial interests of citizens of the US and more specifically the citizens of Texas were served by this anti-corruption enforcement action. Communities in Argentina, Brazil, Ecuador, Mexico, and Venezuela, the countries whose officials were bribed, did not benefit financially. Arguably, their interests could have been protected in other ways, for example if the agreements between their governments and Bridgestone were annulled as a result of the enforcement action, and a new tender opened in which other companies could compete fairly to secure the government contracts. There are no indications that this happened, however. Citizens in the countries where bribes were accepted appear to have been disregarded in the administration of the Bridgestone settlement, an observation that can also be made about the other two enforcement actions that we evaluate.

4.2. VIMPELCOM

Contrary to the US, the Dutch anti-corruption enforcement arena has been relatively inactive in the first decades of the 21st century. The VimpelCom settlement in 2016 was only the third major settlement for foreign bribery in the Netherlands, after SBM Offshore and Ballast Nedam. The investigation into the VimpelCom case started after the Dutch Public Prosecution Service (PPS) received several international requests for legal assistance from European countries. The settlement amount, almost 400 million euros, broke records in the Netherlands. It was the first anti-foreign corruption enforcement action in which authorities published a substantial statement of facts.[40] Parallel investigations, including of

40 Openbaar Ministerie, '*Vimpelcom betaalt bijna 400 miljoen dollar aan Nederland voor omkoping in Oezbekistan [press release]*' (18 February 2016) <https://www.om.nl/actueel/nieuws/2016/02/18/vimpelcom-betaalt-bijna-400-miljoen-dollar-aan-nederland-voor-omkoping-in-oezbekistan> accessed 15 January 2021.

the former VimpelCom chief executive, and board members, failed in Norway.[41] The Norwegian Telenor Group, a former monopolist telecoms provider with a majority state shareholding, managed to avoid liability of any kind.

From the statement of facts, the following can be derived. Headquartered in Moscow, VimpelCom was an international telecommunications provider founded in 1992 and listed on US stock markets since 1996. It moved its headquarters to Amsterdam in 2010 and became one of the world's largest telecommunications companies. The criminal investigation by the PPS revealed that VimpelCom had made corrupt payments to government officials in Uzbekistan through a shell company in connection with its operations in the Uzbek telecommunications market from 2006 until 2012. This included corrupt payments in relation to obtaining telecommunication licenses for 3G and LTE frequencies, payments which constituted the bribery of government officials as well as other criminal law violations. The board of directors of VimpelCom and senior managers were apparently aware that the payments were made and had been involved in the decision-making processes of the bribery scheme.

The press release did not mention the name of the Uzbek public official who was bribed, but it was clear to all involved that the person who was being referred to in the statement of facts was Gulnara Karimova, the daughter of then Uzbek President Islam Karimov. Karimova's name was openly mentioned in the media and she was later personally indicted in the US for her individual role in the bribery scheme.[42] Her involvement was evidence of the high level at which the bribery took place.

The PPS considered the settlement appropriate and explained in the press release how it had come to be this amount: 'It is a punishment that hurts, and it does justice to the significance of the acts committed as well as to the disruption these acts caused to the legal order.'[43] Whether and how much the settlement really hurt the company remains an open question. The agreement regarding exclusive access to the Uzbek telecommunication

---

41 See also Robert Cookson, 'VimpelCom's former chief executive Jo Lunder arrested in Oslo' *Financial Times* (London, 5 November 2015) <https://www.ft.com/content/2f1bd13e-83c7-11e5-8e80-1574112844fd> accessed 15 January 2021, and OECD Working Group on Bribery, 'Implementing the OECD Anti-Bribery Convention, Phase 4 Report: Norway' (14 June 2018) <http://www.oecd.org/corruption/anti-bribery/Norway-Phase-4-Report-ENG.pdf> accessed 15 January 2021.

42 *United States v Gulnara Karimova & Bekhzod Akhmedov* (SDNY 2019) Docket No. 19-CR-00165-KM.

43 Openbaar Ministerie (n 40).

market was not affected by it; in 2016 VimpelCom announced that it would keep its monopoly on the Uzbek market until 2031.[44] Moreover, the settlement did not seem to affect VimpelCom's stock prices.[45]

The VimpelCom case is an example of US involvement with anti-corruption enforcement led by another country. Parallel to the Dutch settlement, VimpelCom also reached settlements with the SEC and DOJ for approximately the same amount, which was also a record high in the US.[46] The two settlements together amounted to more than 800 million euros. On both sides of the Atlantic, law enforcement expressed pride in their close cooperation on the matter. For example, in the SEC press release on the VimpelCom case, the chief of the SEC Enforcement Division's FCPA Unit said:

> International cooperation among regulators is critical to holding companies responsible for all facets of a bribery scheme. This closely coordinated settlement is a product of the extraordinary efforts of the SEC, Department of Justice, and law enforcement partners around the globe to jointly pursue those who break the law to win business.[47]

The VimpelCom enforcement action is still considered an important success in the global fight against corruption, so it particularly relevant to investigate which community interests were served by it.

Community Interests and the VimpelCom Case

The record-high settlement amount led to debates about the destination of the settlement money. Although formally the money involved in the Dutch part of the VimpelCom settlement was divided into three parts (a fine, a confiscation, and a recovery of criminal proceeds), the total amount of 400 million US dollars flowed to the Dutch treasury. Civil society groups and international NGOs including Transparency International argued that all or some of the money should benefit the population

44 'VimpelComs Uzbekistan license extended to 2031' *VEON* (Amsterdam, 22 July 2016) <https://www.veon.com/media/media-releases/2016/vimpelcom-s-uzbekistan-license-extended-to-2031/> accessed 15 January 2021.

45 Macrotrends, 'VEON – 24 Year Stock Price History' <https://www.macrotrends.net/stocks/charts/VEON/vimpelcom/stock-price-history> accessed 15 January 2021.

46 US Securities and Exchange Commission, 'VimpelCom to Pay $795 Million in Global Settlement for FCPA Violations [press release]' (Washington, 18 February 2016) <https://www.sec.gov/news/pressrelease/2016-34.html> accessed 15 January 2021.

47 ibid.

of Uzbekistan.[48] They argued that financial gains for the prosecuting country (The Netherlands) were at odds with the international anti-bribery regime, as contained in the UNCAC and the OECD Anti-Bribery Convention, both of which allowed for victim compensation. Similarly, the Dutch criminal justice system provided that payments ordered by a criminal court should first benefit victims, before they benefitted the state (article 36f, Dutch Criminal Code). Their argument was partly built upon the poverty in Uzbekistan – between 2002 and 2012, more than half of the population of 25 million in Uzbekistan lived on less than 2 dollars per day – and the logic that the Uzbek population was paying too much for their telecommunications because of the corrupt monopoly in place. However, because of the novelty of such a large settlement, there was no policy regarding the destination of the settlement money in the Netherlands. All the money (from the fine, confiscation, and recovery of criminal proceeds) in the 400 million US dollar settlement has to some extent or another benefited the Dutch treasury. Similarly, the US settlement funds flowed into the US treasury.

It bears mentioning that in investigations related to the Dutch-American enforcement action against VimpelCom, Switzerland confiscated assets belonging to Gulnara Karimova and returned 130 million Swiss Francs to Uzbekistan.[49] This would appear to be a step in the direction of protecting local community interests in multinational anti-corruption efforts. However, it was not met with much enthusiasm from Uzbek civil society activists. They argued that the same Uzbek government that had accepted a bribe from VimpelCom in the first place would now be receiving those same funds after confiscation in order that Switzerland could plausibly deny being associated with the corruption. In their view, asset return to the government of Uzbekistan should be guided by human rights standards and should occur only after anti-corruption reforms were implemented in practice and the rule of law was established.[50]

---

48 Transparency International Nederland, 'Brief betreft bestemming gelden Vimpelcom e.a' (19 August 2018) <https://www.transparency.nl/wp-content/uploads/2018/08/2018-8-9-TI-brief-Vimpelcom.pdf> accessed 15 January 2021.

49 Office of the Attorney General of Switzerland 'Uzbekistan: CHF 130 million seized by the Office of the Attorney General of Switzerland to be returned [press release]' (Bern, 24 June 2019) <https://www.admin.ch/gov/en/start/documentation/media-releases.msg-id-75453.html> accessed 15 January 2021.

50 Association for Human Rights in Central Asia, 'Civil Society Activists of Uzbekistan Call for Justice in the Return of Gulnara Karimova's Ill-Gotten Assets' (25 July 2019)

4.3. PETROBRAS

US anti-corruption law enforcement appears to be sensitive to critiques regarding jurisdictional overreach and targeting foreign companies for large settlements. We may be witnessing the beginning of a policy change with the case of Petrobras. This was the first major anti-corruption case with US involvement where the majority of the settlement funds flowed to the country whose officials were bribed.

Petrobras was a state-owned Brazilian energy company that reached a settlement with the DOJ and the SEC as well as Brazilian authorities in 2018 to resolve FCPA violations involving bribes to politicians and political parties in Brazil. It was the largest corruption scandal in the history of Brazil, implicating politicians from Brazil's largest parties, including three former presidents, as well as presidents of the chamber of deputies and the federal senate, state governors, and businesspeople from large Brazilian companies. Petrobras executives (who were also politicians) allegedly accepted bribes in return for awarding contracts to construction firms at inflated prices.

The non-prosecution agreement (NPA) included a criminal penalty of 853.2 million US dollars. Under the NPA, Petrobras would pay 10 percent or 85.3 million US dollars of the criminal penalty to the DOJ and another 10 percent to the SEC. Petrobras would pay the remaining 80 percent or 682.5 million dollars to the Brazilian authorities.[51]

Community Interests and the Petrobras Case

On the US side of the settlement, the money collected by the SEC in part flowed to investors. Monetary penalties imposed by the SEC fell into two categories: civil money penalties and disgorgements. The latter were meant to restore the funds received through the illegal activities. Until 2002, civil money penalties generally went to the US Department of the Treasury. With the passing of the Sarbanes-Oxley Act in 2002, enacted as a reaction to several major corporate and accounting scandals, including Enron and WorldCom, the SEC was given the ability to distribute

<https://ahrca.eu/uzbekistan/rule-of-law/1019-civil-society-activists-of-uzbekistan-call-for-justice-in-the-return-of-gulnara-karimova-s-ill-gotten-assets> accessed 15 January 2021.

51 US Department of Justice, 'Non-Prosecution Agreement Re: Petróleo Brasileiro S.A. Petrobras' (26 September 2018) Criminal Division <https://www.justice.gov/opa/press-release/file/1096706/download> accessed 15 January 2021.

disgorgement money (plus interest) and civil money penalties received for the victims of securities law violations through the Fair Funds for Investors provision. The term 'victims' referred only to 'injured investors', or in other words, to owners of stock or other securities in the company involved in the enforcement action.[52] In cases in which a fair fund for investors is not set up, the money still flows into the Treasury.

In the Petrobras case, the SEC's administrative order stated that the 85.3 million US dollars the agency was collecting would go into a fair fund for harmed Petrobras investors. The SEC saw these investors as victims because Petrobras 'misrepresented its assets, infrastructure projects, the integrity of its management, and the nature of its relationships with its majority shareholder, the Brazilian government.'[53]

The SEC FCPA enforcement division took pride in being able to return high sums of money to investors. Protecting the 'main street investor' was the first principle that the SEC enforcement division reports on in its annual report:

> The Division of Enforcement is focused on protecting the interests of the Main Street, or retail, investor. These are market participants who need and deserve the attention of the Commission. [...] Importantly, Division personnel again worked diligently to return substantial sums to harmed investors – this year $794 million.[54]

Through the fair fund, one community whose interests were protected by the Petrobras enforcement action was the community of investors on the US stock markets.

On the Brazilian side of the settlement, Petrobras said the 682.6 million US dollars it was paying to the Brazilian authorities would be deposited by Petrobras into a special fund in Brazil to be used in strict accordance

52 US Securities and Exchange Commission, 'SEC Rules on Fair Fund and Disgorgement Plans' (21 April 2004) 17 CFR 201.1100ff <https://www.sec.gov/about/fairfund042104.htm> accessed 15 January 2021.

53 *In the Matter of Petróleo Brasileiro SA – Petrobras* (Order Instituting Cease-And-Desist Proceedings Pursuant to Section 8a of the Securities Act of 1933 and Section 21c of the Securities Exchange Act of 1934) (27 September 2018) Administrative Proceeding File No 3-18843 (United States of America before the Securities and Exchange Commission) <https://www.sec.gov/litigation/admin/2018/33-10561.pdf> accessed 15 January 2021.

54 US Securities and Exchange Commission, 'Annual Report. Division of Enforcement' (2018) <https://www.sec.gov/files/enforcement-annual-report-2018.pdf> accessed 15 January 2021.

with the terms and conditions of the consent agreement, including for various social and educational programs to promote transparency, citizenship, and compliance in the public sector.[55] Similar to the situation in the US, the Brazilian authorities said that some of the money may also be used by Petrobras to compensate its investors.[56] The precise agreements regarding the money's destination remain unclear. Until early 2020 there was no public information regarding the money, and there did not appear to be parliamentary oversight or civil society involvement in the spending process.

4.4. EVALUATING COMMUNITY INTERESTS

From the three cases above, two communities whose financial interests were clearly protected by extraterritorial anti-corruption enforcement actions stand out: citizens of countries whose enforcement agencies were active, including citizens of US federal states where bribing companies had offices, and shareholders of multinational corporations listed on US stock markets.

In the case of both communities, controversy arose in relation to their benefiting from anti-corruption enforcement. The US practice of paying settlement money to investors appears to be in contrast with efforts to hold investors indirectly liable for aiding and abetting the commission of human rights violations abroad, under the federal Alien Tort Statute.[57] Moreover, financial gains for the enforcing country are at odds with the international anti-bribery regime, as contained in the United Nations Convention Against Corruption (UNCAC) and the OECD Anti-Bribery

---

55 Petrobras, 'Petrobras Reaches Coordinated Resolutions with Authorities in the United States and Agreement to Remit Bulk of Associated Payments to Brazil [press release]' (27 September 2918) <http://www.petrobras.com.br/en/news/petrobras-reaches-coordinated-resolutions-with-authorities-in-the-united-states-and-agreement-to-remit-bulk-of-associated-payments-to-brazil.htm> accessed 21 January 2021.

56 *Latin Lawyer*, Brazil to create social fund with Petrobras settlement money [press release]'. Pinheiro Neto Advogados (27 September 2018) <http://www.pinheironeto.com.br/imprensa/brazil-to-create-social-fund-with-petrobras-settlement-money> accessed 15 January 2021.

57 *Filártiga v Peña-Irala*, 630 F2d 876 (United States Court of Appeals, 2d Cir 1980) set the precedent for US federal courts to punish non-US citizens for tortious acts committed outside the US that were in violation of public international law. See also: Michael D Ramsey 'International Law Limits on Investor Liability in Human Rights Litigation' (2009) 50 Harvard International Law Journal 271.

Convention, both of which value victim compensation. Although individual victims may formally be able to file claims in some of the countries keeping the money, in practice it is almost impossible for them to participate in a meaningful way. It is unlikely that victims will be aware of either the ongoing procedures or their rights as victims, since settlement negotiations take place behind closed doors. Even if they were aware, it would be extremely difficult and expensive to prove their individual damage in a court of law.

This brings us to a community whose interests were not as clearly protected: citizens of the countries whose officials were bribed by multinational corporations. It can be argued that they collectively form a community of victims because their governments mismanaged their finances for personal financial gain. However, unlike the shareholders of the bribing corporations, who are offered direct protection and have access to financial compensation, these communities are only offered indirect protection at best. They are presumed to benefit from anti-corruption measures in general terms, particularly in relation to a lower level of corruption in their country, but this is not evaluated and there is no legal recourse.

Although the VimpelCom case prompted some corrupt assets to be returned to Uzbekistan, there are many open questions about if and how this benefits the Uzbek population. Similarly, although the Petrobras settlement money may be invested in Brazil, there has been no transparency about the spending and the decision-making process. In general, the global anti-corruption regime offers no guidelines on how large settlement funds can benefit local communities.

As mentioned above, it may be argued that the global anti-corruption regime protects local communities in other than financial ways, by providing justice and creating opportunities for bona fide businesses. In the three cases analyzed here, however, the contracts that had resulted from the bribes remained largely untouched. For example, as discussed earlier in the case of VimpelCom, even though the company settled for a record amount, it continued to have a monopoly on the Uzbek telecoms market. Under these circumstances Ii is difficult to see how the Uzbek population was protected by this enforcement action. Moreover, there was no evidence that any of the three enforcement actions had a substantial impact on improving the rule of law and integrity in the affected countries.[58]

[58] Brazil's score on Transparency International's Corruption Perceptions Index decreased slightly from 37 points in 2017 to 35 points in 2019. Uzbekistan's score, although there

5. CONCLUDING OBSERVATIONS

Critical law and development scholarship elucidates how foreign states' jurisdictional assertions over corrupt practices, even if doctrinally grounded in accepted principles of jurisdiction and well-intentioned, can strengthen vested interests[59] and even misfire[60] by entrenching the very inequality they are supposed to tackle. In a damning indictment of US extraterritoriality regarding foreign corrupt practices, Ellen Gutterman has recently argued that 'US extraterritoriality acts as a brake on global anti-corruption efforts,' citing the focus of FCPA enforcement on 'specific actors and instances of corrupt transactions rather than tackling the embedded networks and practices in which opportunities for corruption are cultivated in the global economy'.[61] Others have highlighted how the replacement of local views regarding the place of anti-corruption in national development strategies may amount to neocolonial or imperial imposition of Western views on what good governance should look like.[62]

Similarly, when the combat of corruption is presented as serving the 'national interest', the national interest referred to is generally that of Western states – because, for example, anti-corruption safeguards the competitive opportunities of bona fide domestic businesses, there is a risk

was a slight increase from 21 points in 2016, remained very low at 25 points in 2019. Data retrieved from Transparency International, 'Corruption Perceptions Index' (2020) <https://www.transparency.org/en/cpi/2019/results/tkm> accessed 15 January 2021.

59 See 'A qui profite la lutte anticorruption?' (*Le Monde Diplomatique* Special issue September 2019) 13.

60 See for the classic work on the 'unforeseen consequences, blind spots, and biases' of (Western) humanitarianism: David Kennedy, *The Dark Side of Virtue: Reassessing International Humanitarianism* (Princeton University Press 2005).

61 Ellen Guttermann, 'Extraterritoriality as an Analytic Lens. Examining the Global Governance of Transnational Bribery and Corruption', in Daniel S Margolies and others (eds), *The Extraterritoriality of Law: History, Theory, Politics* (Routledge 2019) 192–193.

62 Davis (n 23) 511 ('taking concerns about sovereignty into account suggests that enforcement priorities should be shaped by actors based in the jurisdiction most affected by corrupt activity'); Davis (n 30) 231 ('It is reasonable to expect only a partial moral consensus about how to respond to allegations of corruption. In the absence of such a consensus, legal regulation and the associated moral judgments are best left to local actors.'); Morag Goodwin and Kate Rose-Sender, 'Linking Corruption and Human Rights: An Unwelcome Addition to the Development Discourse' in Martine Boersma and Hans Nelen (eds), *Corruption & Human Rights: Interdisciplinary Perspectives* (Intersentia 2010) 235–236; Benoît Bréville and Renaud Lambert, 'Sermonner le monde ou le changer' (*Le Monde Diplomatique*, Special Issue September 2019) 13.

that tolerating foreign corruption abroad may further domestic corruption by the same businesses, or the instability in foreign states caused by corruption may spill over borders (such as in the form of migratory streams).[63]

If the global anti-corruption regime is to genuinely advance the interests of local communities, a first step would be for participants in major anti-corruption settlement negotiations to acknowledge the existence of local communities. A standard clause in settlement agreements could explicitly state that the agreement does not affect the rights of citizens of the countries whose officials accepted bribes to hold the company and their government accountable. This would be in line with the official commentary on Article 3 of the OECD convention regarding sanctions, which states that the article's third paragraph is without prejudice to rights of victims. Second, 'fair funds for victims' as they exist in the US as well as ad hoc funds such as that created in Brazil in the Petrobras case could be expanded to become accessible to local communities. At the same time, transparency and community participation in the decision-making about such funds could be improved, which would be in line with Article 13 of UNCAC on the participation of society. In the future, such funds could potentially be managed by either development cooperation departments of the enforcing country, or – to ensure more democratic control for local communities – by international organisations, if they do so in a transparent manner and with meaningful community participation. Finally, the analysis of the cases discussed in this chapter shows that it is problematic that the deals that had their origin in bribery remained intact even after extraterritorial enforcement actions took place. The argument that such enforcement actions contribute to more ethical business practices and thus protect community interests would be more convincing if the corrupt deals were dismantled as part of the settlement procedure.

---

63 See on self-interest and the prosecution of foreign corrupt practices: Kevin E Davis, 'Self-interest and Altruism in the Deterrence of Transnational Bribery' (2002) 4 American Law and Economics Review 314.

GOOD GOVERNANCE OF NATURAL RESOURCES AS AN INDICATOR OF A COMMUNITY-BASED APPROACH TO PEACEBUILDING

Lessons from Iraq

Saeed BAGHERI*

1. INTRODUCTION

In countries located upon valuable energy reserves, such as oil and natural gas, instability resulting from armed conflict and loss of control over territory impedes governments' ability to exercise sovereignty over their natural resources. The occupation of the oil-rich city of Kirkuk in northern

* Lecturer in Law, School of Law, Global Law at Reading, University of Reading, United Kingdom.

Iraq by the militant group "Islamic State"[1] in 2014 indicated that the group found access to energy resources important for the success of its main objective of creating an Islamic caliphate. Islamic State seemed to put itself in a unique position to achieve its goals by taking control of oil resources in Iraq, which would generate an income to enhance its economic and military capabilities.

The unpredicted military resistance of the Peshmerga, the military forces of Iraqi Kurdistan,[2] then repelled the Islamic State's advance in northern Iraq; the Iraqi Kurds took effective control over Kirkuk through an enduring military campaign against Islamic State.[3] This success provided a strategic advantage to the Kurdish Regional Government (KRG) leadership, which has frequently complained about the central government's discriminatory behaviour and failure to provide the KRG with a fair share of energy resources and national income.[4] Yet the Peshmerga's presence in the oil-rich region around Kirkuk after the defeat of Islamic State escalated existing tensions and fueled another conflict between the Kurdish and Iraqi forces. The Iraqi forces intensified military operations against the Kurds and recaptured the city. In the aftermath of the ceasefire between the Iraqi Kurds and the central government in Baghdad, it is necessary to seek paths to peacebuilding and post-conflict reconstruction in the country.

This chapter builds on the premise that the divisions and conflicts that have arisen in Iraq, particularly after the fall of Islamic State, have

---

1 Eric Robinson and others, *When the Islamic State Comes to Town: The Economic Impact of Islamic State Governance in Iraq and Syria* (RAND Corporation 2017) xvi; Robin Mills, *Under the Mountains: Kurdish Oil and Regional Politics* (Oxford Institute for Energy Studies 2016) 3.

2 According to Article 117 of the Iraqi Constitution, the only legal militia in the Iraqi system are the Iraqi armed forces and security services. Therefore, militias outside the framework of the armed forces are prohibited, but Regions such as the Iraqi Kurdistan are permitted to raise regional security forces and guards. In view of this, the KRG established the Peshmerga as its militia. However, the Peshmerga's status (as part of the Iraqi defence system or a separate regional security force) is still a subject of controversy between the Iraqis and Kurds. See Crispin Smith, 'Independent Without Independence: The Iraqi Kurdish Peshmerga in International Law' (2018) 59(1) Harvard International Law Journal 245, 254. See also Dennis P Chapman, *Security Forces of the Kurdistan Regional Government* (Center for Strategic and International Studies 2009).

3 International Energy Agency, *Iraq Energy Outlook: World Energy Outlook Special Report* (IEA Publications 2012) 23; Ellen Scholl, *Shaping Iraq's Oil and Gas Future* (Atlantic Council's Global Energy Centre 2018) 1.

4 Bilal A Wahab, *Iraq and KRG Energy Policies: Actors, Challenges and Opportunities* (The Institute of Regional and International Studies 2014) 16.

roots in the weak governance and mismanagement of oil resources. Good, sustainable management of these resources is key to ensuring and enhancing equality and political stability in federal Iraq's ethnically diverse society. After focusing on the peacebuilding measures that are necessary in post-Islamic State Iraq, the chapter draws attention to the state's responsibility to protect the interests of its citizens. Just as public interests are central to national legal orders, the common interests of the international community as a whole, including not only states but all human beings, are the principal focal point of international law. As Judge Simma has pointed out, community interests 'correspond to the needs, hopes and fears of all human beings, and attempt to cope with problems the solution of which may be decisive for the survival of entire humankind'.[5] The common interests of the international community are subject to international law, and are to be protected in compliance with the rule of law and the principle of equality.

The chapter then clarifies why good governance of resources in conflict-affected regions, through community initiatives ensuring equality, human rights, and the rule of law, is important. The norms of international law can arguably help fulfill the common interests of members of all ethnic communities in societies across the world – such as sustainable access of a whole society to resources, sustainable management and use of natural resources, economic solidarity, the protection of the natural environment, peace and security, and human rights – which are the major factors in reducing tensions in communities.[6] Certainly, resource management in line with the rule of law and the principle of equality inherently protects community interests, which in turn makes peacebuilding achievable.

Focusing on the priority of common interests in natural resources, which belong to the whole community and to its individual members,

---

5 Bruno Simma, 'Universality of International Law from the Perspective of a Practitioner' (2009) 20(2) European Journal of International Law 265, 268; Bruno Simma, 'From Bilateralism to Community Interest in International Law' (1994) 250 Recueil des Cours de l'Académie de Droit International 217, 244. For a discussion, see Benedict Kingsbury and Megan Donaldson, 'From Bilateralism to Publicness in International Law' in Ulrich Fastenrath and others (eds), *From Bilateralism to Community Interest: Essays in Honour of Bruno Simma* (Oxford University Press 2011) 79–89.

6 Samantha Besson, 'Community Interests in International Law: Whose Interests Are They and How Should We Best Identify Them?' in Eyal Benvenisti and Georg Nolte (eds), *Community Interests Across International Law* (OUP 2018) 43–44. See in general Rüdiger Wolfrum, 'Identifying Community Interests in International Law: Common Spaces and Beyond' in Eyal Benvenisti and Georg Nolte (eds), *Community Interests Across International Law* (OUP 2018) 19–35.

over governments' interests, this chapter examines its case study: how the uneven sharing of resources and the withholding of the regional government's proceeds from the national budget by the Iraqi central government disappointed the KRG as part of the Iraqi community. It argues that ensuring trust and cooperation between the Iraqi government and the KRG is the basis for fairly sharing and protecting the common interests of the various ethnic communities in the country's natural resources, which is in turn the most effective way to achieve stability and peacebuilding in post-war Iraq. The chapter puts forward the pathways which can serve natural resource-based conflict resolution and thereby reach these ambitious goals.

Finally, the chapter evaluates several issues related to peacebuilding in Iraqi society after Islamic State as a matter of the *jus post bellum* and the good governance of energy resources as subject to the protection of community interests.

2. THE LEGAL FRAMEWORK: EXPLORING PEACEBUILDING AS A MATTER OF *JUS POST BELLUM*

As part of conflict resolution, the parties to a conflict need to create and maintain conditions that will achieve a sustainable peace. At this stage, the concept of peacebuilding, which means eliminating the root causes of conflict and establishing a lasting environment of peace, comes to the fore. A sustainable peace settlement will ideally endeavour to achieve a higher level of the rule of law, human rights protection, constitutional power-sharing, transparency and accountability in the management and sustainable use of natural resources, and transitional justice than in the period before the resort to armed force.[7] Sustainable management of natural resources has generally been defined as using resources at a rate that will enable them to be available to future generations. It is a key concern at all levels of society, on a global as well as a local scale,

[7] Jacob Bercovitch and Richard Jackson, *Conflict Resolution in The Twenty-first Century: Principles, Methods, and Approaches* (University of Michigan Press 2009) 168; Carsten Stahn, '"Jus ad bellum", "Jus in bello" … "Jus post bellum"? – Rethinking the Conception of the Law of Armed Force' (2006) 17(5) EJIL 921, 936.

because human development provides the greatest threat to the resilience of ecosystems. Sustainable development provides resources for the use of present populations without causing environmental damage that challenges the survival of other species and natural ecosystems. In other words, it meets the needs of the present without compromising the ability of future generations to meet their own needs.[8] It is worth noting here that sustainable management of natural resources is also an indication of the 'no harm' rule, which provides that states' rights to use their territories and resources are limited by an obligation to avoid significant transboundary harm, but neighbouring states must tolerate harm that remains below that threshold. As the International Court of Justice (ICJ) made clear in its 1996 Advisory Opinion on the Legality of the Threat or Use of Nuclear Weapons, 'the general obligation of states to ensure that activities within their jurisdiction and control respect the environment of other states or of areas beyond national control is now part of the corpus of international law relating to the environment'.[9]

The United Nations (UN) Agenda for Peace of 1992, which has played a significant role in increasing international interest in the peacebuilding concept, addresses it as identifying and supporting structures likely to strengthen and solidify peace in order to avoid a relapse into conflict. Preventive diplomacy seeks to resolve disputes before violence breaks out; peacemaking and peacekeeping are required to halt conflicts and preserve peace once it is attained. If successful, they increase the opportunity for post-conflict peacebuilding, which can prevent the recurrence of violence among nations and peoples.[10] The peace-building process is also seen as involving actions towards establishing a governance structure that

---

8 See in general, Victoria Jenkins, 'Sustainable Management of Natural Resources: Lessons from Wales' (2018) 30(3) Journal of Environmental Law 399; Helle T Anker and Birgitte E Olsen, 'Legal Approaches to Sustainable Management of Natural Resources' in Helle T Anker and Birgitte E Olsen (eds), *Sustainable Management of Natural Resources: Legal Instruments and Approaches* (Intersentia 2018) 3–10; United Nations General Assembly, 'Report of the World Commission on Environment and Development' (11 December 1987) UN Doc A/RES/42/187.

9 See *Legality of the Threat or Use of Nuclear Weapons* (Advisory Opinion) [1996] ICJ Rep 226, para 29; Jutta Brunnée, 'International Environmental Law and Community Interests: Procedural Aspects' in Eyal Benvenisti and Georg Nolte (eds) *Community Interests Across International* (OUP 2008) 156.

10 UN Secretary-General, 'An Agenda for Peace: Preventive Diplomacy, Peacemaking and Peace-Keeping' (17 June 1992) UN Doc A/47/277, para 21 <http://www.un-documents.net/a47-277.htm> accessed 15 January 2021.

can provide an alternative to war by eliminating the causes of war.[11] It is important to note that the concept of peacebuilding has been developed as a result of UN initiatives through its substantial reports, including the Supplement to an Agenda for Peace (1995) and Report of the Panel on UN Peace Operations (2000). Further to this, in 2005 the UN established the Peacebuilding Commission to assist governments in conflict-affected countries in the post-conflict era and provide the necessary resources for peacebuilding in such societies.[12]

Peacebuilding is a basis of *jus post bellum*, a subject of renewed interest in the context of international involvement and administration of territories in post-war societies,[13] especially in terms of challenges facing international and regional organizations such as the UN, the UN Security Council (UNSC), the UN Peacebuilding Commission, and the World Bank. *Jus post bellum* norms are significant for decisions related to various aspects of peacebuilding practice, including political and legal strategies; cooperating with domestic civil society; taking an inclusive and context-specific approach to their activities; sequencing and prioritization; and creating and interpreting mandates.[14]

In the aftermath of the Cold War, in which the international community has been confronted with an increased number of the inter-state conflicts and civil wars, a variety of developments can be identified in the concept of peacebuilding. As a result, the functions of peacebuilding and peacekeeping operations have considerably expanded; they now include the creation of buffer zones, overseeing borders, and maintaining ceasefires. The engagement of civilian personnel is one factor that has given peacebuilding operations a much broader function.[15]

Fundamental rights protection, the rule of law, and the free-market economy have been promoted through peacebuilding programs in conflict-affected societies. However, the experience of countries affected by civil wars between 1989 and 1999 demonstrate that local actors and their interests were ignored in the majority of peacebuilding programmes,

---

11 Johan Galtung, 'Three Approaches to Peace: Peacekeeping, Peacemaking and Peacebuilding' in Johan Galtung (ed), *Peace, War and Defence: Essays in Peace Research* (Ejlers 1976) 298.

12 Stephen Ryan, 'The Evolution of Peacebuilding' in Roger M Ginty (ed.), *Routledge Handbook of Peacebuilding* (Routledge 2013) 25.

13 Jens Iverson and others, 'Epilogue: Jus Post Bellum – Strategic Analysis and Future Directions' in Carsten Stahn and others (eds) *Jus Post Bellum: Mapping the Normative Foundations* (OUP 2014) 545.

14 ibid.

15 UN Secretary-General (n 10) paras 29, 47.

which focused on building a state instead of peace. Scholarship shows that peace programmes without the participation of local actors have actually triggered new conflicts in the regions in question.[16] It has been argued that building peace in countries affected by civil wars would be achievable and sustainable if the primary focus was conflict resolution instead of state-building. Such peacebuilding operations would be largely carried out by local actors, with international organizations focused on providing assistance.[17]

Despite the theoretical and practical controversies around the implementation of peacebuilding in post-war societies, it is generally accepted that there is an obvious connection between democratic practices – such as the rule of law and transparency in decision-making – and the achievement of true peace and security in any new and stable political order. These are the major elements of effective and good governance that need to be promoted in all international and national political communities.[18] International assistance organizations have insisted on the concepts of good governance and of building trust in government in post-war societies. The role and function of governments, particularly their capacity to manage and govern their natural resources, have always been at the centre of good governance.

In post-war societies, good governance is seen as eliminating all forms of violence, with a special focus on building and transforming sustainable relationships among conflicting sectors and cultures to promote cooperation between them. As Stahn has argued, this is a matter of the 'just peace' concept, as part of *jus post bellum*, which requires conflicting parties to end a dispute in a fair and just fashion irrespective of the cause of the resort to force. A 'just peace' must be framed by reference to certain objective rules and standards that regulate guidelines for peacebuilding in the interest of people and individuals affected by conflict.[19] This is particularly important in energy-rich countries affected by civil wars,

16 Roland Paris, *At War's End: Building Peace after Civil Conflict* (Cambridge University Press 2004) 155; Oliver P Richmond, 'The Problem of Peace: Understanding the "Liberal Peace"' (2006) 6(3) Conflict, Security and Development 291.

17 Roger M Ginty (ed), *Routledge Handbook of Peacebuilding* (Routledge 2013) 3.

18 UN Secretary-General (n 10) para 59. See also Matthias Ruffert, 'The Administration of Kosovo and East-Timor by the International Community' (2001) 50(3) International and Comparative Law Quarterly 613, 620–622.

19 Stahn (n 7) 936. See also Mark Evans, 'At War's End: Time to Turn to *Jus Post Bellum*?' in Carsten Stahn and others (eds), *Jus Post Bellum: Mapping the Normative Foundations* (OUP 2006) 26–42.

where public resources have largely been managed in the absence of all stakeholders in the country.

However, good governance in such societies requires practical community initiatives in decision-making, ensuring legal and procedural transparency, efficiency in the use and sharing of resources, and accountability. These concepts have developed over time in international law through UN General Assembly (UNGA) and UNSC resolutions and reports, and have been put into practice in various cases. The UNGA has emphasized the rule of law as a key element of conflict resolution, transitional justice, and peacebuilding.[20] The rule of law itself requires measures to ensure adherence to a number of additional principles, including supremacy of law, equality before the law, accountability to the law, fairness in the application of the law, separation of powers, participation in decision-making, legal certainty, avoidance of arbitrariness, and procedural and legal transparency.[21]

The UNGA has recognized the importance of the assistance and contribution of the international community, including the UN, upon the countries' request, as they may face special challenges during their transition.[22] This may be particularly necessary in post-war societies which lack procedural and legal transparency between local and central governments, as in Iraq. Given the difficulties of natural resource management due to institutional weakness and the absence

---

20 See UNGA, Res 71/148: 'The Rule of Law at the National and International Levels: Resolution Adopted by the General Assembly on 13 December 2016' (20 December 2016) UN Doc A/RES/71/148; UNGA, Res 72/119: 'The Rule of Law at the National and International Levels: Resolution Adopted by the General Assembly on 7 December 2017' (18 December 2017) UN Doc A/RES/72/119; UNGA, Res 73/207: 'The Rule of Law at the National and International Levels: Resolution Adopted by the General Assembly on 20 December 2018' (11 January 2019) UN Doc A/RES/73/207; UNGA, Res 74/191: 'The Rule of Law at the National and International Levels: Resolution Adopted by the General Assembly on 18 December 2019' (30 December 2019) UN Doc A/RES/74/191; UNGA, 'Strengthening and Coordinating UN Rule of Law Activities: Report of the Secretary-General' (11 July 2019) UN Doc A/74/139; UNGA, 'The Rule of Law at the National and International Levels: Report of the Sixth Committee' (11 November 2016) UN Doc A/71/515.

21 UNSC, 'The Rule of Law and Transitional Justice in Conflict and Post-Conflict Societies: Report of the Secretary-General' (23 August 2004) UN Doc S/2004/616, para 6. See also Thomas Fitschen, 'Inventing the Rule of Law for the United Nations' (2008) 12 Max Planck Yearbook of United Nations Law 347, 351–352.

22 UNGA, Res 67/1: 'Declaration of the High-level Meeting of the General Assembly on the Rule of Law at the National and International Levels: Resolution Adopted by the General Assembly on 24 September 2012' (30 November 2012) UN Doc A/RES/67/1, para18.

of governmental authority in post-war societies, evidence suggests that political priorities tend to be economic recovery and maintaining peace instead of sustainable development.[23] In such cases, international assistance may be able to accelerate the adoption of natural resource management techniques as part of good governance.

Similarly, the UNSC has emphasized that peace and stability cannot prevail in the absence of the rule of law and good governance. Peacebuilding requires that the population perceive that politically charged issues – such as ethnic discrimination, unequal distribution of wealth, abuse of power, and the denial of the right to property or citizenship – can be addressed in a legitimate and fair manner.[24] The absence of responsive government in these societies would turn the population into belligerents for their justice and security needs, and post-war societies marked by ineffective governance and repressive policies pose significant threats to international peace and security.[25]

A lack of the rule of law, illegal exploitation of natural resources, and unfair distribution of resource revenues have often fueled new conflicts in post-war societies. The UNSC's measures against the illegal exploitation of natural resources have been significant in preventing this.[26] The administration of Kosovo under the UNSC Resolution 1244 (10 June 1999)[27] and East-Timor under the UNSC Resolution 1272 (25 October 1999)[28] by the international community shed light on the significance of good governance and public administration in transitioning to peace and ending violence. In both countries, the primary objective of the UN-administered peacebuilding processes was the creation of independent political entities and balancing the interests of the conflict parties. This approach was used to serve the interests and needs of the population of the territory, namely, to reconstruct and realize

23 Carl Bruch and others, 'Post-Conflict Peace Building and Natural Resources' (2008) 19(1) Yearbook of International Environmental Law 58, 88.

24 UNSC (n 21) para 4.

25 ibid para 7.

26 See, for instance, UNSC, 'Security Council Condemns Illegal Exploitation of Democratic Republic of Congo's Natural Resources', 4317th and 4318th meetings (3 May 2001) UN Doc SC/7057 <https://www.un.org/press/en/2001/sc7057.doc.htm> accessed 15 January 2021; UNSC, 'Security Council Underscores Need for Peacekeeping Mandates to Consider Helping States Prevent Illegal Exploitation of Natural Resources from Fuelling Conflict', 5705th meeting (25 June 2007) <https://www.un.org/press/en/2007/sc9060.doc.htm> accessed 15 January 2021.

27 UNSC, Res 1244 (10 June 1999) UN Doc S/RES/1244.

28 UNSC, Res 1272 (25 October 1999) UN Doc S/RES/1272.

human rights as a reflection of good governance.[29] The engagement of international organizations in re-establishing a comprehensive peaceful environment indicates the internationalized legal and political status of the administered post-war society. In both Kosovo and East Timor, the law was internationalized through the incorporation of directly applicable international legal norms and acts into the domestic legal system.[30] The UN established peacebuilding missions to support the government of East Timor and relevant institutions with a view to stability, enhancing a culture of democratic governance and facilitating political dialogue among stakeholders in their efforts towards national reconciliation.[31] In Kosovo, the UN mission showed more willingness to establish mechanisms of shared governance and administration by transferring legislative and executive powers to the domestic authorities.[32] Perhaps the most distinct difference between the two cases is that local participation was further developed in East Timor (i.e. the National Consultative Council, composed by a third of UN representatives, was replaced by the National Council with 36 members from parties and municipal social groups only).[33] In some ways this was a people-centred mission seeking to advance the efficiency of peacebuilding measures at the national level.

Aligning internal and external factors in transitional justice and building peace can enable governments in post-war societies to transparently and lawfully manage natural resources, especially through clarifying the chain of responsibility in that management and through providing panels of experts to oversee implementation. If national conditions do not allow for or limit the effectiveness of transitional justice and peace-building measures, the UN seeks to support activities that encourage and lay the foundations for effective mechanisms and processes, including dialogue, to assist national stakeholders to promote interest in and understanding

---

29 Carsten Stahn, 'The United Nations Transitional Administrations in Kosovo and East Timor: A First Analysis' (2001) 5 Max Planck Yearbook of United Nations Law 105, 180–181. Daniel Silander, 'The United Nations and Peace Building: Lessons from the UN Transitional Administrations in East Timor and Kosovo' (2009) 28(2) Social Alternatives 23.

30 UNSC, Res 1704 (25 August 2006) UN Doc S/RES/1704, para 4. See also Stahn (n 29) 154.

31 UNSC, Res 1745 (22 February 2007) UN Doc S/RES/1745; UNSC, Res 1802 (25 February 2008) UN Doc S/RES/1802; UNSC, Res 1867 (26 February 2009) UN Doc S/RES/1867.

32 Stahn (n 29) 151.

33 See, for a more detailed description, Matthias Ruffert (n 18) 625.

of such measures.[34] In both Kosovo and East Timor, UN peacebuilding measures engaged with the local actors and their direct participation in governing structures.[35]

Even though the Iraqi government has not practically requested UN assistance in transitioning to peace and peace talks between the central government and the KRG, the UN missions in Kosovo and East Timor can be considered the basis of peacebuilding measures at the national level in post-war Iraq. Obviously, natural resources as drivers or causes of violence in both Kosovo and East Timor bear similarities to the Iraqi case, where the national relationship between the central and regional governments would be shaped by the relational dynamics between national and international actors. The next three sections will show how post-war Iraq can achieve sustainable peace, like the UN peacebuilding missions at the national level, through good governance of natural resources.

3. GOOD GOVERNANCE OF NATURAL RESOURCES AS A MEANS OF POST-CONFLICT RECONSTRUCTION

The ultimate purpose of fair and just peacebuilding is to remove the causes of violence and oppression; this may require positive transformations of a society's domestic order.[36] As Jimmy Carter rightly pointed out, 'the peace it establishes must be a clear improvement over what exists'.[37] In this

---

34 UN Secretary-General, 'Guidance Note of the Secretary-General: United Nations Approach to Transitional Justice' (2010); UNSC, 'Statement by the President of the Security Council' (25 June 2007) UN Doc S/PRST/2007/22. See also Cindy Wittke (former Daase), 'The Redistribution of Resources in Internationalized Intra-State Peace Processes by Comprehensive Peace Agreements and Security Council Resolutions' (2011) 3(1) Goettingen Journal of International Law 23, 32.

35 Sergio Vieira de Mello, 'Introductory Remarks and Keynote Address' in Nassrine Azimi and Chang Li Lin (eds), *The United Nations Transitional Administration in East Timor (UNTAET): Debriefing and Lessons* (Brill | Nijhoff 2003) 19; Astri Suhrke, 'Peacekeepers as Nation-Builders: Dilemmas of the UN in East Timor' (2001) 8(4) International Peacekeeping 1, 13.

36 Stahn (n 7) 936; Gary J Bass, 'Jus Post Bellum' (2004) 32(4) Philosophy and Public Affairs 384, 385.

37 Jimmy Carter, 'Just War – or Just a War?' *The New York Times* (9 March 2003) <https://www.nytimes.com/2003/03/09/opinion/just-war-or-a-just-war.html> accessed 15 January 2021.

regard, governments in conflict-affected energy-rich countries need to take responsibility for the governance of national resources and must be held accountable for past abuses and governance failures, which tend to be the major causes of violence and social division due to direct violations of civil and political rights. The likelihood of achieving sustainable peace in post-Islamic State Iraq will thus increase through improvements to the political and constitutional order as the core components of democratic resilience and preventing (or at least minimizing) systemic failures in the legal and political system.

The following steps might be considered part of an extensive framework which encompasses the substantive requirements for transition from war to peace in Iraq.

3.1. ACCOUNTABILITY IN RESOURCE GOVERNANCE

Considering the complexity of the political situation in post-war societies and the relationships between the central and regional governments and other groups, such as non-state actors, it is inevitable that all these groups will aspire to ensure their own political and economic interests. Ensuring the political interests of all such entities in federal Iraq, with its large energy resources, is not easy within the context of the process from a very complicated war to a peaceful transition. We know that political regimes in post-war societies must undergo a significant process of political alteration to promote political stability. Various complexities, including political, economic, social, and cultural rights violations and disagreements between the central government and other political entities over governance of natural resources may preclude peacebuilding,[38] defined in the 1992 Agenda for Peace as an 'action to identify and support structures which will tend to strengthen and solidify the peace in order to avoid a relapse into conflict'.[39] Precedents indicate that peace is likely to be lasting only if the security needs of the population are addressed in parallel with the political and socio-economic aspects of post-war reconstruction.[40]

---

[38] Christine Bell, 'Peace Settlements and International Law: From *Lex Pacificatoria* to *Jus Post Bellum*' in Nigel D White and Christian Henderson (eds), *Research Handbook on International Conflict and Security Law: Jus ad Bellum, Jus in Bello and Jus Post Bellum* (Edward Elgar Publishing 2013) 502–503.

[39] UN Secretary-General (n 10) para 21.

[40] Geneva Centre for the Democratic Control of Armed Forces, 'Security Sector Reform in Post-Conflict Peacebuilding' (2009) DCAF Backgrounder, 2.

In addition, post-war countries with considerable high-value natural resources such as oil generally face a very complex situation with respect to energy resource governance due to constraints relating to a recurrence of conflict.[41] Ensuring stability and peace in these societies requires stabilizing fragile peace arrangements and strengthening weak structures within the social and constitutional order.[42]

Because armed conflicts often weaken the institutional capacities[43] of post-war societies, including governmental authority to control the national economy, 'effective governance' based on increased transparency of natural resource management, accountability, and fair distribution of resources and resource revenues[44] (wealth-sharing) among diverse members of a society is the surest pathway towards peace and stability.[45] This enables governments to resolve existing armed conflicts as a primary step towards peace and preventing them from relapsing into conflict in the future.[46] Indeed, a development process governed by the 'principle of permanent sovereignty over natural resources' was adopted by the UNGA in 1962, providing that every state has a right to dispose of its natural wealth and resources in accordance with its national interests and with

---

41 Graham Brown and others, 'A Typology of Post-Conflict Environments' (2011) Centre for Research on Peace and Development, Working Paper No 1, 3.

42 Anna Ohanyan, *NGOs, IGOs, and the Network Mechanisms of Post-Conflict Global Governance in Microfinance* (Palgrave Macmillan Press 2008) 24.

43 Bruch and others (n 23) 88.

44 Fair and equitable sharing of resource and resource revenues involves questions of distributive justice. In that sense, it is interpreted as an equal overall allocation of access to all members of a society – either because such a distribution is seen as desirable in its own right (e.g. a belief that people deserve equal shares of common resources), or because equitability is seen as a prerequisite for effective institutional functioning to reduce free-riding and maximise compliance. Moreover, mutual benefits from shared natural resources act as an incentive for sustained peaceful dialogue, which in turn can generate cooperation among states, communities, and people. See Alex Evans, 'Resource Scarcity, Fair Shares and Development' (2011) A WWF/Oxfam Discussion Paper 11–12; UN Secretary-General, 'Sharing Benefits of Natural Resources Helps Conflict Prevention, Sustainable Development, Secretary-General Tells Security Council' (16 October 2018) Press Release, UN Doc SG/SM/19303-SC/13541-ENV/DEV/1896 <https://www.un.org/press/en/2018/sgsm19303.doc.htm> accessed 15 January 2021.

45 Susan Rose-Ackerman, 'Corruption and Post-Conflict Peace-Building' (2008) 34(2) Ohio Northern University Law Review 405; Carl Bruch and others, 'Facilitating Peace or Fuelling Conflict? Lessons in Post-Conflict Governance and Natural Resource Management' in Carl Bruch, Carroll Muffett and Sandra S Nichols (eds) *Governance, Natural Resources and Post-Conflict Peacebuilding* (Routledge 2016) 960–995.

46 Daniëlla Dam-de Jong, *International Law and Governance of Natural Resources in Conflict and Post-Conflict Situations* (CUP 2015) 426.

respect for the economic independence of states as primary subjects of international human rights.[47]

As it is generally recognised that the UNGA resolutions pertaining to states' permanent sovereignty over their natural resources reflect rights and duties that already existed under international law and the position of a majority of the states acting in enlightened self-interest, it can be concluded that the principle of permanent sovereignty over natural resources has a legal impact on the existing body of international law,[48] which has compelled the ICJ to confirm its customary nature.[49] The right of peoples and nations to permanent sovereignty over their natural wealth and resources must be exercised in the interest of their national development and the well-being of the people of the state concerned.[50] This right, contained in Article 1 of the 1966 International Covenant on Civil and Political Rights (ICCPR) and the 1966 International Covenant on Economic, Social and Cultural Rights (ICESCR), is the economic dimension of the right to self-determination.[51]

It can hardly be disputed that self-determination is a universal human right which constitutes an example of *jus cogens*[52] or that the protection of human rights is a community interest which entails corresponding obligations. The reference to human rights in the UN Charter and the universality of membership in human rights treaties validate

---

47 UNGA, Res 1803(XVII): 'Permanent Sovereignty over Natural Resources' (14 December 1962) UN Doc A/RES/1803(XVII).

48 Sangwani P Ng'ambi, 'Permanent Sovereignty over Natural Resources and the Sanctity of Contracts, from the Angle of Lucrum Cessans' (2015) 12(2) Loyola University Chicago International Law Review 153, 158–159; Karol N Gess, 'Permanent Sovereignty over Natural Resources: An Analytical Review of the United Nations Declaration and Its Genesis' (1964) 13(2) International and Comparative Law Quarterly 398, 448; Robert Dufresne, 'The Opacity of Oil: Oil Corporations, Internal Violence, and International Law' (2004) 36(2) New York University Journal of International Law and Politics 331, 354.

49 *Case Concerning Armed Activities on the Territory of the Congo (Democratic Republic of the Congo v Uganda)* (Judgment) [2005] Judgment, ICJ Rep 168, para 244.

50 UNGA (n 47) para 1.

51 James N Hyde, 'Permanent Sovereignty over Natural Wealth and Resources' (1956) 50(4) The American Journal of International Law 854, 855; Gess (n 48) 414; Ng'ambi (n 48) 155.

52 Cindy Holder, 'Self-Determination as a Universal Human Right', (2006) 7(4) Human Rights Review 5; Hurst Hannum, 'The Right of Self-Determination in the Twenty-First Century' (1998) 55(3) Washington and Lee Law Review 773; UNGA, 'Self-Determination Integral to Basic Human Rights, Fundamental Freedoms, Third Committee Told as It Concludes General Discussion' (5 November 2013) UN Doc GA/SHC/4085.

this statement.[53] In this sense, given that the people of every sovereign state have a permanent right to choose their government, they are entitled to insist that natural resources be exploited on their behalf and for the sake national development, as a reflection of states' accountable exercise of sovereignty in accordance with Article 1 (2) of the ICCPR and ICESCR, which serve as the guarantors of basic human rights.[54] More precisely, states have the power to control and use their natural wealth and resources, but they are not allowed to use their natural resources or the proceeds from those resources against their own people or to refrain from the fair and equitable sharing of the revenues generated from those resources. That is to say, states' power to control their resources is limited, and they 'are obligated to act in accordance with recognized principles of international law as well as international agreements and with due regard for existing legal rights or interests'.[55] Furthermore, a state is legally responsible for ensuring that any 'activities within its activity or control do not cause damage to the environment of other states or to areas beyond national jurisdiction or control'.[56] As the substantive environmental law principle, the prohibition against causing damage to other states has attained customary status endorsed by subsequent state practice. Traditional supporters of this clear and absolute prohibition lie in the various political, military, economic, industry, and other common interests of the international community that influence the process of adopting general principles in the protection of the natural environment.[57]

It is widely accepted that state sovereignty exercised by people exercising self-determination is a matter that needs to be protected as an example

53 Héctor Gros Espiell, 'Self-Determination and Jus Cogens' in Antonio Cassese (ed), *UN Law/Fundamental Rights: Two Topics in International Law* (The Sijthoff and Noordhoff 1979) 170–171; Wolfrum (n 6) 29. For a discussion, see Marija Batistich, 'Right to Self-Determination and International Law' (1995) 7(4) Auckland University Law Review 1013, 1017–1019.

54 Antonio Cassese, 'Self-Determination of Peoples' in Louis Henkin (ed), *The International Bill of Rights: The Covenant on Civil and Political Rights* (Columbia University Press 1981) 103; Dam-de Jong (n 46) 424; Ng'ambi (n 48) 155–157; Father R Araujo, 'Sovereignty, Human Rights, and Self-Determination: The Meaning of International Law' (200) 24(5) Fordham International Law Journal 1476, 1492.

55 Hyde (n 51) 867.

56 'Report of the United Nations Conference on the Human Environment [Stockholm Declaration]' (16 June 1972) UN Doc A/CONF.48/14/ Rev.1; UNGA, Res 2995 (XXVII): 'Co-operation between States in the Field of the Environment' (15 December 1972) UN Doc A/RES/2995(XXVII).

57 See, in general, Andrea Laura Mackielo, 'Core Rules of International Environmental Law' (2009) 16(1) ILSA Journal of International and Comparative Law 257, 262–277.

of basic human rights; the international community will not accept any breach of those rights.[58] Basic and fundamental human rights are pivotal community interests in the international community.

As Human Rights Watch has pointed out, if energy resource revenues are managed and shared fairly and transparently, post-war Iraq could become a model for other petroleum economies because it would prove that it is possible to benefit from oil wealth without sacrificing human rights or democratic freedoms, or fueling massive corruption.[59] Further, integrating sustainable natural resource management into peacebuilding would avert uncontrolled exploitation of resources in the aftermath of any conflict.[60] Transparency and accountability of a government to society in the management of natural resources and the administration of resource revenues are the primary requirements of sustainable development, and have been addressed by the UNSC in various contexts.[61] They be achieved through the free participation of the people in the governance of their polity and in decisions about their economic, social, and cultural policies, reaffirmed in common Article 1 of the ICCPR and ICESCR.[62]

Conversely, unfair and unequal distribution of the resources and the revenues from them reflect mismanagement and unaccountability in rescource management that might pave the way to instability, conflict, and threats to the peace in the energy-rich countries. Effective governance will therefore be achieved through the collaboration of stakeholders, transparency in production and export records, and explicit objectives in maintaining a sustainable economy. In itself, a sustainable economy is one which reduces absolute poverty through providing lasting and secure

---

58 See Theodor Meron, 'On a Hierarchy of International Human Rights' (1986) 80(1) The American Journal of International Law 1, 22; Hyde (n 51) 854–867.

59 Human Rights Watch, 'Considerations for the Management of Oil on Iraq: A Human Rights Watch Background Briefing' (April 2003) 2.

60 David Jensen and Steve Lonergan (eds), *Assessing and Restoring Natural Resources in Post-Conflict Peacebuilding* (Routledge 2012) 9.

61 UNSC (n 34) para 6; UNSC, Res 1607 (21 June 2005) UN Doc S/RES/1607, para 4; UNSC, Res 1647 (20 December 2005) UN Doc S/RES/1647, para 3(a); Daniëlla Dam-de Jong, 'Standard-Setting Practices for the Management of Natural Resources in Conflict-Torn States: Constitutive Elements of Jus Post Bellum' in Carsten Stahn and others (eds), *Environmental Protection and Transitions from Conflict to Peace: Clarifying Norms, Principles, and Practices* (OUP 2017) 169–191.

62 Dorothée Cambou and Stefaan Smis, 'Permanent Sovereignty over Natural Resources from a Human Rights Perspective: Natural Resources Exploitation and Indigenous Peoples' Rights in the Arctic' (2013) 22(1) Michigan State International Law Review 347, 358; Dam-de Jong (n 46), 427.

livelihoods that minimize resource depletion, environmental degradation, cultural disruption, and social instability.[63]

In a post-war society in which energy resources have frequently been the subject of disagreements, such as Iraq, the potential for destabilization is particularly high. Iraq's oil is located in regions dominated by the Kurdish and Shi'ite populations, underlining the need for resource governance to be part of broader political integration efforts.[64] Broadly speaking, divisions and tensions among Sunnis, Shia, and Kurds have often complicated political debates in Iraqi society, as each group worries about the others gaining an advantage.[65] In view of this, political integration through the promotion of interfaith dialogue and avoidance strategies and policies that harden social divisions will help stabilize Iraq only if all groups are seen as part of Iraqi society.[66]

Collaboration between the KRG and the central government of Iraq is thus the primary requirement for achieving sustainable peace, along with effective structures of oversight and shared economic decision-making that takes peacebuilding necessities into consideration. Policy decisions in other areas would then happen by recognizing the importance of economic sustainability in the longer run.[67] Transparency in exploiting, producing, and sharing by the central government of Iraq and the KRG are the preconditions to achieve these objectives. These objectives will not be achieved unless the central government changes from an authoritarian, violent, oppressive, and exclusionary regime to a less authoritarian, less violent, and more accountable regime, which is more tolerant towards the other political entities in the Iraqi political system. Indeed, one might argue that Iraq has undergone a transition from a purely authoritarian system to one with an elected government after the fall of Saddam Hussein's statue on 9 April 2003. However, organized violence, oil-funded state patronage and the use of communal differences for 'divide and rule'

---

63 See Edward B Barbier, 'The Concept of Sustainable Economic Development' (1987) 14(2) Environmental Conservation 101, 103.

64 For more information, see Virginia Haufler, 'The Private Sector and Governance in Post-Conflict Societies' in Derick W Brinkerhoff (ed), *Governance in Post-Conflict Societies: Rebuilding Fragile States* (Routledge 2007) 153.

65 See Peter S Henne, 'Economic Integration and Political Reconciliation in Iraq' (17 April 2018) Center for American Progress <https://www.americanprogress.org/issues/security/reports/2018/04/17/449687/economic-integration-political-reconciliation-iraq/> accessed 15 January 2021.

66 ibid.

67 Astri Suhrke and others, *Peacebuilding: Lessons for Afghanistan* (Michelsen Institute 2002) 111; Bass (n 36) 408.

strategies as the major levers of power still remain crucial factors in Iraqi's political system.[68]

Clearly, peacebuilding is tied to the ending of autocratic, undemocratic, and oppressive regimes, and directed towards the ideal of 'popular sovereignty' held by individuals instead of states or elites.[69] In this respect, accountable and people-centred governance will provide an operational framework for making democracy work in conflict-affected Iraqi society.[70] At the same time, political entities such as the KRG must be restrained within the context of a new political and democratic constitutional order as the primary support of the transition from war to the peace and the builder of the new political regime, thus reducing the risk of new conflicts and tensions through the regulation of the division and balance of power among central, federal, and regional government. In other words, building peace and democracy in a post-war federal society depend on new rules that ensure equality and the protection of citizens' core rights from potential violations.[71] Moreover, the new order would serve long-term peace objectives if its political and legal institutions take responsibility for past constitutional and human rights violations and identify the authorities who may make decisions about policies in the transition from war to peace and post-war reconstruction.[72] Responsibility for the troubled past in states involved in armed conflict and mass violence is a matter of justice and facilitates the transition from war to peace. Authorities' responsibility for past constitutional and human rights violations can be categorized as a core component in expediting the peacebuilding processes.[73]

Opting for federalism as a recipe for heterogeneous societies which include very diverse populations of multiple ethnicities means devising federal political arrangements that address the needs and demands of sub-national groups and regions of dispersed and national minorities.

---

68 Claire Spencer, Jane Kinninmont and Omar Sirri (eds), *Iraq Ten Years On* (Chatham House 2013) xi. See also Marisa Sullivan, *Maliki's Authoritarian Regime* (Institute for the Study of War 2013) 9.

69 Stahn (n 7) 941.

70 CK Lal (ed), *Human Rights, Democracy and Governance* (ActionAid International Asia 2010) 46.

71 Izabela Pereira Watts, 'From War to Peace: When Democracy Prevails?' 35 (2016) Saint Louis University Public Law Review 351, 378.

72 See, in general, Bell (n 38) 503.

73 For further information about the accountability for the past crimes and violations in post-conflict societies and post-authoritarian regimes, see Jemima García-Godos, 'It's About Trust: Transitional Justice and Accountability in the Search for Peace' in Cecilia M Bailliet and Kjetil M Larsen, *Promoting Peace Through International Law* (OUP 2015) 321–343.

These arrangements include conflict resolution, ensuring peaceful settlements, promoting dialogue, building peaceful road-maps and encouraging inclusive democracy – resulting in the recognition of diversity and equality as the source of strength and integration rather than the source of conflict and division.[74]

This does not mean that federalism and autonomy are methods of conflict resolution, however. Considering the particular case of Iraqi Kurdistan, an autonomous region recognised by the Iraqi 2005 Constitution, it can be argued that autonomy was the basis of aspirations for secessionism, which in turn triggered armed conflict between the central and the autonomous government. Evidence indicates that, thanks to the mismanagement of energy resources and revenues, this is the most prevelent type of conflict in areas that cover a large portion of energy resources with poor governance. A lack of accountability in the context of natural resource revenue management in these areas precludes peacebuilding processes. Accordingly, the creation of an enabling peacebuilding environment in these societies is contingent on fair and equitable sharing of the resources and resource revenues between all their members, irrespective of their political aspirations, ethnic and religious identities, and social background. As subject to community interests, natural resources need to be managed as commons instead of being privatised. Fairness and reciprocity are crucial for effective cooperation between central and regional governments. Fairness is both an outcome of a well-managed commons and part of what makes it work. Given the limited availability of natural resources in all societies, it is not possible for everyone to use them equally, but everyone should receive equal shares of the income derived from selling them.[75]

Of course, effective cooperation needs community knowledge and support, which entails equal participation of the whole of a society in decision-making processes to decentralize the management of resources. This will also help people to articulate and enforce their common interests through equal access and sustainable use of resources. Indeed, unequal access is a product of the failure of economic and social justice in divided societies. which anversely affects the common interest. Moreover, as discussed above, sustainability in natural resource use ensures future generations' access to resources, meeting the needs of the present without causing serious damage to the natural environment.

---

74 Arshi Khan, 'Contesting Democratic Politics in the Interest of Federalism' (2012) 363 Journal of Studies on European Integration and Federalism 251, 253.

75 Evans (n 44) 14.

3.2. TRANSPARENCY IN RESOURCE GOVERNANCE AS A MATTER OF HUMAN RIGHTS

Political oppression or large-scale violations of the human rights of people or groups, through preventing them access the national budget and legal institutions, may trigger substantial damages to existing political integrity. This is, in fact, one of the most crucial factors triggering a dependent people's aspirations to freedom and independence from their former masters in ethnically diverse societies with widespread human rights violations, political and economic discrimination, injustice, and oppression. In constitutionally recognised autonomous regions within the Iraqi political system, such as the KRG, all peoples of the region have the right to freely determine their political status and pursue their economic, social, and cultural development.

Transparency in government operations is an important precondition for macroeconomic fiscal sustainability, good governance, and overall fiscal rectitude.[76] The non-transparency of both the central government and the KRG in making and applying their policies and operations, including regional and international energy deals in violation of Article 110 of the Iraqi Constitution, has driven a wedge between the KRG and Baghdad. This was particularly emanated when the Kurdistan parliament passed a regional law in 2007, creating the KRG's ministry of natural resources with an authorization to sign contracts with international oil companies. However, the federal government considered the KRG's oil law unconstitutional, its contracts illegal, and its exports smuggling.[77]

According to Article 110, the 'exclusive authorities of the federal government' include formulating foreign policy and diplomatic representation; negotiating, signing, and ratifying international treaties and agreements; negotiating, signing, and ratifying debt policies; drawing up the national budget of the state; and formulating economic and trade policies. However, the Iraqi Constitution does not give exclusive authority over the energy resources to the Iraqi central government. The federal government, in association with the producing governorates and regional governments, is to undertake the management of oil and gas extracted from present fields, provided that it distributes its revenues in a fair

---

[76] George Kopits and Jon Craig, 'Transparency in Government Operations' (1996) International Monetary Fund Occasional Paper 158, 1.

[77] See Bilal A Wahab (n 4) 15.

manner in proportion to the population distribution in all parts of the country and this shall be regulated by law. Given that 'oil and gas are owned by all the people of Iraq in all the regions and governorates' (Article 111 of the Iraqi Constitution), the Iraqi central government should formulate 'the necessary strategic policies to develop the oil and gas wealth in a way that achieves the highest benefit to the Iraqi people' (Article 112 of the Iraqi Constitution) using the most advanced techniques of the market and encouraging investment in conjunction with the regional and governorate governments.[78] As the primary revenue source of the state's economy, the energy revenue from the various regions of the country is to be managed transparently under the effective control of the central government.

Evidence indicates that the lack of transparency of the KRG and central government in formulating and implementing economic and trade policies, particularly their decisions to distribute the revenue from natural resources unequally, paved the way for divisions within federal Iraq as a country, with an economy in transition, which has recently evolved to a federation under a new permanent constitution approved by a national plebiscite in October 2005.[79] As a result of the non-transparency of the central government in sharing the total revenue and its cutting of the KRG's proceeds from the national budget in 2014, the KRG started take control of and market the resources, prompting an increase in tensions between the two parties. The tension also stemmed from the Iraqi government's inefficient temporary budget allocations and contracting practices, in lieu of establishing an effective legal framework to govern the management of the energy resources. Building trust in the central government requires an effective legal framework and the publication of the annual national petroleum accounts, reconciling all revenues and company costs and profits to clearly show how the federal energy revenues are derived.[80]

Given the constitutional values and norms of Iraq's political system, the central and regional governments are responsible for the violation and

78 See Justin Dargin, 'Securing the Peace: The Battle over Ethnicity and Energy in Modern Iraq', (2009) 7 Oil, Gas and Energy Law Intelligence 1, 26; David Romano, 'Iraq's Descent into Civil War: A Constitutional Explanation' (2014) 68(4) Middle East Journal 547, 556.

79 Kopits and Craig (n 76) 16.

80 Keith Myers, 'Breaking Iraq's Oil-Law Stalemate' (2011) Petroleum Economist 12, 13 <https://resourcegovernance.org/sites/default/files/Iraq%20Myers_5.pdf> accessed 15 January 2021; Erik G Jensen, 'Introduction to the Laws of Iraq and Iraqi Kurdistan' (2013) Stanford Law School, Iraq Working Paper Series, 18–21.

infringement of the interests of their citizens. Bearing in mind that the central government is the primary authority responsible for promoting and protecting its citizens' fundamental rights, while the regional government has only a complementary role to play, the state may delegate implementation thereof to lower tiers of government, including regional authorities, upon ratifying international treaties. In order to establish procedures and controls to ensure that the state's human rights obligations are implemented at the regional level, the regional authorities may require power and financial resources.[81] In practice, the above-mentioned budget allocations and contracting practices did not ensure transparency and efficiency, prompting the KRG to manage Kirkuk's regional resources. To this end, the KRG started a contract-signing spree-by December 2013, independently of Baghdad in order to improve its economic capabilities.[82]

Handling the energy industry and energy policy untransparently and preventing a certain group of people from access to energy revenues contributed to the re-emergence of tensions between the KRG and Baghdad. These constitutional abuses are directly attributable to the Iraqi central government, since it is responsible for protecting the fundamental human rights of its citizens as a reflection of the concept of sovereignty. The adequate implementation of economic, social, and cultural rights by the regional authorities required financial resources. Accordingly, denying the regional government any income from energy resources in post-war Iraq might be regarded as an obvious violation of the central government's obligation to protect the international human rights of the Iraqi citizens nationally and regionally.

Whatever powers are conferred on a regional government, they would not be effective in protecting constitutional rights and human rights if no financial resources were available to carry them out.[83] In essence, as the major factor in preventing recurrence of violence, increased implementation of the state's constitutional and human rights obligations depends on closer interaction and institutionalized cooperation between

---

81 UNGA, 'Role of Local Government in the Promotion and Protection of Human Rights-Final Report of the Human Rights Council Advisory Committee' (7 August 2015) UN Doc A/HRC/30/49, para 21.

82 'Oil and Borders: How to Fix Iraq's Kurdish Crisis' (2017) Crisis Group Middle East, Briefing No 55, 5; Volkan Özdemir and Slawomir Raszewski, 'State and Substate Oil Trade: The Turkey-KRG Deal' (2016) 23(1) Middle East Policy 125; Bilal A Wahab (n 4) 15.

83 UNGA (n 81) para 22.

the central and regional governments on political, economic, and social rights.[84]

3.3. THE EFFECTIVE APPLICATION OF THE CONSTITUTIONAL NORMS

Establishing a new democratic constitutional order to eliminate monopolies of power, reduce the risk of new conflicts, and restrain the uncontrolled behaviour of political entities would be a milestone in changing the Iraqi government from an authoritarian, violent, oppressive, and exclusionary regime to a less authoritarian, less violent regime with more tolerance towards people from all ethnic, religious, and cultural backgrounds and other political entities in the Iraqi political system. Within the new order, officials must be subject to the rule of law.

Importantly, a new political and democratic constitutional order requires identifying the authorities and allocating particular responsibilities and decision-making powers. In addition to the role of political entities, particular attention to ethnic, gender, and religious diversity and the inclusion of all minority groups in political and public life will ensure precious opportunities for their involvement in decision-making processes. For instance, in post-war Iraq no major social roles are available to women, but women as well as minorities have a central role in consolidating peace.[85] Strengthening the capacity of women's organisations has a multiplying effect in securing improved observance of human rights and the rule of law.[86]

Although the rule of law and ethnic equality are guaranteed by the Iraqi Constitution in Article 14, their effective implementation has not been evident either before or after the war on Islamic State, especially in 'the ideal use and division of the federal financial resources' contained in Article 106 and 'the management of oil and gas extracted from present

84 ibid para 21. See also International Institute for Democracy and Electoral Assistance, *The Global State of Democracy Exploring Democracy's Resilience* (International IDEA Publications 2017) 257.

85 DCAF Backgrounder (n 40) 7; Ohanyan (n 42) 41.

86 Office of the High Commissioner for Human Rights, 'Rule-of-Law Tools for Post-Conflict States: Mapping the Justice Sector' (2006) HR/PUB/06/2, 30. See also Fionnuala Ní Aoláin and Michael Hamilton, 'Gender and the Rule of Law in Transitional Societies' (2009) 18(2) Minnesota Journal of International Law 380, 395.

fields, provided that it distributes its revenues in a fair manner in proportion to the population distribution in all parts of the country' under Article 112, as parts of the general guarantee of equality. While constitutional equality encourages cooperation between the groups, individual accountability and a quest for comprehensive understanding of the past would allow for peace and stability between them.[87]

Iraqi Kurds have never been allowed to hold a referendum in Kirkuk within the context of 140 (2) of the Iraqi Constitution, which seeks normalization for Iraq's ethnic groups providing that the responsibility placed upon the executive branch of the Iraqi Transitional Government, stipulated in Article 58 of the Transitional Administrative Law, shall extend and continue to the executive authority elected in accordance with the constitution, provided that it accomplishes normalization, a census, and a referendum in Kirkuk and other disputed territories to determine the will of their citizens by a date not exceeding December 31, 2007. As discussed earlier, the Iraqi Kurds had lost their political power in the country and the regional government after the entire budget of the KRG was cut by the central government.

Accordingly, it appears that a democratic constitutional order approving the fundamental rights of ethnic groups based on ethnic equality (in the positive sense of ethnic identity) is crucial in the transition to peace. Article 1 (1) of the Declaration on the Rights of Persons Belonging to National or Ethnic, Religious and Linguistic Minorities (1992)[88] states that achieving this objective requires protecting the existence and the national or ethnic cultural, religious and linguistic identity of minorities within their respective territories through the adoption of appropriate legislative and other measures (Article 1/2), including the planning and implementation of national policies and programmes to promote the possibility of the full participation in social, political and economic progress and development in the country without any form of discrimination (Articles 4–7). This is the basis and the prerequisite of democracy: important decisions are to be made only after the wide participation of the public and deliberative procedures which ensure respect for law and freedom of criticism before and after the

---

87 Louis M Santander, 'Reconciliation: A Critical Approach to Peacebuilding in Bosnia-Herzegovina' (2016) Journal of Peace, Conflict and Development 77, 84.

88 UNGA, Res 47/135: 'Declaration on the Rights of Persons Belonging to National or Ethnic, Religious and Linguistic Minorities' (18 December 1992) UN Doc A/RES/47/135.

decision is made. This ultimately serves to increase public trust in state institutions.[89]

More importantly, the recognition of ethnic identities irrespective of their culture, religion, and language is attainable through a democratic constitutional order that provides a balance between the powers of the central and regional government. This means approving the fundamental rights of ethnic groups based on the principle of equality; the planning and implementation of substantial and effective national policies to ensure the full participation of minorities and ethnic groups in social, political, and economic progress and development without any form of discrimination; and in this case the application of Article 20 of the Iraqi Constitution, in which the right to participate in public affairs and enjoy political rights including the right to vote, elect, and run for office are the requirements of citizenship.

The constitutional balance between shared rule (participation of regional governments in the decision-making procedure of central governments) and self-rule (making decisions on policies, legislation, and taxation under within regional parliaments) is the essence of a federal political regime. To ensure a combination of shared rule and self-rule, the federal regime needs an entrenched constitution; guaranteed powers and functions for national and state governments; a bicameral parliament in which the states are represented; and oversight by the judiciary. These are the significant preconditions that reduce the likelihood or severity of ethnic conflicts, communal tensions, and the massive exploitation of the mandates obtained.[90] In other words, the constitutional balance and combination of shared and self-rule have a demonstrable utility in peacebuilding.[91]

A combination of self-rule and shared rule in post-war Iraq would ensure the equality, diversity management, and the rule of law as the prerequisites for sharing the power to govern the peacebuilding process. Constitutional and legal equality would encourage cooperation between the central and regional government in governing natural resources in a

89 Quincy Wright, *A Study of War (Volume II)* (The University of Chicago Press 1942) 842. See also Secretary General of the Council of Europe, 'State of Democracy, Human Rights and the Rule of Law: Populism – How Strong Are Europe's Checks and Balances?' (2017) 82.

90 Khan (n 74) 252; Bertus De Villiers, 'Federations: Shared Rule and Self-rule in the Search for Stable Governance' (2012) 39(3) Politikon 391, 407.

91 Daniel J Elazar (ed), *Federal Systems of the World: A Handbook of Federal, Confederal and Autonomy Arrangements* (2nd edn, Longman 1994) 2; De Villiers (n 90) 391–410.

transparent manner. Moreover, responsibility for past violations, abuses, and misconduct due to non-transparency in resource governance would make reconciliation and the transition to justice achievable. This is subject to constitutional reforms that ensure mechanisms for addressing past abuses and upholding the rule of law.[92] In other words, peacebuilding operations must include efforts to protect human rights, equality, and the rule of law through reforming or strengthening the political and constitutional order.

Of course, the state's accountability and transparency in resource governance, and its effective application of the constitutional norms, would ensure its individual ineterets through promoting higher standards of living, full employment, and economic and social progress. What matters most is that the creation of the conditions of stability and well-being, as subject to Article 55 of the UN Charter, would also ensure 'peaceful and friendly relations between states', which constitutes a pivotal example of international community interests. More precisely, security, stability, and development are essential to ensuring an equal voice for people in deciding how to protect common interests in international law.

4. LESSONS LEARNED

Iraq is an ethnically diverse and energy-rich country with a variety of political, cultural, and ethnic dimensions which have been affected by both Islamic State and the regional Iraqi-Kurdish conflict. If the central government's mismanagement of natural resources was a source of the emergence of the Iraqi-Kurdish conflict, efficient resource management must be at the centre of the peacebuilding talks and negotiations. Energy resource governance has always been a central concern in the transition from war to peace in energy-rich societies. It is important to note, however, that post-conflict management methods, strategies, and policies need to be changed and improved in the direction of reconstruction and recovery.

To achieve a successful transition to peace, a government must provide the basis for trust and confidence between itself and other parties involved in peacebuilding, including peace talks and negotiations for rebuilding the country in all aspects. Having identified accountability and transparency in natural resource governance and the effective application of the

[92] Santander (n 87); Democratic Progress Institute, 'Accountability and Reconciliation in Peace Processes' (2015) 10.

constitutional norms as the fundamental steps towards ensuring peace in energy-rich post-war Iraq, this chapter discussed the pivotal role of natural resources in the transition to a sustainable peace after Islamic State.

Applying the rule of law in the exploitation and distribution of natural resources – ensuring the supremacy of law, equality, accountability to the law, avoidance of arbitrariness, and legal transparency – is an indicator of good governance in the transition to peace. Considering the results obtained in post-war societies, particularly if the international organizations involved in the process take on lessons learned from the previous cases, such as Kosovo and East Timor, would significantly improve the peacebuilding measures in post-war Iraq. In this regard, the lessons learned from the mentioned cases might be summarized as follow:

a) *Decentralized management decisions:* If energy resource mismanagement was a core factor in the disagreement between the KRG and Baghdad, peacebuilding in post-Islamic State Iraq is largely dependent on the good governance of those resources. This requires decentralized management decisions and shared policies. Cooperation between the KRG and the Iraqi central government will thus indicate a common desire to reach a sustainable peace for the whole society.

b) *Building public trust:* Given the damage to the political, financial, cultural, and ethnic dimensions of society as a result of failed governance, the transition to peace will be complicated. However, regional and central governments' shared financial management and sustainable energy resource management would build public trust.

c) *Internationalisation of peacebuilding efforts:* Ethnic divisions can make post-war peacebuilding more difficult than estimated. Establishing a parallel political structure in the local context through international assistance can therefore be invaluable.[93] This is subject to the internationalized legal and political status of the society, through the incorporation of directly applicable international legal norms and acts in the domestic legal system and appealing to the assistance of international organisations such as the UN.

---

93 See, for a more detailed description, Nicolas Lemay-Hébert, 'Coerced Transitions in Timor-Leste and Kosovo: Managing Competing Objectives of Institution-Building and Local Empowerment' (2012) 19(3) Democratization 465; Lise M Howard, 'Kosovo and Timor-Leste: Neotrusteeship, Neighbors, and the United Nations' (2014) 656(1) ANNALS of American Academy of Political and Social Science 116.

d) *Common interests:* If energy resources are the major revenue source in energy-rich countries, sustainable peace in these societies might be coordinated based on a perception of natural resources as a source for common interests instead of tensions. In that sense, rapidly eradicating poverty, enhancing human well-being, and transitioning to a low-carbon energy system in line with national development goals come to the fore. Access to resources should be affordable, reliable, and sustainable. Carbon-based energy systems have been the foundation of modern industrial development, but require sustainable emissions reductions to address climate change and other environmental concerns.[94] Peacebuilding initiatives in post-war societies based on these common grounds will undoubtedly create a positive climate for peace talks to reach an all-encompassing agreement which guarantees all citizens' lawful interests and rights.

e) *New and effective legal order:* Given the challenges of applying, implementing, and enforcing the current law, post-war societies might consider a new and more effective legal order that captures more aspects of public interests, in order to operate an effective framework based on the interests of all citizens as per the principle of equality.

Though maintaining international peace and security and protecting human rights are considered essential community interests,[95] the experiences of Kosovo and East Timor indicate that constructiveness of the peacebuilding operations does not depend only on the involvement of the international community.[96] A successful war-to-peace transition also depends on the variable capacity available and actions taken under ever different circumstances. Yet the achievements of previous cases with or without the direct participation of the international organizations might be taken into consideration and included in the assessment of

94 See Ahmad O Al Khowaiter and Yasser M Mufti, 'An Alternative Energy Transition Pathway Enabled by the Oil and Gas Industry' (2020) 121 Oxford Energy Forum 14.

95 Kingsbury and Donaldson (n 5) 81; Simma, 'From Bilateralism to Community Interest in International Law' (n 5) 235.

96 Dahlia Simangan, *International Peacebuilding and Local Involvement: A Liberal Renaissance?* (Routledge 2019) 80–143. For a discussion on the international intervention in the peacebuilding operations, see Mats Berdal and Spyros Economides (eds), *Nations Interventionism, 1991–2004* (CUP 2007); Simon Chesterman, *You, the People: The United Nations, Transitional Administration, and State-Building* (OUP 2004); Jane Stromseth, David Wippman and Rosa Brooks (eds), *Can Might Make Rights? Building the Rule of Law after Military Interventions* (CUP 2006).

peacebuilding measures in post-war Iraq. Besides the lessons discussed above, the perspectives and proposals of the UN Peacebuilding Commission (PBC) Working Group on Lessons Learned[97] could be a significant foundation for substantial improvements in the peacebuilding process in Iraq after Islamic State.

5. CONCLUSION

Rebuilding Iraq and establishing a peaceful environment after the devastating fight against Islamic State can be achieved through compromise based on effective governance of energy resources as the country's main independent source of revenue. Ensuring respect for the rule of law, fundamental rights, and equality creates a peaceful society and allows a state to protect common interests such as peace and security, human rights, sustainable management and use of natural resources, the protection of the natural environment, and economic solidarity.

This chapter demonstrated that reconstruction and transition to peace in post-war and ethnically diverse societies where energy resources have been subject to mismanagement requires inclusive negotiations for a more lasting agreement. The effective implementation of constitutional norms, or their renegotiation in order to create a new political and constitutional order, respectful of justice and the equitable sharing of energy resources among diverse members of a society to reduce inequalities, would make peace more accessible. Social and economic stability will obviously come through ensuring ethnic equality and diversity management as well. Spreading the rule of law and deepening respect for human rights are seen as central to durable peace and security in post-war societies.[98] With this

---

97 See, for instance, Peacebuilding Commission Working Group on Lessons Learned, *Resource Mobilization for Peacebuilding Priorities and Improved Coordination Among Relevant Actors* (6 April 2011), *Lessons Learned from National Dialogue in Post-Conflict Situations* (14 October 2009), *Comparative Experiences in Developing National Capacities after Conflict* (15 December 2008), *Comparative Lessons from the UN Rule of Law Assistance* (20 October 2008), *Key Insights, Principles, Good Practices and Emerging Lessons in Peacebuilding* (12 June 2008), *Justice in Times of Transition* (26 February 2008), *Local Governance and Decentralization in Post-War Contexts* (13 December 2007) <https://www.un.org/peacebuilding/documents> accessed 15 January 2021.

98 Office of the High Commissioner for Human Rights (n 86) 4; Antony Blinken, Norman Ricklefs and Ned Parker 'Is Iraq on Track? Democracy and Disorder in Baghdad' (2012) 91(4) Foreign Affairs 152, 156.

in mind, the chapter has argued that accountability and transparency as indicators of good governance of natural resources would promote higher standards of living, full employment, and economic and social progress. Moreover, creating the conditions for stability and well-being plays a significant role in promoting security, stability, and development, which would ensure an equal voice to people in deciding on the most adequate way to protect human rights and peace as common interests of the international community.

From a human rights perspective, resource governance in deference to the community interests in the resource-rich society of Iraq will require the Iraqi central government and the KRG to respect peoples' right to dispose of the energy resources in an accountable and transparent way. As collective agents of the international community, states are obliged to act in compliance with the rule of law to ensure the adequate protection of people's fundamental rights and common values, and here it would ensure a peaceful post-war society, serving both the individual and common interests of the international community.

Maintaining the peace and stability in post-war Iraq depends on exercising governance through a highly decentralized political system balancing competing demands for democracy and unity in society. Having analysed decentralization as a means to vertical power-sharing between the central and regional governments, this chapter provided an explanation of how to avoid the recurrence of major disagreements and conflicts in energy-rich and ethnically diverse Iraq in the aftermath of the war on Islamic State.

As the war on Islamic State in Iraq created the grounds for increasing tensions between the Kurds and the Iraqi central government, this chapter put forward effective pathways to peacebuilding in northern Iraq, based on regional conditions stemming from energy resource governance and lessons learned from related cases. The war on Islamic State carried crucial advantages and disadvantages for the KRG, giving it the economic leverage to take a concrete step towards establishing a Kurdish state, much against the wishes of the Iraqi central government. For this reason, the peacebuilding process in post-Islamic State Iraq was gradually overcome by violence. Citing the primary factors triggering the tensions between the Kurds and Baghdad, this chapter discussed the importance of decentralized management decisions, building public trust, identifying common interests, and establishing an effective legal order as the primary pathways towards more sustainable peace in northern Iraq.

PART III

HUMAN RIGHTS AND SECURITY RELATED ISSUES

THE RIGHT TO SELF-DETERMINATION AND THE PROLONGED OCCUPATION OF PALESTINIAN TERRITORY

Matthew SAUL*

---

* Associate Professor, Inland Norway University of Applied Sciences, Norway. Guest researcher at PluriCourts – Centre for the Study of the Legitimate Roles of the Judiciary in the Global Order, Faculty of Law, University of Oslo, Norway. This chapter draws on an expert opinion prepared by the author for the Diakonia International Humanitarian Law Resource Centre in Jerusalem (July 2019). Thanks to Geir Ulfstein, Gentian Zyberi, and the anonymous reviewer for very helpful comments on earlier drafts.

1. INTRODUCTION

The law of occupation limits the scope for changes to an occupied territory, its demography, and its infrastructure. In so doing, the law of occupation protects the occupied people's right to self-determination. However, the law of occupation expects temporary occupations. In prolonged occupations, extending over many years, it may not be viable to conserve the circumstances of the occupied territory in the way envisaged by the law of occupation. One way to respond to this potential inadequacy is to give more attention to the function of the right to self-determination as a fundamental principle of international law.[1]

The right to self-determination may inform interpretations of the law of occupation. Scholars refer to the right to self-determination in order to support arguments for modifying components of the law of occupation concerning participation in decision-making processes;[2] change of infrastructure;[3] usufruct;[4] and the end of occupation.[5] The right to self-determination is thus one element among others in the discussion about how to interpret components of the law of occupation.[6]

The right to self-determination may also serve as a standalone basis for assessing the conduct of the occupier. The International Court of Justice (ICJ) took this approach in its 2004 advisory opinion on the Legal Consequences of the Construction of a Wall in the Occupied Palestinian

1 For a general account of the role of fundamental principles in the creation and practice of international law, see Roman A Kolodkin, 'Fragmentation of International Law? A View from Russia' in Roland St John Macdonald and Douglas M Johnston, *Towards World Constitutionalism: Issues in the Legal Ordering of the World Community*, (Martinus Nijhoff 2005) 227–228.

2 Eyal Benvenisti, *The International Law of Occupation* (2nd edn, Oxford University Press 2012) 79–80; Eyal Benvenisti, *The International Law of Occupation* (Princeton University Press 1993) 171, 215.

3 Alain Pellet, 'The Destruction of Troy Will Not Take Place' in Emma Playfair (ed), *International Law and the Administration of Occupied Territories: Two Decades of Israeli Occupation of the West Bank and Gaza Strip* (Clarendon Press 1992) 169.

4 Iain Scobbie, 'Natural Resources and Belligerent Occupation: Mutation Through Permanent Sovereignty' in Stephen Bowen (ed), *Human Rights, Self-Determination and Political Change in the Occupied Palestinian Territories* (Martinus Nijhoff 1997) 221, 249.

5 Iain Scobbie, 'An Intimate Disengagement: Israel's Withdrawal from Gaza, the Law of Occupation and of Self-Determination' (2004) 11(1) Yearbook of Islamic and Middle Eastern Law 3, 21.

6 Such factors include evidence from the occupier of a concern for the best interests of the local population, see scholars cited by Marco Longobardo, 'The Palestinian Right to Exploit the Dead Sea Coastline for Tourism' (2015) 58 German Yearbook of International Law 317, section III A at footnote 41.

Territory.[7] The ICJ provided only a brief account of the meaning and reach of the right to self-determination.[8] This is understandable in light of the question asked by the UN's General Assembly, but it gives little guidance on whether it is advisable to focus on using the right to self-determination as an aid in interpreting the law of occupation or elaborating its function as a standalone legal framework.

How should we understand the function of the right to self-determination in situations of prolonged occupation? To shed light on this question, the first part of this chapter examines doctrine on the meaning of the right in international law and its relation to the law of occupation. It explains how the right to self-determination may serve as part of the law of occupation's interpretative framework, but also as a standalone component of the international legal framework for prolonged occupations. The second part of this chapter examines the prolonged occupation of Palestinian territory from the perspective of the right to self-determination. Specific attention is given to the Oslo Accords, circumstances in Gaza, population movement, and natural resource usage. The analysis brings more fully into focus the distinct nature of the two functions of the right to self-determination and illustrates the importance of keeping them separate. The third part of the chapter examines the legal consequences that follow from denying the right to self-determination. The focus is on the right's importance for the international community of states and the obligations this generates.

The chapter argues that when circumstances add complexity and uncertainty to the operation of a specialised legal regime, it is important to recognise that fundamental principles of international law continue to operate as a baseline securing protection of international community interests. The right to self-determination as a precept of non-domination provides legal protection in situations of prolonged occupation regardless of the haze that can form around the meaning and application of the law of occupation. The right to self-determination precludes practices that will pre-empt the choices available to the people at the end of an occupation with regard to the territory's organization, utilization,

---

7 *Legal Consequences of the Construction of a Wall in the Occupied Palestinian Territory* (Advisory Opinion) [2004] ICJ Rep 136; see also Jean-François Gareau, 'Shouting at the Wall: Self-Determination and the Legal Consequences of the Construction of a Wall in the Occupied Palestinian Territory' (2005) 18 Leiden Journal of International Law 489.

8 *Israeli Wall case* (n 7) [88], [115–122] and [159]; See also the Separate Opinion of Judge Higgins [29–30].

and status. Attempts to make sense of the law of occupation in situations of prolonged occupation should not come at the expense of attending to the meaning of, and legal consequences that result from, denial of the right to self-determination.

2. THE MEANING OF THE RIGHT TO SELF-DETERMINATION

One of the purposes of the United Nations is to pursue the development of friendly relations among nations 'based on respect for the principle of equal rights and self-determination of peoples'.[9] The development of the legal right to self-determination occurred subsequent to the signing of the UN Charter, as part of the movement for decolonisation during the 1960s.[10] Thus the core meaning of the legal right to self-determination centres on the idea of freedom from foreign subjugation.[11]

The legal status of the right to self-determination is grounded in several UN General Assembly Resolutions,[12] and its inclusion as common

9 Charter of the United Nations (opened for signature 24 June 1945, entered into force 24 October 1945) 1 UNTS XVI (UN Charter) art 1(2); see Rosalyn Higgins, *Problems and Process: International Law and How We Use It* (Clarendon Press 1994) 111.

10 See Marc Weller, *Escaping the Self-Determination Trap* (Brill | Nijhoff 2009) 35; Jean Salmon, 'Internal Aspects of the Right to Self-Determination: Towards a Democratic Legitimacy Principle?' in Christian Tomuschat (ed), *Modern Law of Self-Determination* (Martinus Nijhoff 1993) 253, 254–255.

11 UN General Assembly, 'Resolution 1514 (XV): Declaration on the Granting of Independence to Colonial Countries and Peoples' (14 December 1960) UN Doc A/RES/1514(XV). The Declaration specifies that 'the subjection of peoples to alien subjugation, domination and exploitation constitutes a denial of fundamental rights, [and] is contrary to the Charter of the United Nations'. It also provides that 'all peoples have the right to self-determination' (numeral 1) and that 'by virtue of their right they freely determine their political status and freely pursue their economic, social and cultural development' (numeral 2). This is the basis for a people subject to colonial rule to be given the choice of how they wish to be constituted: independence, integration, or association, which is specified in GA Res. 1541; see *Legal Consequences for States of the Continued Presence of South Africa in Namibia (South West Africa) Notwithstanding Security Council Resolution 276 (1970)* (Advisory Opinion) [1971] ICJ Rep 56 paras 52–53.

12 UNGA (n 11); UNGA, Res 1541 (XV): 'Principles Which Should Guide Members in Determining Whether or Not an Obligation to Transmit the Information Called for Under Article 73 e of the Charter' (15 December 1960) UN Doc A/RES/1541(XV); UNGA, Res 2625 (XXV): 'Declaration on Principles of International Law Concerning Friendly Relations and Co-operation Among States in Accordance with the Charter of the United Nations' (24 October 1970) UN Doc A/RES/2625(XXV).

Article 1 in the two International Covenants of Human Rights.[13] These instruments do not limit the legal right to self-determination to the colonial context.[14] Still, the broad formulation of 'all peoples have the right freely to determine, without external interference, their political status and to pursue their economic, social and cultural development', which is repeated in almost all the relevant UN documents, means that the meaning of the right has been and continues to be a source of contestation.[15] To clarify the meaning of the legal right to self-determination, let us consider how it relates to self-determination as a political principle.

As a political principle, it has at least three key dimensions. One is that the people of a state as a whole should be free, within the boundaries of the state, to determine, without outside interference, their social, political, economic, and cultural infrastructure.[16] Another is that each ethnically or culturally distinct group should be free to choose how it constitutes itself.[17] A third is that a state should be constituted along democratic lines to enable the people – including distinct groups – to participate in the state's social, political, economic, and cultural systems.[18] Attempts have been made, with varying levels of success, to identify each of these dimensions within the international legal concept of self-determination.

The most successful of the political components, in terms of the acceptance by states of its international legal status, has been the first. Not only is it politically important, but it is also an international legal requirement that the population of a state as a whole be free to 'determine, without external interference, their political status and to pursue their

13 International Covenant on Civil and Political Rights (adopted 16 December 1966, entered into force 23 March 1976) 999 UNTS 171 (ICCPR); International Covenant on Economic, Social and Cultural Rights (adopted 16 December 1966, entered into force 3 January 1976) UNTS 93 (ICESCR).

14 See Gareau (n 7) 500.

15 Weller (n 10) 23; see also Deborah Z Cass, 'Re-Thinking Self-Determination: A Critical Analysis of Current International Law Theories' (1992) 18(1) Syracuse Journal of International and Comparative Law 21, 22–23.

16 Jeremy Waldron, 'Two Conceptions of Self-Determination' in Samantha Besson and John Tasioulas (eds), *The Philosophy of International Law* (OUP 2010) 397, 406.

17 ibid 398.

18 See Michla Pomerance, 'The United States and Self-Determination: Perspectives on the Wilsonian Conception' (1976) 70(1) The American Journal of International Law 1, 17 and 20; Antonio Cassese, *Self-Determination of Peoples: A Legal Reappraisal* (Cambridge University Press 1995) 19; Thomas D Musgrave, *Self-Determination and National Minorities* (Clarendon Press 1997) 22–24; see also Weller (n 10) 23.

economic, social and cultural development'.[19] The core accepted meaning of the right to self-determination overlaps with the right of a sovereign state to 'freely choose and develop its political, social, economic and cultural systems'.[20] This overlap supports the idea of popular sovereignty.[21]

Advocates of popular sovereignty posit that sovereignty is now better seen as the consummation of the self-determination of people, rather than something that is worth protecting for its own sake. Yet in spite of a long history of governments subscribing to the concept of popular sovereignty,[22] it has yet to be fully reflected in international law, which continues to separate the rights of the state from the rights of the people.[23] Accordingly, it is possible to view the right to self-determination as generating an additional prohibition on interference in the internal affairs of a state.[24]

The question to be asked when determining whether external involvement in a territory is consistent with the right to self-determination is this: does the external involvement prevent the people in question from freely determining their political status and pursuing their economic, social, and cultural development? To identify the threshold at which the engagement of a third state on a state's territory constitutes a breach of the right to self-determination requires a factual assessment, specific to the case in point. It is clear, though, that an imposed governance arrangement is such a breach,[25] as this hinders enjoyment of all of the elements covered

19 UNGA UN Doc A/RES/2625(XXV) (n 12); common article 1 (2) of the ICCPR and ICESCR; see also UN Human Rights Committee (HRC), 'General Comment No. 12: Article 1 (Right to self-determination)' (13 April 1984) para 6; Higgins (n 9) 104; Cassese (n 18) 59; Rein Müllerson. *International Law, Rights and Politics: Developments in Eastern Europe and the CIS* (Routledge 1994) 90–91.

20 UNGA, UN Doc A/RES/2625(XXV) (n 12).

21 See Brad R Roth, 'The Enduring Significance of State Sovereignty' (2004) 56 Florida Law Review 1017, 1042; Christian Tomuschat, 'International Law: Ensuring the Survival of Mankind on the Eve of a New Century' (1999) 281 Recueil des Cours de l'Académie de Droit International 9, 165; Müllerson (n 19); Allan Rosas, 'Internal Self-Determination' in Christian Tomuschat (ed), *Modern Law of Self-Determination* (Martinus Nijhoff 1993) 250–251.

22 Brad R Roth, 'Popular Sovereignty: The Elusive Norm' (1997) 91 Proceedings of the American Society of International Law Annual Meeting 363.

23 Maziar Jamnejad and Michael C Wood, 'The Principle of Non-Intervention' (2009) 22(2) Leiden Journal of International Law 345, 369; see also Cassese (n 18) 55; Benedetto Conforti, 'The Principle of Non-Intervention' in Mohammed Bedjaoui (ed), *International Law: Achievements and Prospects* (Martinus Nijhoff 1991) 467.

24 Wouter G Werner, 'Self-Determination and Civil War' (2001) 6(2) Journal of Conflict and Security Law 171; Brad R Roth, *Sovereign Equality and Moral Disagreement: Premises of a Pluralist International Legal Order* (OUP 2011) 81.

25 See Gregory H Fox, *Humanitarian Occupation* (CUP 2008) 208–209; Richard D Caplan, 'Transitional Administration' in Vincent Chetail (ed), *Post-Conflict*

in the standard definition of the right. It also triggers application of the law of occupation. The circumstances of occupation change how we think about the right to self-determination. They put the focus on ending the occupation, but also on preserving the occupied territory, its demography, and its infrastructure, so that it is possible for self-determination to eventually resume.

3. THE LAW OF OCCUPATION AND THE RIGHT TO SELF-DETERMINATION

The law of occupation is a regulatory framework that applies in warfare if a state comes into uninvited effective control of the territory of a third state.[26] Its content has been informed by rationales such as servicing the humanitarian needs of the people and preserving the occupied state's sovereignty.[27] This section explains how the law of occupation is also a means of protecting the occupied population's right to self-determination.

The primary sources of treaty law regulating situations of occupation are the Regulations Annexed to the Hague Convention IV 1907 (Hague law/Hague Regulations),[28] in particular Articles 42–56; and Geneva Convention No. IV 1949 (Geneva law/GC IV),[29] in particular Articles 27–34 and 47–78. As the 'Hague law' was created at a time when there was no general prohibition on the use of force[30] or a legal right of all peoples to

Peacebuilding: A Lexicon (OUP 2009) 359, 364; UNGA, 'Universal Realization of the Right of Peoples to Self-Determination: Resolution adopted by the General Assembly on 22 December 2003' (2 March 2004) UN Doc A/RES/58/161, para 2; Steven Wheatley, 'The Security Council, Democratic Legitimacy, and Regime Change in Iraq' (2006) 17(3) European Journal of International Law 531, 540.

26 *Prosecutor* v *Mladen Naletilić and Vinko Martinović* (Judgment) ICTY IT-98-34-T (31 March 2003), para 217.

27 See Adam Roberts, 'Prolonged Military Occupation: The Israeli-Occupied Territories since 1967' (1990) 84(1) The American Journal of International Law 44, 46.

28 Hague Convention (IV) Respecting the Laws and Customs of War on Land, with Annex of Regulations (adopted 18 October 1907, entered into force 26 January 1910) TS No 539 (Hague Regulations).

29 Fourth Geneva Convention Relative to the Protection of Civilian Persons in Time of War (adopted 12 August 1949, entered into force 21 October 1950) 75 UNTS 287 (GC IV).

30 See Christopher Greenwood, 'The Administration of Occupied Territory in International Law' in Emma Playfair (ed), *International Law and the Administration of Occupied Territories* (Clarendon Press 1992) 242, 245.

self-determination,[31] meaning that title to territory could still be acquired through the use of force, one might doubt its contemporary relevance as a legal framework for safeguarding sovereign rights. There was, however, a rule that during warfare, when territory of a state came under the authority of an army whose government did not have title to that territory, its annexation was not permitted until the cessation of hostilities.[32] This created a transitional phase in which a legal framework for the preservation of sovereign rights was deemed necessary to prevent further deterioration in relations between the belligerents and hopefully increase the likelihood of a peace treaty.[33]

This rationale, an understanding based on contemporary experience that occupations were not prolonged in nature, and a belief that occupiers were not particularly interested in civilian affairs, or would not need to be, help to explain why the Hague law does not concentrate on matters related to the civilians.[34] Instead, it concentrates on issues pertinent to the displaced sovereign. One example is Article 55, which classifies the occupier as only the administrator of public properties,[35] which it must do according to the rules of usufruct (prudent administration).[36] Another example is Article 43, which requires that the existing laws must be respected unless pursuit of 'public order and safety [civil life]' absolutely prevents doing so.

The 1949 Diplomatic Conference in Geneva was a response to developments in the nature of the state and in the conduct of warfare up to and during the world wars, which had demonstrated the inadequacies of the Hague law with regard to human welfare.[37] The 'Geneva law' provisions of the law of occupation supplemented rather than replaced the Hague law.[38] The humanitarian rationale of the Conference greatly shaped the

---

[31] See Gerry J Simpson, 'The Diffusion of Sovereignty: Self-Determination in the Post – Colonial Age' (1996) 32 Stanford Journal of International Law 255.

[32] Georg Schwarzenberger, 'The Law of Belligerent Occupation: Basic Issues' (1960) 30 Nordic Journal of International Law 10, 12–14.

[33] Doris Appel Graber, *The Development of the Law of Belligerent Occupation 1863–1914 – A Historical Survey* (Columbia University Press 1949) 37–40.

[34] Eyal Benvenisti, *International Law of Occupation* (Princeton University Press 1993) 20–21.

[35] Hague Regulations (n 28) art 55.

[36] This provision is returned to below in the discussion on the use of natural resources in the oPt.

[37] See Benvenisti (n 34) 23–27.

[38] See Jean S Pictet (ed), *Commentary: The Fourth Geneva Convention Relative to the Protection of Civilian Persons in Time of War* (International Committee of the Red Cross 1958) 614.

content of the law, which is focused on the plight of civilians during occupation, typified in provisions such as the requirement not to create unemployment (Article 52),[39] and provisions regarding labour conditions (Article 51).[40]

The law of occupation imposes obligations on the occupier and gives rights to the occupied in relation to how the administration is conducted. For example, Article 50 GC IV establishes obligations pertaining to education of children, Article 55 GC IV to the supply of foodstuffs and medical supplies to the civilian population,[41] and Article 48 of the Hague Regulations[42] governs collection of taxes. There is an emphasis on the indication of areas where administration must be conducted rather than on change or development.[43] The expectation is that change will be deferred until the occupation ends,[44] meaning that any attempts to make permanent changes would be of doubtful legality.[45] There are, however, limited circumstances in which the law of occupation allows for making temporary legislative changes.[46]

Article 43 Hague Regulations,[47] as supplemented with Article 64 GC IV,[48] is thought to embody the *raison d'être* of the law of occupation: the 'conservationist principle'.[49] Article 43, as noted above, requires that the existing laws must be respected unless this is absolutely prevented by the pursuit of 'public order and safety [civil life]'. The key term in Article 43 is 'absolutely prevented'. The nature of the phrase is aptly described by Stone: 'It has never been taken literally; and unless it is so taken, the boundaries of the occupant's legislative powers are still to be drawn.'[50] It has been seen as a matter of military necessity only,[51] but most texts

39 GC IV (n 29) art 52.
40 ibid art 51.
41 ibid art. 50 and 55.
42 Hague Regulations (n 28) art 48.
43 Greenwood (n 30) 246.
44 See Gregory H Fox, 'The Occupation of Iraq' (2005) 36(2) Georgetown Journal of International Law 195, 234–240.
45 Greenwood (n 30) 245.
46 See Hilaire McCoubrey and Nigel D White, *International Law and Armed Conflict* (Dartmouth Publishing 1992) 287.
47 Hague Regulations (n 28) art 43.
48 GC IV (n 29) art 64.
49 See McCoubrey and White (n 46) 286.
50 Julius Stone, *Legal Controls of International Conflict* (Reinhart and Company 1954) 698.
51 See Edmund H Schwenk, 'Legislative Power of the Military Occupant under Article 43, Hague Regulations', (1945) 54 The Yale Law Journal 393 and the many citations therein.

now link it with both military necessity and necessity for public order and safety, or civil life, depending on language.[52]

The preceding account indicates that the law of occupation protects the right to self-determination by essentially freezing its exercise while the occupation continues. The justification may be found in the following logic: attempts to exercise elements of self-determination, such as acts involving the depletion of the capital of natural resources, will be susceptible to direct and indirect influence from the occupier; thus such acts should be prevented, as they are not acts of free determination, given the representation problem. In addition, they should be prevented because they will pre-empt or distort the self-determination choices available once the occupation has ended. This is the pre-emption problem. An occupier's adherence to the law of occupation should ensure that an occupied people are in a position to resume self-determination once the occupation ends. This logic is most persuasive in a shorter-term occupation. A prolonged occupation, to which we now turn, challenges the feasibility of freezing change and development of the state and civil infrastructure.

4. THE RIGHT TO SELF-DETERMINATION IN A PROLONGED OCCUPATION

In a prolonged occupation, extending over many years, the right to self-determination continues to generate an obligation for the occupier to end the occupation.[53] Moreover, adhering to the law of occupation will continue to protect the right to self-determination. Yet the sufficiency of this approach – protecting self-determination through preserving the circumstances of the territory – will likely reduce as time passes. In an occupation that spans many years, limiting the scope for changing and developing the territory may start to pre-empt matters of self-determination. Infrastructure will start to become outdated, for example. In addition, if resources are to be utilized or preserved effectively, choices

52 See Michael Bothe, 'Occupation, Belligerent', *Encyclopedia of Public International Law* 3 (1997) 765; McCoubrey and White (n 46) 284; for a broader reading see Benvenisti (n 2) 79.

53 See Ralph Wilde, 'Expert Opinion on the Applicability of Human Rights Law to the Palestinian Territories with a Specific Focus on the Respective Responsibilities of Israel, as the Extraterritorial State, and Palestine, as the Territorial State' Diakonia International Humanitarian Law Resource Centre in Jerusalem (9 February 2018) 13.

must be made about what steps to take and about which actors should make those choices. For such reasons, prolonged occupation challenges the idea that the conservationist approach in the law of occupation is an optimal response to matters of self-determination. Scholars have addressed how the conservationist principle should be understood in circumstances of prolonged occupation.[54]

This debate includes Pellet's proposal for reading the conservationist principle in light of the right to self-determination. Pellet has argued that the law of occupation was originally intended to protect the rights of the displaced sovereign. Consequently, the principle of conservation should determine the validity of any changes made in the interest of military or humanitarian necessity. Now, however, because it is the people who are sovereign, the limit should be the right to self-determination.[55] Hence, for Pellet, changes linked to humanitarian interests can be pursued to the extent that they do not affect the right to self-determination.[56] This, Pellet argues, would allow such changes up to the point of 'physical character, demographic composition, institutional structure, or status of […] territories.' In this reading, self-determination sets the limits on change and development. Such an approach foresees scope for more invasive changes than under the conservationist principle, but prevents foundational changes in the areas covered by the right to self-determination. One challenge is that a collection of small changes could cumulatively have an overall impact on the scope for exercise of the right to self-determination following the end of the occupation. Also, because this proposal gives the occupier greater discretion, it increases the risk of changes being made to favour the interests of the occupier.

This analysis suggests reasons to doubt that the right to self-determination is an adequate replacement for the conservationist principle. It would therefore be preferable to have a specific rendering of the conservationist principle for situations of prolonged occupation. Longobardo has proposed a test based on an assessment of 'the concrete advantage of the new policy: If it benefits only the occupying power, it should be considered unlawful, whilst if it benefits the local population,

---

54 See work cited in Longobardo (n 6) section III A.

55 Pellet (n 3) 186.

56 ibid 202; see also Pål Wrange, 'Self-Determination, Occupation and the Authority to Exploit Natural Resources: Trajectories from Four European Judgments on Western Sahara' (2019) 52(1) Israel Law Review 3, 19, contemplating the merger of aspects of the law of occupation with the UN law for non-self-governing territories.

there is room to argue that it is lawful, provided that it does not strengthen the occupying power's claims over the territory.'[57] One challenge with such an approach is how to assess whether the new policy in fact benefits the local population. Benvenisti's scholarship suggests that the significance of this sort of challenge may be reduced through a focus on local participation in the decision-making: 'The more occupation policies are shaped and implemented with the effective input of the local population, the more credibility will be given to the occupant's assertions of pursuing legitimate goals.'[58] A challenge here would be determining which local actors should participate and under what sort of conditions. There will remain a risk that the local actors involved will be chosen because of potential alignment with the preferences of the occupier.

The debate surrounding the scope and content of the conservationist principle in general, but especially in relation to prolonged occupations, is one reason why it is important to remember that the right to self-determination also functions separately from the law of occupation. The right to self-determination operates in the background of the law of occupation, providing baseline protection for the fundamental international community interest by ensuring that people are free from domination in how they exercise fundamental societal choices. This protection is especially relevant when contestation over the meaning of the law of occupation for a particular set of circumstances undermines its effectiveness as a source of legal protection. The subsequent sections develop this argument through a case study of the prolonged occupation of the Palestinian territory.

5. SELF-DETERMINATION OF THE PALESTINIAN PEOPLE

Israel occupied the Palestinian territory, consisting of the Gaza Strip and the West Bank, including East Jerusalem, in 1967.[59] Having now lasted for over 50 years, it is the longest military occupation existing today.[60]

---

57 Longobardo (n 6) section III A.

58 Benvenisti (n 37) 79.

59 See, for a succinct account on the history of the occupation, *Israeli Wall case* (n 7) [70–77].

60 Other situations which may be argued to constitute prolonged military occupations include the territories of: Moldova (by Russia since 1992), Azerbaijan

This section assesses particular aspects of the occupation that can help illuminate the nature and significance of the legal backstop role of the right to self-determination in circumstances of prolonged occupation. The discussion proceeds in the following order: (A) the circumstances of the occupation overall; (B) the Oslo Accords; (C) circumstances in Gaza; (D) the settlements and the wall; and (E) the use of natural resources.

5.1. THE OVERALL OCCUPATION AND THE RIGHT TO SELF-DETERMINATION

The analysis in the preceding sections focused on one state occupying another state. The circumstances of the prolonged occupation of Palestinian territory diverge from this model in two main respects. First, while the people of Palestine exist and have the right to self-determination, as recognised in major, widely supported international instruments,[61] there is contestation among certain states as to whether Palestine has yet the status of a state.[62] This disagreement complicates Palestine's ability to rely on state-based rights and obligations under international law, and raises the importance of the right to self-determination as a basis for legal protection from external interference.

Second, the Green Line from the armistice agreement of 1949 between Israel and Jordan 'is currently internationally recognised as the

(by Armenia since 1991), Western Sahara (by Morocco since 1975), Cyprus (by Turkey since 1974). There are other occupations that face the possibility of a prolonged reality, such as the territory of Ukraine (by Russia since 2014).

61 *Israeli Wall case* (n 7) [118].

62 In November 2012, the UN General Assembly decided, by 138 votes to 9 with 41 states abstaining, 'to accord to Palestine non-member observer State status in the United Nations'. 'Status of Palestine in the United Nations: Resolution adopted by the General Assembly on 29 November 2012' (4 December 2012) UN Doc A/Res/67/19, 3; see Andreas Zimmerman, 'Palestine and the International Criminal Court Quo Vadis? Reach and Limits of Declarations under Article12(3)' (2013) 11(2) Journal of International Criminal Justice 303, 304; note also that after referral from Palestine, and the conclusion of the preliminary investigation by the International Criminal Court (ICC) prosecutor, ICC Pre-Trial Chamber I is preparing a jurisdictional ruling on the scope of the territorial jurisdiction of the ICC under article 12(2)(a) of the Rome Statute in Palestine; Palestine has also initiated a case at the ICJ, which will spotlight its claim to statehood, *Relocation of the United States Embassy to Jerusalem (Palestine v United States of America)* (Application Instituting Proceedings) [2018] General List No 176; see Nathaniel Berman, 'Jerusalem before the International Courts: Utopias 2020' (*Opinio Juris*, 10 August 2020) <https://opiniojuris.org/2020/08/10/jerusalem-before-the-international-courts-utopias-2020/> accessed 15 January 2021.

eastern limit of Israeli sovereignty',[63] yet 'Israel has never recognised the Green Line as an international border and maintains it has claims to the West Bank.'[64] At the same time, Israel's annexation of East Jerusalem lacks international recognition.[65] The dispute over exact territorial borders and the failure to resolve it contributes to an explanation for the prolonged occupation.[66] The right to self-determination requires that an occupation be brought to an end, which would normally entail withdrawal of the occupier. In the context of the occupied Palestinian territories (oPt), exercise of the right to self-determination has come to focus on the resolution of the political dispute over the territorial claim. The right to self-determination requires that such negotiations proceed in good faith.[67]

In the pursuit of a political resolution, adherence to the law of occupation protects the right to self-determination.[68] Its conservationist principle conserves political, economic, social, and cultural conditions, so that these matters may be freely determined when the occupation ends. Disregard for the law of occupation in order to make changes in these areas may infringe the right to self-determination. However, it may be possible that violations of the conservationist principle – centred on an assessment of military necessity and necessity for public order and safety or civil life – do not reach a sufficient level to infringe on the right to self-determination. What matters for the right to self-determination is whether the occupier's actions lead to pre-emption of the choices available to the people on the organization, utilization, and status of the territory following the end of the occupation.

The contestation surrounding whether or not the people of Palestine have self-determined to the status of a state generates additional self-determination-based obligations for third states. In particular, there is an obligation on third states to be respectful of the on-going process of

---

63 Michael Sfard, 'B – Border/Barrier' in Orna Ben-Naftali, Michael Sfard and Hedi Viterbo, *The ABC of the OPT: A Legal Lexicon of the Israeli Control over the Occupied Palestinian Territory* (CUP 2018) 46.

64 ibid 46.

65 ibid 49.

66 Gareau (n 7) 512.

67 Vienna Convention on the Law of Treaties (adopted 23 May 1969, entered into force 27 January 1980) 1155 UNTS 332 (VCLT) art 26.

68 It is generally agreed, although disputed by Israel in relation to Geneva law, that both of the main instruments of occupation apply to the oPt (although Israel still claims to follow Geneva law), see *Israeli Wall case* (n 7) [89–101].

determination.[69] This could involve not acting in such ways that would pre-empt the choice of final status: for example, removal or blocking of ties with a third state; or taking actions that have implications for the disputed territorial boundary.

5.2. THE OSLO ACCORDS

In 1993, by putting aside the question of the dispute's final settlement, the parties were able to agree on an interim settlement which came to be known as the Oslo Accords. This provided for a degree of self-government for a five-year transitional period, which would lead to further negotiations on a permanent settlement.[70] The framework for the interim period was set out in the Declaration of Principles (DoP) negotiated in Oslo,[71] and elaborated on in subsequent interim agreements.[72] The DoP provided for immediate transfer of limited authority to an interim Palestinian Authority (PA). This PA was to be appointed by the Palestinian Liberation Organisation (PLO) with Israeli approval,[73] with further authority being gradually transferred to an elected Palestinian Council,[74] such as has been provided for in subsequent agreements.[75] The process has recently been described by a UN Special Rapporteur as 'lifeless'.[76] Yet the Accords have had a major impact on the infrastructure for governance,[77] and continue to be referred to in judicial practice.[78]

---

69 See Gareau (n 7) 516; also, *Israeli Wall case* (n 7) [159].

70 See Avi Shlaim, *The Iron Wall: Israel and the Arab World* (Norton 2000) 516–523.

71 'Declaration of Principles on Interim Self-Government Arrangements' (13 September 1993) 32 ILM 1525 (DoP).

72 See, e.g., 'Israeli-Palestinian Interim Agreement on the West Bank and the Gaza Strip' (28 September 1995) UN Doc A/51/889 and S/1997/357 (Oslo II).

73 DoP (n 71) art VI.

74 DoP (n 71) art III.

75 See, e.g., for the long list of areas, Annex III, Oslo II (n 72).

76 UNGA, 'Situation of Human Rights in the Palestinian Territories Occupied Since 1967' (22 October 2018) UN Doc A/73/45717 para 47; on the legal status of the Oslo Accords, compare G R Watson, 'The 'Wall' Decisions in Legal and Political Context' (2005) 99(1) The American Journal of International Law 6, 22–24, with Yuval Shany, 'Faraway, so Close: The Legal Status of Gaza after Israel's Disengagement' (2006) 8 Yearbook of International Humanitarian Law 369, 381.

77 See Christine Bell, *Peace Agreements and Human Rights* (OUP 2003) 157; on the jurisdictional allocations, see Omar M Dajani, 'Israel's Creeping Annexation' (2017) 111 The American Journal of International Law Unbound 51.

78 See section 5.E below.

The Oslo Accords do not mention the law of occupation.[79] They involve topically and geographically limited transfer of authority to the PA,[80] leading to speculation about an end to or reduction in the scope of the application of the law occupation.[81] Yet Israel 'remained the source of all powers and responsibilities, and retained residual powers in all spheres where no such transfer had been effected,'[82] underpinning the view that the territory remains occupied and fully subject to the law of occupation.[83] This is the position of the ICJ.[84] Still, the Oslo Accords are an important element in Gross' thesis that there are layers of indeterminacy surrounding the question of whether and to what extent the law of occupation continues to apply to the oPt.[85] This heightens the importance of the right to self-determination as an additional, standalone legal basis for assessing practices concerning the oPt.

How do the Oslo Accords relate to the right to self-determination? On the one hand, the arrangements they introduce were intended to be temporary, not pre-empting the right to self-determination but rather functioning as a preparatory step towards its realisation.[86] They were also agreed to by the PLO. At the time the PLO was a national liberation movement,[87] an umbrella organisation for several factions[88] which had received widespread international recognition as the representative of the people's right to self-determination.[89] On the other hand, the

---

79 The Interim Agreement directs the limits on Palestinian authority to be gauged by reference only to the provisions of 'the DoP, this Agreement, or any other agreement that may be reached between the two sides' Oslo II (n 72) art XVIII 4(a).

80 Aeyal Gross, *The Writing on the Wall: Rethinking the International Law of Occupation* (CUP 2017) 182–183.

81 See, e.g., Benvenisti (n 37) 211; Peter Malanczuk, 'Some Basic Aspects of the Agreements between Israel and the PLO from the Perspective of International Law' (1996) 7 EJIL 485, 487; see also discussion in ibid 192–193.

82 Gross (n 80)184.

83 ibid.

84 See *Israeli Wall case* [77]; also, Iain Scobbie, 'Gaza' in Elizabeth Wilmshurst (ed), *International Law and the Classification of Conflicts* (OUP 2012) 280, 298.

85 Gross (n 80) 189.

86 See Gross (n 80) 197; Bell (n 77) 153.

87 Frank L M Van de Craen 'Palestine Liberation Movement' (1990) 12 Encyclopedia of Public International Law 278.

88 See Adrien Katherine Wing, 'The Palestinian Basic Law: Embryonic Constitutionalism' (1999) 31(2) Case Western Reserve Journal International Law 383, 392.

89 In 1974, the UN General Assembly recognised the PLO as 'the principal party to the question of Palestine.' UNGA, 'Invitation to the Palestine Liberation Organization' (14 October 1974) A/Res/3210(XXIX).

arrangements put in place by the Accords have been long-lasting and connect to actions concerning settlements and natural resources,[90] which impede the right to self-determination (see sections below). This is a reason to take greater interest in the adequacy of the PLO's consent as an expression of the will of the people.

The PLO received recognition as the representative of a people with a right to self-determination under circumstances of occupation.[91] There is limited practice to draw upon to make sense of the limits on such a representative's authority. The circumstances of occupation generate a risk that the occupier will dominate their decision-making.[92] Article 47 GC IV addresses this by precluding any changes to political institutions or agreements between the occupied and occupier that would deprive protected persons of the benefits of the GC IV.[93]

Consider also the ICJ's recent advisory opinion on the Legal Consequences of the Separation of the Chagos Archipelago from Mauritius in 1965. The ICJ was of the view that the consent of the representatives of the Mauritian people to the ceding of territory to the UK, while Mauritius was a non-self-governing territory and therefore under the authority of the UK, was not a 'free and genuine expression of the will of the people concerned.'[94] The ICJ did though hint that that a more thorough attempt to ascertain the will of the people could have generated consistency with the right to self-determination.[95] Similar reasoning can help make sense of the requirements of the right to self-determination under circumstances

---

90 Gross (n 80) 187.

91 See also Gareau (n 7) 498.

92 See Pictet (n 38) 67; for the argument that elections and international recognition offset this risk, see Benvenisti (n 37) 210.

93 Pictet (n 38) 272–276.

94 *Legal Consequences of the Separation of the Chagos Archipelago from Mauritius in 1965* (Advisory Opinion) [2019] ICJ Rep 95, para 172.

95 ibid; 'heightened scrutiny should be given to the issue of consent in a situation where a part of a non-self-governing territory is separated to create a new colony.' The ICJ does not specify what would be sufficient as a free and genuine expression of the will of the people; in other recent judicial practice from the UK and the EU concerning non-self-governing territories, evidence of consultation with the people (which was absent) has been treated as a requirement for the validity of agreements between the governing authority and a third party for the use of natural resources, see Wrange (n 56) 19; consultation with the people has also been a feature of the practice for determining the future status of a territory subject to colonial rule, Ralph Wilde, *International Territorial Administration: How Trusteeship and the Civilising Mission Never Went Away* (OUP 2008) 160–161.

of occupation. The individuals who are treated as the representatives of the occupied people should not be assumed to have a mandate to consent to actions that will pre-empt the right to self-determination. Additional evidence of a free and genuine expression of the will of the people is needed. This was not present for the Oslo Accords.[96] At minimum, this reduces the strength of the argument that the Accords can justify actions that pre-empt the right to self-determination.

5.3. GAZA

In September 2005, Israel withdrew its settlements and military installations from the Gaza Strip. The Prime Minister Ariel Sharon, in an address to the UN General Assembly, claimed that this represented 'the end of Israeli control over and responsibility for the Gaza Strip.'[97] Yet Israel has continued to exercise control over the territory in a variety of ways. The Israeli NGO Gisha, in a still accurate report from 2007,[98] highlighted and described the following elements:

- Substantial control of Gaza's land crossings;
- Control on the ground through incursions and sporadic ground troop presence ('no-go zone');
- Complete control of Gaza's airspace;
- Complete control of Gaza's territorial waters;
- Control of the Palestinian population registry (including who is a 'resident' of Gaza);
- Control of tax policy and transfer of tax revenues;

---

96 The Oslo process grew out of a secret channel of negotiations among leading Palestinians and Israelis, which were subsequently upgraded to official negotiations, see Norwegian Ministry of Foreign Affairs, 'Report: Norway's involvement in the peace process in the Middle East' (31 October 1999) <https://www.regjeringen.no/en/dokumenter/involvement/id420034/> accessed 15 January 2021; It is also reported that there was a significant level of opposition to the Accords amongst Palestinians, and that the PLO Executive Committee was split, making it a struggle for Yasser Arafat, Chairman of the Executive Committee, to muster the necessary majority amongst the 18 members, see Shlaim (n 70) 521.

97 Gisha, 'Disengaged Occupiers: The Legal Status of Gaza: Executive Summary (Executive Summary)' (2007) 8 <http://www.gisha.org/UserFiles/File/publications_english/Publications_and_Reports_English/ExecutiveSummary.pdf> accessed 15 January 2021.

98 See UNGA (n 76).

- Control of the ability of the Palestinian Authority to exercise governmental functions;
- Control of the West Bank, which, together with Gaza, constitute a single territorial unit.[99]

The absence of a complete end to Israeli control has prompted debate about whether the law of occupation is no longer applicable.[100] Israel has argued before the Israeli High Court of Justice (HCJ) that its application has ended;[101] the HCJ accepts this argument but does not consider all of the occupier's obligations to be extinguished.[102] The academic literature includes several approaches,[103] including arguments for the continued application of the law of occupation based on the right to self-determination.[104]

Reflecting on the academic debate, Gross recognises that:

> One might argue that, given the lack of full and substantive self-determination (which in the Palestinian case must include effective self-government in both the West Bank and Gaza), it is better to characterize the situation as one of occupation, consistently including the full scope of duties associated with occupation.

However, Gross also asks: 'is reinforcing the occupant's right and duty to intervene always desirable?'[105] Gross argues instead 'for a functional approach, in which the occupier only has obligations for elements where control continues'.[106] The functional approach has practical relevance. How does it relate to the right to self-determination?

In reducing its involvement in the territory, Israel may be argued to have created some autonomous space for what goes on in the territory to be determined by the people of Palestine, and thereby to have reduced the level of infringement of the Palestinians' right to self-determination that

---

99 Gisha (n 97) 10; Gross (n 80) 234 discussing how the sum of control is bigger than the parts.
100 See Gross (n 80) 204–215.
101 ibid 212.
102 ibid 216–17.
103 Compare Shany (n 76) 378, 383, with Scobbie (n 5) 24–25, 29, 31.
104 Scobbie (n 5) 24–25, 29, 31.
105 See also Gross (n 80) 214 discussing the double edge sword involved in arguing for the continued application of the law of occupation.
106 ibid 215.

Israel's presence represents. Under such an interpretation, the continued application of the law of occupation to the whole of the territory and to all public functions might be viewed as no longer necessary from a self-determination perspective. However, there are reasons to query the quality of the autonomous space created as a result of Israel's partial disengagement. There is now greater autonomy, yet it is questionable whether the identity of those actors with authority in Gaza would be the same if Israel did not still exercise the level of control that it does. That is, the circumstances within the Gaza Strip that are connected to Israel's continued control might help to explain why it is that Hamas, specifically, has been able to rise to and sustain authority. Moreover, the control that Israel continues to exert has an influence on the governance decisions taken by Palestinians with authority in the Gaza Strip. For instance, decisions concerning the energy sector are affected by Israel's control of the electricity supply.[107]

The fact that the quality of the autonomous space in the Gaza Strip is not equivalent to an unoccupied territory is a basis to argue for the continued application of the whole of the law of occupation to the whole of the territory.[108] However, accepting a functional approach to the law of occupation does not necessarily coincide with a view that the right to self-determination is being realised in areas where the law of occupation no longer applies. The right to self-determination continues to operate as a standalone basis for assessing the circumstances. Especially when taken as a whole, the control that Israel exercises continues to prevent the exercise of the right to self-determination in the Gaza Strip. It is possible to make sense of the situation legally by accepting the functional approach to the application of the law of occupation, while at the same time attending more closely to how the control that Israel continues to exercise denies the right to self-determination.

---

107 See The World Bank, 'Cash-Strapped Gaza and an Economy in Collapse Put Palestinian Basic Needs at Risk: Press Release' (Jerusalem, 28 September 2018) <https://www.worldbank.org/en/news/press-release/2018/09/25/cash-strapped-gaza-and-an-economy-in-collapse-put-palestinian-basic-needs-at-risk> accessed 15 January 2021.

108 Matthew Saul, 'The Functional Approach to the Occupation of the Gaza Strip and the Right to Self-Determination' (*Opinio Juris*, 25 April 2012) <http://opiniojuris.org/2012/04/25/the-functional-approach-to-the-occupation-of-the-gaza-strip-and-the-right-to-self-determination/> accessed 15 January 2021.

5.4. ALTERING THE DEMOGRAPHIC COMPOSITION, CHARACTER, AND STATUS OF THE PALESTINIAN TERRITORY

The UN Security Council has a long line of resolutions concerning the occupation of Palestinian Territory.[109] To take a recent example, in Resolution 2334 (2016), the UNSC condemns:

> all measures aimed at altering the demographic composition, character and status of the Palestinian Territory occupied since 1967, including East Jerusalem, including, *inter alia*, the construction and expansion of settlements, transfer of Israeli settlers, confiscation of land, demolition of homes and displacement of Palestinian civilians, in violation of international humanitarian law and relevant resolutions.

This quote from the resolution encompasses various actions undertaken by Israel,[110] including the establishment and expansion of settlements in East Jerusalem and the West Bank,[111] but also the establishment of a wall or security barrier which the UN Secretary General describes as deviating 'more than 7.5 kilometres from the Green Line in certain places to incorporate settlements, while encircling Palestinian population areas.'[112]

The rest of this section addresses the settlements and the wall together, in order to indicate the relevance of the right to self-determination as a basis for assessing specific actions that affect the demographic composition, character, and status of the Palestinian territory.[113]

In its advisory opinion, the ICJ found that the settlements represent a breach of Article 49 paragraph 6 of the Fourth Geneva Convention, which provides: 'The Occupying Power shall not deport or transfer parts

---

109 Including resolutions 242 (1967), 338 (1973), 446 (1979), 452 (1979), 465 (1980), 476 (1980), 478 (1980), 1397 (2002), 1515 (2003), and 1850 (2008), as cited in UN Security Council, 'Resolution 2334, Adopted by the Security Council at its 7853rd meeting, on 23 December 2016' (23 December 2016) Un Doc S/RES/2334.

110 See Committee on the Elimination of Racial Discrimination (CERD), 'Consideration of reports submitted by States parties under article 9 of the Convention' (3 April 2012) UN Doc CERD/C/ISR/CO/14-16, para 25.

111 See UNGA (n 76) 14; CERD (n 110), directing Israel to eliminate any policy of 'demographic balance' from its planning and zoning policy in the West Bank.

112 UNGA, 'Report of the Secretary-General prepared pursuant to General Assembly resolution ES-10/13,' (24 November 2003) UN Doc A/ES-10/248, para 7.

113 For an account of the HCJ's jurisprudence, see Gross (n 80) 262.

of its own civilian population into the territory it occupies.' The ICJ found that:

> [the] provision prohibits not only deportations or forced transfers of population such as those carried out during the Second World War, but also any measures taken by an occupying Power in order to organize or encourage transfers of parts of its own population into the occupied territory.[114]

The ICJ also addressed the settlements in combination with the wall from the perspective of the right to self-determination. It found that:

> the construction of the wall and its associated régime create a 'fait accompli' on the ground that could well become permanent, in which case, and notwithstanding the formal characterization of the wall by Israel, it would be tantamount to *de facto* annexation.[115]

Here, the Court indicates that it does not view the annexation of territory as having yet occurred. Others argue that it has.[116] Annexation is a contravention of the right to self-determination.

The ICJ found also that:

> the route chosen for the wall gives expression in *loco* to the illegal measures taken by Israel with regard to Jerusalem and the settlements, as deplored by the Security Council ... There is also a risk of further alterations to the demographic composition of the Occupied Palestinian Territory resulting from the construction of the wall inasmuch as it is contributing ... to the departure of Palestinian populations from certain areas. That construction, along with measures taken previously, thus severely impedes the exercise by the Palestinian people of its right to self-determination, and is therefore a breach of Israel's obligation to respect that right.[117]

In the absence of a decisive finding that annexation has yet occurred, the finding of breach of the right to self-determination stems from actions that pre-empt the choices available for the Palestinian people at the end of occupation.[118] The settlements are changing, and will potentially continue

---

114 *Israeli Wall case* (n 7) [120].
115 ibid [121].
116 For arguments that there is annexation see Special Rapporteur on the situation of human rights in the Palestinian territories UNGA (n 76) para 32; Dajani (n 77) 51, 53.
117 *Israeli Wall case* (n 7) [122].
118 Gareau (n 7) 516.

to change, the territory's demographic, so that the population on the territory is no longer as it was at the commencement of the occupation. They also impede the exercise of the right to self-determination in the sense that they take or have the potential to take land and other resources away from Palestinian exercise.[119] The construction of the wall compounds these elements: it creates conditions that lead or may lead to further departures of Palestinians from the territory, and strengthens the hold of Israel over the land.

The ICJ's approach brings into focus the argument that Israel, as the occupier, is duty-bound to refrain from actions that actually or potentially pre-empt the process of self-determination.[120] This argument is also relevant with regard to specific actions concerning resources on the territory.

5.5. EXPLOITING NATURAL RESOURCES

The UN General Assembly has expressed grave concern about a range of practices negatively impacting Palestinian natural resources.[121] The precise relevance of the law of occupation and the right to self-determination for acts affecting natural resources is exemplified by the practice of quarrying the land for the production of gravel.[122]

This practice was addressed by the HCJ in a case from 2011.[123] Israeli NGO Yesh Din petitioned the HCJ to order the cessation of quarrying in Israeli-owned quarries in the West Bank and of the development of new quarries. The petition was dismissed. The HCJ recognised that the quarries were opened in the 1970s after the commencement of the occupation. It assessed them for consistency with Article 55 of the Hague Regulations:

> The occupying State shall be regarded only as administrator and usufructuary of public buildings, real estate, forests, and agricultural estates belonging to the hostile State, and situated in the occupied country. It must safeguard the

119 See Gross (n 80) 279, 284.

120 Gareau (n 7) 516.

121 UNGA, 'Permanent Sovereignty of the Palestinian People in the Occupied Palestinian Territory, Including East Jerusalem, and of the Arab Population in the Occupied Syrian Golan Over Their Natural Resources: Resolution Adopted by the General Assembly on 22 December 2011' (29 March 2012) UN Doc A/RES/66/225. This includes the destruction of agricultural land and orchards, and the destruction of water pipelines and sewage networks, which negatively affects the water supply.

122 See also Longobardo (n 6).

123 HCJ 2164/09 *Yesh Din – Volunteers for Human Rights v Commander of the IDF Forces in the West Bank and others* (26 December 2011).

> capital of these properties, and administer them in accordance with the rules of usufruct.

The essence of this provision is 'that an occupying state is entitled to reap the fruits of the occupied territory's assets but must not deplete their "capital" by harming the assets themselves.'[124] The HCJ saw that the practice affected the capital,[125] but found it justified in light of the prolonged occupation, which required adjustment of the traditional laws of occupation to allow for economic development and growth.[126] This reading of the law has been criticised for undervaluing the objectives and principles of the law of occupation anchored in Article 43 'Hague law', which should have been the starting point for the interpretation.[127] The HCJ also supported its position with reference to the terms of the Oslo Accords.[128] Specifically, Article 31 of the first Schedule to Appendix 3 (the civil appendix) of the Interim Agreement, which provides for transfer of the quarries to the Palestinians and an agreement that the quarries would remain active in the interim.[129] This position is criticised in light of the absence of attempts to transfer the quarries to the Palestinians.[130] In addition, it is criticised on the basis of the block the law of occupation places on curtailing the rights of the occupied population on the basis of agreement with the occupier.[131]

It likewise pre-empts the right to self-determination when the occupier opens new quarries; it means that once the people are in a position to self-determine, the resource will no longer be available in the same form for the people to determine how it should be used.

6. LEGAL CONSEQUENCES FROM DENIAL OF THE RIGHT TO SELF-DETERMINATION

The preceding discussion highlighted how the exercise of the right to self-determination in the oPt has come to focus on the resolution of the

124 Gross (n 80) 199.
125 *Yesh Din* (n 123) [8].
126 ibid [10].
127 See Guy Harpaz and others, 'Expert Legal Opinion on HCJ 2164/09 Yesh Din in Support of the Petitioner's Motion for an *En Banc* Review' (January 2012) para 101.
128 *Yesh Din* [6].
129 ibid.
130 Gross (n 80) 201.
131 ibid 201; GC IV (n 29) art 47.

political dispute over the territorial claim through negotiations which the law requires proceed in good faith. The discussion also highlighted occupier actions, in relation to resources and settlements, which challenge the presumption of good faith and independently infringe the right to self-determination by pre-empting the choices available for the Palestinian people at the end of occupation. This section identifies and examines some of the legal consequences that follow from denial of the right to self-determination under the law of state responsibility, especially what is possible and required of third states in light of the right's elevated normative status.[132]

6.1. *ERGA OMNES*

In the *Barcelona Traction* case of 1970, the ICJ found that there are obligations in international law that are owed by states 'towards the international community as a whole', and that, consequently, 'all States can be held to have a legal interest in their protection'.[133] This is the concept of obligations *erga omnes*, which 'must be fulfilled regardless of the behavior of other states in the same field' and 'give rise to a claim for their execution that accrues to any other member of the international community.'[134] Authoritative bodies assert that the right of all peoples to self-determination is a norm with *erga omnes* status.[135] This provides for any third state to invoke state responsibility in relation to denial of the right to self-determination.

---

132 See also Longobardo (n 6) Section VI.

133 *Barcelona Traction, Light and Power Company Limited (Belgium v Spain)* (Judgment) [1970] ICJ Rep 3 [33].

134 Cassese (n 18) 134.

135 *Case Concerning East Timor (Portugal v Australia)* (Judgment) [1995] ICJ Rep 90 para 29; *Israeli Wall case* (n 7) [88] and [156]; see, Gentian Zyberi, 'Self-Determination Through the Lens of the International Court of Justice' (2009) 56(3) *Netherlands International Law Review* 429, 432; consider also the *erga omnes partes* nature of the obligations created by human rights instruments such as the ICCPR. Israel is a state party to the ICCPR. This means that it is open to any other state party to invoke responsibility for a breach of the treaty, regardless of whether or not it is directly injured; International Law Commission (ILC), 'Articles on State Responsibility ILC, 'Draft Articles on Responsibility of States for Internationally Wrongful Acts, with commentaries' (ARSIWA) in *Report of the International Law Commission on its 53rd Session* (23 April–1 June and 2 July–10 August 2001) UN Doc A/56/10, art 48; see also ICCPR art 41.

The scope for invoking responsibility includes demanding cessation and calling for reparation for the injured party. Such steps can serve as part of a strategy to encourage a non-compliant occupier to become compliant. Signalling that the occupier is not complying with its international legal obligations can affect its legitimacy both domestically and internationally.[136] For this to affect the occupier requires that a concern for its legitimacy exists, as well as an understanding that complying with the law is a means to improving its legitimacy. It also requires that, from the perspective of the occupier, any such legitimacy concerns outweigh the strategic benefits derived from maintaining the occupation.

Article 54 of the ILC Articles on Responsibility of States for Internationally Wrongful Acts (ARSIWA) provides a basis for countermeasures to coerce compliance, but the specific nature of the measures permissible in this context remains uncertain. The general practice of countermeasures includes examples of economic sanctions and cessation of certain types of relations.[137] The fact that the amount of practice is limited is connected to the absence of a clear incentive for third states to monitor and enforce human rights around the world.[138] Still, in recent years, Libya, Syria, and Russia have all been subject to significant third-party counter measures from, among others, EU member states.[139] Reasons given for why third states condemn but do not issue sanctions against Israel for specific breaches of international law include a concern that they will not be constructive in the search for a political resolution to the dispute over the territorial claim.[140] In this respect, it is important to reflect on the *jus cogens* status of the right to self-determination, as serious breaches of *jus cogens* norms generate obligations for third states.

---

136 See, generally, Beth A Simmons, *Mobilizing for Human Rights: International Law in Domestic Politics* (CUP 2009) 124.

137 See ILC, (n 135) 137, para 3 (commentary on art 54); see also Christian J Tams and Antonios Tzanakopoulos, 'Barcelona Traction at 40: The ICJ as an Agent of Legal Development' (2010) 23(4) Leiden Journal of International Law 781, 793–794.

138 See Simmons (n 136) 122.

139 See Martin Dawidowicz, 'Third-Party Countermeasures: A Progressive Development of International Law?' (2016) 29 Questions of International Law, Zoom In 3 <http://www.qil-qdi.org/third-party-countermeasures-progressive-development-international-law/> accessed 15 January 2021.

140 See, eg., 'The German parliament has called on Israel to halt its plans to annex settlements in the occupied West Bank. However, it has ruled out the use of sanctions against Israel' in 'Germany rejects Israel's West Bank annexation plans as illegal' *Deutsche Welle* (1 July 2020) <https://www.dw.com/en/germany-rejects-israels-west-bank-annexation-plans-as-illegal/a-54019730> accessed 15 January 2021.

6.2. *JUS COGENS*

The establishment of the concept of *jus cogens* norms (peremptory norms) in international law occurred through the 1969 Vienna Convention on the Law of Treaties (VCLT). Article 53 of the VCLT provides:

> [A] peremptory norm of general international law is a norm accepted and recognized by the international community of States as a whole as a norm from which no derogation is permitted and which can be modified only by a subsequent norm of general international law having the same character.

Article 53 also indicates the consequence that a treaty 'is void if, at the time of its conclusion, it conflicts with a peremptory norm of general international law.' Scholarly attention has since been given to other legal consequences of the acceptance of a norm as *jus cogens*.[141] In the view of the ILC, if a state fails to fulfil an obligation that has a *jus cogens* status in a gross or systematic manner, all other states are prohibited from recognizing as lawful the resulting situation, and from rendering aid or assistance in maintaining it.[142] The ILC specifies that '[t]his not only refers to the formal recognition of these situations, but also prohibits acts which would imply such recognition'.[143]

In its commentary to its articles on state responsibility, the ILC includes the right to self-determination as an example of a norm with *jus cogens* status. The ILC is not precise in its wording or explanation for this status, relying on a quote from the ICJ in the *East Timor* case – a quote which does not refer directly to peremptory norm (*jus cogens*) status.[144] The strength of the argument on *jus cogens* status varies depending on how the notion of *jus cogens* is understood and on which components of the right to self-determination are in focus.[145] The strongest arguments limit the

141 See Antonio Cassese, *International Law* (2nd edn, OUP 2005) 205–208.

142 ILC (n 135) art. 40 and 41.

143 ILC (n 135) 114, art 41, para 5.

144 ILC (n 135) art 40, para 6; in the *East Timor case* (135), the ICJ states that '[t]he principle of self-determination … is one of the essential principles of contemporary international law'.

145 See Matthew Saul, 'The Normative Status of the Right to Self-Determination: A Formula for Uncertainty in the Scope and Content of the Right?' (2011) 11(4) *Human Rights Law Review* 609; also, Matthew C R Craven, 'The European Community Arbitration Commission on Yugoslavia' (1995) 66(1) *British Yearbook of International Law* 333, 383.

claim to colonial and alien domination and supplement state practice with appeal to the moral strength of the obligation.[146] This covers situations of prolonged occupation. Indeed, the ILC has specified in its work on state responsibility that states' obligation to desist from recognition 'applies to "situations" created by these breaches, such as, for example, attempted acquisition of sovereignty over territory through the denial of the right of self-determination of peoples.'[147]

The ICJ's opinion on the consequences of a denial of the right to self-determination in relation to the construction of the wall in the oPt does not directly use the terminology of *jus cogens*,[148] but identifies obligations consistent with those flowing from a serious breach of *jus cogens* norms under ARSIWA Article 40:

> Given the character and the importance of the rights and obligations involved, the Court is of the view that all States are under an obligation not to recognize the illegal situation resulting from the construction of the wall in the Occupied Palestinian Territory, including in and around East Jerusalem. They also are under an obligation not to render aid or assistance in maintaining the situation created by such construction. It is also for all States, while respecting the United Nations Charter and international law, to see to it that any impediment, resulting from the construction of the wall, to the exercise by the Palestinian people of its right to self-determination is brought to an end.[149]

7. CONCLUSION

This chapter has examined the relevance of the right of all peoples to self-determination in the context of prolonged occupations with a specific focus on the oPt. The conclusion provides a summary of key points that are important in relation to the chapter's three main parts. It also notes several policy implications that follow from the analysis.

---

146 See Saul (n 145) 636–637.

147 ILC (n 135) 114, art 41, para 5; Dajani (n 77) 55.

148 For criticism of the approach taken by the ICJ in the Wall Opinion for appearing to merge the *erga omnes* concept with the concept of *jus cogens*, see James Crawford, 'International Crimes of States' in James Crawford, Alain Pellet, Simon Olleson, and Kate Parlett (eds), *The Law of International Responsibility* (OUP 2010) 411–412; see also Gareau (n 7) 520.

149 *Israeli Wall case* (n 7) [159]; see also Gareau (n 7) 517.

What is the function of the right of all peoples to self-determination in the context of a prolonged occupation?

The right to self-determination may be used as an interpretative aid, giving meaning to provisions of the law of occupation. This may provide a basis for certain expansive interpretations of aspects of the law of occupation, such as the conservationist principle, to allow greater change and development of state and civil infrastructure, which could help avoid pre-emption of the right to self-determination through the time-related decay of its objects. However, the test associated with the right to self-determination – that is, whether a change would pre-empt the choices available at the end of occupation – is more lenient than the standard test of necessity for public order or civil life under the conservationist principle. The risk of the occupier manipulating the law of occupation to suit its interests is heightened.

The right to self-determination is also relevant as a standalone basis for assessing the occupation. This is true in two ways. First, occupation in and of itself is a breach of the right to self-determination, which provides a legal requirement that the occupation must cease. Under a more traditional invasion of a territory by a third state, this simply requires withdrawal. When complicating factors exist, such as uncertainty about the status of components of the occupied territory, the right to self-determination points towards a political process undertaken in good faith.

Second, the right to self-determination may also be used as basis for assessing specific aspects of the practice of the occupier. In a shorter-term occupation, this feature may not emerge, as the terms of the law of occupation focused on conservation of existing infrastructure may be sufficient to protect the right to self-determination. The relevance of the right to self-determination emerges in situations of prolonged occupation or other circumstances that lead to uncertainty about whether the law of occupation applies in its entirety or where adherence to the law is simply neglected. In such circumstances, the right to self-determination serves a backstop role. It precludes practices that will pre-empt the choices about the organization, utilization, and status of a territory available to the people at the end of the occupation.

How is the right to self-determination relevant in the oPt?

The political process aimed at ending the overall occupation of the oPt has led to significant developments, such as the occupier granting a degree of authority for self-governance to Palestinians through the PA, although the PA remains subject to the influence of the occupier in the vast majority of its public functions. These developments add complexity to law of occupation-based questions about the nature and extent of the obligations established for the respective parties. Such circumstances generate a heightened need to pay attention to the right to self-determination as a legal backstop, precluding actions that would pre-empt the eventual exercise of self-determination following the end of the occupation. Israeli actions that pre-empt and thereby breach the Palestinians' right to self-determination include the settlements and the wall, along with the opening and operation of gravel quarries. The strength of the Oslo Accords as a possible legal justification for actions that pre-empt the right to self-determination has been challenged in this chapter due to the lack of a direct mandate from the Palestinian population for such actions. If a future peace process addresses issues concerning the status, infrastructure, and resources of the territory,[150] its consistency with the right to self-determination will increase in line with the extent to which it reflects a free and genuine expression of the will of the Palestinian people.

What are international legal consequences and remedies for denial of the right to self-determination?

The right to self-determination has *erga omnes* status. This gives all states a basis to invoke responsibility and call for an end to acts in breach of the right. It also has *jus cogens* status, requiring states to desist from recognition of the situation created by the right's breach. It places states under an obligation not to render aid or assistance in the maintenance of the situation. States should also cooperate to end a situation that constitutes a breach to the right of self-determination. This can be facilitated in situations of prolonged occupation through a greater focus not only on the occupation overall but also on how specific actions of the occupier and occupied relate to the right to self-determination.

[150] See, eg., France's initiative in Ministère de L'Europe et des Affaires Étrangères, 'France Diplomacy – Initiative for the Middle East Peace Process' <https://www.diplomatie.gouv.fr/en/country-files/israel-palestinian-territories/peace-process/initiative-for-the-middle-east-peace-process/> accessed 15 January 2021.

REPATRIATING FOREIGN (TERRORIST) FIGHTERS AND THEIR FAMILY MEMBERS

A Legal, Moral, and Security Conundrum

Francesca CAPONE*

1. INTRODUCTION

In the aftermath of the military defeat of the Islamic State of Iraq and the Levant (ISIL), many states have faced the thorny question of how to deal with citizens who went to Syria and Iraq as foreign terrorist fighters (FTFs),

* Assistant Professor of Public International Law at the Sant'Anna School of Advanced Studies, Italy. Ph.D. Sant'Anna School of Advanced Studies and Tilburg University. Email: f.capone@santannapisa.it.

and their family members.[1] This issue represents a clear challenge and real conundrum in light of the need to protect a key community interest, namely human security,[2] while also respecting the human rights of everyone, including those designated terrorists. Given the complex interplay between these two goals and the lack of balance that often characterises the implementation of counter-terrorism legislation, it is important to explore ways of better reconciling certain values and interests that initially appear incompatible.

As is well known, international counter-terrorism law (ICTL) – the set of provisions scattered throughout universal and regional conventions and UN Security Council Resolutions – does not exist in a legal vacuum, but heavily relies on other subfields of international law to face the multifaceted threats posed by international terrorism.[3] Over the past few years, in particular with ISIL's establishment, the rise of the FTFs phenomenon has further exacerbated the tension between global security and state sovereignty. With the fight against and the defeat of ISIL, the focus has gradually shifted from outgoing FTFs to incoming FTFs.[4] According to the most widely cited data, in a very short amount of time 41,490 international citizens from 80 countries became affiliated with ISIL.[5] Some 5,000 men, women, and children travelled from Europe to Syria and Iraq for this

---

1 Francesca Capone, 'The Children (and Wives) of Foreign ISIS Fighters: Which Obligations upon the States of Nationality?' (2019) 60 Questions of International Law 69.

2 Rhonda Callaway and Julie Harrelson-Stephens, 'Toward a Theory of Terrorism: Human Security as a Determinant of Terrorism' (2006) 29 Studies in Conflict & Terrorism 679; Wolfgang Benedek, 'Human Security and Prevention of Terrorism' in Wolfgang Benedek and Alice Yotopoulos-Marangopoulos (eds), *Anti-Terrorist Measures and Human Rights* (Martinus Nijhoff Publishers 2004) 171–184.

3 Ben Saul, 'Attempts to Define "Terrorism" in International Law' (2005) 52(1) Netherlands International Law Review 57; Todd Sandler, 'Terrorism and Counterterrorism: An Overview' (2015) 67 Oxford Economic Papers 1; Larissa Van Den Herik and Nico Schrijver (eds), *Counter-Terrorism Strategies in a Fragmented International Legal Order: Meeting the Challenges* (Cambridge University Press 2013).

4 OSCE Office for Democratic Institutions and Human Rights, 'Guidelines for Addressing the Threats and Challenges of "Foreign Terrorist Fighters" within a Human Rights Framework' (2018) <https://www.osce.org/odihr/393503?download=true> accessed 15 January 2021; United Nations Security Council Counter-Terrorism Committee Executive Directorate (CTED), 'The Challenge of Returning and Relocating Foreign Terrorist Fighters: Research Perspectives' (Trends Report, CTED 2018) <https://www.un.org/sc/ctc/wp-content/uploads/2018/04/CTED-Trends-Report-March-2018.pdf> accessed 15 January 2021.

5 Joana Cook and Gina Vale, 'From Daesh to "Diaspora": Tracing the Women and Minors of Islamic State' (International Centre for the Study of Radicalisation 2018) 7, <https://icsr.info/wp-content/uploads/2018/07/ICSR-Report-From-Daesh-to-'Diaspora'-Tracing-the-Women-and-Minors-of-Islamic-State.pdf> accessed 15 January 2021.

reason starting in 2012. An estimated 1,500 individuals have returned to Europe,[6] but precise information is lacking about those who were either born in Syria or Iraq, died, fled elsewhere, or are currently detained.

Despite the lack of accurate information, it is possible to affirm that in Syria the Syrian Democratic Forces (SDF) still hold about 12,000 men and boys suspected of ISIL affiliation, including 2,000 to 4,000 foreigners from almost 50 countries, in overcrowded prisons. The group also holds about 100,000 Syrian and foreign women and children who are family members of ISIL suspects – some of whom may be ISIL members themselves – in squalid camps.[7] The SDF, a non-state actor (opposed to the current Syrian Government) which exercises governmental functions in part of the Syrian territory with the support if not the control of the US, has declared on various occasions that is not willing or able to prosecute FTFs and it is equally incapable of managing the camps where FTFs' family members are held.[8] In contrast, the Iraqi Government is relying on its sovereign right to prosecute adult FTFs,[9] both men and women, but is asking states of origin to repatriate children, many of whom are detained on national security-related charges for their alleged association with ISIL.[10]

---

6 Francesca Capone, 'Is Trump Right? Foreign Fighters and the States' Obligation to Repatriate Them' (*Verfassungsblog*, 10 March 2019), <https://verfassungsblog.de/is-trump-right-foreign-fighters-and-the-states-obligation-to-repatriate-them/> accessed 15 January 2021; Thomas Renard and Rik Coolsaet (eds), Returnees: Who are They, Why Are They (Not) Coming back and how Should We Deal with Them? Assessing Policies on Returning Foreign Terrorist Fighters in Belgium, Germany and the Netherlands (Paper 101, *Egmont* 2018) <http://www.egmontinstitute.be/content/uploads/2018/02/egmont.papers.101_online_v1-3.pdf?type=pdf/> accessed 15 January 2021 [3].

7 Belkis Wille, 'ISIS Suspect Transfers to Iraq Replete with Risks', *Just Security* (1 November 2019) <https://www.justsecurity.org/66789/isis-suspect-transfers-to-iraq-replete-with-risks/> accessed 15 January 2021.

8 'SDF Calls for International Tribunal for ISIL Detainees' *Aljazeera* (25 March 2019) <https://www.aljazeera.com/news/2019/03/sdf-calls-international-tribunal-isil-detainees-190325140845893.html> accessed 15 January 2021.

9 UN General Assembly, 'Report of the Special Rapporteur on Extrajudicial, Summary or Arbitrary Executions on Her Mission to Iraq' (20 June 2018) UN Doc A/HRC/38/44/Add.1; Council of Europe (Committee on Legal Affairs and Human Rights) 'Addressing the issue of Daesh foreign fighters and their families returning from Syria and other countries to the member States of the Council of Europe' (4 February 2020) AS/Jur (2020) 03, 3–4 <http://www.assembly.coe.int/LifeRay/JUR/Pdf/DocsAndDecs/2020/AS-JUR-2020-03-EN.pdf> accessed 15 January 2021.

10 Belkis Wille, 'Unfair ISIS Trial in Iraq Hands Women Harshest Sentences: Foreign Defendants Receive Harsh Penalties for Non-Violent Acts' *Human Rights Watch* (21 February 2018) <https://www.hrw.org/news/2018/02/21/unfair-isis-trial-iraq-hands-women-harshest-sentences>.

The presence of FTFs in Syria, Iraq, and, to a far lesser extent, Libya triggers a number of questions that states, individually and collectively, seem unequipped or unwilling to address, especially now that the Covid-19 pandemic provides a solid excuse to avoid dealing with other problems. One of the most difficult aspects is represented by the claim, eloquently summarised in a famous tweet from former US President Donald Trump in February 2018,[11] that there exists an obligation, incumbent upon FTFs' states of nationality, or more broadly of origin, to repatriate them. The alleged obligation to 'take them back' clearly hints that a proactive approach should be adopted – that is, measures should be implemented to facilitate the repatriation or extradition of individuals when the legal conditions are fulfilled. This proactive approach needs to be distinguished from states' obligation to readmit their nationals and allow them to enter their territory in accordance with customary international law and international human rights law.

Since no extradition treaties have been concluded with either Iraq or Syria and no formal mechanisms exist to govern the fate of those imprisoned or held, the states whose citizens became FTFs – including European states – have adopted heterogeneous and even contradictory strategies in relation to repatriating them. Although the situation has been addressed before several international bodies, like the Human Rights Committee (HRC)[12] and the Committee on the Rights of the Child,[13] many states have tried to avoid facing the question of whether they are acting in compliance with the existing international legal framework. Therefore, after clarifying who falls within the FTF category and which specific issues emerge in relation to their accompanying family members, this chapter reflects on whether or not an obligation to repatriate FTFs and their families can be inferred from one or more subfields of international law. On the one hand, it is possible to claim that international counter-terrorism law can contribute – in light of a 'common-sense obligation rooted in community morality that morphed

---

11 'Trump Tells European Countries to Take back IS Fighters' *BBC News* (17 February 2019) <https://www.bbc.com/news/world-middle-east-47269887> accessed 15 January 2021.

12 See Human Rights Committee, 'Concluding observations on the sixth periodic report of Belgium', (6 December 2019) CCPR/C/BEL/CO/6, paras 12–14; HRC, 'Concluding observations on the fifth periodic report of the Netherlands' (22 August 2019) CCPR/C/NLD/CO/5, paras 50–51.

13 *LH et al v France*, Admissibility Decision Adopted by the Committee on the Rights of the Child Concerning Communications No 79/2019 and No 109/2019 (2 November 2020) UN Doc CRC/C/85/D/79/2019–CRC/C/85/D/109/2019.

into international obligation'[14] – to shaping a duty incumbent upon states of nationality to repatriate FTFs suspected of or convicted for terrorist crimes and/or terrorist-related conduct, especially when willingness to exercise territorial jurisdiction is lacking. On the other hand, the situation of foreigners, in particular women and children, deprived of liberty outside formal arrest and detention, appears much more complex and requires a closer look at states' obligations under the law of diplomatic and consular relations, as well as human rights law, which come into play when FTFs' origin states are called on to protect their nationals abroad. This second approach serves as the basis of this chapter. Finally, since the repatriation of FTFs is not just a legal challenge, but also triggers important moral and security considerations, this article will, to the maximum degree possible, incorporate these perspectives too.

2. DEFINITIONS AND KEY ISSUES: ARE ALL FOREIGN FIGHTERS 'TERRORISTS'?

In the aftermath of the caliphate's defeat, the question of what would happen next resonated everywhere. Over the past six years, the events and violations taking place in a caliphate the size of Britain have often been overlooked in order to avoid the possible threats that FTFs could pose to their countries of origin. Security concerns inform every decision-making process since ISIL lost the last pocket of territory in Syria it controlled. The foreigners who joined ISIL and survived have been detained, while their family members are held in 'restricted' sections of displacement camps in the northern-eastern part of Syria and in detention sites in Iraq.[15] Whereas the SDF in Syria seeks to draw a distinction between detained fighters and family members held in displacement camps, Iraqi authorities are more inclined to regard all foreigners as terrorist fighters, with the possible exception of children, should their countries of origin claim them back.[16]

---

14 Michael A Newton, 'Terrorist crimes and the *aut dedere aut judicare* obligation' in Larissa van den Herik and Nico Schrijver (eds), *Counter-Terrorism Strategies in a Fragmented International Legal Order: Meeting the Challenges* (CUP 2013) 70.

15 Human Rights Watch, '"Bring Me Back to Canada" Plight of Canadians Held in Northeast Syria for Alleged ISIS Links' (29 June 2020) <https://www.hrw.org/report/2020/06/29/bring-me-back-canada/plight-canadians-held-northeast-syria-alleged-isis-links> accessed 15 January 2021.

16 Bill Van Esveld, 'Iraq/KRG: 1,400 Women, Children from ISIS Areas Detained: Investigate Killings, Abductions of Foreign Men' *Human Rights Watch* (20 September 2017) <https://www.hrw.org/news/2017/09/20/iraq/krg-1400-women-children-isis-areas-detained> accessed 15 January 2021.

The assumption that all foreigners are terrorists is clearly incorrect, but it is reflected in the constant use, at all levels, of an inconsistent terminology, with the terms 'foreign fighters' (FFs) and 'foreign terrorist fighters' often used interchangeably. The former have been defined as 'individuals, driven mainly by ideology, religion and/or kinship, who leave their country of origin or their country of habitual residence to join a party engaged in an armed conflict.'[17] This definition places the accent on the individuals' departure from their state of origin in order to support an actor engaged in an armed conflict of international or internal character: an armed group or the state's armed forces.[18] In the case of the armed conflicts in the Middle East, it is very difficult to determine who joined which party, as foreign fighters from all over the world have supported either government forces or insurgents.[19] When the insurgents that the foreign fighters join are identified as a terrorist group in accordance with the existing legal framework, or when the foreign fighters become involved in the preparation or commission of terrorist offences, then we speak of 'foreign terrorist fighters', which, according to UNSC Resolution 2178 (2014), means 'individuals who travel to a State other than their States of residence or nationality for the purpose of the perpetration, planning, or preparation of, or participation in, terrorist acts or the providing or receiving of terrorist training, including in connection with armed conflict.'[20]

UNSC Resolution 2178(2014) calls on member states to deal specifically with those who travel abroad with 'terrorist intent' as opposed to those who travel abroad only to 'fight', suggesting the latter's direct participation in hostilities[21] without the purpose of committing a terrorist offence. When the terrorism element is lacking, the predominant

---

17 See Andrea de Guttry, Francesca Capone and Christophe Paulussen, 'Introduction' in Andrea de Guttry and others (eds), *Foreign Fighters under International Law and Beyond* (Asser Press 2016) 2.

18 On the difference between international armed conflicts and non-international armed conflicts see, generally, Sandesh Sivakumaran, 'Re-envisaging the International Law of Internal Armed Conflict' (2011) 22(1) EJIL 219, 221. See also Dieter Fleck, 'The Law of Non-International Armed Conflict' in Dieter Fleck (ed) *The Handbook of International Humanitarian Law* (3rd ed, Oxford University Press 2013) 603.

19 See International Crisis Group, 'New Approach in Southern Syria' (Report N°163, 2 September 2015) <https://www.crisisgroup.org/middle-east-north-africa/eastern-mediterranean/syria/new-approach-southern-syria> accessed 15 January 2021.

20 See United Nations Security Council (UNSC), Res 2178 (24 September 2014) UN Doc S/RES/2178, preamble.

21 On the definition of 'direct participation in hostilities' see Nils Melzer, 'Interpretive Guidance on the Notion of Direct Participation in Hostilities under International Humanitarian Law' (2009) *International Committee of the Red Cross* <https://www.icrc.org/en/doc/assets/files/other/icrc-002-0990.pdf> accessed 15 January 2021 [43].

set of rules to take into consideration is that provided under the international humanitarian law (IHL) framework. As is well known, the direct participation in hostilities of both nationals and foreign fighters is in principle 'unlawful' in a non-international armed conflict (NIAC), whereas in an international armed conflict (IAC) it is regarded as a lawful activity,[22] regardless of the combatant's nationality or permanent residency status. Without lingering on the characterisation of the armed conflicts in Syria and Iraq – the former certainly raises a wider range of questions due to the plethora of actors involved – it is worth stressing that under IHL depicting an armed group as 'terrorist' does not really mean anything,[23] nor does labelling an individual a foreign terrorist fighter. Given the current lack of agreement on the breadth and exact meaning of 'terrorism',[24] the definition of foreign terrorist fighters enshrined in Resolution 2178 fails to provide member states with sufficient guidance on whom exactly falls within this category.[25] As a result it is likely that states will implement different, and in some cases even abusive, responses, thus jeopardising the chance of effectively and legitimately countering the phenomenon of foreign terrorist fighters and the threat they may pose to maintaining international peace and security.

In light of the fact that it is extremely difficult to determine whether an individual has committed terrorist offences while in Syria and Iraq, states usually base their initial assessment on 'affiliation' with groups labelled 'terrorist'.[26] Twenty-two states in the EU – and many more around the

22 See Emanuele Sommario, 'The Status of Foreign Fighters under International Humanitarian Law' in Andrea de Guttry and others (eds), *Foreign Fighters under International Law and Beyond* (Asser Press 2016) 147–149.

23 Ben Saul, 'Terrorism and International Humanitarian Law' in Ben Saul (ed), *Research Handbook on International Law and Terrorism* (OUP 2014) 231; Bibi van Ginkel, 'Combating Terrorism: Proposals for Improving the International Legal Framework' in Antonio Cassese (ed), *Realizing Utopia: The Future of International Law* (OUP 2012) 461.

24 Francesca Capone, 'Countering "Foreign Terrorist Fighters": A Critical Appraisal of the Framework Established by the UN Security Council Resolutions' (2015) 25 Italian Yearbook of International Law (ItYIL) 227, 237–242.

25 Mercenaries, as defined by Article 47 of Additional Protocol (AP) I to the Geneva Conventions, do not belong to the category of foreign fighters, because the latter fights by definition for private gain, while a foreign fighter mostly pursues an ideological or religious motivation. On the definition of mercenaries under IHL, see Knut Ipsen, 'Combatants and Non-combatants' in Dieter Fleck (ed) *The Handbook of International Humanitarian Law* (3rd ed, OUP 2013) 84.

26 Kai Ambos, 'Our Terrorists, your Terrorists? The United Nations Security Council Urges States to Combat "foreign terrorist fighters"', but Does not Define "Terrorism"' (*EJIL: Talk!*, 2 October 2014) <http://www.ejiltalk.org/our-terrorists-your-terrorists-the-united-nations-security-council-urges-states-to-combat-foreign-terrorist-fighters-but-does-not-define-terrorism/> accessed 15 January 2021.

world – have criminalised *tout court* participation in or leadership of a terrorist group,[27] or even attempts to enter a given territory of a foreign country where certain groups are active.[28] Therefore, virtually in every case and under every domestic jurisdiction, foreigners affiliated with ISIL will be prosecuted as FTFs and not simply as foreign fighters. It follows that women and children, who do not necessarily perform military tasks, may also fall within the category of foreign terrorist fighters because activities like the preparation of terrorist activities and the provision of training – which in accordance with UNSC Res. 2178 (2014) includes both providing *and receiving* terrorist training – are defined quite vaguely so as to encompass activities that in normal contexts would not raise suspicion. Yet the Security Council itself has asked states to assist women and children associated with foreign terrorist fighters who may be victims of terrorism, and to take into account gender and age sensitivities while doing so.[29] Furthermore, in the Key Principles for the Protection, Repatriation, Prosecution, Rehabilitation and Reintegration of Women and Children with Links to United Nations Listed Terrorist Groups, the UN Secretary General points out that there are specific international law obligations applicable to member states' actions in relation to women and children with links to UN-listed terrorist groups, and provides member states with guidance on the main issues to take into consideration in order to align governments' decisions with the current international legal framework.[30]

With regard to women, it should be underscored that during the first two waves of returnees, in 2013–2014 and early 2015 respectively,[31] a lenient approach was implemented towards female FTFs, based on the

27 Bibi van Ginkel and Eva Entenmann, 'The Foreign Fighters Phenomenon in the European Union – Profiles, Threats and Policies' (Report, *International Centre for Counter-Terrorism* 1 April 2016), <https://icct.nl/publication/report-the-foreign-fighters-phenomenon-in-the-eu-profiles-threats-policies/> accessed 15 January 2021 [6].

28 UNSC, 'Analysis and Recommendations with regard to the Global Threat from Foreign Terrorist Fighters' (19 May 2015) UN Doc S/2015/358, para 54; France, for example, has broadly criminalized 'having been abroad in a theatre of operations of terrorist groups', see van Ginkel and Entenmann (n 27) 32.

29 UNSC, Res 2396 (21 December 2017) UN Doc S/RES/2396, para 31.

30 UN Secretary-General, 'Key Principles for the Protection, Repatriation, Prosecution, Rehabilitation and Reintegration of Women and Children with Links to United Nations Listed Terrorist Groups' (April 2019) <https://www.un.org/counterterrorism/sites/www.un.org.counterterrorism/files/key_principles-april_2019.pdf> accessed 15 January 2021.

31 European Parliamentary Research Service (EPRS), 'The Return of Foreign Fighters to EU Soil Ex-post Evaluation' (15 May 2018) <http://www.europarl.europa.eu/thinktank/en/document.html?reference=EPRS_STU(2018)621811> accessed 15 January 2021.

assumption that they only played ancillary roles and therefore could not pose a significant threat to national security.[32] The evolving understanding of female FTFs now evidences that their depiction as 'jihadi brides' or *muhajirat* (female migrants) is not adequate to grasp the complexity of women's contribution to ISIL and more generally their role as active participants in Islamist insurgencies.[33] A similar discourse – although perhaps not yet so widely shared – concerns children recruited by terrorist groups like ISIL, as the traditional, yet hard-fought for, victim-oriented approach to child soldiers is challenged on the basis of security concerns.[34] The subsequent sections will shed further light on the situation of FTFs' accompanying family members, before addressing the question of whether an obligation to repatriate all FTFs, or at least women and children who joined them, exists under the current international legal framework.

3. THE ROLE OF WOMEN AND CHILDREN ASSOCIATED WITH FOREIGN TERRORIST FIGHTERS

It is perhaps trivial to underscore that, when dealing with FTFs and their family members, states should assess if and to what extent each individual poses a security threat on a case-by-case basis. In reality, however, there is a widespread tendency to categorise and depersonalise, in practice but also across the relevant studies and literature. Keeping this caveat in mind and acknowledging that every experience is different and deserves to be properly singled out, this section addresses the role of women and then of children associated with FTFs. In particular, the aim is to shed more light on how these two groups contributed and/or were involved in ISIL activities.

3.1. WOMEN

As anticipated above, a more repressive approach has been recently adopted towards female FTFs.[35] During the first waves of returns, women

---

32 ibid 36.

33 Meredith Loken and Anna Zelenz, 'Explaining Extremism: Western Women in Daesh' (2017) 3(1) European Journal of International Security 45, 51.

34 Francesca Capone, '"Worse" than Child Soldiers? A Critical Analysis of Foreign Children in the Ranks of ISIL' (2017) 17(1) International Criminal Law Review 161.

35 EPRS (n 31) 36.

were generally perceived as harmless 'victims', capable of playing only a limited logistical role. Recent studies present a different and more disturbing picture that challenges the narrow-minded narrative of females as hopeless, passive individuals lured to the Middle East and forced to join ISIL against their will.[36] The proactive role of women and girls has been attributed to a shift in ISIL's position on the status of women in combat, which occurred between 2015 and 2018. It was the group itself – weakened by armed attacks and increasing military defeats – that allowed women to perform more active roles, including a recent statement that 'it is obligatory for women to take up arms'.[37]

In fact, it has been ascertained that ISIL women have often received sniper training, carried Kalashnikovs, and worn suicide vests; they have become members of the Al-Khansaa brigade and been actively involved in propaganda and recruitment, grooming other women and girls online.[38] Girls recruited into ISIL have been also trained in how best to support husbands, to whom they may have been married from the age of nine. While they may have not engaged in combat roles, girls have been generally referred to as 'sisters of the Islamic State' alongside adult females. Accordingly, they may have been also involved in activities such as recruitment and dissemination of propaganda when it was deemed that they were mature enough.[39]

Recent insights into women's increasing involvement in recruitment and other activities have resulted in changing practices in several different countries of origin, including across Europe. A 2018 study by the Egmont Institute – featuring analyses of policies for returnees in Belgium, Germany, and the Netherlands by several prominent scholars of counter-terrorism – confirmed that in those three EU member states '[u]ntil recently, women were treated with more clemency, but this has now come to an end'.[40] For example in Germany for several years male FTFs were automatically subject to criminal investigation upon arrival, whereas evidentiary thresholds were much higher to investigate women upon return. However, starting from December 2017, Germany's federal judicial authorities announced a tougher judicial stance on female returnees to

---

36 Loken and Zelenz (n 33) 52–53.

37 Cook and Vale (n 5) 28.

38 Amy-Jane Gielen, 'Exit Programmes for Female Jihadists: A Proposal for Conducting Realistic Evaluation of the Dutch Approach' (2018) 33 International Sociology 454, 455–456.

39 EPRS (n 31) 37.

40 Renard and Coolsaet (n 6) 4.

remove gender discrepancies in investigation and prosecution practices.[41] This entails that, upon return or following repatriation, female FTFs are likely to face criminal investigation – if not already initiated in *absentia* – and administrative and/or criminal measures. The widespread perception of foreign women in the ranks of ISIL as a major security threat and the fact that they are well placed to switch from the role of facilitators to perpetrators explain, but perhaps does not justify, the reluctant approach adopted by their states of origin towards their repatriation.[42]

3.2. CHILDREN

Generally speaking children associated with armed forces or armed groups get into that position in one of three ways: they are abducted or conscripted through force or serious threats; they present themselves and become enlisted/enrolled; or they are born into armed forces or groups.[43] In the case of ISIL, research shows that the children in its ranks belong to various categories, i.e. they are the sons and daughters of foreigners who joined the fight, the children of supportive locals, abandoned children found in ISIL-controlled orphanages, children coercively taken from parents, and runaway children or adolescents, in some instances foreigners, who volunteered for service to ISIL.[44]

Thus there were at least three main categories of foreigners under the age of 18 years affiliated with ISIL during the caliphate. First, teenagers motivated by the desire to belong somewhere who travelled to Syria by themselves, often lured by a precursor who facilitated the trip. Second, foreign jihadists leaving in family groups, that is, those who participated in 'family jihad', whose ambition was to live in a 'true Islamic society' and

---

41 EPRS (n 31) 46.

42 See Andrew Roth, '"We aren't dangerous": Why Chechnya Has Welcomed Women Who Joined ISIS' *The Guardian* (2 March 2019) <https://www.theguardian.com/world/2019/mar/02/we-arent-dangerous-why-chechnya-has-welcomed-women-who-joined-isis> accessed 15 January 2021. See Ilya Arkhipov 'Putin Shows Rare Soft Spot to Rescue Russia's ISIS Children' *Bloomberg* (1 February 2019) <https://www.bloomberg.com/news/articles/2019-02-01/putin-shows-rare-soft-spot-to-rescue-russia-s-isis-children> accessed 15 January 2021. See also 'Kazakhstan Repatriates 156 Children of ISIS Fighters from Syria' *The Defense Post* (10 May 2019) <https://thedefensepost.com/2019/05/10/kazakhstan-repatriates-156-isis-children/> accessed 15 January 2021.

43 Marc A Drumbl, *Reimagining Child Soldiers in International Law and Policy* (OUP 2012) 132.

44 Capone (n 34) 175–176.

escape from what they perceived as discrimination and harassment in their Western countries of residence. Third, children born in Syria and Iraq to one foreign parent or two. Family units tended to remain intact, as many adults who moved to the caliphate took their families along or started a family there.[45] Within these networks, fighters were encouraged to train their children to become the next-generation of jihadists, 'lion cubs' (*ashbal*),[46] allowing ISIL to forge and groom more loyal members. There is compelling evidence that children in the ranks of ISIL were exposed to jihadi indoctrination as early as six and received military training as early as nine.[47] Even though the declared approach followed by states of origin towards children still stranded in Syria and Iraq is to consider them victims rather than perpetrators, the decisions they have taken so far display a completely different story.[48]

Belgium, for example, has openly declared its willingness to readmit all children under the age of 10, without actively pursuing their repatriation but by simply allowing relatives to bring them back, and to treat the older ones on a case-by-case basis.[49] The case of Shamima Begum, and her baby who died from pneumonia in a Syrian camp soon after the UK government decided not to bring them back home and stripped Ms Begum of her British citizenship,[50] sparked an intense national debate in Britain, without resulting as yet in the adoption of a strategy to the benefit of other women

---

45 See Mia Bloom and John Horgan, 'The Rise of the Child Terrorist' (9 February 2015) *Foreign Affairs* <https://www.foreignaffairs.com/articles/middle-east/2015-02-09/rise-child-terrorist> accessed 15 January 2021.

46 Noman Benotman and Nikita Malik, 'The Children of Islamic State' (2016) *Quilliam* <https://www.quilliaminternational.com/shop/e-publications/the-children-of-islamic-state/> accessed 15 January 2021 [25].

47 Asaad Almohammad, 'ISIS Child Soldiers in Syria: The Structural and Predatory Recruitment, Enlistment, Pre-Training Indoctrination, Training, and Deployment' (Research Paper, *ICCT* 19 February 2018) <https://icct.nl/publication/isis-child-soldiers-in-syria-the-structural-and-predatory-recruitment-enlistment-pre-training-indoctrination-training-and-deployment/> accessed 15 January 2021 [19–22].

48 See 'Daesh Suspects to Return to Sweden after Escape from Syria Camp' *MEMO Middle East Monitor* (2 November 2020) <https://www.middleeastmonitor.com/20201102-daesh-suspects-to-return-to-sweden-after-escape-from-syria-camp/> accessed 15 January 2021.

49 Thomas Renard and Rik Coolsaet, 'Children in the Levant: Insights from Belgium on the Dilemmas of Repatriation and the Challenges of Reintegration' (Security Policy Brief, *Egmont* 2018) <http://www.egmontinstitute.be/content/uploads/2018/07/SPB98-Renard-Coolsaet_v2.pdf?type=pdf> accessed 15 January 2021 [4–5].

50 UK Parliament, '"No Easy Answers" Home Secretary on Shamima Begum's Case' (11 March 2019) <https://www.parliament.uk/business/news/2019/march/shamima-begum-subject-of-urgent-question-following-the-death-of-her-baby/> accessed 15 January 2021.

and children in the same conditions. Notably, the situation of Ms Begum took an unexpected turn when the Court of Appeal said she had been denied a fair hearing because she could not make her case from the Syrian camp, and should thus be allowed to return to the UK to fight the decision to remove her British citizenship.[51] The ruling means the UK government must now find a way to allow Ms Begum, who is currently in Camp Roj in northern Syria, to appear in court in London despite repeatedly saying it would not assist removing her from Syria.[52]

In Germany, domestic courts have started to order the government to repatriate German children as well as their mothers or guardians. On 6 November 2019, the Higher Administrative Court of Berlin-Brandenburg (OVG Berlin-Brandenburg) confirmed the decision of the lower court and held that the German government must repatriate a German citizen who, in 2014, travelled from Germany to territory held by ISIL in Syria, together with her three minor children.[53] More in detail, the Court found that the situation in the SDF camp constituted a danger to the lives of the children, and therefore the state had no room for discretion with regard to its duty to protect its nationals abroad. The mother was allowed to travel back to Germany with her children *in primis* because it was in their best interests and because the government failed to prove that she constituted a threat to public safety. In particular, the government did not provide evidence on her exact role under ISIL or how she would constitute a concrete danger to citizens living in Germany. According to the Court, claiming that a general danger can result from the return of ISIL fighters is insufficient to outweigh the fundamental protection of family ties, as enshrined in the German Constitution.[54]

France too is struggling with its lack of clear commitment towards its nationals detained or located in Syria and Iraq. The French government has repatriated from Syria only five orphaned children of French jihadists, and French media have reported that the grandparents of two French children detained with their jihadist mother in Syria have brought a

---

51 *Shamima Begum v SIAC and the Secretary of State for the Home Department* [2020] EWCA Civ 918, paras 121–122.

52 Billy Perrigo, 'Woman Who Ran Away to Join ISIS As Teenager Can Return to U.K. to Fight Citizenship Decision, Court Rules' *Time* (16 July 2020) <https://time.com/5867626/shamima-begum-uk/> accessed 15 January 2021.

53 OVG 10 S 43.19 of 6 November 2019 (Higher Administrative Court of Berlin-Brandenburg, Germany).

54 ibid paras 33–41; Basic Law for the Federal Republic of Germany in the revised version published in the Federal Law Gazette Part III, classification number 100-1, as last amended by Article 1 of the Act of 28 March 2019 (Federal Law Gazette I p 404), art 6.

case before the European Court of Human Rights (ECtHR).[55] The claimants contend that France is allowing the children to be exposed to inhumane and degrading treatment in a camp beset by illness and malnutrition in violation of Article 3 of the European Convention of Human Rights (ECHR)[56] and Article 3(1) of its Protocol No. 4,[57] according to which no one shall be deprived of the right to enter the territory of the state of which they are a national. The question of whether such claims are well-founded, and more generally whether international law imposes upon the states of origin the obligation to repatriate at least women and children affiliated to ISIL who did not commit or participate in terrorist activities, will be addressed in the following section.

4. STATES' OBLIGATION TO REPATRIATE FOREIGN TERRORIST FIGHTERS AND THEIR FAMILY MEMBERS UNDER INTERNATIONAL LAW

Prior to discussing whether the current international legal framework governs the repatriation of FTFs and their family members, an important caveat is needed: demanding the repatriation of FTFs is not the same thing as claiming that if ISIL foreign members and their families are released from detention and travel back to their countries of origin they must be allowed entry. This scenario is thought to be implausible, although recent episodes have showed otherwise,[58] but also easier to solve. Under both customary international law and human rights law, admission to a state primarily depends on nationality.[59] The essence of nationality, which has been eloquently defined as 'an institution of domestic law [that] has

55 Marc Daou, 'France Taken to Court for Refusing to Repatriate the Children of Jihadists' *France 24* (7 May 2019) <https://www.france24.com/en/20190507-france-taken-court-over-repatriating-children-jihadists> accessed 15 January 2021.

56 Convention for the Protection of Human Rights and Fundamental Freedoms (European Convention on Human Rights, as amended) (opened for signature on 4 November 1950, entered into force on 3 September 1953) ETS 5.

57 Protocol 4 to the European Convention for the Protection of Human Rights and Fundamental Freedoms, securing certain Rights and Freedoms other than those already included in the Convention and in the First Protocol thereto (opened for signature 16 September 1963, entered into force 2 May 1968) ETS 46.

58 For evidence of women and children escaping from the SDF camps, see Nisan Ahmado and Mutlu Civiroglu, 'IS Foreign Women Smuggled Out in Northeastern Syria Camp' *Voice of America* (1 October 2019) <https://www.voanews.com/extremism-watch/foreign-women-smuggled-out-northeastern-syria-camp> accessed 15 January 2021.

59 As is well known, nationality is determined by one's social ties to the country of one's nationality, and when established, gives rise to rights and duties on the part of the

consequences in international law',[60] can be said to lie in the state's duty to admit its nationals and allow them to reside within its territory. Such a duty exists first and foremost vis-à-vis other states, meaning that it is an obligation that is needed to balance states' sovereign prerogative to regulate the presence of foreigners on their territory.[61]

Under international human rights law, the state's obligation to admit its nationals becomes the individual's right to enter and reside free from expulsion in their country of nationality.[62] Pursuant to Article 13(2) of the Universal Declaration of Human Rights (UDHR), 'everyone has the right to leave any country, including his own, and to return to his country'.[63] Article 12(4) of the International Covenant on Civil and Political Rights (ICCPR) further provides that 'no one shall be *arbitrarily* deprived of the right to enter his own country'.[64] The Human Rights Committee (HRC), in its General Comment No. 27, clarified that the reference to the concept of arbitrariness in this context is intended to emphasise that it applies to all state actions and that there are few, if any, circumstances in which restrictions of the right to enter one's own country could be reasonable.[65] The HRC also explained that states parties must not, by stripping a person of nationality, arbitrarily prevent this person from returning to their own country and cannot prevent a person from coming to the country of nationality for the first time if they were born abroad.[66] Notably, most states' nationality laws feature a set of rules – alongside those which elaborate the conditions for acquisition of nationality – which stipulate the grounds upon which a national can lose or be deprived of that nationality. A surge in FTFs mobilising around the world and then seeking to return

state, as well as on the part of the citizen/national. *Nottebohm Case (Liechtenstein v Guatemala)* (Second Phase, Judgment) [1955] ICJ Rep 1955 [4].

60 Ivan Shearer and Brian Opeskin, 'Nationality and Statelessness', in Brian Opeskin, Richard Perruchoud and Jillyanne Redpath-Cross (eds), *Foundations of International Migration Law* (CUP 2012) 93.

61 Alice Edwards, 'The Meaning of Nationality in International Law in an Era of Human Rights', in Alice Edwards and Laura van Waas (eds), *Nationality and Statelessness under International Law* (CUP 2014) 11; Alison Kesby, *The Right to Have Rights Citizenship, Humanity, and International Law* (OUP 2012) 16.

62 ibid 17.

63 Universal Declaration of Human Rights (adopted 10 December 1948) UNGA Res 217 A (III) (UDHR).

64 International Covenant on Civil and Political Rights (adopted 16 December 1966, entered into force 23 March 1976) 999 UNTS 171 (ICCPR) (emphasis added).

65 UN Human Rights Committee (HRC), 'General Comment No 27: Article 12 (Freedom of Movement)' (1999) in 'Note by the Secretariat, General Comments and General Recommendations Adopted by Human Rights Treaty Bodies' (2008) UN Doc HRI/GEN/1/Rev.9 (Vol. I), paras 11–18.

66 Ibid para 19.

to their countries of origin has ignited debate and new questions on denationalisation as a legitimate policy instrument. As explained by van Waas in her analysis of how the emerging state practice is conflicting with international human rights standards,[67] revoking nationality to prevent the return of FTFs is a violation of international law, often combined with the breach of the duty to avoid imposing statelessness and the principle of non-discrimination.[68]

The concept of deprivation of nationality clearly comes into play with regard to the repatriation of FTFs and their families, as resorting to it 'releases' governments from an alleged obligation to intervene to bring back their nationals.

4.1. THE LAW OF DIPLOMATIC AND CONSULAR RELATIONS

An important field of international law relevant to the matter at hand is the law of diplomatic and consular relations, a set of well-established norms of which the Vienna Convention on Diplomatic Relations (VCDR)[69] and the Vienna Convention on Consular Relations (VCCR) constitute the core.[70] When foreigners, including terrorist fighters in an armed conflict, are captured and detained, or simply held in camps, by a third state or non-state actor as in the case of the SDF, questions arise about the possible exercise of diplomatic protection, both in the sense of formal 'diplomatic protection' by one state against another and in the sense of informal diplomatic protection, meaning the 'protection of nationals' as practiced by diplomatic missions and consular posts under customary international law and treaty law.[71]

---

67 Laura van Waas, 'Foreign Fighters and the Deprivation of Nationality: National Practices and International Law Implications' in Andrea de Guttry and others (eds), *Foreign Fighters under International Law and Beyond* (Asser Press 2016) 476–480.

68 See ibid 481; Sandra Mantu, '"Terrorist" Citizens and the Human Right to Nationality' (2018) 26(1) Journal of Contemporary European Studies 28, 31–33. Emblematic in this regard is the UK Government's decision to strip Shamima Begum of her citizenship leaving her *de facto* stateless as a possible second citizenship was denied by the Bangladeshi Government.

69 Vienna Convention on Diplomatic Relations (adopted 18 April 1961, entered into force 24 April 1964) 500 UNTS 95 (VCDR).

70 Vienna Convention on Consular Relations (adopted 24 April 1963, entered into force 19 March 1967) 596 UNTS 261 (VCCR).

71 See Eileen Denza, 'Nationality and Diplomatic Protection' (2018) 65 Netherlands International Law Review 463, 473.

In its formal sense the expression 'diplomatic protection' is defined by the International Law Commission (ILC) in its Draft Articles as meaning 'the invocation by a state, through diplomatic action or other peaceful means, of the responsibility of another state for an injury caused by an internationally wrongful act to a natural or legal person that is a national of the former State with a view to the implementation of such responsibility'.[72] Under customary international law, diplomatic protection, which is exercised by a state following exhaustion of local remedies by one of its nationals, is a right that belongs to states; each state can choose not only the timing and extent of any action, but first and foremost whether it would take any action at all.[73] Notably, a controversial proposal to impose on states a limited duty to exercise diplomatic protection where the fundamental rights of their nationals are violated abroad was rejected by the ILC in 2000, conveying the powerful message that 'the golden rule of state discretion is alive and well'.[74] On the other hand, the domestic laws of most states provide that individuals or enterprises have a 'legitimate expectation' that their state of nationality would give full consideration and react to a claim.[75] In interpreting and applying said laws, the national courts of states such as South Africa, Canada, the UK, and Germany have recognised the legitimate expectation to receive diplomatic protection, but failed to impose a duty on their respective governments to exercise it.[76]

One of the central arguments, which will be further discussed in the next subsection, raised in the most well-documented decisions against the recognition of a duty to exercise diplomatic protection is the notion that a state has no obligation to ensure human rights protection to its nationals while they are outside its territorial boundaries, given the territorial application of international human rights treaties and the sovereignty of

72 ibid 466; See ILC, 'Draft Articles on Diplomatic Protection' (19 May 2006) UN Doc A/CN.4/L 684.

73 Annemarieke Vermeer-Künzli, 'As If: The Legal Fiction in Diplomatic Protection' (2007) 18(1) EJIL 37; Wilhelm Karl Geck, 'Diplomatic Protection' in Rudolf Bernhardt (ed), *Encyclopedia of Public International Law* (Volume 1, North Holland 1992) 1056; Mohamed Bennouna, 'Preliminary Report on Diplomatic Protection' (Documents of the fiftieth session, ILC 4 February 1998) UN Doc A/CN.4/484, paras 19–20.

74 Noura Karazivan, 'Diplomatic Protection: Taking Human Rights Extraterritorially' (2006) 44 Canadian Yearbook of International Law 299, 300.

75 ibid 300. Some States, like Albania, have a constitutionally-grounded obligation to protect their citizens abroad. See Albania's Constitution of 1998 with Amendments through 2016, art 8.

76 See for instance *R (Abbasi) v Secretary of State for Foreign and Commonwealth Affairs and Secretary of State for the Home Department* [2002] EWCA Civ 1598, [2003] UKHRR 76. See also Denza (n 71) 467.

the host state. The other key aspect considered by the national courts that have examined the issue is the wide discretion enjoyed by the executive in setting the state's foreign-policy objectives. Such discretion is not, in principle, immune from judicial scrutiny, although the standard for claiming that a government has failed to respond appropriately to a request for diplomatic protection would be, in the words of the Constitutional Court of South Africa and the Federal Constitutional Court of Germany respectively, the 'irrationality of the government's decision'[77] or its 'total incomprehensiveness'.[78] The decision taken by the governments of several states, including European ones, not to repatriate FTFs has been challenged on these grounds only before French national courts, which have regarded this decision as an 'act of government' that is ultimately not subject to judicial review.

More concretely, on 23 April 2019 France's top administrative court, the *Conseil d'Etat*, rejected demands for repatriation made by two French nationals for their daughter and her children, currently held in Syria.[79] The claimants, who are now seeking justice before the ECtHR after having exhausted domestic remedies, asked the court to, *inter alia*, reverse the decision of the lower court, which applied the theory of the *acte de gouvernement* to justify its lack of jurisdiction,[80] and recognise instead France's obligation to repatriate its nationals, especially in light of the severe human rights violations to which they are exposed while in the SDF-controlled camp. The *Conseil d'Etat* stated that it lacked jurisdiction, as proactively seeking the return of its nationals would require the state's engagement in negotiations with foreign authorities or even intervention on a foreign territory. These actions, according to the Court, fall under the remit of France's international relations,[81] and are therefore exempted from judicial scrutiny.

Furthermore, as anticipated above, the expression 'diplomatic protection' is also used informally to mean the assistance given by diplomatic missions and consular posts to their nationals in order to access and to make use of local remedies. Both the VCDR and the VCCR (under Art. 3 and Art. 5 respectively) list among the basic functions of diplomatic missions and of consular posts 'protecting *in the receiving State* the interests of the sending

[77] Constitutional Court of South Africa, *Kaunda v President of the Republic of South Africa* (2005) 4 South African Law Reports 235 (CC), 44 ILM 173, 35.

[78] 2 BvR419/80 of 16 December 1980, 398 (Federal Constitutional Court of Germany).

[79] Décision N° 429668, Ordonnance du 23 avril 2019 (*Conseil d'Etat* of France).

[80] ibid 2.

[81] ibid 5.

state and of its nationals'. Moreover, the VCCR places particular emphasis on states' duty to safeguard the interests of minors, particularly where any guardianship or trusteeship is required.[82] Missions and consular posts each confront a number of legal, practical, and financial hurdles in in the process of performing a wide range of protective functions. These functions range from sensitive political assistance, which may be required by a person unjustly imprisoned or charged, through administrative functions such as renewal of a passport or registration of a birth or death, to practical assistance with return home or subsistence following a robbery.[83]

The question of whether an obligation to provide assistance to a state's nationals held in Syria is incumbent upon that state's diplomatic and consular services was recently brought before the Belgian courts. The lower court ordered that Belgium should do everything in its powers to bring six children and their mothers, the latter tried and convicted *in absentia* by Belgian courts, back from the Al-Hol camp in Syria. The judge ruled that the interest of the children should be upheld by all Belgian authorities, including the Belgian diplomatic and consular services. According to the Code of Consular Affairs, Belgian citizens are entitled to consular assistance when they find themselves in extreme circumstances, and even though the mothers might no longer be entitled to consular assistance, the same could not be claimed with regard to the children.[84] Therefore, the court ordered Belgium to organise their travel within 40 days of being notified of the decision or pay a daily penalty of 5,000 euros for each child, up to a maximum 1 million euros. The decision, immediately appealed by the Belgian government, which feared that it could set a dangerous precedent, was overturned in February 2019, when the appeals court ruled that Belgium had no obligation to bring back the children and their mothers.[85] In spite of the lack of a legal obligation, the Belgian government reiterated its commitment to differentiating between the mothers and the children, stating that it would allow the latter to enter the country, but without taking responsibility for facilitating and seeking their return, and, even more disturbingly, without considering whether it is in the children's best

82 VCCR art 5(h).

83 See Denza (n 71) 474.

84 Tanya Mehra and Christophe Paulussen, 'The Repatriation of Foreign Fighters and Their Families: Options, Obligations, Morality and Long-Term Thinking' (Perspective, *ICCT* 6 March 2019) <https://icct.nl/publication/the-repatriation-of-foreign-fighters-and-their-families-options-obligations-morality-and-long-term-thinking/> accessed 15 January 2021.

85 ibid 4.

interests to be separated from their mothers.[86] The Belgian lower court's decision, although swiftly reversed, represents an important milestone and may act as a wake-up call for other national courts across Europe. Nonetheless, at the moment – setting aside the fact that most European states have cut off diplomatic relations with Syria and Libya – there is no agreement either on the question of whether a national has a legal right or, again, merely a legitimate expectation, of receiving protection from their own embassy or consular post, nor is there consensus among states, even among EU member states, on the extent of protection offered by individual missions or posts.[87]

4.2. HUMAN RIGHTS LAW

As mentioned above, one of the principal arguments used by national courts to ultimately deny the existence of a duty on states to protect their nationals abroad against violations of their fundamental human rights, is based on the lack of recognition of the extraterritorial application of international human rights treaties.[88] In the words of the South African Constitutional Court 'the exercise of jurisdiction beyond a state's territorial limits would [...] constitute an interference with the exclusive territorial jurisdiction of another state'[89] and hence it would violate international law. In the case of FTFs held in Syria, the SDF declared lack of willingness and capabilities to try alleged foreign terrorists and keep holding their families on the one hand, and the eloquent silence of the Syrian government on the other,[90] suggest that no interference with the State's sovereign rights will be denounced should the states of origin seek to repatriate their nationals. In the case of Iraq, the issue is more complex

86 See UN Secretary-General (n 30) 6: '[t]he best interests of the child must be given primary consideration in all actions concerning them, including in relation to maintaining family unity [...] Member States should seek the free and informed consent of parents before separating children for repatriation, unless separation is decided to be in the child's best interests.'

87 See Denza (n 71) 475.

88 This point was mainly addressed when discussing the extraterritorial application of the ECHR in *Abbasi* (n 76) paras 77–79.

89 *Kaunda* (n 77) 19.

90 Tanya Mehra, *Bringing (Foreign)* 'Terrorist Fighters to Justice in a Post-ISIS Landscape Part I: Prosecution by Iraqi and Syrian Courts' (Perspective, *ICCT* 22 December 2017) <https://icct.nl/publication/bringing-foreign-terrorist-fighters-to-justice-in-a-post-isis-landscape-part-i-prosecution-by-iraqi-and-syrian-courts/>.

as the state is willing to prosecute all crimes committed on its territory and only the repatriation of minors could be regarded as an option that does not impinge on the state's sovereign rights.

Yet the question remains whether international human rights treaties actually provide states with jurisdiction over their nationals, or habitual residents, outside their territories because extraterritorial jurisdiction entails not only the possibility of legitimate exercise of jurisdiction, but also the duty to comply with legally binding obligations, including an alleged obligation to repatriate FTFs. As is well known, the jurisprudence of the ECtHR does not offer a definitive or straightforward solution to the problems that surround the interpretation of Article 1 of the ECHR.[91] So far the ECtHR, in its seemingly inconsistent case law from *Banković* onwards,[92] has confirmed that jurisdiction under Article 1 of the ECHR is 'primarily territorial'[93] and it has also recognised 'a number of exceptional circumstances' outside of territorial boundaries, which could give rise to the establishment of jurisdiction.[94] Said exceptional circumstances can be grouped into two categories, 'state agent authority and control over persons' and 'effective control over an area or territory'.[95] Even though the ECtHR jurisprudence regarding jurisdiction, and thus extraterritoriality, is primarily based on facts rather than on a generalisable principle,[96] it is possible to anticipate that it would be impossible for the Court to find that France,[97] or any other member

91 Marko Milanovic, *Extraterritorial Application of Human Rights Treaties: Law, Principles, and Policy* (Oxford Monographs in International Law 2011); Samantha Besson, 'The Extraterritoriality of the European Convention on Human Rights: Why Human Rights Depend on Jurisdiction and What Jurisdiction Amounts to' (2012) 25(4) Leiden Journal of International Law (LJIL) 857, 862–868; Seunghwan Kim, 'Non-Refoulement and Extraterritorial Jurisdiction: State Sovereignty and Migration Controls at Sea in the European Context' (2017) 30(1) LJIL 49, 53–61.

92 *Banković and Others v Belgium and 16 Other Contracting States* App no 52207/99 (ECtHR, 19 December 2001), paras 31–53.

93 Sarah Miller, 'Revisiting Extraterritorial Jurisdiction: A Territorial Justification for Extraterritorial Jurisdiction under the European Convention' (2010) 20(4) EJIL 1223, 1226–1230.

94 Kim (n 91).

95 *Al-Skeini and Others v United Kingdom* (2011) ECHR 1093, App No 55721/07 paras 133–140.

96 Michael O'Boyle, 'The European Convention on Human Rights and Extraterritorial Jurisdiction: A Comment on "Life after Bankovic"' in Fons Coomans and Menno T Kamminga (eds), *Extraterritorial Application of Human Rights Treaties* (Intersentia 2004) 128.

97 See section 3(b) below.

state, is exercising 'total', 'full', 'exclusive' control or physical power over its nationals stranded or captured in Syria or Iraq.

Considering the scope of application of human rights treaties other than the ECHR,[98] like the ICCPR, the Convention against Torture and Other Cruel, Inhuman or Degrading Treatment or Punishment (CAT),[99] and the Convention on the Rights of the Child (CRC) and its Optional Protocols,[100] in particular the Optional Protocol to the Convention on the Rights of the Child on the Involvement of Children in Armed Conflict (OPAC),[101] can lead to different, or at least less discouraging, conclusions. This is evident in the legal analysis jointly carried out by the Special Rapporteur on the promotion and protection of human rights while countering terrorism and the Special Rapporteur on extrajudicial, summary or arbitrary executions,[102] and is also demonstrated by the Committee on the Rights of the Child in the case of *L.H. et al v. France*, in which the Committee found that France has jurisdiction over children, in SDF-controlled camps in Syria, who are French nationals.[103] The HRC has interpreted Article 2 of the ICCPR as requiring that state parties 'secure the rights under the Covenant for all persons in their territory *and* all persons under their control'.[104] Over the years, the HRC has

98 See Theodor Meron, 'Extraterritoriality of Human Rights Treaties' (1995) 89(1) The American Journal of International Law 78; Vassilis P Tzevelekos, 'Reconstructing the Effective Control Criterion in Extraterritorial Human Rights Breaches: Direct Attribution of Wrongfulness, Due Diligence, and Concurrent Responsibility' (2014) 36(1) Michigan Journal of International Law 129, 132.

99 Convention Against Torture and Other Cruel, Inhuman or Degrading Treatment or Punishment (adopted 10 December 1984, entered into force 26 June 1987) 1465 UNTS 85 (CAT).

100 Convention on the Rights of the Child (adopted 20 November 1989, entered into force 2 September 1990) 1577 UNTS 3 (CRC).

101 Optional Protocol to the Convention on the Rights of the Child on the Involvement of Children in Armed Conflict (adopted 25 May 2000, entered into force 12 February 2002) 2173 UNTS 222.

102 The Special Rapporteur on the promotion and protection of human rights while countering terrorism and the Special Rapporteur on extrajudicial, summary or arbitrary executions, 'Extra-territorial Jurisdiction of States over Children and their Guardians in Camps, Prisons, or elsewhere in the Northern Syrian Arab Republic: Legal Analysis' (2020) <https://www.ohchr.org/Documents/Issues/Terrorism/UNSRsPublicJurisdictionAnalysis2020.pdf> accessed 15 January 2021.

103 *LH et al v France* (n 13).

104 HRC, 'General Comment No 31: The Nature of the General Legal Obligation Imposed on States Parties to the Covenant' (2004) in 'Note by the Secretariat, General Comments and General Recommendations Adopted by Human Rights Treaty Bodies' (2008) UN Doc HRI/GEN/1/Rev.9 (Vol. I), para 12.

consistently affirmed the extraterritorial application of the Covenant to anyone within the power or effective control of that state party, even if not situated within the territory of the state party. Notably, the HRC has also recognised the extraterritorial reach of the Covenant in cases where a state party has control over the facts and events giving rise to human rights violations in breach of its negative obligations,[105] thus opening the door for a wider interpretation of the jurisdiction clause, which could, in principle, find application in the situation of FTFs and their family members with regard to both negative and positive obligations of their states of nationality.[106]

Assuming that FTFs and their families in Syria and Iraq suffer from, or are exposed to, cruel, inhuman, or degrading treatment or punishment, or torture, the CAT Committee seems to expect all states to engage to prevent such serious violations. Consistently with the views expressed by the CAT Committee,[107] the Special Rapporteur on torture and other cruel, inhuman, or degrading treatment or punishment has stated that

> the *jus cogens* non-derogable prohibition against torture and ill-treatment cannot be territorially limited and that any jurisdictional references found in the CAT cannot be read to restrict or limit States' obligations to respect all individuals' rights to be free from torture and ill-treatment, *anywhere in the world*.[108]

Accordingly, the obligation to take preventive measures under Articles 2(1) and 16(1) of the CAT encompasses actions taken by states '*in their own jurisdictions to prevent* torture or other ill-treatment extraterritorially'.[109] Hence a state may also be responsible for 'indirectly attributable extraterritorial wrongfulness' owing to a failure to fulfil its positive human rights obligations.[110] In such scenarios the criterion of 'effective control' may be taken into account to assess the standards of due diligence that

---

105 Martin Scheinin, 'Extraterritorial Effect of the International Covenant on Civil and Political Rights' in Fons Coomans and Menno T Kamminga (eds.), *Extraterritorial Application of Human Rights Treaties* (Intersentia 2004) 76.

106 HRC (n 104) at 6–7.

107 Karen da Costa, *The Extraterritorial Application of Selected Human Rights Treaties* (Martinus Nijhoff Publishers 2012) 255–257; Manfred Nowak and Elizabeth McArthur, *The United Nations Convention Against Torture: A Commentary* (OUP 2008).

108 UNGA, 'Interim Report of the Special Rapporteur on Torture and other Cruel, Inhuman or Degrading Treatment or Punishment' (7 August 2015) UN Doc A/70/303, para 27 (emphasis added).

109 ibid para 33 (emphasis added).

110 ibid para 35.

a state is legally obliged to demonstrate in a given situation.[111] It follows that, in order to effectively protect their nationals from the risk of torture or ill-treatment, repatriation would be a nationality state's main way to take action and fulfil their obligations under the CAT.

In relation to the CRC – and thus with specific reference to the fate of foreign children currently held in Syria and Iraq – the CRC Committee has reiterated on various occasions that the Convention has extraterritorial reach,[112] a position that is also shared, as in the case of the ICCPR, by the International Court of Justice (ICJ).[113] In *L.H. et al v. France*, the CRC Committee observed that 'the State party, as the State of the children's nationality, has the capability and the power to protect the rights of the children in question by taking action to repatriate them or provide other consular responses'.[114] The Committee did not clarify precisely which test of extraterritorial jurisdiction is being applied, although it was likely adopting a functional approach, that is, holding that France has the duty to protect the children because it has the ability to do so, on the basis of numerous contextual factors.[115] In addition to the case against France, in which the CRC Committee unanimously found that states of nationality have a positive obligation to protect the human rights of child nationals in the Syrian camps, despite the fact that these camps are under the control of a non-state armed group; the extraterritorial application of the Convention and of the OPAC has been particularly emphasised with regard to the recruitment and use of child soldiers. This is relevant also with regard to the case under scrutiny as the defeat of ISIL has not neutralised the risk that children – left without protection in war-torn countries – could be recruited by other armed

111 See Tzevelekos (n 98) 142–146.

112 UN Committee on the Rights of the Child, 'Concluding Observations: Israel' (9 October 2002) UN Doc CRC/C/15/Add.195, paras 2, 5, 57–58.

113 Ralph Wilde, 'Human Rights Beyond Borders at the World Court: The Significance of the International Court of Justice's Jurisprudence on the Extraterritorial Application of International Human Rights Law Treaties' (2013) 12(4) Chinese Journal of International Law 639, 663–665.

114 *H et al v France* (n 13) [9.7].

115 See Marko Milanovic, 'Repatriating the Children of Foreign Terrorist Fighters and the Extraterritorial Application of Human Rights' (*EJIL: Talk!* 10 November 2020 <https://www.ejiltalk.org/repatriating-the-children-of-foreign-terrorist-fighters-and-the-extraterritorial-application-of-human-rights/> accessed 15 January 2021.

forces or groups. The CRC Committee – discussing the principle of *non-refoulement* – underscored that

> [...] as underage recruitment and participation in hostilities entails a high risk of irreparable harm involving fundamental human rights, including the right to life, States' obligations stemming from Article 38 of the Convention, in conjunction with Articles 3 and 4 of the OPAC, entail extraterritorial effects and States shall refrain from returning a child in any manner whatsoever to the borders of a State where there is a real risk of underage recruitment [...].[116]

Article 4 of the OPAC, by providing that armed groups that are distinct from the armed forces of a state should not, under any circumstances, recruit or use in hostilities persons under the age of 18 years, recognises that states, as the only parties to the Protocol, are responsible for its implementation and must take effective measures to prevent recruitment and use of children by non-state armed groups, wherever they are located.[117] Furthermore, it is worth stressing that Article 7 of the OPAC affirms that 'States Parties shall cooperate ... in the prevention of any activity contrary to the Protocol', and are requested to create 'legal, administrative and other measures' to implement the Protocol within their jurisdiction. As a result, by overtly providing that states must develop proactive behaviour in the context of due diligence, the OPAC contributes, perhaps more than the other human rights treaties considered, to shaping an obligation to repatriate minor FTFs.

5. CONCLUSIONS

As it has emerged from this analysis, the current international framework does not seem to impose on states a straightforward obligation to repatriate FTFs and their families. The lack of a common and uniform strategy

116 UN Committee on the Rights of the Child, 'General Comment No 6: Treatment of Unaccompanied and Separated Children Outside their Country of Origin' (2005) in 'Note by the Secretariat, General Comments and General Recommendations Adopted by Human Rights Treaty Bodies' (2008) UN Doc HRI/GEN/1/Rev.9 (Vol. II), para 10. See also Capone (n 34) 169–170.

117 Tracey B C Begle, 'The Extraterritorial Obligation to Prevent the Use of Child Soldiers' (2012) 27(3) American University International Law Review 613, 630–633.

across the European states most affected by the FTFs phenomenon – and thus, most 'threatened' by the return of FTFs and their accompanying family members – confirms that there is a certain degree of confusion. A nebulous approach cloaked by (short-term) security concerns is prevailing over humanitarian considerations, and international law needs to come into play to shed light on the obligations that states owe to their nationals abroad, especially women and children. Many states of origin of FTFs are drawing a line between adult FTFs, in light of the recent recognition of women's roles in the ranks of ISIL, and children, yet even when it comes to the latter states have only pursued a proactive approach to repatriating them sporadically and quite unpredictably. The international normative framework regulating diplomatic protection, in both its formal and informal meaning, is still ambiguous on the extent to which states of nationality have an obligation to assist their nationals abroad and perform protective functions. Nonetheless, there is increasing recognition of a legitimate expectation to receive both diplomatic protection, after the exhaustion of domestic remedies, and diplomatic and consular assistance. A refusal to hear and react to its nationals' claims places a state in a position where its conduct could, and should, be submitted to domestic, regional, and international judicial review.

Moreover, in the absence of a clear and precise obligation to exercise protection over their nationals detained or stranded in Syria and Iraq, states can be blamed for indulging in a behaviour that does not comply with international human rights standards. Although the extraterritorial application of human rights treaties remains a controversial topic, whether a human rights treaty protects a particular individual in an extraterritorial context is ultimately a matter of treaty interpretation.[118] Working on this assumption, the chapter has showed that there is an increasing convergence of interpretations that depart from the traditional models of spatial and personal models of jurisdiction and recognise it with regard to negative obligations and, in instances like the CAT and the CRC, positive ones. Based on these positive obligations towards individuals and children at risk of being affected by torture, ill-treatment, and recruitment and use in armed conflict, states of nationality should act and bring FTFs and their family members back home – especially considering, in the case of children, that separation from their mother is rarely in a child's best interests.

[118] Milanovic (n 115).

Implementing repatriation ultimately represents the most effective way to reconcile interests and values that appear to be difficult to balance, like the protection of human rights of all individuals and states' national security. The UK Court of Appeal has adopted this approach in the Begum case,[119] and it can only be hoped that other domestic courts in Europe and beyond will follow in its footsteps.

[119] See *Shamima Begum* (n 51), para 121.

PUSHING THE BOUNDARIES OF HUMAN RIGHTS DISCOURSE

Peasant Rights and Peasant Interests

Corina HERI*

1. INTRODUCTION

International human rights law has regularly been criticised for its failure to adequately reflect a number of fundamental interests and issues that are based on hegemony, relevant beyond national borders, and difficult to resolve by one sovereign state alone. Examples include abuses of corporate power, climate change and other environmental harms, growing global inequality, and neoliberal and neo-colonial policies, which all have impacts on the effective enjoyment of a wide range of human rights. In particular, international law, of which the international human rights system is a subset, is influenced by, complicit

---

* Postdoctoral researcher, University of Zurich. I am grateful to the two anonymous peer-reviewers for their feedback on this chapter. All remaining errors and inaccuracies are, of course, mine.

in, and driven through capitalism.[1] In this regard, Margot E. Salomon has explored the opposing perspectives of nihilism and pragmatism that can be taken in view of an awareness of these capitalist leanings. From a pragmatist perspective, she has argued, human rights law can still serve a partially emancipatory or reformist, although not a revolutionary, purpose within this structure.[2]

One way to seek to address these issues within the framework of human rights law, beyond litigating existing rights, involves the creation of instruments enshrining new or expanded obligations for states and other actors. The recognition of the human rights of peasants and rural dwellers provides a recent and informative example. During this process, self-identified peasants from across the globe came together to contest developments in international trade law and (neo-)liberal trade policies as well as lacunae in the human rights framework that negatively affect peasant communities.

The international peasant movement, which should not be understood as homogenous or unitary despite its well-organised push for rights, is made up of grassroots organisations such as the global La Vía Campesina (LVC), along with the Europe-Third World Centre (CETIM), FIAN International (the Food First Information and Action Network), and many others.[3] In its struggle for the recognition of peasant human rights, the movement has often positioned itself as an outsider, or as the 'other' of free-trade policies or capitalism.[4] At the same time its aims reflect communitarian interests, for example the struggle to control climate change, curb corporate human rights abuses, and protect biodiversity.

---

1 Margot E Salomon, 'Nihilists, Pragmatists and Peasants: A Dispatch on Contradiction in International Human Rights Law' in Emilios Christodoulidis, Ruth Dukes, and Marco Goldoni (eds), *Research Handbook on Critical Legal Theory* (Edward Elgar Publishing 2019).

2 ibid.

3 For example, the fifth and last session of the Working Group to draft the UNDROP featured participation by Alliance for Food Sovereignty in Africa (AFSA), Comité francais pour la Solidarité Internationale, Community Self Reliance Centre (COSEREC), Farmworkers Association of Florida, Indonesian Peasant Union (SPI), Korean Women Peasants Association (KWPA), Red Nacional de Agricultura Familiar (RENAF), SOS Faim, Via Campesina, World Forum of Fisher People (WFFP), and International Federation of Rural Adult Catholic Movements (FIMARC). See Human Rights Council, 'Report of the open-ended intergovernmental working group on a United Nations declaration on the rights of peasants and other people working in rural areas' (13 July 2018) UN Doc A/HRC/39/67, 19.

4 Luis Hernández Navarro and Annette Aurélie Desmarais, 'Crisis y Soberanía Alimentaria: Vía Campesina y el Tiempo de Una Idea' (2009) 153 El Cotidiano 89, 93.

Through a process initiated to a significant extent by grassroots peasant movements, peasant human rights were recognised by the United Nations General Assembly (UNGA) in December 2018, when it adopted a declaration on the rights of peasants and rural dwellers (the UNDROP).[5] This document was prepared on the recommendation of the Human Rights Council Advisory Committee[6] through five sessions of the open-ended intergovernmental working group on the UNDROP,[7] which took place with the extensive collaboration of peasant movements and forums, as well human rights experts and NGO representatives. In its final version, the UNDROP contains 28 articles covering a range of human rights entitlements, some of them novel and subversive,[8] including what Salomon has called 'rights against global capitalism'.[9] To peasant activists, this declaration 'protects the lives and livelihoods of farmers and improves their recognition as political subjects while granting them the right to use, manage and control natural resources'.[10]

The peasant movement for human rights, and the UNDROP itself, have been subject to increasing scholarly analysis in recent years. Priscilla Claeys has written widely about food sovereignty, the process of gaining recognition for peasant rights, and the possibility of losing the subversive potential of those rights.[11] Other scholars, for example Christophe Golay and Adriana Bessa, Noha Shawki, Smita Narula, Sofia Monsalve Suárez, Marc Edelman and Carwil James, Josh Brem-Wilson, Margot E. Salomon,

5 UN General Assembly, Res 73/165: 'United Nations Declaration on the Rights of Peasants and Other People Working in Rural Areas' (21 January 2019) Resolution adopted by the General Assembly on 17 December 2018 UN Doc A/RES/73/165.

6 Human Rights Council, 'Final study of the Human Rights Council Advisory Committee on the advancement of the rights of peasants and other people working in rural areas' (24 February 2012) UN Doc A/HRC/19/75.

7 With the most recent taking place in 2018, see Human Rights Council (n 3).

8 Coline Hubert, 'The United Nations Declaration on the Rights of Peasants' (CETIM 2019) 157.

9 Salomon (n 1).

10 La Vía Campesina, 'Peasants Fighting for Justice: Cases of Violations of Peasants' Human Rights' (2017) <https://viacampesina.org/en/publication-peasants-fighting-for-justice/> accessed 15 January 2021.

11 See, for example, Priscilla Claeys, 'The Creation of New Rights by the Food Sovereignty Movement: The Challenge of Institutionalizing Subversion' (2012) 46(5) Sociology 844; Stefania Errico and Priscilla Claeys, 'Human Rights and the Commons: Exploring Approaches to the Governance of Land and Natural Resources beyond Indigenous Peoples' Rights – The Case of Peasants' (2020) 27(1) International Journal on Minority and Group Rights 1; Priscilla Claeys and Marc Edelman, 'The United Nations Declaration on the Rights of Peasants and Other People Working in Rural Areas' (2019) 47(1) The Journal of Peasant Studies 1, as well as the literature cited throughout this chapter.

Coline Hubert, and Ingeborg Gaarde, have provided analyses of peasant rights and their bearers.[12] A golden thread traversing much of this work is the difficult balance between the radical rights claims that would push back against harmful market forces and state policies, and the risks and trade-offs required when seeking codification in a human rights instrument.

The present chapter will discuss some of the main novelties contained in the UNDROP – significantly, the right to food and seed sovereignty, the peasant right to land, and environmental rights claims – and analyse how, by gaining recognition of these rights specifically and the peasant rights project more generally, the peasant movement is exposing gaps in how human rights law protects interests, and using a human rights frame to seek to fill these lacunae. While unable to do full justice to the developments that have taken place in this context in recent decades, or in related contexts such as those of indigenous peoples' rights and environmental justice, among others, the chapter seeks to make some 'good trouble' for certain core indeterminacies of international law,[13] and specifically of international human rights law. In other words, it will seek

---

12 Christophe Golay and Adriana Bessa, 'The Right to Seeds in Europe: The United Nations Declaration on the Rights of Peasants and Other People Working in Rural Areas and the Protection of the Right to Seeds in Europe' (2018) Geneva Academy of International Humanitarian Law and Human Rights, Academy Briefing No 15; Christophe Golay, 'Towards a Convention on the Rights of Peasants' in Sophia Murphy and Armin Paasch (eds), *The Global Food Challenge: Towards a Human Rights Approach to Trade and Investment* (The Global Food Challenge – Finding New Approaches to Trade and Investment that support the Right to Food Conference, Geneva, November 2008); Noha Shawki, 'New Rights Advocacy and the Human Rights of Peasants: La Vía Campesina and the Evolution of New Human Rights Norms (2014) 6(2) Journal of Human Rights Practice 306; Smita Narula, 'The Global Land Rush: Markets, Rights, and the Politics of Food' (2013) 49(1) Stanford Journal of International Law 101; Sofia Monsalve Suárez, 'The Human Rights Framework in Contemporary Agrarian Struggles' (2013) 40(1) Journal of Peasant Studies 239; Marc Edelman and Carwil James, 'Peasants' Rights and the UN System: Quixotic Struggle? Or Emancipatory Idea Whose Time has Come?' (2011) 38(1) Journal of Peasant Studies 81; Josh Brem-Wilson, 'La Vía Campesina and the UN Committee on World Food Security: Affected Publics and Institutional Dynamics in the Nascent Transnational Public Sphere' (2017) 43(2) Review of International Studies 302; Josh Brem-Wilson, 'Towards Food Sovereignty: Interrogating Peasant Voice in the UN Committee on World Food Security' (2015) 42(1) Journal of Peasant Studies 73; Salomon (n 1); Hubert (n 8); Ingeborg Gaarde, *Peasants Negotiating a Global Policy Space: La Vía Campesina in the Committee on World Food Security* (Routledge 2017).

13 Martti Koskenniemi, *From Apology to Utopia: The Structure of International Legal Argument* (Cambridge University Press 2006).

out key examples of how peasant human rights can help contest not only the usefulness of the concept of community interests, but also some of the widely accepted constraints of liberal, Western, individualistic, universal, and state- and freedom-oriented human rights law through the injection of a mixture of radical, critical, third-world, and Marxist perspectives. In doing so, it will focus largely on the legal writings concerning peasant rights that have emerged in recent years. It cannot offer a complete overview of the peasant rights process or a detailed reflection on the views of peasant activists and transnational movements themselves. Instead it proceeds with mainstream human rights law – what might be called the human rights establishment – in mind, and interrogates the ways in which peasant rights and the movement behind them relate to and challenge the anatomy of that establishment.

2. COMMUNITY INTERESTS, COLLECTIVE INTERESTS, AND THE COMMONS

The present volume concerns the concept of community interests, and this chapter accordingly sets out by asking how that concept relates to the context of peasant rights. In other words, in what ways does the concept of community interests meaningfully describe the issues addressed by the movement, and the gaps or failures in the protection of these interests by the international legal order? In doing so, this chapter refers not only to community interests, but also to collective interests and the commons, although the latter are referred to only tangentially and are not the focus of the contribution.

Community interests have taken on significance in the context of international legal scholarship as a way of delineating the topics that fall under the purview of the international legal order and that have the appeal of universality.[14] The concept has been defined by Eyal Benvenisti and Georg Nolte as serving to explore 'the extent to which states owe duties toward those who are affected by their actions and omissions, and

14 Compare, for example, Eyal Benvenisti and Georg Nolte (eds), *Community Interests Across International Law* (Oxford University Press 2018); Bruno Simma, 'From Bilateralism to Community Interest in International Law' (1994) 250 Recueil des Cours de l'Académie de Droit International 217, 233; Wolfgang Benedek and others (eds), *The Common Interest in International Law* (Intersentia 2014); Mónica García-Salmones Rovira, 'The Politics of Interest in International Law' 25(3) (2014) European Journal of International Law 765.

therefore in a broad sense'.[15] In other words, not only states but also non-state actors, individuals and groups whose interests are insufficiently taken into account in the context of policymaking, can constitute a 'community'.[16] But this definition is exceedingly vague and flexible, meaning that any interest could arguably fall under it. The 'community' element is thus rendered largely moot, allowing the term to be alternatively defined simply as 'interests', and no indication is given for how to prioritise or promote any given interest over any other. This indeterminacy indicates that, for the purposes of ensuring adequate human rights protection (for peasants or otherwise), or for striking a balance between human rights protections and other interests, the meaning contained in the concept is largely negligible.

And yet the concept endures, and so there might be more to it after all. Samantha Besson's effort to more clearly define community interests can help provide some clarity. She has discussed community interests as 'interests … that are common … and/or belong to a community', and linked the interests in question to values that are important or fundamental and shared by collective bearers, that is, by (people in) more than one state.[17] Human rights are frequently cited as an example of community interests, and clearly fall under Besson's understanding of the concept. The indeterminacy persists, however, and any other host of issues might fall under such a term. It is equally possible to argue, for example, that 'international investment law properly construed can be conceptualized as protecting community interests, because it is part of the legal infrastructure necessary for the functioning of the global economy under a rule of law framework', despite the frictions between international investment law and human rights.[18]

In fact, any subfield of the international legal order can fall under this definition, without any indication of how these subfields can or should interact, how to resolve conflicts of interests, and whether there should be any type of hierarchy between them. So, for example, the concept does very little to resolve the long-lasting and intractable deadlock between the

---

15 Eyal Benvenisti and Georg Nolte, 'Introduction' in Eyal Benvenisti and Georg Nolte (eds), *Community Interests Across International Law* (OUP 2018) 3–16.

16 ibid.

17 Samantha Besson, 'Community Interests in International Law' in Eyal Benvenisti and Georg Nolte (eds), *Community Interests Across International Law* (OUP 2018) 38–40.

18 Stephan W Schill and Vladislav Djanic, 'International Investment Law and Community Interests' in Eyal Benvenisti and Georg Nolte (eds), *Community Interests Across International Law* (OUP 2018) 221–248.

human rights system and the World Bank.[19] It is this same malleability and 'tactical polyvalence' – or dependence on the speaker's position of power and the institutional context – that allows human rights to be deployed 'in defence of wealth and power in the period of neoliberal hegemony'.[20] This characteristic is what renders human rights discourse slippery enough to be deployed in order to defend the rights of capital.[21]

In writing about mass land grabs, Jochen von Bernstorff has juxtaposed two sets of 'community interests': human rights (especially socio-economic rights, including the right to housing, to adequate food, and to an adequate standard of living, but also the right to permanent sovereignty over natural resources and freedom from discrimination) and regimes that foster market and trade liberalisations and protect foreign investors.[22] If both of these sets of interests, along with any number of further and potentially contradictory interests, can be described as falling under the vaguely circumscribed category of community interests, then what we inevitably end up with is a balancing exercise in which trade-offs between the market and human dignity are determined *ad hoc* by a multitude of fragmented decision-makers.[23] According to von Bernstorff, because the question of what should and should not qualify as 'community interest' is difficult to establish without a unified vision of global socio-economic justice, we should be cautious about using the notion.[24]

Taking this difficulty on board, the present chapter proceeds on the understanding that the concept of community interests cannot be deployed to any meaningful extent to distinguish between the interests promoted and those contested by the peasant movement.[25] The concept lacks the critical positioning required in order to understand the radical anti-capitalist power of the rights in question. For the purposes of this

19 Dimitri Van Den Meerssche, 'A Legal Black Hole in the Cosmos of Virtue: The Politics of Human Rights Critique Against the World Bank' (2021) 21(1) Human Rights Law Review 80.

20 Jessica Whyte, *The Morals of the Market: Human Rights and the Rise of Neoliberalism* (Verso 2019).

21 Upendra Baxi, *The Future of Human Rights* (3rd edn, OUP 2008).

22 Jochen von Bernstorff, '"Community Interests" and the Role of International Law in the Creation of a Global Market for Agricultural Land' in Eyal Benvenisti and Georg Nolte (eds), *Community Interests Across International Law* (OUP 2018) 294.

23 ibid 294–295.

24 ibid 295.

25 cf Benedict Kingsbury and Megan Donaldson, 'From Bilateralism to Publicness in International Law', in Ulrich Fastenrath and others (eds), *From Bilateralism to Community Interest: Essays in Honour of Bruno Simma* (OUP 2011) 79, 82. For a further critical view of the concept, see von Bernstorff (n 22).

chapter, the concept of community interests will therefore be focused on the collective and fundamental interests captured by Besson's definition. Again, Besson describes interests as 'common' when they have collective holders and are of fundamental or collective character.[26] Here the focus will be on collective concerns about secure access to and administration and protection particularly of land, food, water, and the environment. These are some of the main interests at stake in the peasant rights context, which is at the same time infused with peasant rights advocates' firm conviction that unfettered market liberalisation in a neoliberal capitalist global order is not in the interest of the majority of people the world over.[27]

The collective aspect of the interests at stake is of particular relevance here, and distinctions can be made between individual rights, rights held by all members of a group individually, and rights held collectively by an entity such as an indigenous people or a minority.[28] Many of the interests discussed in the peasant rights context, for example land and tenure rights and environmental concerns, can be examples of collective rights. It should be noted, however, that categorising rights into strict and distinct categories, such as the purely individual and the purely collective, is not necessarily useful. Collective and individual rights can relate to the same resources. Thus the deleterious effects of climate change can impact the enjoyment of both, for example, the collective right to land[29] and the individual right to life. Likewise, as the Inter-American Court of Human Rights has recently noted, the human right to the environment contains both individual and collective elements.[30]

A last term bears mention here. Some but not all collective rights relate to the enjoyment of, participation in, and protection of the commons, specifically the use of natural resources such as land, fisheries, forests, and the natural environment in general, as well as the protection thereof from devastation or depletion. What, then, are the commons under discussion? Stefania Errico and Priscilla Claeys have defined the

26 Besson (n 17) 39.

27 Philip McMichael, 'A Comment on Henry Bernstein's Way with Peasants, and Food Sovereignty' (2015) 42(1) Journal of Peasant Studies 193.

28 Miodrag Jovanović, 'Cultural Rights as Collective Rights' in Cultural Rights as Collective Rights: An International Law Perspective (Brill | Nijhoff 2016) 16.

29 On this, see, for example, *Sawhoyamaxa Indigenous Community v Paraguay*, Judgment (Merits, Reparations and Costs) [2006] IACtHR Series C-146, or *Centre for Minority Rights Development (Kenya) and Minority Rights Group (on behalf of Endorois Welfare Council) v Kenya* [2010] ACHPR Case No 276/03.

30 *Advisory Opinion OC-23/17 on the Environment and Human Rights, requested by the Republic of Colombia* (Advisory Opinion) [2017] IACtHR Series A No 23, 26, para 59.

commons as 'shared resources in which each stakeholder has an equal interest', and discussed the claims of peasants concerning the commons in terms of access to land and other natural resources.[31] The term 'commons' will be used here to refer to these and other natural resources to which peasant rights claims relate. While peasant movements, by lobbying for the UNDROP, chose a path of individual and collective rights rather than a commons-based approach *per se*, their focus on rights is not myopic, for they have also continued to:

> oppose and struggle against the commodification, financialisation and patenting of our commons, such as: land; farmers', traditional and reproducible seeds; livestock breeds and fish stocks; trees and forests; water; the atmosphere; and knowledge. Access to these should not be determined by markets and money. In using common resources, we must ensure the realisation of human rights and gender equality, and that society as a whole benefits. We also acknowledge our responsibility to use our Commons sustainably, while respecting the rights of mother earth. Our Commons should be managed through collective, democratic and community control.[32]

In other words, it can be argued that what is happening here is a novel way of understanding human rights and their relationship to natural resources, including the natural environment.[33]

All of these terms relate to collectively held interests that, as they have been discussed in the peasant rights context, can provide a counterpoint to the vindication of individualism that infuses the Western liberal legal order. This ties into the fact that, as Claeys has noted, peasants pursue an agenda that includes changing many largely accepted constraints of human rights law imposed by the liberal underpinnings of these rights – not only their Western, individualistic basis but also their focus on state obligations (as opposed to those of private actors or transnational corporations (TNCs)) and their emphasis on (economic) liberty.[34] These underpinnings should not be seen as forming a necessary and non-negotiable precondition of human rights, but as the result of a discourse shaped by pro-capital forces.[35]

---

31 Errico and Claeys (n 11).

32 Nyéléni Food Sovereignty Forum, 'Synthesis Report: Nyéléni Forum for Food Sovereignty' (2007), cited in Priscilla Claeys, 'The Right to Land and Territory: New Human Right and Collective Action Frame' (2015) 75(2) Revue Interdisciplinaire d'Etudes Juridiques 115, 124.

33 ibid 123.

34 Priscilla Claeys, *Human Rights and the Food Sovereignty Movement: Reclaiming Control* (Routledge 2015).

35 Whyte (n 20).

Without seeking to provide a clear and final definition of the terms discussed above and while keeping their vague delineation firmly in mind, the following will explore aspects of this challenge to the idea of the individual, decontextualised liberal subject that stems from 'liberal law's enmeshment with liberal capitalism'.[36]

3. A BACKGROUND ON THE MOVEMENT FOR PEASANT RIGHTS

The international peasant movement, as exemplified by grassroots organizations such as LVC, has taken an active role in the Human Rights Council's work to draft a declaration of peasant rights. This document, the United Nations Declaration on the Rights of Peasants and Rural Workers (UNDROP), was adopted by the UNGA in December 2018. It represents a massive milestone for the peasant movement, which began to take its current form in the 1970s and 1980s in the face of neoliberal policies that negatively affected smallholder farming.[37] From the outset, these movements focused on cross-border phenomena – specifically TNCs, international capital flows, and the international trade regulation they influenced – as crucial factors affecting peasant lives and livelihoods.[38]

In a relatively short time, the peasant movement managed to place rural interests on the international agenda, and its positions – originally seen by some as utopian – were quickly proven viable and crucially important by events such as the 2008 food crisis.[39] Who, then, are the peasants represented by LVC and similar organisations?[40] The international peasantry has been described as a vulnerable,[41] disadvantaged, and stereotyped social group.[42] The peasant movement

---

36 Anna Grear, 'The Liberal Subject of Rights, Capitalism and the Corporation' in Anna Grear (ed), *Redirecting Human Rights: Facing the Challenge of Corporate Legal Humanity* (Palgrave Macmillan 2010) 68.

37 Peter Rosset and Maria Elena Martinez, 'Participatory Evaluation of La Via Campesina' (2005) <https://www.norad.no/globalassets/import-2162015-80434-am/www.norad.no-ny/filarkiv/ngo-evaluations/evaluation-of-la-via-campesina-lvc.pdf> accessed 15 January 2021, 7–8; Hernández Navarro and Desmarais (n 4) 91.

38 McMichael (n 27).

39 ibid 91.

40 Claeys (n 11) 853–854.

41 Human Rights Council Advisory Committee (n 6).

42 David Chacón Hernández, '¿Y Qué Hay de los Derechos Humanos Campesinos?' (2018) 100 Alegatos 815.

does not require a strict definition of peasantness or claim exclusive representation of peasants,[43] but the UNDROP defines a peasant as:

> [A]ny person who engages or who seeks to engage alone, or in association with others or as a community, in small-scale agricultural production for subsistence and/or for the market, and who relies significantly, though not necessarily exclusively, on family or household labour and other non-monetized ways of organizing labour, and who has a special dependency on and attachment to the land.[44]

As well as referring to peasants' 'special dependency on and attachment to the land', the UNDROP, in its preamble, notes that peasants disproportionately suffer from poverty, hunger, and malnutrition, as well as suffering the effects of environmental degradation and climate change and facing 'several factors [that] make it difficult (...) to make their voices heard, to defend their human rights and tenure rights'. In other words, the definition invokes a common experience of marginalization.[45] While the essentialism of envisioning peasant 'communities' as homogenous and solidary is contested,[46] it has been argued that unification is needed 'to blunt the singular force and violence of commodification of land, labor, genetic resources and knowledges', as well as small producers' 'tenuous hold' on their land due to the effects of WTO policy and enclosure by mass land grabs.[47]

How do peasant rights activists go about this? In 2005, Peter Rosset and Maria Elena Martinez wrote that LVC's political tactics were 'more "outside" than "inside," and more protest than lobby'.[48] They also noted that LVC was, at the time, deeply distrustful of 'methods that channel and "calm" dissent: that is, of "conflict resolution," "stakeholder dialogue," World Bank "consultations" and "participation," etc.'[49] Since then, however, LVC has chosen to complement its work on the 'outside' with participation in discussions on the 'inside' of the institutions it challenges. Perhaps the most obvious turn to the 'inside' is its decision to seek recognition of its claims within the existing human rights framework.

---

43 cf, for example, Hannah Wittman, 'Interview: Paul Nicholson, La Vía Campesina' (2009) 36(3) Journal of Peasant Studies 676, 680.

44 UN General Assembly (n 5) art 1.

45 Corina Heri, 'Justifying New Rights: Affectedness, Vulnerability, and the Rights of Peasants' (2020) 21(4) German Law Journal 702.

46 Henry Bernstein, 'Food Sovereignty Via the 'Peasant Way': A Sceptical View' (2014) 41(6) Journal of Peasant Studies 1031, 1044, 1046 and 1056.

47 McMichael (n 27) 199.

48 Rosset and Martinez (n 37) 13.

49 ibid 12.

The following will argue that, by gaining recognition of these rights, the peasant movement is not only proposing an amended understanding of the human rights subject, but is also lobbying for and exposing gaps in the protection of community interests by human rights law, and using a human rights frame to fill them.

4. PEASANT RIGHTS AND THE PROTECTION OF PEASANT INTERESTS

Through the process of obtaining recognition of peasant-specific human rights, the peasant movement has engaged with and advanced the criticism that international human rights law in its current iteration fails to adequately contest and remedy elements of social, global, and environmental justice, business responsibility for human rights, and the effects of neoliberalism.[50] (Here, neoliberalism is synonymous with a market fundamentalism divested of connections to lived realities in human societies that promotes unfettered markets and designs institutions and laws that protect or serve the market.[51]) In other words, this is the understanding that human rights are 'powerless companions' to neoliberalism, and social rights a consolation prize in the absence of social justice. It is a criticism that has been questioned and enriched notably through the work of Jessica Whyte, who recasts human rights not as separate from neoliberalism but instead as a tool shaped by the latter in order to allow its proliferation,[52] and Paul O'Connell, who reminds us that human rights actors and activists are not a homogenous body and that inequality is part and parcel of capitalism.[53]

Several of the rights claims formulated by the peasant movement represent a pushback against these shortcomings, including the proposed rights to land and seeds and a novel understanding of the right to food informed by the concept of food sovereignty. One of the main claims

---

50 cf on this Samuel Moyn, *Not Enough: Human Rights in an Unequal World* (Harvard University Press 2019).

51 cf Quinn Slobodian, *Globalists: The End of Empire and the Birth of Neoliberalism* (Harvard University Press 2018) 5–6.

52 Whyte (n 20).

53 Paul O'Connell, 'Capitalism, Inequality, and Human Rights', (*LPE Project Blog*, 6 April 2018) <https://lpeproject.org/blog/capitalism-inequality-and-human-rights/> accessed 15 January 2021.

of the peasant movement is that peasants and their lands and crops are negatively impacted by the international legal order and the inequalities and market-oriented positions it allows or even encourages. This, in turn, is used as a springboard for the recognition of peasant-specific rights (both of substance and participation) on the same hierarchical level as the source of that impact, namely the international legal order. To put it differently, the struggle for peasant rights is a struggle for self-determination concerning a number of issues that are key to peasant life.[54] At the same time, stratifications of peasant interests, claims, and movements and should be acknowledged, and any analysis should proceed with the awareness that there is harm in essentialism or reductionism.

As discussed, this contribution explores the concept of 'community interests' through a focus on collective concerns about certain access to and administration of land, food, water, and the environment and a pushback against the commodification of these goods – concerns related primarily to the effects of the neoliberal world order on human life. So what exactly is new about peasant human rights claims, and how do they contest these issues? Certainly, not everything about peasant human rights claims as enshrined in the UNDROP is novel. Many of the demands made in this context are simply restatements of existing rights. Indeed, the UNDROP restates and partially expands a number of the human rights enshrined both in regional and international human rights treaties and in relevant UNGA resolutions, including the right to life, liberty, and security of persons,[55] the right to freedom of thought, belief, conscience, religion, opinion, expression, and peaceful assembly,[56] and the right to discrimination-free access to justice,[57] to name just a few. The novelty lies not in the content of these rights, but in pointing out the exclusions of legal subjectivity and the fact that peasants have, in their own assessment and that of UN bodies,[58] not been adequately protected by them.

---

54 Errico and Claeys (n 11) 4.

55 Human Rights Council, Res 39/12: 'United Nations Declaration on the Rights of Peasants and Other People Working in Rural Areas (UNDROP), Resolution Adopted by the Human Rights Council on 28 September 2018' (8 October 2018) UN Doc A/HRC/RES/39/12, art 6.

56 ibid art 8.

57 ibid art 12.

58 See, for example, Human Rights Council Advisory Committee (n 6).

Other elements of the rights claimed by peasants are not part of the human rights enshrined in the International Bill of Human Rights at all,[59] although there are many overlaps between these claims and existing rights such as the right to food, health, just and favourable work conditions, social security, an adequate standard of living, non-discrimination, and housing, as well as the right to water,[60] indigenous peoples' rights, and the idea of resource sovereignty.[61]

In short, while formulating these claims as separate from existing rights may allow peasants to shape those rights' meaning and gain leverage concerning their content and impact, some of the rights claims made by peasants do not go beyond – or far beyond – existing rights as interpreted today by the relevant bodies. The following will touch on some of the elements that *do* push the boundaries of the codified human rights law by centring the resources essential to peasant lives and livelihoods, and the knowledges that arguably constitute the greatest commons of peasant communities.[62]

4.1. FOOD AND SEED SOVEREIGNTY

A rallying cry of LVC's rights claims is the right to food sovereignty. LVC itself developed and popularised this concept. In 1996, it defined food sovereignty as 'the right of each nation to maintain and develop its own capacity to produce its basic foods respecting cultural and productive diversity', which in turn means that peasants claim 'the right to produce our own food in our own territory.'[63] Since then the concept has evolved and become a cornerstone of peasant rights. As a collective entitlement,[64]

---

59 Meaning the Universal Declaration of Human Rights (adopted 10 December 1948) UNGA Res 217 A(III) (UDHR), the International Covenant on Civil and Political Rights (adopted 16 December 1966, entered into force 23 March 1976) 999 UNTS 171 (ICCPR) and the International Covenant on Economic, Social and Cultural Rights (adopted 16 December 1966, entered into force 3 January 1976) UNTS 93 (ICESCR).

60 UNGA, Res 64/292: 'The Human Right to Water and Sanitation' (3 August 2010) UN Doc A/RES/64/292, declaring safe and clean drinking water and sanitation a human right essential to the full enjoyment of life and all other human rights.

61 UNGA, Res 1803 (XVII): 'Permanent Sovereignty over Natural Resources' (14 December 1962).

62 Edith Carolina Pineda Pinzón, 'Saberes Campesinos y Experiencias de Gobierno Comunitario en Colombia' (2020) 2 Revista Ucronías 77, 79.

63 'The Right to Produce and Access to Land', a Statement by La Vía Campesina to the Rome Civil Society Organisation Forum held in Rome, Italy (11–17 November 1996).

64 See on this Chacón Hernández (n 42) 831.

it encompasses or is linked to a range of other peasant rights, including the right of access to land, the right to seeds, the protection of cultural identity, and the idea that all forms of life should be protected from being patented.[65]

The right to food sovereignty goes undefined in LVC's own 2009 draft of a declaration of peasant rights,[66] appearing instead as a foundational principle underlying the document. The final text of the UNDROP, by contrast, grants peasants 'the right to determine their own food and agriculture systems, recognized by many states and regions as the right to food sovereignty', as well as participation rights in public policy-making related to food security, food sovereignty, and the right to food.[67] It also, in Article 19, enshrines a right to seeds that includes the protection of traditional knowledge related to plants' genetic material and the right to save, use, exchange, and sell farm-saved seeds. This right, the campaign for which has to a significant extent been female-led, has been described elsewhere as pushback against 'patriarchy, capitalism, food empires, absolute and militarized control of resources, and environmental crises'.[68] Both these rights relate to control or sovereignty, and therefore to taking back power from the state and from international and regional actors.

For a long time LVC was 'wary of institutionalizing the right to food sovereignty at the international level' due to the risk of 'containment and cooption', and focused instead on undermining the institutions it saw as responsible for international trade law, such as the WTO.[69] The shift occurred in recent years after lengthy debates within the movement about institutionalizing a legally binding international human right to food sovereignty.[70] This involved peasant organisations making a clear distinction between those international and regional actors deemed worthwhile partners in seeking to protect peasants, and those – like the WTO – considered inimical to peasant interests.[71]

---

65 Hernández Navarro and Desmarais (n 4) 95.

66 LVC, 'Declaration of the Rights of Peasants – Women and Men' (2009) <https://viacampesina.org/en/declaration-of-rights-of-peasants-women-and-men/> accessed 15 January 2021.

67 UNDROP art 15(4)–(5).

68 Ivonne Vizcarra Bordi, '*Mad Max* y las Defensoras de las Semillas: Mujeres Indígenas y Campesinas en los Movimientos Sociales de Lucha por las Soberanías' (2019) 4(7) Revista Interamericana de Estudios Rurales 210, 210. Translation from the original Spanish by the author.

69 Claeys (n 11) 853.

70 ibid 852–853, citing interviews with members of the movement.

71 Claeys and Edelman (n 11).

Food sovereignty is a radical concept because it allows LVC to position its interpretation as an alternative to existing understandings of human rights, including the right to food, and to present what seems to be a more human-centred or subject-centred rights discourse while controlling the relevant narrative. The reference to sovereignty is in itself provocative: it evinces a space free of the state within which peasants demand to be the sovereign decision-makers. Peasants' demand for sovereignty is revolutionary given the dictates of current markets and the top-down nature of food and agricultural policy. Unsurprisingly given the nature of these demands, food sovereignty was a highly debated issue of the UNDROP drafting process, with EU delegates in particular suggesting replacement of the remaining references to food sovereignty in the text with references to food security, which is a very different concept that largely lacks food sovereignty's participatory elements.[72]

Peasants were far from willing to abandon the concept. In the context of the Working Group, efforts to strike the concept from the draft text were resoundingly contested by peasant rights advocates and several states that have been won over to some degree by the peasant rights agenda, including Bolivia and Ecuador. Yet the process did lead to the formulation of less radical claims. In past versions of the UNDROP, the right to food sovereignty was enshrined as a separate right that reiterated aspects of the right to access adequate food. States' objections meant that it has been softened to a 'right to adequate food',[73] which includes a peasant right to 'determine their own food and agriculture systems, recognized by many states and regions as the right to food sovereignty'.[74]

As indicated by this phrasing, food sovereignty has found recognition elsewhere as well. The Economic Community of West African States (ECOWAS) has recognised this right, as has the Organization of American States (OAS) to some extent.[75] Numerous states also have their own food sovereignty policies, including Bolivia, Ecuador, Nepal, Mali, Senegal, and Venezuela.[76] A set definition of the term is not easy

72 5th Session of the Working Group on the UNDROP, Palais des Nations, Geneva, 9–13 April 2018.

73 UNDROP art 15.

74 ibid art 15(4).

75 Economic Community of West African States (ECOWAS), 'Agriculture & Environment', <https://www.ecowas.int/ecowas-sectors/agriculture/> accessed 15 January 2021; OAS General Assembly, Declaration of Cochabamba on 'Food Security with Sovereignty in the Americas' (Adopted on 5 June 2012) AG/DEC. 69 (XLII-O/12).

76 Nadia C S Lambek, Priscilla Claeys, Adrienna Wong, and Lea Brilmayer (eds) *Rethinking Food Systems: Structural Challenges, New Strategies and the Law* (Springer 2014) 47; Wittman (n 43).

to come by, but what is clear is that it entails 'a call for peoples' rights to shape and craft food policy' and was 'very specifically intended as a foil to the prevailing notions of food security', which is shaped in turn by the search for efficiency in securing access to adequate, safe and nutritious food.[77] The 1996 LVC definition of food sovereignty as 'the right of each nation to maintain and develop its own capacity to produce its basic foods respecting cultural and productive diversity'[78] implies that food sovereignty is in fact not a collective interest, in the sense that universal solutions are inappropriate. But if food sovereignty is understood as a policy proposal that seeks alternatives to free-market industrial agriculture, it can be understood as a clear challenge to the idea that there is a collective interest in a liberalised market approach to food and to the related resource of seeds. Instead of a direct challenge to the existing right to food,[79] it should therefore be seen as a demand for a rebalancing of international policy-making that affects food production by tackling the effects of enclosure through patent rights over seeds, loss of land, and the commodification of food.

4.2. LAND RIGHTS

Another area in which LVC, through a rights frame, has positioned itself not only in opposition to economic forces but also to the mainstream approach to socio-economic rights is the area of land rights and, more broadly, the understanding of property that has shaped the liberal legal order. Since the drafting of the Universal Declaration of Human Rights, the right to property has been focused on individual rights over collective ones, to the disappointment of delegates who had pushed for a right to own property 'alone or collectively' as opposed to the accepted wording, which concerns the right to own property 'alone or in association with others'.[80] In other words, the right to property as understood today is focused on preserving existing ownership rights, not on redistribution

---

77 Raj Patel, 'Food Sovereignty' (2009) 36(3) Journal of Peasant Studies 663, 663 and 665.

78 ibid 665, citing a statement by Via Campesina at the World Food Summit (1996).

79 As interpreted in UN Committee on Economic, Social and Cultural Rights, 'General Comment No 12: The Right to Adequate Food (Art. 11 of the Covenant)' (1999) in 'Note by the Secretariat, General Comments and General Recommendations Adopted by Human Rights Treaty Bodies' (2008) UN Doc UN Doc HRI/GEN/1/Rev.9 (Vol. I).

80 UNGA, 'Summary Record of the Ninety-Third Meeting' (1948) UN Doc A/C.3/SR.93, 9–10; UDHR art 17(1).

or the guarantee of a minimum of property needed for a life with dignity. And while legal security of tenure and the prohibition of forced evictions are elements of the right to housing,[81] in practice tenure rights are not available to all, may discriminate by gender, can fall prey to market forces, and can be pitted against property rights.[82] In fact, it has been shown that almost half of the world's rural populations do not enjoy security of tenure.[83]

In current discourse, it is not unusual to see property owners' individual liberty, that is their right to property, being raised as in need of urgent protection without mention of inequality or lack of access to housing.[84] Self-responsibility, enclosure, and individualism run rampant, and land tenure rights were not just a casualty but also a specific target of the architects of the neoliberal global order. For example, in 1957, members of the Chicago school of economics expressly advocated abolishing communal land tenure and replacing it with individual property rights, arguing that this would free individuals from customary and family obligations while encouraging personal initiative and individualism.[85]

The peasant movement advances visions of individual *and* collective sustainable use of land that opposes the vision of land as a commodity and the enclosure that has shaped modern legal systems. LVC's own 2009 draft of a declaration on the rights of peasants contains a separate right to land and territory in its Article IV, which *inter alia* contains a peasant right 'to own land, collectively or individually' and 'to toil on their own land', as well as 'to toil and own the non-productive state land on which they depend for their livelihood'.[86] The provision also enshrines a right to 'reject all kinds of land acquisition and conversion for economic purpose' and 'to security of tenure and not to be forcibly evicted from their lands and territories'. It provides for a prohibition of *latifundia* and states that '[l]and has to fulfill its social function', for which reason it requires the introduction of land ownership ceilings 'whenever necessary in order to ensure an equitable access to land'.

---

81 UN Committee on Economic, Social and Cultural Rights, 'General Comment No 4: The Right to Adequate Housing (Art. 11 (1) of the Covenant)' (1991) in 'Note by the Secretariat, General Comments and General Recommendations Adopted by Human Rights Treaty Bodies' (2008) UN Doc HRI/GEN/1/Rev.9 (Vol. I).

82 Jérémie Gilbert, 'Land Rights as Human Rights: The Case for a Specific Right to Land' (2013) 10(18) Sur International Journal on Human Rights 115; Hubert (n 8) 165.

83 Gilbert (n 82) 116.

84 Whyte (n 20) 12–13.

85 Peter Thomas Bauer and Basil S Yamey, *The Economics of Under-Developed Countries* (CUP 1957) 68.

86 LVC (n 66).

Such a right to land, which was largely inconceivable two decades ago, along with the accompanying recognition that access to land can, in many cases, be a prerequisite for the fulfillment of socio-economic rights, has now made its way into academic discourse and UN documents alike.[87] The recognition of the peasant right to land in the UNDROP provides that peasants 'have the right to land, individually and/or collectively, [...] including the right to have access to, sustainably use and manage land and the water bodies, coastal seas, fisheries, pastures and forests therein, to achieve an adequate standard of living, to have a place to live in security, peace and dignity and to develop their cultures.'[88] States thereby have an obligation to 'take appropriate measures to provide legal recognition for land tenure rights, including customary land tenure rights not currently protected by law, recognizing the existence of different models and systems' and to prevent peasants from being 'arbitrarily or unlawfully evicted'.[89] This right to land also means that 'States shall recognize and protect the natural commons and their related systems of collective use and management', as well as a range of other rights regarding protection against displacement, eviction, and expropriation or arbitrary deprivation of lands, a right to return to land thus appropriated, agrarian reforms facilitating broad and equitable access to land and other necessary natural resources, and the limitation of 'excessive concentration and control of land, taking into account its social function'.[90]

While the UNDROP envisions a 'right to land', and not a right to *own* land, peasant rights frame land, water, seeds, and the food grown with them as natural resources, not commodities, that small-holders should be able to access and use without undue restriction by virtue of their human rights entitlements. This draws attention to the lack of adequate protection provided for their interests under international law as it stands, which allows other interests to trump or undermine human rights-related entitlements in this area. And it speaks to the thinking behind the UNDROP, which is 'to let peasants stay peasants', a goal that is only achieved if they can retain access to land and, if evicted or displaced, can reobtain access to the productive resources necessary for their livelihoods.[91] The peasant right to land is thus a pushback against

87 See UNGA, 'Report of the Special Rapporteur on the Right to Food' (11 August 2010) UN Doc A/65/281.
88 UNDROP art 17(1).
89 UNDROP art 17(3).
90 UNDROP art 17(3)–(6).
91 Hubert (n 8) 163.

enclosure and against the logic of enrichment through dispossession.[92] Crucially, it centres communities and not states as the beneficiaries of rights over natural resources, as has been argued for in the context of Third World Approaches to International Law (or TWAIL) scholarship.[93] While questions remain – such as, by analogy, those raised by the African Court on Human and Peoples' Rights in the *Ogiek* case concerning the ability of indigenous peoples to sell their communally managed resources,[94] or those discussed by the Inter-American Court of Human Rights when faced with a potential conflict between indigenous and peasant rights[95] – this represents a powerful counter-move to policies of eviction, displacement, and enclosure.

5. PEASANT RIGHTS AND THE ENVIRONMENT

Perhaps one of the greatest contemporary failures of states to act in the collective interest is the current and impending harm caused by climate change and other environmental damage.[96] Measures agreed upon by the international community are indispensable in this area, and collective action is in the interest of all involved.[97]

The UNDROP contains various rights that relate to the environment. As noted above, its preamble notes that peasants disproportionately suffer the effects of environmental degradation and climate change. Article 16(4) UNDROP, which restates the right to an adequate standard of living, also enjoins states to 'transition to sustainable

---

92 Joana Salém Vasconcelos, 'Tierra y Derechos Humanos en Chile: la Contrarreforma Agraria de la Dictadura de Pinochet y las Políticas de Reparación Campesina' (2020) 80 Historia Agraria 209.

93 Olivier de Schutter and Balakrishnan Rajagopal, 'Property Rights from Below: An Introduction to the Debate', in Olivier de Schutter and Balakrishnan Rajagopal (eds), *Property Rights from Below: Commodification of Land and the Counter-Movement* (Routledge 2019).

94 *African Commission on Human and Peoples' Rights v the Republic of Kenya* (Judgment) [2017] ACtHPR Case No 006/2012, para 127.

95 *Case of the Indigenous Communities of the Lhaka Honhat (Our Land) Association v Argentina* (Judgment) [2020] IACtHR Series C 400.

96 See on this, for example, UNGA, 'Climate Change and Poverty: Report of the Special Rapporteur on Extreme Poverty and Human Rights' (17 July 2019) UN Doc A/HRC/41/39.

97 Jutta Brunnée, 'The Rule of International (Environmental) Law and Complex Problems' in Heike Krieger, Georg Nolte, and Andreas Zimmermann (eds), *The International Rule of Law: Rise or Decline?* (OUP 2019).

modes of agricultural production', as well as stipulating that they shall 'stimulate sustainable production, including agroecological and organic production, whenever possible, and facilitate direct farmer-to-consumer sales.' Article 17(7) requires states to 'take measures aimed at the conservation and sustainable use of land and other natural resources used in their production'.[98] Article 18(1) UNDROP gives peasants the right to 'the conservation and protection of the environment and the productive capacity of their lands, and of the resources that they use and manage.' Article 18(2) UNDROP stipulates that 'States shall take appropriate measures' to ensure that peasants enjoy a 'safe, clean and healthy environment'.

The UNDROP further contains references to strengthening the resilience of peasants against natural disasters[99] and to the duty to conduct a social and environmental impact assessment before exploiting natural resources.[100] It enjoins states to comply with their international obligations to combat climate change, and gives peasants the right to participate in the design and implementation of relevant policies.[101] It prohibits the disposal or storage of hazardous waste on peasant lands and addresses transboundary environmental harms[102] as well as environmental harms by non-state actors.[103]

By focusing so strongly on environmental protection, the peasant movement seems to be going beyond simply protecting that environment for the benefit of human individuals, and may be seen as advocating for a closer connection between humans and the natural world, and even a protection of nature in its own right. This indicates a possible transcendence of definitionally anthropocentric human rights.

At the same time, the UNDROP does not retain the language contained in LVC's original draft of a peasant rights declaration, which enshrined a human right to a healthy environment.[104] The UN has not yet formally recognised that right in a universal legal instrument.[105] Proponents of its

98 UNDROP art 17(7).
99 UNDROP art 16(5).
100 UNDROP art 5(2)(a).
101 UNDROP art 18(3).
102 UNDROP art 18(4).
103 UNDROP art 18(5).
104 LVC (n 66) art 11.
105 UNGA, 'Report of the Special Rapporteur on the Issue of Human Rights Obligations Relating to the Enjoyment of a Safe, Clean, Healthy and Sustainable Environment' (19 July 2018) UN Doc A/73/188, para 37.

recognition argue that it would not only raise the profile of environmental protection and the fight against climate change and reinforce the interconnectedness of effective enjoyment of human rights and the environment. It would also arguably open up access to legal remedies and policy-setting to 'citizens seeking to protect both their individual right to a healthy environment and society's collective interest in a healthy environment.'[106]

David R. Boyd, before taking office as the UN Special Rapporteur on human rights and the environment in 2018, wrote that 'protecting the environment is impossible if we continue to assert human superiority and universal ownership of all land and wildlife to pursue endless economic growth. Today's dominant culture and the legal system that supports it are self-destructive'.[107] The peasant rights promulgated in the UNDROP are thus a challenge to the neoliberal global order, and a statement of the incompatibility of environmental protection with the status quo. They make a case for reimagining the dominant approach to property rights and legal personality, so that nature and the environment as a whole can be part of the collectives or communities whose interests are taken into consideration.[108] In other words, the approach to justice, rights, and collective interests that is required here is not one that is justified from an exclusively anthropocentric perspective.

The adoption of the UNDROP also remedies a particular disadvantage facing peasants in the climate change context. Peasant organizations have long sought to oppose the logics of appropriation that are integral to certain aspects of climate change discourse,[109] but struggled to do so because of the absence of an international human rights instrument on which to base their claims.[110] In this and other contexts, the UNDROP provides an essential basis and a touchstone for the defense and elevation of peasant interests.

---

106 ibid para 42.

107 David R Boyd, *The Rights of Nature: A Legal Revolution That Could Save the World* (ECW Press 2017).

108 See, Kaloyan Kirilov, 'A Human Rights-Based Approach to Protecting the Environment: Status, Critique and Alternative' (master's thesis, University of Helsinki 2019) 36.

109 Priscilla Claeys and Deborah Delgado Pugley, 'Peasant and Indigenous Transnational Social Movements Engaging with Climate Justice' (2017) 38(3) Canadian Journal of Development Studies / Revue Canadienne d'études Du Développement 325, 333, referring to ETC Group, GRAIN, and La Vía Campesina, *Climate Summit: Don't Turn Farmers into 'Climate Smart' Carbon Traders! News Release* (ETC Group 2013).

110 ibid.

6. PEASANT RIGHTS AND PEASANT INTERESTS

From the start, peasant organisations have resisted absorption into broader and less change-oriented movements. The founding meeting of LVC was funded by a Dutch development NGO, the Paulo Freire Foundation, which intended to incorporate peasant activists into the International Federation of Agricultural Producers (IFAP).[111] LVC's rupture with the foundation evidences peasants' desire for political and peasant-centric change rather than dialogue or an NGO-style approach, as do representatives' statements that involvement with NGOs is a 'yoke'.[112] At the same time, Claeys has written about how indispensable support from small NGOs and academics has been for the peasant movement, which has managed to work with these gatekeepers to international attention on its own terms.[113]

The UNDROP shows us what human rights can look like when they are claimed in a bottom-up manner and less decisively fettered by concerns about the market and economic growth, instead focusing on enabling people to live the lives they want to live in the best possible way, or at least without interference by powerful actors, specifically the market and market-oriented structures. It also reconnects these peasant lives to the building blocks of living such lives: land, seeds, a clean and healthy environment, water, and food. For peasants, in the words of Belgian peasant rights activist Victor Delobel, '[h]uman rights may be one of our last lines of defence at a time when our disappearance seems inevitable'.[114]

In this context, the UNDROP has been described as an important advocacy tool, as a benchmark and as a reference.[115] When reduced to its essence, though, the peasant push for rights can also be read as a searing indictment of the values and priorities emphasised by the international legal order as shaped for and by neoliberalism. Or, conversely, it can be seen as pushback against attacks on traditional values that have shaped

---

111 Delphine Thivet, 'Défense et Promotion des "Droits des Paysans" aux Nations Unies: Une Appropriation Oblique de l'*Advocacy* par La Vía Campesina' (2015) 67(2) Critique Internationale 67.

112 ibid.

113 Priscilla Claeys, 'The Rise of New Rights for Peasants. From Reliance on NGO Intermediaries to Direct Representation' (2018) 9(3–4) Transnational Legal Theory 386.

114 Vincent Delobel, 'The Peasant Farm: Dignity, Respect and Mother Earth in the Declaration' (2019) 47(1) Journal of Peasant Studies 13, 15.

115 Coline Hubert, 'Adoption par l'Assemblée Générale de la Déclaration sur les Droits des Paysans et des Autres Personnes Travaillant en Zones Rurales' (2019) La Revue des Droits de l'Homme.

peasant lives and livelihoods for generations and that preexisted the advent of the international legal order as we know it. This framing connects the work of the international peasant movement to a long history of peasant uprisings. Maywa Montenegro de Wit, for example, has linked current peasant claims for seed sovereignty to peasant uprisings over the price of bread in the eighteenth century, which 'were less about bread *per se* than about emergent capitalism abridging customary social protocols.'[116]

In essence, peasant human rights claims are arguably about more than peasants, or even humans, and they allow an opportunity to reflect normatively on human rights law. The peasant rights agenda contests many largely accepted constraints of human rights law that have been imposed by or in the interest of the liberal underpinnings of these rights – their Western, individualistic basis, their focus on state obligations, and their emphasis on (economic) liberty.[117] The need for change in this regard is suggested by the fact that, despite the ongoing work of a range of actors, initiatives, and treaty bodies, hard human rights law has by no means succeeded in eliminating the human rights impacts of climate change, corporate activities, or global inequality,[118] and by some accounts it enables the persistence of these impacts.[119] Against this background, peasants are reimagining what human rights can do for them, and by doing so they are challenging the 'neoliberal fixation on personal responsibility' in favour of a legal subject that recognises and incorporates their needs and realities, but also those of the environment on which they depend for survival.[120] This strips away the neutral framing of concepts like

---

116 Maywa Montenegro de Wit, 'Beating the Bounds: Inside the Struggle to Make Open Source Seed', in Anna Grear and David Bollier (eds), *The Great Awakening: New Modes of Life Amidst Capitalist Ruins* (Punctum Books 2020) 165, citing E P Thompson, 'The Moral Economy of the English Crowd in the Eighteenth Century' (1971) 50(1) Past and Present 78.

117 Claeys (n 34).

118 See, for example, the words of Philip Alston in UNGA (n 96), the impacts addressed by the UN, 'Guiding Principles on Business and Human Rights: Implementing the United Nations "Protect, Respect and Remedy" Framework' (2011) HR/PUB/11/04, or the UN Special Rapporteur on Human Rights and the Environment describing the ways in which the Paris Agreement falls short of what is necessary in order to address climate change, in UNGA, 'Report of the Special Rapporteur on the Issue of Human Rights Obligations Relating to the Enjoyment of a Safe, Clean, Healthy and Sustainable Environment' (1 February 2016) UN Doc A/HRC/31/52, paras 76–77.

119 Whyte (n 20) On the facilitation of mass land grabs by the international legal system, see von Bernstorff (n 22) 281–284.

120 Martha Albertson Fineman, 'Equality and Difference – The Restrained State' (2015) Emory University School of Law, Legal Studies Research Paper Series, Research Paper No. 15-348.

collective interests, and it positions some interests (those of capital and commodity) as harmful and oppressive while elevating others. Peasant interests clearly contain the critical lens that the concept of community interests lacks.

The gaps highlighted by the peasant rights movement, broadly speaking, stem from the fact that the liberal conception of international and regional human rights is predominantly an individual-oriented one decisively shaped or constrained through the decades by a market-oriented capitalist world view. To be more concrete, human rights standards, especially those rights that can be the subject of cases or communications brought to human rights treaty bodies by individuals, focus heavily on individual rights. This type of procedure comes with certain intrinsic hurdles to defending collective interests, not least its inability to offer much in terms of compensatory relief, along with difficulties of enforcement and of deterring future harm.[121] Yet individual human rights and the procedures safeguarding them may provide argumentative fodder and momentum for change.[122] Indeed, the peasant rights movement interrogates not just how we see specific community interests relevant to the lives and agricultural livelihoods of peasants and rural dwellers, but what we are willing to accept as a valid community interest and the way in which these interests relate to each other in case of friction.

This framing presumes that human rights law does not in its current form adequately serve peasants' – legitimate and valuable – purposes, and that peasants' self-formulated claims are a more legitimate manner of addressing these purposes. What it also demonstrates, however, is a positive outlook or at least a hope for what human rights can do, or their potential and value for protecting the same peasants who currently consider themselves excluded from adequate protection under this framework. This means that the peasant rights movement speaks to various universals, including the need for food and the vulnerability of both our fragile human form and our environment. These are addressed by focusing on a particular group, however loosely that group is defined – in this case, peasants. How this group-focused approach and the universality element can coexist deserves some further attention.

---

121 Annalisa Savaresi and Juan Auz, 'Climate Change Litigation and Human Rights: Pushing the Boundaries' (2019) 9 (3) Climate Law 244.

122 ibid.

During negotiations on the UNDROP text, the EU representative argued against the Declaration as a whole, submitting that the recognition of new rights applicable only to persons living and working in rural areas would undermine the universality of rights.[123] This argument can be swiftly rejected as unconvincing: human rights for specific groups have been recognised any number of times, and these efforts are all ultimately about ensuring human dignity for every person, universally but as required by the exigencies of specific situations, risks, and dependencies. The argument does make more sense however when the content and context of the peasant movement for rights is seen as a direct and unequivocal challenge to neoliberalism and the idealised legal subject. It troubles the 'potent founding fiction of the liberal social contract, folded into the foundations of which is a highly particular subject – a specific kind of person – the "man of property/classic contractor"'.[124] A movement led, without compromise, by the real, contextualised people it represents – who face specific non-negligible harms because they depend on the natural world for their lives and livelihood – exposes this idealised subject as what it is, namely a fiction or imaginary, and not one that serves those it arguably represents particularly well.

In addition, it should be made clear that the framing of peasant rights as rights being demanded by a small but aggressive group seeking special treatment and unmerited advantages is disingenuous. First, peasant rights potentially apply to a huge number of people. It has been estimated that there are more than 570 million farms world-wide, for example, and that of these more than 500 million are family farms.[125] While the definition of peasants is broader than just smallholder farmers, this provides an indication of the huge number of individuals who might be described as peasants. Even leaving that aside, true universals exist here. For example, talking about food and its production in the way that peasants do means talking about something that affects all humans. Similarly, it is difficult to distinguish a universal right to land – which would likely have to be applied so as to ensure that those who will work the land have access to it – from a peasant right to land, given that peasants and indigenous

---

123 Based on the author's own notes of the session, held in Geneva from 9 to 13 April 2018.

124 Anna Grear, 'Legal Imaginaries and the Anthropocene: "Of" and "For"' (2020) 31 Law and Critique 351.

125 Sarah K Lowder, Jakob Skoet, and Terri Raney, 'The Number, Size, and Distribution of Farms, Smallholder Farms, and Family Farms Worldwide' (2016) 87 World Development 16.

peoples are often the ones working the land. We can accordingly see land as a resource that, in certain circumstances, enables the fulfilment of a range of other universal rights. Lastly, more generally speaking, questioning the neoliberal underpinnings of international law and politics – that is, the ways in which a free-market, capital-forward point of view dominates and shapes these fields – is an undertaking that aims to shift the accepted rules of the game in a way that can affect all people the world over.

It has therefore been argued that peasantness, like indigenous identity and the relevant rights, is being used to push back against globalisation, 'cultural uniformity', the effects of colonialism, and corporate exploitation.[126] By stepping into the human rights framework, peasants are confronting that framework with their demands in a way that unsettles accepted approaches to how we view land and how we understand the role of human rights vis-à-vis certain challenges. By demanding sovereignty over their productive resources, particularly land and seeds, and the food they produce with them, the peasant movement can also be understood as challenging the adequacy and legitimacy of state regulation that relies equally on sovereignty-based arguments but does not in fact deliver protection to affected persons. It seems to pose the question of how the state can assert sovereignty over goods it has mismanaged and failed to protect from the assault of market forces.

Peasant rights claims over resources related to community interests or the commons are, in essence, claims for change in terms of how these are governed, including in relation to other interests such as those of the market, big agribusiness, and corporate seed producers. These human rights claims, now recognised in the UNDROP, are a far cry from Garret Hardin's 'tragedy of the commons', the idea that the predominance of self-interest in individual gains will necessarily undermine the state of the commons.[127] In any event, that is a notion now relativised or even debunked to no uncertain extent by research such as that of Elinor Ostrom[128] and scores of scholars in a variety of fields.[129] Examples of modern-day commons that defy Hardin's thesis include initiatives to share

126 Ronald Niezen, *The Origins of Indigenism: Human Rights and the Politics of Identity* (University of California Press 2003) 2 and 5.

127 Garrett Hardin, 'The Tragedy of the Commons' (1968) 162(3859) Science 1243.

128 Elinor Ostrom, *Governing the Commons: The Evolution of Institutions for Collective Action* (CUP 1990); Montenegro de Wit (n 116).

129 Montenegro de Wit (n 116).

seeds in the public domain free of the constraints imposed by corporate seed giants.[130]

These efforts, imperfect though they may be in terms of safeguarding indigenous and peasant traditions and forms of ownership,[131] improve upon and diversify a landscape of rights fundamentally shaped by efforts to promote and safeguard the freedom of the market.[132] Peasant rights can be described as claims to freedom *from*, thereby appropriating the approach to human rights that enables and was fomented by neoliberalism and its predecessors.[133] This is, in other words, a freedom *from* enclosure, although not one that trumps other interests such as the protection of indigenous peoples' rights to land or the protection of the environment.[134] They are also claims that shift the balance away from the neoliberal logic linking freedom in the human rights sense to the market's freedom from state control and disconnecting it from nationalization and redistribution of wealth.[135] This is the logic that focuses attention on corporate gains instead of human harms, that fails to recognise the irreconcilability of human dignity and inequality, and that allows the private property interests of capitalism's winners to obfuscate the social and economic rights of those in need.

The UNDROP is already making first waves in the domestic context[136] and in the work of human rights bodies. The Inter-American Court of Human Rights has considered the vulnerability and rights of Creole peasants living on indigenous land, for example, by referring to the UNDROP.[137] In 2019, the UNDROP was cited in a landmark environmental case before the Human Rights Committee.[138] It has also featured in the ongoing discussions about a General Comment on land governance and the human right to land before the Committee on Economic, Social and Cultural Rights, where questions of tenure, development-induced displacement, corporate human rights impacts,

130 On the Open Source Seed Initiative, see ibid, particularly 160–161.
131 Montenegro de Wit ibid 177–179.
132 Whyte (n 20).
133 ibid.
134 *Our Land* (n 95).
135 ibid.
136 See the interview with Diego Montón ('We Want the Declaration to Come to Life') in Claeys and Edelman (n 11) 40–43.
137 *Our Land* (n 95) [136].
138 *Portillo Cáceres v Paraguay*, Views Adopted by the Human Rights Committee under article 5(4) of the Optional Protocol, Concerning Communication No 2751/2016 (20 September 2019) UN Doc CCPR/C/126/D/2751/2016, footnote 49.

free and informed consent, and the advantages and exclusions of customary forms of tenure are at stake, including the gender dimensions of tenure.[139] Challenges certainly remain, such as the risk that peasant rights may be pitted against indigenous rights, thereby diluting their transformative potential. But while the putting into practice of the UNDROP only started relatively recently, these early references indicate that the challenges raised and demands made in the context of peasant human rights have begun to be heard by human rights bodies.

At the same time, there are clearly limits to what can be expected of the UNDROP in terms of radical transformational potential. In the words of Salomon, while the UNDROP enshrines 'rights against global capitalism', it also retains the regimes that sustain global capitalism and provides for benefit-sharing, which is per definition premised on logics of commodification and exclusive property rights.[140] This is perhaps an inevitable consequence of participation in the form and system of international law, but it leaves room to expect a certain transformation of that system. In other words, it 'provides a glimpse of hope that multilateralism can be centered on human rights, anti-colonialism, justice and solidarity.'[141]

7. CONCLUSION

The peasant movement's approach to human rights is revolutionary on multiple levels: it claims new rights in terms of substance, champions collective rights in the context of a framework largely oriented towards individual rights, promotes the obligations of all involved actors, including TNCs, in a primarily state-oriented context, contests a capital-dominated approach to agriculture, and provides a focus beyond definitionally anthropocentric human rights. The legitimacy generated by the reclamation of peasant identity, radical self-representation and the momentum created by grassroots activists seem to be driving these developments. While it has faced pushback from certain states, the salience

139 Committee on Economic, Social and Cultural Rights, 'Issues Paper', Day of General Discussion on Governance of Land Tenure (4 October 2019) <https://www.ohchr.org/Documents/HRBodies/CESCR/Discussions/2019/Issues_paper.pdf> accessed 15 January 2021.

140 Salomon (n 1).

141 See statement by Andrea Nuila, Philip Seufert, Sofía Monsalve, and Ana María Suárez Franco ('Defying the Conventional Way of Lobbying the United Nations') in Claeys and Edelman (n 11) 29.

of the peasant critique of human rights is undeniable – and, notably, it seems hopeful about the future of the human rights system.[142] In the words of Henry Saragih, there is hope that the UNDROP can become 'a reference point for human rights and a framework for the future of food and of agrarian life.'[143]

As noted above, framing any claims as human rights claims means to some extent accepting the constraints imposed by the liberal underpinnings of these rights.[144] It also means stepping into an international legal order that is supportive of extractive global commodity-based capitalism. However, rights framing has a uniting power, and can legitimise and lend visibility to the claims in question.[145] More than that, it represents an opportunity to challenge human rights law's constraints. The peasant movement has brought such a challenge by making claims that aim to expand the very foundations of rights: from individual to collective, from state-oriented to addressed toward all relevant actors, from rooted in economic liberty to based on resource-sharing, accessibility, inclusivity, and sustainability, from something that is created top-down to an entitlement that is demanded bottom-up by those who are affected, from patriarchal to gender-equal and inclusive.[146] They seem to be inviting us to look at shared resources from a fresh perspective unfettered by the constraints of the neoliberal world order.

From a peasant rights perspective, the concept of community interests as currently deployed seems neither useful nor particularly concrete. Its indeterminacy does not allow for distinguishing oppressive interests from those of the oppressed. In a context of power imbalances, this makes the concept a falsely neutral one. Reading the UNDROP in its context, namely with regard to the counter-capitalist rights and arguments of peasants, proposes an alternative way of prioritising interests: a peasant way, but also a way that focuses on global and environmental justice.

---

142 Delobel (n 114).

143 See the interview with Henry Saragih ('A Declaration that is Truly the Voice of the Movement') in Claeys and Edelman (n 11) 19.

144 Claeys (n 34).

145 Wittman (n 43) 679.

146 On this last part, cf Nettie Wiebe, 'Women of La Via Campesina: Creating and Occupying Our Rightful Spaces' in *La Via Campesina's Open Book: Celebrating 20 Years of Struggle and Hope* (La Via Campesina 2013) <https://viacampesina.org/en/wp-content/uploads/sites/2/2013/05/EN-01.pdf> accessed 15 January 2021. Expressing concerns that gender issues did not receive sufficient attention in the final draft of the UNDROP, see the interview with Sandra Moreno Cadena in Claeys and Edelman (n 11) 63.

PART IV

CONCLUDING REMARKS

THE PROTECTION OF COMMUNITY INTERESTS IN INTERNATIONAL LAW

Some Reflections on Potential Research Agendas

Gentian Zyberi*

* Head of the Norwegian Centre for Human Rights, University of Oslo; member of the UN Human Rights Committee (2019–2022). I am grateful for the useful feedback received during the book conference organized in Oslo on 3 June 2019 and the insights received from colleagues during presentations at Koç University Law School (Istanbul, 3 May 2018) and at Peking University (Wang Tieya Lecture Series of International Law, 24 May 2018). Opinions expressed here are my own.

1. INTRODUCTION

This chapter provides an analysis of the concept of 'community interests' in international law, before presenting a potential research agenda concerning three areas, namely ensuring *collective human security*, managing *collective natural resources*, and preserving *world cultural heritage*. While displaying different degrees of normative intensity and institutional development, these areas involve the provision of various important global public goods. The organized international community is facing these contemporary global challenges, while trying to end the COVID-19 pandemic and eventually prevent others from occurring. Recent decades have seen many active armed conflicts worldwide, of high, medium, or low intensity,[1] which have caused extensive loss of life and material damage as well as forced displacement. These conflicts have occurred in Syria, Afghanistan, Libya, South Sudan, and Ukraine, to mention just a few places. Tens of millions of people have received humanitarian assistance over these decades, with the numbers increasing steadily, reaching about 235 million people needing humanitarian assistance and protection in 2021.[2] Meanwhile there is growing concern about the effects of climate change,[3] the depletion of shared natural resources,[4] and major industrial accidents involving oil spills and nuclear accidents causing lasting damage, including the Chernobyl disaster in April 1986, the BP oil spill in April 2010, and the Fukushima nuclear power plants disaster in March 2011. Last but

---

1 For more information, see, inter alia, Uppsala Conflict Data Program and Peace Research Institute Oslo, 'UCDP/PRIO Armed Conflict Dataset' <www.prio.org/Data/Armed-Conflict/UCDP-PRIO> accessed on 15 April 2021, and Uppsala University, Department of Peace and Conflict Research, 'Uppsala Conflict Data Program' <https://ucdp.uu.se/encyclopedia> accessed on 15 April 2021. The War Report published by the Geneva Academy informs that 13 international armed conflicts (IACs) and 36 non-international armed conflicts (NIACs) took place in 2016, 17 IACs and 38 NIACs took place in 2017, and 18 IACs and 51 NIACs took place in 2018, see Annyssa Bellal (ed), 'The War Report 2018: Armed Conflicts in 2018' (*Geneva Academy of International Humanitarian Law and Human Rights 2018*, April 2019) <www.geneva-academy.ch/research/publications/detail/471-the-war-report-2018> accessed 15 April 2021.

2 For more details, see United Nations Office of Coordination of Humanitarian Affairs (UNOCHA), 'Global Humanitarian Overview 2021' <https://gho.unocha.org> accessed 15 April 2021.

3 For more information, see, inter alia, United Nations Environment Programme at <www.unep.org/climatechange>, United Nations (UN), 'Climate Action' at <www.un.org/en/climatechange> accessed 15 February 2021, and UN, 'Global Action – Climate Change' at <www.un.org/en/global-issues/climate-change> accessed 15 April 2021.

4 See, inter alia, UN, 'EU-UN Partnership on Land, Natural Resources and Conflict Prevention' <www.un.org/en/land-natural-resources-conflict> accessed 15 April 2021.

not least, armed conflicts in the former Yugoslavia, Syria, Iraq, Yemen, Mali, and other places,[5] but also lack of attention, resources, and expertise in various countries, have caused the destruction of tangible and intangible world cultural heritage.

The question of whether and to what extent international law protects community interests stands at the centre of numerous current debates. Recent examples include those around whether community interest in the punishment of mass atrocity crimes and providing reparations to victims should supersede the immunity of senior state officials and state immunity; whether peremptory norms embodying community interest such as that of preventing and punishing genocide[6] should supersede treaty reservations to treaty enforcement mechanisms; whether states or state officials should enjoy immunity for serious violations of human rights and humanitarian law before foreign domestic courts; whether mining in the deep seabed or polar regions should be allowed, despite the risk of pollution and damage to wildlife; and whether responsibility for the deleterious effects of climate change can be adequately apportioned and, if so, how.

Doubts remain as to how far one can take a 'community interest', provided it is legally enforceable in the first place. If we consider the United Nations Security Council as empowered to enunciate and enforce common interests with binding effect for all states in the context of international peace and security, could that possibly include, under extreme circumstances, the sacrificing of the very existence of a sovereign state?[7] Should the Security Council be allowed to not intervene in a specific situation on behalf of a population at risk, when the state concerned is manifestly failing its responsibility to protect? Is economic integration of the type of the European Community, or some kind of political integration, a prerequisite for the emergence and effective protection of 'community interests'? Is the invocation of our common humanity and destiny enough for such 'community interests' to materialize and be given legal and institutional expression? Answering these difficult questions creates the potential to chart new territories in

5 For more information, see, inter alia United Nations Educational Scientific and Cultural Organization (UNESCO) 'World Heritage Centre' <http://whc.unesco.org> accessed 15 April 2021.

6 See, among others, Andreas Zimmermann, 'The Obligation to Prevent Genocide: Towards a General Responsibility to Protect' in Ulrich Fastenrath and others (eds), *From Bilateralism to Community Interest: Essays in Honour of Bruno Simma* (Oxford University Press 2011) 629–645.

7 Bruno Simma, 'From Bilateralism to Community Interest in International Law' (1994) 250 Recueil des Cours de l'Académie de Droit International 217, 253.

international law and international relations, and providing necessary guidance on important issues for policy and decision-makers.

The bilateral-minded nature of traditional international law is largely reflected in the law of state responsibility and traditional dispute-settlement mechanisms such as the International Court of Justice (ICJ), based primarily on the principle of consent and the correlative rights and obligations of its subjects.[8] The concept of 'common interest' carries the promise of transforming international law into a system which serves the interest of the collective, as opposed to solely those of states *ut singuli*.[9] The formulation of international law itself constitutes a much wider process than the formulation and acknowledgement of its 'formal sources', seeking the legitimacy of international norms through the expression of the *opinio juris communis* (going well beyond the subjective element of custom), as well as the fulfilment of the public interest and the realization of the common good of the international community as a whole.[10] The sections below will first explore the concept of community interest, and then outline briefly a research agenda for the three selected areas, namely *collective human security*, *collective natural resources*, and *world cultural heritage*, before providing some concluding remarks.

---

8 See, among others, James Crawford, 'Responsibility to the International Community as a Whole' (2001) 8(2) Indiana Journal of Global Legal Studies 303, 322, stating: 'We have not yet succeeded in ridding ourselves of the notion that legal obligations in international law can always be analogized to bilateral legal obligations, and their breach to bilateral wrongs.'

9 For a pioneering and extensive discussion on the topic of 'community interest', see Simma (n 7). See also Santiago Villalpando, 'The Legal Dimension of the International Community: How Community Interests Are Protected in International Law' (2010) 21(2) European Journal of International Law 387; Ulrich Fastenrath and others (eds), *From Bilateralism to Community Interest: Essays in Honour of Bruno Simma* (OUP 2011); André Nollkaemper, 'International Adjudication of Global Public Goods: The Intersection of Substance and Procedure' (2012) 23(3) EJIL769; Wolfgang Benedek and others (eds), *The Common Interest in International Law* (Intersentia 2014); Claire Buggenhoudt, *Common Interests in International Litigation: A Case Study on Natural Resource Exploitation Disputes* (Intersentia 2017); Eyal Benvenisti and Georg Nolte (eds), *Community Interests Across International Law* (OUP 2018); Giorgio Gaja, 'The Protection of General Interests in the International Community' (2013) 364 Recueil des Cours 9. On the issue of global values, see, inter alia, Otto Spijkers, *The United Nations, the Evolution of Global Values and International Law* (Intersentia 2011). Spijkers argues that a common desire to eradicate war, poverty, inhuman treatment, and to halt the exploitation of peoples, has led to an affirmation of the values of peace and security, social progress and development, human dignity and the self-determination of all peoples.

10 Antônio Augusto Cançado Trindade, *International Law for Humankind: Towards a New Jus Gentium* (2nd edn, Brill | Nijhoff 2010) 638.

2. COMMUNITY INTEREST: WHAT IS IN A CONCEPT?

Although the terms 'international community' and 'community interest' occasionally surface within international law, their nature and scope remain somewhat ephemeral and vague.[11] The same can be said about such related concepts as 'global values' and the 'common challenges' facing humankind. Agreeing on what these 'global values'[12] are and what constitute the most urgent 'common challenges' presently facing the international community is not easy, and both depend on whom you ask. The concept of 'international community', on which the 'community interest' concept is based, comprises not only states but also international and regional organizations[13] and, arguably, prominent non-state actors.[14] Ultimately, despite these differences, the international community is the depository of values that transcend the state understood *ut singuli* that is being referred to.[15] That said, arguably the international community is a legal fiction comprising at least all UN member states, and it is at a minimum these states collectively that are the holders of identified 'common interests'.

Various terms are used to denote community interests. Gaja has used the term 'general interest'.[16] Villalpando and Nollkaemper have used 'global public goods'.[17] 'Goods' can be seen as problematic because common interest could include enforcing common global values, such as protecting populations through the prohibition of genocide, as well as managing

11 See, among others, Bruno Simma and Andreas L Paulus, 'The "International Community": Facing the Challenge of Globalization' (1998) 9(2) EJIL 266; Anne-Laure Vaurs-Chaumette, 'The International Community as a Whole' in James Crawford, Alain Pellet, and Simon Olleson (eds) *The Law of International Responsibility* (OUP 2010) 1023–1028.

12 For a thorough discussion of this issue, see, among others, Spijkers (n 9) 13–59.

13 See, among others, UNGA, 'Fourth Report on State Responsibility by Mr. James Crawford, Special Rapporteur' (2 April 2001) International Law Commission fifty-third session UN Doc A/CN.4/517, para 36; Simma and Paulus (n 11); Jan Klabbers, 'What Role for International Organizations in the Promotion of Community Interests? Reflections on the Ideology of Functionalism' in Eyal Benvenisti and Georg Nolte (eds), *Community Interests Across International Law* (OUP 2018) 86–100.

14 See, among others, Andrea Bianchi, 'The Fight for Inclusion: Non-State Actors and International Law' in Ulrich Fastenrath and others (eds), *From Bilateralism to Community Interest: Essays in Honour of Bruno Simma* (OUP 2011) 39–57.

15 Anne-Laure Vaurs-Chaumette, 'Peoples and Minorities' in James Crawford, Alain Pellet, and Simon Olleson (eds), *The Law of International Responsibility* (OUP 2010) 1024.

16 Gaja (n 9) 20–22.

17 See, respectively, Villalpando (n 9) 387–419; Nollkaemper (n 9).

collective material goods, such as ocean resources or the commons more generally. Moreover, the two qualities which Villalpando identifies as characterizing these public goods – they must be 'non-excludable' and 'non-rivalrous'[18] – do not easily apply to certain common interests, since access to and use of some of them can be established and maintained by some members of the international community to the detriment or even exclusion of others. This broader discussion about the emergence and protection of 'community interests' is neither theoretical nor utopian, since community interests are already being enforced at international and regional levels.[19] Many of these questions clearly have a tangible practical side: for example, those about who should profit from the melting of the Polar ice caps and who should be indemnified for the deleterious effects of climate change; who should be held responsible for not preventing or stopping ongoing mass atrocities; and who is responsible for the loss of world cultural heritage.

A correct understanding of the nature and scope of the 'international community' and 'community interest or interests' is therefore necessary in order to be able to properly assess whether and to what extent such interests are being safeguarded. This chapter confines itself to three broad areas, which can be described as *collective human security*, *collective natural resources*, and *world cultural heritage*. They are expressed in legal terms in these ways:

a) Collective human security is expressed in the concepts of human security and the responsibility to protect doctrine, and related institutional arrangements including the UN and regional and security organizations.
b) Collective natural resources management is expressed in the concept of the common heritage of mankind and shared natural resources, and the related institutional arrangements.
c) World cultural heritage is expressed in the notion of world heritage and related institutional arrangements, especially UNESCO.

---

18 See Villalpando (n 9) 392, identifying 'non-excludable' as describing those goods which, once they are made available, cannot be kept away from users' consumption – anyone can have access to them – and 'non-rivalrous' as their enjoyment by one consumer does not deprive any other user of the commodity, nor does it reduce the amount of the good available for consumption by others.

19 See, among others, Simma (n 7) 217–384; Erika de Wet, 'The International Constitutional Order' (2006) 55 International & Comparative Law Quarterly 51; Villalpando (n 9) 387–419; Nollkaemper (n 9).

The following subsections critically evaluate the nature and scope of the concepts of 'international community' and 'community interests', and analyze the process through which certain issues of common international concern become 'community interests'. This process entails the elevation of a specific community interest to the level of representing common legal obligations incumbent upon the international community as a whole, and its fostering and protection through appropriate institutional mechanisms or arrangements.

2.1. TRACKING DOWN THE CONCEPTS OF 'INTERNATIONAL COMMUNITY' AND 'COMMUNITY INTEREST', MAINLY THROUGH AN ICJ LENS

As the principal international organisation, the United Nations (UN) is widely considered to represent the organised international community. Its existence and activities are intrinsically associated with the concept of international community and with the formulation and protection of community interests. The three main purposes of the UN, as expressed in Article 1 of the UN Charter, include maintaining international peace and security and developing friendly relations, solving problems of economic, social, cultural, or humanitarian character, and promoting respect for human rights and fundamental freedoms without discrimination. Additionally, from an organizational perspective, as reflected in Article 1(4) of the Charter, the UN is expected to function as a centre for harmonizing the actions of nations towards the attainment of these *common ends*. The starting point for the development of 'community interests' should therefore be tracked down to these 'common ends' of the organized international community, for whose attainment the UN serves as a centre of coordination. Article 1(4) of the Charter envisages the transformation of the society of states into a community of states, a transformation facilitated by the sharing of common goals, as well as by the means through which these goals are to be achieved (cooperation, development of friendly relations based upon certain principles, settlement of disputes, and adjustment of disputes and situations in conformity with the principles of international law and justice).[20] Admittedly, the legal formulation chosen by the drafters

[20] Rüdiger Wolfrum, 'Article '1' in Bruno Simma and others (eds), *The Charter of the United Nations: A Commentary* (2nd edn, OUP 2002) 44.

of the UN Charter also leaves open the pursuance of these common ends through other mechanisms operating alongside the UN system.

Although the ICJ, a main organ and the principal legal organ of the UN, has made reference to the concept on several occasions, the nature and scope of 'common interest' remain questionable. Moreover, the 'interest' concerned has variously involved the state parties to an international treaty, the international community as a whole,[21] a people,[22] or an international organisation.[23] In its 1951 advisory opinion, the ICJ found that:

> In such a convention [Genocide Convention] the contracting States do not have any interests of their own; they merely have, one and all, a *common interest*, namely, the accomplishment of those high purposes which are the *raison d'être* of the convention.[24]

In the much-celebrated dictum of the *Barcelona Traction* case, the ICJ introduced a distinction between international obligations of a bilateral and of a community interest nature by stating that:

> [A]n essential distinction should be drawn between the obligations of a State towards the international community as a whole, and those arising vis-à-vis another State in the field of diplomatic protection. By their very nature the former are the *concern of all States*. In view of the importance of the rights involved, all States can be held to have a legal interest in their protection; they are obligations *erga omnes*.[25]

The Court has identified certain principles of international law that are part of the obligations owed by individual states to the international

21 *United States Diplomatic and Consular Staff in Tehran* (*United States of America v Iran*) (Judgment) [1980] ICJ Rep 3, 43, para 92.

22 *Legal Consequences for States of the Continued Presence of South Africa in Namibia (South West Africa) Notwithstanding Security Council Resolution 276 (1970)* (Advisory Opinion) [1971] ICJ Rep 56, 16 (*Namibia case)*; *Western Sahara* (Advisory Opinion) [1975] ICJ Rep 12; *Legal Consequences of the Construction of a Wall in the Occupied Palestinian Territory* (Advisory Opinion) [2004] ICJ Rep136 *Israeli Wall* case.

23 *Legality of the Use by a State of Nuclear Weapons in Armed Conflict* (Advisory Opinion) [1996] ICJ Rep 66; *Legality of the Threat or Use of Nuclear Weapons* (Advisory Opinion) [1996] ICJ Rep 226; *Israeli Wall* case (n 22) 136; *Accordance with International Law of the Unilateral Declaration of Independence in Respect of Kosovo* (Advisory Opinion) [2010] ICJ Rep 403.

24 *Reservations to the Convention on the Prevention and Punishment of the Crime of Genocide* (Advisory Opinion) [1951] ICJ Rep 15, 23.

25 *Barcelona Traction, Light and Power Company, Limited (Belgium v. Spain)* (Judgment) [1970] ICJ Rep 3, 32, para 33 (*Barcelona Traction*) (emphasis added).

community as a whole, implying that there is a 'common interest' for such obligations to be properly discharged by each state. In the words of the Court:

> Such obligations derive, for example, in contemporary international law, from the outlawing of acts of aggression, and of genocide, as also from the principles and rules concerning the basic rights of the human person, including protection from slavery and racial discrimination. Some of the corresponding rights of protection have entered into the body of general international law (Reservations to the Convention on the Prevention and Punishment of the Crime of Genocide, Advisory Opinion, I.C.J. Reports 1951, p. 23); others are conferred by international instruments of a universal or quasi-universal character.[26]

Two other legal terms used by the Court that are inherently linked to the concept of 'common interest', if not explicitly meant to give expression to it, are 'sacred trust of civilization' and 'elementary considerations of humanity'. The term 'sacred trust of civilization' has been used in cases concerned with the process of decolonisation and the self-determination of peoples, as expressing the 'common interest' of the international community that such processes be finalized in accordance with the genuine will of the people concerned.[27] In a recent advisory opinion, the ICJ held that: 'Since respect for the right to self-determination is an obligation *erga omnes*, all states have a legal interest in protecting that right'.[28] 'Elementary considerations of humanity' was originally meant to express a basic standard of expected state conduct *vis-à-vis* all members of the international community,[29] and then extended to the substantive protection of individuals during an armed conflict under Common Article 3 to the Geneva Conventions and the fundamental general principles of humanitarian law.[30]

In a case concerning diplomatic staff protection, the Court drew the attention of 'the entire international community' to the irreparable harm that could be done by the hostage-taking of diplomatic and

26 ibid para 34.

27 See, among others, *Namibia case* (n 22) 16. See, among others, Gentian Zyberi, 'Self-Determination Through the Lens of the International Court of Justice' (2009) 56(3) Netherlands International Law Review 429.

28 *Legal Consequences of the Separation of the Chagos Archipelago from Mauritius in 1965* (Advisory Opinion) [2019] ICJ Rep 95, 139, para 180.

29 *Corfu Channel case (United Kingdom of Great Britain and Northern Ireland v Albania)* (Merits) (Judgment) [1949] ICJ Rep 4, 22.

30 *Military and Paramilitary Activities in and against Nicaragua* (*Nicaragua v United States of America*) (Merits) (Judgment) [1986] ICJ Rep 14, 114, para 218; *Legality of the Threat or Use of Nuclear Weapons* (n 23) paras 79 and 95.

consular staff. It stated that such acts undermine the edifice of law that has been carefully constructed by mankind over a period of centuries, the maintenance of which is vital for the security and well-being of the complex international community of the present day; accordingly, it is more essential than ever that the rules developed to ensure the ordered progress of relations between its members are constantly and scrupulously respected.[31] Here, besides emphasizing the specific value of the immunity and inviolability of diplomatic and consular staff for the maintenance of peace and friendly relations, the Court pointed to the common interest of safeguarding the system of international law itself from grossly unlawful behavior on the part of individual states.

In the *Obligation to Prosecute or Extradite* case, the ICJ found that in compliance with the relevant obligations under the Convention against Torture, the common interest implies the entitlement of each state party to the Convention to make a claim concerning the cessation of an alleged breach by another state party.[32] This finding has important consequences for the enforcement of international human rights norms that have attained a *jus cogens* status, and it can potentially be seen as a reversal of the Court's earlier position in the *South West Africa* case.[33] The Court restated a similar position concerning the prohibition of genocide in the *Application of the Genocide Convention* case, by finding that:

> In view of their shared values, all the States parties to the Genocide Convention have a *common interest* to ensure that acts of genocide are prevented and that, if they occur, their authors do not enjoy impunity. That *common interest* implies that the obligations in question are owed by any State party to all the other States parties to the Convention … [a]ny State party to the Genocide Convention, and not only a specially affected State, may invoke the responsibility of another State party with a view to ascertaining the alleged failure to comply with its obligations *erga omnes partes*, and to bring that failure to an end.[34]

This brief review of the ICJ's case law shows that 'community interest', especially concerning human security and accountability for mass

31 *USA v Iran* (n 21) 43.

32 *Questions Relating to the Obligation to Prosecute or Extradite* (*Belgium v Senegal*) (Judgment) [2012] ICJ Rep 422 para 69.

33 *South West Africa* (*Ethiopia and Liberia v South Africa*) (Judgment, Second Phase) [1966] ICJ Rep 6, 32, para 44.

34 *Application of the Convention on the Prevention and Punishment of the Crime of Genocide* (*The Gambia v Myanmar*) (Order of 23 January 2020) ICJ Rep 69, para 41 (emphasis added).

atrocity crimes,[35] has been gaining in importance in the cases brought before the principal judicial organ of the UN.

2.2. THE NATURE AND SCOPE OF THE CONCEPTS OF 'INTERNATIONAL COMMUNITY' AND 'COMMUNITY INTEREST'

Although the term 'international community' is used frequently, debates continue around whether at this stage of organisation we can speak of an 'international community', or whether 'international society' is more appropriate.[36] The concept of 'community' presupposes that its members largely share their interests, as opposed to the looser concept of a 'society' where members have contact, but do not necessarily share common interests. Depending on the respective system established to protect the common interest in the three selected areas, namely collective human security, collective natural resources, and world cultural heritage, an assessment needs to be made about whether it is proper to speak about community interests or whether a different categorization needs to be developed and used. An example of a sufficiently organized community is the European Union, which has a complex institutional system for ensuring compliance with what are identified as community interests. At an international level, it seems suitable to speak of a 'community' and 'community interests' when the level of organization achieved is of such a degree that the relevant interest is protected through institutional mechanisms which are not voluntary and whose decisions are binding.

A definition of the 'international community' or 'community interest' does not appear in either the ICJ's findings or the work of the International Law Commission (ILC),[37] whose function is to develop and

---

35 See, among others, Bruno Simma, 'Human Rights Before the International Court of Justice: Community Interest Coming to Life?' in Christian J Tams and James Sloan (eds), *The Development of International Law by the International Court of Justice* (OUP 2013) 301–325; Gentian Zyberi 'The Interpretation and Development of International Human Rights Law by the International Court of Justice' in Martin Scheinin (ed), *Human Rights Norms in 'Other' International Courts* (Cambridge University Press 2019) 28–61.

36 For a detailed discussion of this concept, see, among others, Simma and Paulus (n 11); Vaurs-Chaumette (n 11); Gaja (n 9) 26–33.

37 See Georg Nolte, 'The International Law Commission and Community Interests' in Eyal Benvenisti and Georg Nolte (eds), *Community Interests Across International Law* (OUP 2018) 101–117.

codify international law. In giving a tentative definition of 'community interest', Simma perceives it as a consensus according to which respect for certain fundamental values is not left to the free disposition of states individually or *inter se* but is recognized and sanctioned by international law as a matter of concern to all states.[38] Further, Simma notes that 'the identification of common interests does not derive from scientific abstraction but rather flows from the recognition of concrete problems. Besides, the articulation of community interests occupies a permanent place on the agenda of the UN and other international bodies or conferences.'[39] As Simma puts it, by sheer necessity, the quest to realize community interests has led to an even stronger institutionalization, or organisation, of international society.[40] Yet questions remain as to the breadth and depth of that institutionalisation process. The comprehensive impact of community interest visible today also reveals a fundamental tension in contemporary international law – the tension between the need to make international law express and support what are assumed to be universally held moral beliefs and the need to make it firmly reflect its political context.[41] While that tension is here to stay, the normative and institutional developments of international law, especially in the period after the end of the Cold War, that is the past three decades, provide ample ground to assess the its effects and its impact upon the emergence and subsequent protection of 'community interests'. The description of the emergence of community interests in international law requires a departure from a purely legal perspective in order to examine the social environment in which community interests have arisen – that is, how states in their mutual relations have been driven to ensure the protection of certain community interests beyond their individual sphere – and the effects which this phenomenon has had in international law.[42]

While the ICJ is perhaps more reserved than the other main organs of the UN in referring to 'international community' or 'community interests' due to the largely bilateral nature of most of the disputes brought before it, it is difficult to state with certainty in which instances the term 'international community' is used in the sense of an 'international community of states' and when it is used in a more general sense, and whether the term 'common interest' means a legally protected value or

38 Simma (n 7) 233 and footnote 15 (emphasis added).
39 ibid 235.
40 ibid.
41 ibid 249.
42 Villalpando (n 9) 390.

simply encompasses a desirable standard of state behaviour.[43] In any case, it is clear that community interest and the obligations arising under it for the concerned stakeholders are not one-way, from an individual state towards the community of states, but ultimately also impose certain obligations on the part of the latter.[44] The importance of generating a general consensus in the process of identifying and protecting 'community interests' is expressed in the 1969 Vienna Convention on the Law of the Treaties in relation to peremptory norms of international law which need to be accepted and recognized by the 'international community as a whole'.[45] All of these *jus cogens* norms, as identified by the International Law Commission in its work on the Draft Conclusions on Peremptory Norms of General International Law (*Jus Cogens*),[46] can be considered as encapsulating community interests.

2.3. WHICH INTERESTS, WHOSE, AND TO WHAT EXTENT?

A number of questions arise with regard to the process of identifying and protecting 'common interests' at an international level. How best to articulate and promote collective concerns of the international community

43 A search for the exact words 'international community' among all documents at the official website of the ICJ yielded about 1055 results, whereas a similar search with the exact words 'common interest' yielded about 203 results (accessed 15 April 2021). The results include court decisions and individual opinions, submissions of parties to legal proceedings before the court, and speeches of the Court's presidents and vice-presidents.

44 That is clear in the 'responsibility to protect' doctrine, where the international community assumes the obligation to protect a population from genocide, war crimes, ethnic cleansing, and crimes against humanity, when a state is manifestly failing to exercise its primary responsibility. See, for more details, UN General Assembly, '2005 World Summit Outcome. Resolution Adopted by the General Assembly on 16 September 2005' (24 October 2005) UN Doc A/Res/60/1, paras 138–139.

45 Vienna Convention on the Law of Treaties (adopted 23 May 1969, entered into force 27 January 1980) 1155 UNTS 332 (VCLT) art 53.

46 In its non-exhaustive list, the ILC includes the following *jus cogens* norms: (a) The prohibition of aggression; (b) The prohibition of genocide; (c) The prohibition of crimes against humanity; (d) The basic rules of international humanitarian law; (e) The prohibition of racial discrimination and apartheid; (f) The prohibition of slavery; (g) The prohibition of torture; (h) The right of self-determination. See UNGA, Annex to the Draft Conclusions on Peremptory Norms of General International Law (*Jus Cogens*) (Chapter V), in 'Report of the International Law Commission, Seventy-First Session, General Assembly Official Records' (29 April–7 June and 8 July–9 August 2019) UN Doc A/74/10, 208.

in a decentralized legal order focused mainly on the rights and obligations of sovereign states? Can international law mediate effectively between competing individual and collective concerns in a world where the socio-economic and political differences between states are enormous, and where the pressure on human and natural resources is steadily increasing? Despite its emphasis on the rights and duties of individual states, international law has also supported efforts aimed at encouraging and strengthening international cooperation and solidarity among states. However, as Simma rightly cautions, the rise and recognition of community interests is one thing, and their impact on the real world is quite another.[47] It also remains unclear whether those things labelled 'common interests' should command an appeal similar to that inherent in bonds such as nationality, religion, or historical ties before they could qualify as such. Villalpando argues that the late emergence of community interests historically is explained by the fact that 'communitarian' relations among states are not inspired by the same forces characterizing inter-individual communities (common blood, affection, proximity, or traditions), but rather result from an advanced stage of cooperation.[48] Villalpando thus seems to discount aspects of the complex web which ties together the international community, or constituent parts of it, and which partly laid the basis for this advanced stage of cooperation. These kinds of ties are still relevant and form the basis of certain organizations.

Is there a list of requirements to be fulfilled before an interest becomes a 'community interest', just as there are necessary requirements to be fulfilled for a legal norm to qualify as a norm of customary international law? Among other scholars, Simma cautions that there is reason to be concerned about new conceptions being grafted upon universal international law without support through, and serious attempts at, adequate institution-building.[49] In noting and explaining their importance, Simma has emphasized the potential of multilateral treaties to serve as workhorses of community interest.[50] After the 1945 United Nations Charter, the 1982 United Nations Convention on the Law of the Sea (UNCLOS) was the first significant step towards creating suitable mechanisms for fostering community interests; it subjects the seabed and ocean floor and the subsoil thereof which are

47 Simma (n 7) 247.
48 Villalpando (n 9) 393.
49 Simma (n 7) 249.
50 ibid 322–376, especially at 322–325.

beyond the jurisdiction of states to a regime designed for the benefit of the international community as a whole.[51] Other efforts at fostering community interest are those included in the Outer Space Treaty and the Antarctic Treaty System.[52] Simma points out that the intensity of such interests will not be the same everywhere due to differences in the geographical positions or economic potential of the states involved.[53] In a finding relevant to the issue of human security, the ICJ has confirmed this by asserting that the responsibility of states to prevent genocide depends on a number of factors, including

> [t]he capacity to influence effectively the action of persons likely to commit, or already committing, genocide. This capacity itself depends, among other things, on the geographical distance of the State concerned from the scene of the events, and on the strength of the political links, as well as links of all other kinds, between the authorities of that State and the main actors in the events. The State's capacity to influence must also be assessed by legal criteria, since it is clear that every State may only act within the limits permitted by international law; seen thus, a State's capacity to influence may vary depending on its particular legal position vis-à-vis the situations and persons facing the danger, or the reality, of genocide.[54]

The need for a proper understanding of 'community interest' and the ensuing rights and duties in this regard for the members of the international community is of both theoretical and practical value. A practical example is provided by the Arctic, as climate change has created a real possibility for using the natural resources in that area.

---

51 United Nations Convention on the Law of the Sea (adopted 10 December 1982, entered into force 16 November 1994) 1833 UNTS 397 (UNCLOS), see, respectively, Part VII on the High Seas (arts 86–89) and Part XI, Subsection 4, on the International Sea-bed Authority (arts 156–158).

52 There are a number of UN treaties on outer space, including UNGA, 'Resolution 2222 (XXI): Treaty on Principles Governing the Activities of States in the Exploration and Use of Outer Space, Including the Moon and Other Celestial Bodies' (adopted 19 December 1966, entered into force 10 October 1967) 610 UNTS 205, and UNGA, 'Resolution 34/68: Agreement Governing the Activities of States on the Moon and Other Celestial Bodies' (5 December 1979) 1363 UNTS 3; for the key documents of the Antarctic Treaty System, see <www.ats.aq/e/key-documents.html> accessed on 15 April 2021.

53 Simma (n 7) 242.

54 *Application of the Convention on the Prevention and Punishment of the Crime of Genocide (Bosnia and Herzegovina v Serbia and Montenegro)* (Judgment) [2007] ICJ Rep 43, 221, para 430.

Numerous international institutions have been established over time with the aim of safeguarding community interests rather than the interests of individual states.[55] However, both between and within the three broad areas selected for this chapter, the comprehensiveness and strength of the legal framework and the effectiveness of the institutions created under them differ. The next section and subsections will briefly outline potential research agendas under the three areas, namely *collective human security*, *collective natural resources*, and *world cultural heritage*.

3. THE PROTECTION OF COMMUNITY INTERESTS AS A PROMISING RESEARCH AREA

International law has continuously expanded over the last century, the pace of its growth depending on the political and socio-economic circumstances prevailing at a given time. As Simma has pointedly noted, international law is finally overcoming the legal as well as moral deficiencies of bilateralism and maturing into a much more socially conscious legal order.[56] Evidently, an international law that properly formulates and adequately protects community interests carries the promise of a law of and for humankind.[57] A re-orientation of international law from co-existence and cooperation to co-progressiveness,[58] aimed at ensuring human flourishing and protecting the interest of collectives and peoples, is bound to emerge in the coming decades if the processes of globalization and further political and economic integration continue apace – including, arguably, as a response to them and their (un)intended consequences.

---

55 With regard to institutions relevant to collective human security, we can mention the UN Security Council and the UN Peacebuilding Commission; with regard to institutions relevant to the common heritage of mankind we can mention the International Seabed Authority (established under UNCLOS), the Marine Environment Protection Committee of the International Maritime Organization (IMO) and the Regional Fishery Bodies (RFB) of the Food and Agriculture Organization of the United Nations (FAO); and, with regard to institutions relevant to common cultural heritage, we can mention the World Heritage Committee and the International Centre for the Study of the Preservation and Restoration of Cultural Property (ICCROM) of UNESCO.

56 Simma (n 7) 234.

57 ibid; See also Cançado Trindade (n 10).

58 See Sienho Yee, *Towards an International Law of Co-Progresiveness* (Martinus Nijhoff 2004) 1–26.

Several areas of common interest to the international community as a whole are readily apparent. That fact that in the areas of collective human security, collective natural resources management, and world cultural heritage community interest is not an abstract notion but already part and parcel of international law can be illustrated, among other examples, by the responsibility to protect a population against mass atrocity crimes, incumbent upon the international community when the state concerned is manifestly failing that duty; the international efforts made to address climate change and manage collective natural resources; and the international efforts to safeguard world cultural heritage through UNESCO and other means. These issues are not limited only to discussions in relevant international fora, but can potentially be brought before international (quasi) judicial mechanisms for adjudication.[59] Not so long ago there was a discussion about the possibility of Palau requesting an advisory opinion from the ICJ with regard to the joint responsibility of the international community if climate change causes some island states to disappear from the map.

The safeguarding and pursuance of community interests in the selected areas are conferred on a number of international institutions operating largely within the UN system, as well as outside it, and are also pursued at a regional level. Topics related to preventing or assigning responsibility for the transboundary harm arising through hazardous activities (for example the cross-border effects of a Chernobyl-type explosion), protecting persons in the event of disasters, the law of transboundary aquifers, and so on figure prominently in the agenda of the ILC.[60] However, as Nolte has noted, the picture which emerges from the work of the ILC is that of an institution which has accompanied the development of international law in a way which fits the narrative of 'from self-interest to community interest' only to a certain extent.[61]

---

59 See, among others, Buggenhoudt (n 9) 81–147; Eyal Benvenisti, 'Community Interests in International Adjudication' in Eyal Benvenisti and Georg Nolte (eds), *Community Interests Across International Law* (OUP 2018) 70–85.

60 See, respectively, the topics 'Prevention of Transboundary Damage from Hazardous Activities', 'International Liability in Case of Loss from Transboundary Harm Arising out of Hazardous Activities', 'Shared Natural Resources (Law of Transboundary Aquifers)', 'Protection of Persons in the Event of Disasters', and 'Shared Natural Resources (Oil and Gas)' (discontinued). For more information, see ILC, 'Analytical Guide to the Work of the International Law Commission' <https://legal.un.org/ilc/guide/gfra.shtml> accessed 15 April 2021.

61 Nolte (n 37) 117.

It is clear that the everyone-for-their-own approach cannot solve some of the greatest challenges facing international community, such as the depletion of non-renewable natural resources and the degradation of the environment, climate change, threats to global human security, and damage to world cultural heritage. International solidarity might be a valuable starting point, but does not seem to provide a strong enough vehicle to cope with these challenges, as the COVID-19 pandemic has shown. If solidarity is understood as the common ascription to a common good, it follows that forestalling self-interested behaviour that gravely threatens the collective good can be characterized as a kind of super-self-interest.[62] Yet international solidarity seems based mainly on goodwill and not on a sense of legal obligation.

Over these three broad areas of community interests, different specific normative and procedural systems and institutional mechanisms have developed. It is important to test the adequacy and strength of these systems entrusted with safeguarding 'community interests' based on a number of variables, including considerations of system coherence, legal certainty, and suitable enforcement mechanisms. The first step in such an inquiry would be to make an inventory of the normative bases, institutional mechanisms, and oversight systems for safeguarding common interest in the three areas. The second step will be to assess the effectiveness and adequacy of existing mechanisms and procedures in protecting the common interest of the international community as a whole. The third and final step must be to provide recommendations with a view to strengthening and improving the current systems, in order to ensure that the common interest is duly formulated and protected.

Importantly, research on these issues will also have to deal head-on with double standards when dealing with the issue of adequate enforcement of 'community interest'. Why do states continue to tolerate oppression and starvation, disease and poverty, human cruelty and suffering, human misery and human indignity, of all kinds and on a scale they could not tolerate within their internal societies, and at the same time occasionally evoke community interest?[63] While double standards erode the moral bases which support claims based on common interest, the

---

62 See, inter alia, Roland St John MacDonald, 'Solidarity in the Practice and Discourse of Public International Law' (1996) 8(2) Pace International Law Review 259, 301. See also Rüdiger Wolfrum and Chie Kojima (eds), *Solidarity: A Structural Principle of International Law* (Springer 2010).

63 See Philip Allott, *Eunomia: New Order for a New World* (OUP 2001) 248.

legal basis for such claims is established through an elaborate framework of international treaties spanning multiple areas of international law.

This in-depth exploration of the formulation and protection of community interests will have three interrelated aspects. First, the theoretical bases of 'community interest' and its understanding in the three selected international law areas need to be fully explored and explained. Second, the institutional framework and mechanisms established to protect and safeguard community interest must be analyzed and their adequacy and effectiveness assessed. Third, the research will necessarily address the challenges and prospects for ensuring community interests, be they concerned with efficiently managing public goods or with protecting common values. The three inter-related questions which thus emerge are:

1. What is community interest, how does it emerge, and does understanding of it differ from one selected area of international law to another?
2. Which regulatory framework provides for a better realisation of community interests?
3. What are the challenges and prospects of realising community interests in these three selected areas of international law?

Answering these questions will show whether the selected areas reflect real and mature 'common interests' of the international community, or whether the language of 'common interests' is simply used to conceal the inability of international law to serve as a useful tool in facing current common challenges to humankind. The institutional framework under these areas of international law should be analyzed through four dimensions: regime formation, regime attributes, regime consequences, and regime dynamics.[64] A related, subsequent part of the research in this field is to study the effectiveness of the international regimes created under the three broad areas and to measure the progress made in protecting

---

64 See, among others, Marc A Levy, Oran R Young, and Michael Zürn, 'The Study of International Regimes' (1995) 1(3) European Journal of International Relations 267; Helmut Breitmeier, Oran R Young, and Michael Zürn, *Analyzing International Environmental Regimes: From Case Study to Database* (MIT Press 2006); Ronald B Mitchell and others (eds), *Global Environmental Assessments: Information and Influence* (MIT Press 2006); Olav Schram Stokke and Geir Hønneland (eds), *International Cooperation and Arctic Governance: Regime Effectiveness and Northern Region Building* (Routledge 2007).

identified 'community interest'.[65] To that aim, such research would need to address issues of regime formation, regime consequences, and regime effectiveness. The methodology of research in these areas would need to combine traditional international law theories and approaches with other methods, including constitutionalism and global governance, feminism, third world approaches, and legal pluralism, to mention a few.[66] The complexity of the dilemmas, involving politics, international relations, and economics, among other aspects, would necessitate, where possible, the use of mixed methods and research groups combining various backgrounds and knowledge from these fields.[67] The following subsections will briefly elaborate on the three selected topics for a research agenda, namely *collective human security*, *collective natural resources*, and *world cultural heritage*.

3.1. FIRST RESEARCH AREA: COLLECTIVE HUMAN SECURITY AND THE RESPONSIBILITY TO PROTECT

Human security is an approach that assists UN member states in identifying and addressing widespread and cross-cutting challenges to the survival, livelihood, and dignity of their people.[68] Related to that, the current collective security system is premised on the common interest to ensure international peace and security and aims to protect that interest by concentrating force in order to induce compliance. Human security has a broad and a narrow understanding, and it is the more narrow understanding of freedom from violence which is of

65 With regard to the issue of effectiveness, see, among others, Levy, Young, and Zürn (n 64). With regard to the issue of progress in international law, see, among others, Russell Miller and Rebecca Bratspies, *Progress in International Law* (Martinus Nijhoff 2008); Thomas Skouteris, *The Notion of Progress in International Law Discourse* (Asser Press 2010).

66 Andrea Bianchi, *International Law Theories: An Inquiry Into Different Ways of Thinking* (OUP 2016).

67 Malcolm Langford, 'Interdisciplinarity and Multimethod Research' in Bård A Andreassen, Hans-Otto Sano, Siobhán McInerney-Lankford (eds), *Research Methods in Human Rights: A Handbook* (Edward Elgar Publishing 2017) 161–191.

68 UNGA, 'Follow-up to Paragraph 143 on Human Security of the 2005 World Summit Outcome. Resolution Adopted by the General Assembly on 10 September 2012' (25 October 2012) UN Doc A/RES/66/290. More generally, see United Nations Trust Fund for Human Security, 'What is Human Security?' <https://www.un.org/humansecurity/what-is-human-security/> accessed 15 April 2021.

main concern here.[69] Primary responsibility for the maintenance of international peace and security is invested in the Security Council of the UN.[70] Regional organizations and security organizations, as the Organisation for Security and Cooperation in Europe (OSCE, civilian) and North-Atlantic Treaty Organisation (NATO, military), also have a role to play in collective security,[71] but only when there is general agreement among the international community about the necessary steps.

Sadly, the collective security system has repeatedly failed to provide adequate responses to mass atrocities committed against populations.[72] The vulnerability and the essentially fluctuating nature of the engagement of the UN and, in particular, of the Security Council for the defense of collective interests, as the perfectly random way in which it condemns certain violations of obligations arising from peremptory norms to turn a blind eye on others just as serious, structurally prohibit the pursuit of the daydream of the initial codifiers of responsibility for crimes.[73] It was this inability and failure of the organized international community to respond in a timely and efficient manner to mass atrocities unfolding in various parts of the world that gave rise to the doctrine of the responsibility to protect (RtoP) in 2001 and its subsequent adoption by the international community in the 2005 World Summit Outcome document.[74] Based on the principle of

---

69 See, among others, Hisashi Owada, 'Human Security and International Law' in Ulrich Fastenrath and others (eds) *From Bilateralism to Community Interest: Essays in Honour of Bruno Simma* (OUP 2011) 505–520; Mary Martin and Taylor Owen (eds), *Routledge Handbook of Human Security* (Routledge 2013); Cedric Ryngaert and Math Noortmann (eds), *Human Security and International Law: The Challenge of Non-State Actors* (Intersentia 2013).

70 For more information on the UN Peace and Security System, see <www.un.org/en/global-issues/peace-and-security> accessed 15 April 2021. See, among others, Thomas G Weiss (ed), *Collective Security in a Changing World* (Lynne Rienner 1993); Ademola Abass and Mashood A Baderin, 'Towards Effective Collective Security and Human Rights Protection in Africa: An Assessment of the Constitutive Act of the New African Union' (2002) 49(1) Netherlands International Law Review 1; Alexander Orakhelashvili, *Collective Security* (OUP 2011); Gary Wilson, *The United Nations and Collective Security* (Routledge 2014); Ramesh Thakur, *The United Nations, Peace and Security: From Collective Security to the Responsibility to Protect* (2nd edn, CUP 2016).

71 See Tarcisio Gazzini, 'NATO's Role in the Collective Security System' (2003) 8(2) Journal of Conflict and Security Law 231.

72 See, among others, Joseph C Ebegbulem, 'The Failure of Collective Security in the Post World Wars I and II International System' (2011) 2(2) Transcience 23.

73 Pierre-Marie Dupuy, L'Unité de l'Ordre Juridique International: Cours Général de Droit International Public (2000) 297 Recueil des Cours 9, 376–377.

74 Some of the most important documents include: International Commission on Intervention and State Sovereignty, 'Responsibility to Protect: Report of the International

complementarity, this doctrine places the primary responsibility for the protection of populations from genocide, war crimes, ethnic cleansing, and crimes against humanity upon individual states, and when a state manifestly fails in that duty, the responsibility passes on to the international community.

While a lot has been written on the RtoP since its inception in 2001, the work of the institutional mechanisms concerned with translating it into practice is in urgent need of further exploration. The main UN organs, regional and security organizations, international courts and tribunals, and regional human rights systems all have important roles to play in operationalizing RtoP and ensuring that it is transformed from promise into practice. As the process of building a suitable and acceptable model is a work in progress, taking stock of existing institutional procedures and mechanisms and designing and establishing more effective procedures and mechanisms to carry out RtoP obligations provide new challenges but also new opportunities. The RtoP operational model needs to be one in which domestic, regional, and international mechanisms are well-connected and synchronized in their actions, whereby decisions on addressing RtoP situations are taken through well-informed and meaningful deliberations, and the commitment to protect the populations at risk of mass atrocities is matched by the necessary material and human resources and political will.[75]

Commission on Intervention and State Sovereignty' (International Research Centre 2001) and 2005 World Summit Outcome (n 44), paras 138–140; UN Secretary-General Reports 2009–2020 and other key documents are available at United Nations Office on Genocide Prevention and the Responsibility to Protect, 'Key Documents' <https://www.un.org/en/genocideprevention/key-documents.shtml> accessed 15 April 2021. See, among others, Gareth Evans, *The Responsibility to Protect: Ending Mass Atrocity Crimes Once and for All* (Brookings Institution Press 2008); Jared Genser and Irwin Cotler, *The Responsibility to Protect: The Promise of Stopping Mass Atrocities in Our Time* (OUP 2011); Julia Hoffmann and André Nollkaemper (eds), *Responsibility to Protect: From Principle to Practice* (Amsterdam University Press 2011); Gentian Zyberi (ed), *An Institutional Approach to the Responsibility to Protect* (CUP 2013); Alex J Bellamy, *Responsibility to Protect: A Defense* (OUP 2014); Susan Breau, *The Responsibility to Protect in International Law: An Emerging Paradigm* (Routledge 2016); Alex J Bellamy and Tim Dunne (eds), *The Oxford Handbook of the Responsibility to Protect* (OUP 2016); Ramesh Thakur, *Reviewing the Responsibility to Protect: Origins, Implementation and Controversies* (Routledge 2018).

75 Gentian Zyberi, 'Sharing the Responsibility to Protect: Taking Stock and Moving Forward' in Gentian Zyberi (ed), *An Institutional Approach to the Responsibility to Protect* (CUP 2013) 530.

3.2. SECOND RESEARCH AREA: COLLECTIVE NATURAL RESOURCES

Adequate management of natural resources has long been an international concern.[76] The concept of the 'common heritage of mankind' is seen as one of the major advances made in international law, especially in terms of fostering 'common interests' and governing the commons.[77] Despite the old semblance given by the use of terms as *res communis humanitatis*, *res publica internationalis*, *res communis omnium*, *res extra commercium*, and *res unitas communis*, the concept of the common heritage of mankind is fairly recent. This area of international law could also be called international or common resources administration. Baslar notes that although the scope of the common heritage concept is uncertain, it is widely agreed to provide certain elements that are characteristic when applied to common space areas: (1) areas designated as common heritage shall not be appropriated; (2) use of the areas and their resources which fall under the common heritage regime will be governed and managed by an international authority; (3) benefits derived from the exploitation of the common heritage area and its resources will be actively and equitably shared; (4) the areas and resources concerned will be used peacefully; and (5) the given resources will be protected and preserved for the benefit and interest of humankind.[78] The concept of common heritage of mankind applies at a minimum to international regimes on the high seas,[79] Antarctica,[80] outer space and celestial bodies.[81] The main idea behind this concept is

---

76 See, among others, Elinor Ostrom, *Governing the Commons: The Evolution of Institutions for Collective Action* (CUP 2015).

77 See, generally, Stephen Gorove, 'The Concept of "Common Heritage of Mankind": A Political, Moral or Legal Innovation?' (1972) 9 San Diego Law Review 390; Rüdiger Wolfrum, 'The Principle of the Common Heritage of Mankind' (1983) 43 ZaöRV/HJIL 312; Kemal Baslar, *The Concept of the Common Heritage of Mankind in International Law* (Martinus Nijhoff 1997) 12; Erkki Holmila, 'Common Heritage of Mankind in the Law of the Sea' (2005) 1 Acta Societatis Martensis 187. See also Benvenisti and Nolte (n 9) 121–187 (Part III Community Interests and Natural Resources, with chapters by Ranganathan, Park, Brunnée, and Casini).

78 Baslar (n 77) xx–xxi.

79 *ibid* 205–243; Holmila (n 77).

80 Baslar (n 77) 243–277.

81 ibid 159–205. Some of the relevant treaties include UNGA, Resolution 2222 (XXI) (n 52); UNGA, 'Resolution 2345 (XXII): Agreement on the Rescue of Astronauts, the Return of Astronauts and the Return of Objects Launched into Outer Space' (adopted 19 December 1967, entered into force 3 December 1968) 672 UNTS 119; UNGA, 'Resolution 2777 (XXVI): Convention on International Liability for Damage Caused by Space Objects' (adopted 29 November 1971, entered into force 1 September 1972)

the peaceful use and an equitable share of resources for the benefit of all humankind.

Oceans cover almost three-quarters of the Earth's surface, comprise nine-tenths of its water resources, and are home to over 97 per cent of all life.[82] According to the 2002 Report *Oceans: The Source of Life*, the economic value and potential of oceans is considerable: marine minerals – including offshore oil and gas, gold, tin, diamonds, sand and gravel – were estimated to generate nearly one trillion USD every year, while the combined value of ocean resources and uses was estimated to be about seven trillion USD per year.[83] Another issue which needs to be addressed in the framework of such research is the rise in the global average sea level by 10 to 25 centimetres over the past 100 years, with models projecting a further rise of 15 to 95 cm by 2100 (with the 'best estimate' at 50 cm).[84] The impact of climate change might mean that certain island states cease to exist, not to speak of the damage to densely inhabited coastal areas.[85] Climate change, loss of biodiversity, and potential for serious environmental pollution[86] require the international community to establish a viable regime for the exploration, preservation, and exploitation of collective natural resources for the benefit of all humankind and present and future generations.

An international legal basis for space activities has been built up over the last five decades.[87] The legal regime established aims to ensure use of

---

961 UNTS 187; UNGA, 'Resolution 3235 (XXIX): Convention on Registration of Objects Launched into Outer Space' (adopted 12 November 1974, entered into force 15 September 1976) 1023 UNTS 15; UNGA, Resolution 34/68 (n 52).

82 'Oceans: The Source of Life' Published on the Occasion of the 20th Anniversary (1982–2002) of the United Nations Convention on the Law of the Sea, 13 <www.un.org/Depts/los/convention_agreements/convention_20years/oceanssourceoflife.pdf> accessed 15 April 2021.

83 ibid.

84 ibid 14.

85 See, among others, Nico Schrijver, 'The Impact of Climate Change: Challenges for International Law' in Ulrich Fastenrath and others (eds), *From Bilateralism to Community Interest: Essays in Honour of Bruno Simma* (OUP 2011) 1278–1297; Human Rights Committee, *Ioane Teitiota v. New Zealand* (24 October 2019) communication No 2728/2016, CCPR/C/127/D/2728/2016, especially paras 9.10–9.12.

86 See, among others, International Tribunal on the Law of the Sea, *Responsibilities and Obligations of States Sponsoring Persons and Entities with Respect to Activities in the Area* (Advisory Opinion) [2011] ITLOS Rep 10.

87 See, among others, Frans G von der Dunk and Fabio Tronchetti (eds), *Handbook of Space Law* (Edward Elgar Publishing 2015); Francis Lyall and Paul B Larsen, *Space Law: A Treatise* (2nd edn, Routledge 2017). See also Vladimír Kopal, 'The Progressive Development of International Space Law by the United Nations (Lecture Series on the Law of Outer Space)' (2008) UN Audiovisual Library of International Law <http://legal.un.org/avl/ls/Kopal_LOS.html> accessed 15 April 2021.

the Moon and other celestial bodies for peaceful purposes. To that aim, Article 4 of the 1979 Agreement Governing the Activities of States on the Moon and Other Celestial Bodies provides that 'the exploration and use of the Moon shall be the province of all mankind and shall be carried out for the benefit and in the interests of all countries, irrespective of their degree of economic or scientific development. Due regard shall be paid to the interests of present and future generations as well as to the need to promote higher standards of living and conditions of economic and social progress and development in accordance with the Charter of the United Nations.' The United Nations Office for Outer Space Affairs (UNOOSA) implements the decisions of the General Assembly and of the Committee on the Peaceful Uses of Outer Space (COPUOS) and is responsible for promoting international cooperation in the peaceful uses of outer space.[88] COPUOS was created in 1958, shortly after the launching of the first artificial satellite, Sputnik-1, and is one of the largest UN committees. The challenges facing the international community in administering the common heritage of mankind are multifaceted, and research should provide useful guidance to those professionals interested in this broad area.

3.3. THIRD RESEARCH AREA: WORLD CULTURAL HERITAGE

Several international treaties aim at protecting world cultural heritage, both tangible and intangible.[89] Diverse aspects of the protection of world

---

88 For more information, visit the website of the United Nations Office for Outer Space Affairs (UNOOSA) <www.oosa.unvienna.org> accessed 15 April 2021.

89 Namely, Convention for the Protection of Cultural Property in the Event of Armed Conflict (adopted 14 May 1954, entered into force 7 August 1956) 249 UNTS 215; Protocol to the Convention for the Protection of Cultural Property in the Event of Armed Conflict (adopted 14 May 1954, entered into force 7 August 1956) 249 UNTS 358; Second Protocol to the Hague Convention of 1954 for the Protection of Cultural Property in the Event of Armed Conflict (adopted 26 March 1999, entered into force 9 March 2004) 2253 UNTS 172; Convention on the Means of Prohibiting and Preventing the Illicit Import, Export and Transfer of Ownership of Cultural Property (adopted 14 November 1970, entered into force 24 April 1972) 823 UNTS 231); Convention Concerning the Protection of the World Cultural and Natural Heritage 1972 (adopted 16 November 1972, entered into force 17 December 1975) 1037 UNTS 151 (UNESCO World Heritage Convention); Convention on the Protection of the Underwater Cultural Heritage 2001 (adopted 2 November 2001, entered into force 2 January 2009) 2562 UNTS 3 (UNESCO Underwater Heritage Convention); Convention for the Safeguarding of the Intangible Cultural Heritage (adopted 17 October 2003, entered

cultural heritage are dealt with in the literature.[90] Besides cooperation at an international level, mainly under the framework of the United Nations Education, Scientific and Cultural Organization (UNESCO),[91] there is also regional cooperation in the framework of ASEAN, the Council of Europe, the EU, and so on. A lot of world cultural heritage has been damaged and looted due to armed conflicts in former Yugoslavia, Iraq, Afghanistan, and elsewhere. In 2012, UNESCO frequently urged all warring parties to respect and protect Syria's great cultural legacy, which constitutes a source of identity and fulfilment for its people, and to abide by their international obligations in the area of culture.[92] The Operational Guidelines for the Implementation of the World Heritage Convention aim to facilitate the implementation of the Convention concerning the Protection of the World Cultural and Natural Heritage (UNESCO World Heritage Convention) by setting forth the procedure for: (a) the inscription of properties

into force 20 April 2006) 2368 UNTS 3 (UNESCO Intangible Heritage Convention); Convention on the Protection and Promotion of the Diversity of Cultural Expressions (adopted 20 October 2005, entered into force 18 March 2007) 2240 UNTS 346; Council of Europe Framework Convention on the Value of Cultural Heritage for Society (adopted 27 October 2005, entered into force 1 June 2011) CETS No 199.

90 See, among others, Guido Camarda and Tullio Scovazzi (eds), *The Protection of the Underwater Cultural Heritage: Legal Aspects* (Giuffrè 2002); Kevin Chamberlain, *War and Cultural Heritage: An Analysis of the 1954 Convention for the Protection of Cultural Property in the Event of Armed Conflict and Its Two Protocols* (Institute of Art and Law 2004); Janet E Blake, *Commentary on the 2003 UNESCO Convention on the Safeguarding of the Intangible Cultural Heritage* (Institute of Art and Law 2006); Francesco Francioni (ed), *The 1972 World Heritage Convention: A Commentary* (OUP 2008); James AR Nafziger and Tullio Scovazzi (eds), *The Cultural Heritage of Mankind* (Martinus Nijhoff 2008); Francesco Francioni and James Gordley *Enforcing International Cultural Heritage Law* (OUP 2013); Janet E Blake, *International Cultural Heritage Law* (OUP 2015); Lucas Lixinski, *International Heritage Law for Communities: Exclusion and Re-Imagination* (OUP 2019); Francesco Francioni and Ana Filipa Vrdoljak (eds), *The Oxford Handbook of International Cultural Heritage Law* (OUP 2020); Lorenzo Casini, 'Cultural Sites Between Nationhood and Mankind' in Eyal Benvenisti and Georg Nolte (eds), *Community Interests Across International Law* (Oxford University Press 2018). See also Judge Abdulqawi A Yusuf, 'The Notion of Cultural Heritage in International Law (Lecture Series on Cultural Heritage)' UN Audiovisual Library of International Law <http://legal.un.org/avl/ls/Yusuf_CH.html> accessed 15 April 2021.

91 For more information on the activity of the World Heritage Centre of UNESCO, see <http://whc.unesco.org> accessed 15 April 2021.

92 See, for instance, UNESCO WHC, 'The Director-General of UNESCO Appeals for the Protection of the World Heritage City of Aleppo' (27 July 2012) <https://whc.unesco.org/en/news/915> accessed 15 April 2021, and UNESCO WHC, 'UNESCO Director-General Deplores Continuing Destruction of Ancient Aleppo, a World Heritage Site' (24 April 2013) <https://whc.unesco.org/en/news/1002/> accessed 15 April 2021.

on the World Heritage List and the List of World Heritage in Danger; (b) the protection and conservation of World Heritage properties; (c) the granting of International Assistance under the World Heritage Fund; and (d) the mobilization of national and international support in favor of the Convention.[93] The challenges facing UNESCO and its member states in protecting world cultural heritage are multifaceted, and research on these issues would be beneficial for them and other relevant actors working in this field.

4. CONCLUDING REMARKS

At a time when public expectations for global justice are high and the challenges for meeting these expectations substantial,[94] a critical need exists for further developing and entrenching a novel understanding of international law as a means for articulating and protecting community interests and providing global public goods. An international law based on furthering community interests engages a broader set of common goods and values, which better represent the interests of states, international organizations, and non-state actors operating on the international stage.[95] Such an approach will move the discipline of international law in a new direction and toward an understanding which better reflects the present needs of the international community. One potential impact of further research in this field is a major shift towards and further elaboration of an international law of collectives and a system of global governance guided by an enlightened self-interest based on the proper articulation and protection of community interests. A major contribution of such research concerns answering the question of whether international law can serve as

93 UNESCO WHC, 'Operational Guidelines for the Implementation of the World Heritage Convention' (2012) <http://whc.unesco.org/archive/opguide12-en.pdf> accessed 15 April 2021.

94 See, inter alia, Simon Caney, *Justice Beyond Borders: A Global Political Theory* (OUP 2005); Jeffrey L Dunoff and Joel P Trachtman (eds), *Ruling the World? Constitutionalism, International Law, and Global Governance* (CUP 2009); Charlotte Ku, *International Law, International Relations, and Global Governance* (Routledge 2012); Carlo Focarelli, *International Law as Social Construct: The Struggle for Global Justice* (OUP 2012); Malcolm Langford and others (eds), *Global Justice, State Duties: The Extraterritorial Scope of Economic, Social and Cultural Rights in International Law* (CUP 2013).

95 See, among others, Steven R Ratner, *The Thin Justice of International Law: A Moral Reckoning of the Law of Nations* (OUP 2015) 415–434.

the *gentle civilizer* of nations[96] and if community interests are the vehicle which could facilitate that major societal transformation towards a just and peaceful global order.

The protection of community interests should encourage closer cooperation, solidarity, and cohesion among states and more widely within the international community, while at the same time facilitating systemic changes of the international legal order. However, rivalries among big powers and normative and institutional deficiencies may negatively affect these developments and possibly even reverse some of the positive developments achieved in more recent decades, at least temporarily. Community interest has already manifested itself at the heart of several major areas of contemporary international law, such as state responsibility, environmental law, and international criminal law, and underpins successful new concepts invoked in contemporary debates on collective human security, the responsibility to protect, and the international rule of law.[97] Despite the increasingly central place community interest has come to occupy in contemporary international law, fundamental questions remain about what it is, how it emerges, and whether its understanding differs from one selected area of international law to another. What regulatory frameworks are necessary for an effective realization of community interests? And what are the challenges and prospects of realizing community interests in the three selected areas of international law? The increasing pressure on scarce natural resources, technological advances, climate change, an ageing population, and other relevant factors are going to require a set of decisions that strike the right balance between the individual and collective interests of states. As suggested by Judge Simma in the preface, research based on international law theories, combined with multi- or inter-disciplinary approaches on the processes of formulation and protection of community interests, can provide useful insights and answers to these important questions for the future of humankind.

96 See, generally, Martti Koskenniemi, *The Gentle Civilizer of Nations: The Rise and Fall of International Law 1870–1960* (CUP 2004). See also John R. Morss, *International Law as the Law of Collectives: Toward a Law of People* (Routledge 2013).

97 See, among others, Villalpando (n 9) 389.

INDEX

ABOUT THE EDITOR

Gentian Zyberi is a Professor of International Law and Human Rights and Head of Department of the Norwegian Center for Human Rights at the University of Oslo, Norway. He is a member of the UN Human Rights Committee (CCPR, 2019–2022) and a member of the Permanent Court of Arbitration, The Hague, the Netherlands (2016–2022).

Over the past two decades, he has carried out research, published and taught in the areas of international human rights, international humanitarian law, international criminal law and public international law at various universities in the Netherlands, Albania, China, the US and Norway. He has served as Co-Editor-in-Chief at the Nordic Journal of Human Rights and a member of the Board of Advisors to the Editorial Board of the Yearbook of International Humanitarian Law (TMC Asser Institute, The Hague).

In 2008, he was awarded the Second Prize for the 2008 Max van der Stoel Human Rights Award by Tilburg University and the Netherlands School of Human Rights Research for his PhD dissertation. His research interests include the role of international courts and tribunals in developing international human rights law, international humanitarian law, and international criminal law; the protection of community interests in international law; operationalization of the responsibility to protect doctrine; and transitional justice, with a focus on the Balkans.

www.ingramcontent.com/pod-product-compliance
Ingram Content Group UK Ltd.
Pitfield, Milton Keynes, MK11 3LW, UK
UKHW021846100926
8556IPUK00019B/1072

9 781839 701122